Classic
Walks
in Britain

More than 200 walks
in the best-loved
areas of Britain

Produced by AA Publishing
© Automobile Association Developments Limited 2005
Illustrations © Automobile Associations Developments Limited 2005

Published by AA Publishing (a trading name of Automobile Association
Development Limited, whose registered office is Fanum House, Basing View,
Basingstoke, Hampshire RG21 4EA; registered number 1878835)

ISBN 0-7495-4805-3

A02675

A CIP catalogue record us available from the British Library

With thanks to The Estate Office, Sandringham, for their permission
to use mapping data belonging to the Estate Office, Sandringham to
compile walk 74.

Some of these routes may appear in other AA Publishing walks books.

Visit the AA Publishing website at www.theAA.com

Printed in China

Classic
Walks
in Britain

More than 200 walks
in the best-loved
areas of Britain

AA

Contents

CENTRAL ENGLAND

NORTHERN ENGLAND

SCOTLAND

Using this Book

Each walk is shown on an illustrated map. Many of these will stand up to being used alone to navigate your way around the walk, and the book is specially designed for you to use in this way. However, some detail is lost because of the restrictions imposed by scale. Particularly in the upland areas, we recommend that you use them in conjunction with an Ordnance Survey map. In poor visibility, you should not attempt the walks in upland areas unless you are familiar with bad weather navigation in the hills.

Feature walks

These are easy-to-follow, unmapped walks however we recommend that you take the relevant Ordnance Survey map with you.

Information Panels

Each walk has an information panel giving distance, total ascent, terrain, gradients, conditions under foot and parking. The parking suggestions given have been chosen to minimise the impact of leaving cars parked in the countryside. They do not imply that motorists have a guaranteed right to park in the places suggested. Please park your vehicle with due consideration for other traffic and countryside users, especially agricultural access. Refreshment places mentioned in the text are suggestions by field researchers for their convenience to the route. Listing does not imply that they are AA inspected or recognised, though they may coincidentally carry an AA classification.

Grading

The walks have been graded 1, 2 or 3 to give an indication of their difficulty. Easier walks, such as those around towns, or with little total ascent and over shorter distances are rated 1. The hardest walks, either because they include a lot of ascent, greater distances, or are in mountainous or otherwise difficult terrain, are rated 3. Moderate walks are rated 2. These gradings are relative to each other and for guidance only.

Access

All the walks in this book are on rights of way, permissive paths or on routes where de facto access for walkers is accepted. On routes in England and Wales which are not on legal rights of way, but where access for walkers is allowed by local agreements, no implication of a right of way is intended.

Safety

Although each walk here has been researched with a view to minimising the risk to the walkers who follow its route, no walk in the countryside can be considered to be completely free from risk. Walking in the outdoors will always involve a degree of common sense and judgement to ensure that it is as safe as possible.

• Be particularly careful on cliff paths and in mountainous terrain, where the consequences of any slip can be very serious.

• Remember to check tidal conditions before walking on the seashore.

• Some sections of route are by or cross busy roads, so take care here and remember traffic is a danger even on minor country lanes.

• Be careful around farm machinery and livestock, especially if you have children with you.

• Be aware of the consequences of changes in the weather and know the weather forecast.

Southwest England

The southwest of England tapers into a long and remarkably varied peninsula, stretching from the rural heart of England to the broken cliffs and coves of the Lizard and Land's End. Tiny fishing coves and smugglers' haunts contrast with bustling seaside resorts such as Newquay and Penzance, and the rolling farmland of central Devon. Despite the extensive granite uplands rising inland, you're never far from the sea, which means this corner of England gets its fair share of mist and rain – but the warming effects of the Gulf Stream also give the region more hours of sunshine than almost anywhere else.

The Southwest is blessed with a continuous coastal path from Minehead to Poole Harbour, no mere seaside stroll but one of the most varied and interesting walks in Britain. Trodden by excisemen and smugglers over the centuries, this path takes in a succession of rugged cliffs and coves.

The area boasts two national parks: the wild upland bogs of Dartmoor and the coastal cliffs and rolling heaths of Exmoor. Further protected areas encompass large stretches of the Cornish coast, Bodmin Moor, parts of Devon and Dorset, as well as the Quantock Hills and North Wessex Downs. There's a wealth of natural history to explore in the uncultivated land of the Cotswold escarpment, or the rugged gorges of the Mendips.

This is an area rich in legend. To the east the hills of the Dorset and Wessex Downs are scored by ancient earthworks and decorated with chalk figures. Cornwall was a last bastion of Celtic culture in England, and this is also the legendary homeland of King Arthur. Our ancient forebears trod along the crest of the downs when Britain was a wild and wooded place, and so there is no shortage of footpaths and trackways. At the opposite end of the scale, attractive historic towns offer the walker a rich urban landscape to discover.

The literary tradition is strong in the Southwest, and Thomas Hardy's novels contain some of the best descriptions ever of the English countryside. Other literary works lead you through Exmoor in search of Lorna Doone and Tarka the Otter, or almost anywhere in Cornwall after Daphne du Maurier's characters.

Best of the Rest

Lyme Regis and Dorset Coast Meryl Streep brought the image of the Cobb in Lyme Regis to cinema screens all over the world. The Dorset seaside town is the setting for John Fowles' international bestseller *The French Lieutenant's Woman*, and was used extensively in the film version. From Lyme walks extend along the beautiful coast in both directions, with nearby Golden Cap, the highest point on the south coast, a notable highlight.

Bedruthan Steps The flat, unremarkable Cornish countryside that lies inland from Bedruthan Steps belies the stupendous nature of the area's coastline. At the foot of tall cliffs lies dramatic rock islands that at high tide are besieged by crashing waves and at low tide, spring from a smooth expanse of golden, sea-damp sand. This was Victorian 'picturesque' at its most melodramatic and the area was popular with 'excursionists' in the late 19th century.

Forest of Dean A remote corner of Gloucestershire, nestling up to the Welsh border, it became rich through the exploitation of its mineral wealth. Now time has healed its industrial scars, leaving a legacy of excellent footpaths and bridleways through beautiful forest and, at Symond's Yat, a breathtaking view of the River Severn meandering along a wooded gorge.

Bath The Romans understood the importance of Bath's therapeutic waters, but it took the commercial savvy and aesthetic brilliance of the Georgians to create this upmarket watering hole of the 18th century. There are famous tourist sights in Bath, but it is a walk around the lesser known parts which will bring the true history of the city to life. The squalor of the servants' living quarters and the expedient shortcuts in construction are shown up by a walk around the passages and alleys.

Slaughters For many the Cotswolds are epitomised by the chocolate-box images of Upper and Lower Slaughter. But away from the tourist coaches a network of excellent paths connects these idyllic settlements and gives the walker a unique view of this most English of landscapes.

The Somerset Coal Canal Hidden in the valleys which connect with the Avon near Bath is a lost industrial relic, a testament to a time when the Industrial Revolution touched every remote corner. To extricate coal from the Somerset coalfield for industrialising Bristol, a branch was built from the great Kennet and Avon waterway up the Cam valley to Paulton. Geology made the coal hard won, and railways soon slashed the price of heavy transport. A walk along the canal's remnants is a reminder of a bygone pioneering spirit.

ABOUT • GEEVOR

In this walk you will discover another side of scenic Cornwall – its 2000-year-old history as a tin mining area, which was at its peak during the Victorian era. While you're there visit the Geevor Heritage Centre, the largest preserved mine site in Britain.

Southwest England

DISTANCE • 5 miles (8km)

TOTAL ASCENT • 246ft (75m)

PATHS • undulating coast path, gritty tracks and field paths

TERRAIN • coastal cliffs and farmland

GRADIENTS • some non-strenuous ascents and descents on coast path; inland paths fairly level

REFRESHMENTS • Queen's Arms, Botallack; The North Inn and The Radjel Inn in Pendeen; café at Geevor Tin Mine

PARK • free parking at Pendeen lighthouse, signed off the B3306 at Pendeen (St Just to St Ives road)

DIFFICULTY • 2

Around a Cornish Tin Mine at Geevor

❶ Walk inland up the lane for ¼ mile (400m). Opposite Enys, No 6 of the row of whitewashed cottages, turn right signed Cape Cornwall. Follow the marked path downhill, descend stone steps to cross a stream, then up and over two stiles to a wooden bench at the top of a steep slope (views of the tin workings ahead). Follow coast path signs through the workings, ignoring signs to Geevor.

❷ Continue along the coast path to pass Levant Beam Engine, right. Walk straight through the car park and along a gritty track, following a coast path sign, to meet and walk by a wall, left.

❸ Keep on the coast path for ¾ mile (1.2km), ignoring tracks leading inland, to reach Roscommon Cottage and then the remains of Botallack mine, marked by two big chimney stacks (left and right), and a huge metal headworks gantry, left. Just before the gantry, at a coast path sign, bear right on the narrow path and descend. In 50yds (46m) reach a flat area with views down to the restored engine houses of the Crowns mine. Return to the track.

❹ Continue ahead on the main route and in a few yards pass Botallack Count House Workshop. Continue to Botallack Manor Farm, left. Just beyond the farmhouse, where the lane bends right, turn left (right of way, not signed) along a grassy path to the right of the entrance to farmyard. Continue for a few yards by a stone hedge on the right, then join a track. In 300yds (274m) emerge between stone hedges, bear left and descend gently. A solitary granite

chimney stack lies ahead. Ignoring side tracks, keep on the main track for 400yds (366m) to reach the entrance to a field.

❺ Go through the entrance, turn right, go up stone steps and over a stile. Walk along the top of the next field, which you leave between two walls. Walk round the top edge of the next field (houses and buildings, right); keep on to cross the stone bank (right) and cross the next field, keeping the wall on your right. Cross a wooden stile, a track and a stone stile, to join a narrow path.

❻ Turn left. The path joins a track. Turn right then keep right at a junction to meet Levant Road and turn right. Just past the 30mph sign at Hillside, turn left by

Pentrew and follow the lane straight on past Merivale House, left. Keep straight on through the farm. The lane becomes a track, then a narrow path, which you follow to pass Geevor Tin Mine. The path ends at a T-junction with a huge boulder, left. Go up and over the bank ahead and walk downhill (wire fence, right) to rejoin the coast path at the Levant/Geevor signpost (Point ❷).

❼ Turn right, retrace your steps along the coast path to your car.

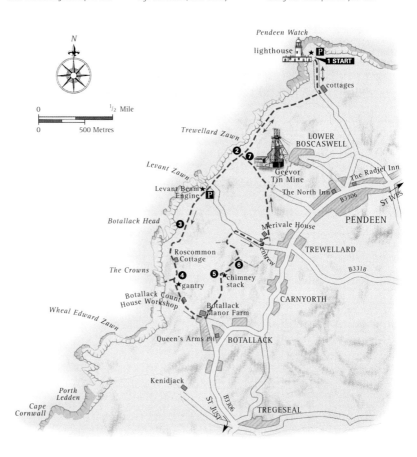

Zennor and the Spectacular Coast Path

Traverse the Cornish coast's front line, defiantly facing the mighty Atlantic Ocean

WALK
2

Distance: 5½ miles (9km)
Total ascent: 800ft (244m)
Paths: mostly good but can be very muddy, particularly between Tregerthen and Wicca
Terrain: fields, farm tracks, coast path
Gradients: steep in places on the coast path
Refreshments: Tinners Arms and Old Chapel Café, Zennor
Park: car park, Zennor, on B3306 betweeen St Ives and St Just
Difficulty: 2

Cornish stile

Carn Naun Point

The Carracks

River Cove

Pen Enys Point

N

½ mile

0

½ km

TREVALGAN

B3306

Mussel Point

5

TREVEAL

4

TREVEGA

St Ives

Wicca Pool

Boscubben Farm

TENDRINE

Gala Rocks

6

Wicca Farm

3

Rosewall Hill

Zennor Head

Porthzennor Cove

TREGERTHEN

Tendrine Hill ▲ 244

8

7

Tremedda Farm

B3306

2

Giant's Rock ●

church

Tinners Arms PH 🅿 **1** ZENNOR

Mermaid, Zennor

B3306

Trewey Hill

Zennor

St Just

Penzance

1 Turn left out of the car park and head up the hill. Immediately after the church turn right by some railings and take the footpath over the fields, crossing several stiles, to Tremedda Farm.

2 Cross the farm track via two stiles, continue across open fields to the hamlet of Tregerthen and cross another track. Follow the narrow, muddy track through thickets until it opens out to fields which lead to Wicca Farm.

3 Take the stile between the farmhouse and the barn, going straight through the farmyard and continuing along the road. Just after Boscubben Farm, turn left down the track to Treveal. At the hamlet take the right-hand fork at the footpath sign, where the track turns back on itself and leads down to a cattle grid.

4 Take the path signed River Cove down the wooded valley to the stream, where the path starts to rise and then descends to the coast. Veer left and follow the coast path, which eventually rises steeply to some prominent rocks at the summit of Mussel Point.

5 Continue round the point and follow the path across the open, grassy hillside. After a prominent boulder on the right the path drops steeply into a small valley. Cross the stream on stepping stones to a stile.

6 Cross the stile and turn right, following the coast and descending slightly before ascending to a small point. The path then zigzags steeply down, almost to sea level. Continue along a flatter section for ½ mile (800m), then bear inland and uphill steeply, over one stream and on to another.

7 Continue at the same level to a waymark where the path drops to the right. Descend steeply and then begin a long ascent to a cluster of boulders at the summit of the point. Continue along a broad, grassy track to Zennor Head.

8 Head back inland, rising slightly, to a stile. Follow the narrow path for 50yds (46m), to where it meets the road above a white house. Take the road back to Zennor and the car park.

ABOUT • ST IVES

This walk starts at the coast to the west of the town and reveals the aspects of light and landscape that has inspired artists to visit and paint here since the early 1920s. While you're in St Ives visit the Tate Gallery St Ives and the Barbara Hepworth Museum.

Southwest England

DISTANCE • 7 miles (11.3km)
TOTAL ASCENT • 607ft (185m)
PATHS • rocky coast path, lanes, farm tracks and fields
TERRAIN • undulating coast path, narrow town lanes and farmland
GRADIENTS • some fairly steep, short ascents on coast path and in St Ives;

REFRESHMENTS • pubs, restaurants, and cafés in St Ives; coffee shop and restaurant at Tate St Ives; the Tinner's Arms at Zennor
PARK • small car park by the National Trust sign for Rosewall Hill on the B3306 St Ives to St Just road, ½ mile (800m) past the sign to Trevalgan Farm (right)
DIFFICULTY • 2

Aspects of Light at St Ives

❶ Cross the road and follow the path across Little Trevalgan Hill (NT) past a huge boulder and memorial to artist Peter Lanyon. Continue downhill to a field; turn right to the bottom corner, and cross the wall into the lane.

❷ Turn left and in ½ mile (800m) reach Trevega Wartha Farm; 100yds (91m) beyond turn right down a signed bridleway between hedges. Cross a grassy track and follow footpath signs straight on, to walk downhill through a metal gate and over a stream to Trevail Mill. Walk up the drive.

❸ Past the cattle grid turn right, signed River Cove. Follow the path through a wood to meet the coast path. Turn right and continue for 2 miles (3.2km) where it branches. Go left past a sign for Hellesveor Cliff and continue to Clodgy Point.

❹ Continue right along the coast path for ¾ mile (1.2km) to reach a car park above Porthmeor Beach (toilets). At the road keep straight on to pass the Tate St Ives (right).

❺ Follow the road round right, then left at a junction, passing

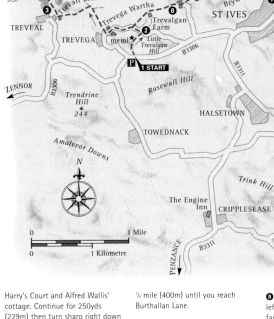

• DON'T MISS •

The Wayside Folk Museum, Cornwall's oldest private museum, in Zennor, a little further west along the B3306. Here you can see and experience the life and customs of past generations in this isolated part of West Cornwall where, until the 1800s, goods were transported by pack animals and sledges.

Harry's Court and Alfred Wallis' cottage. Continue for 250yds (229m) then turn sharp right down Fish Street to the harbour. Turn right along Wharf Road to reach West Pier and the lifeboat house.

❻ Turn right up Lifeboat Hill; take the second lane right (Back Street) to the entrance to the Barbara Hepworth Museum. Turn left up Ayr Lane and across a junction to a T-junction (Kenwyn Place sign). Turn right, and left at the top of the hill. Keep on this road for

¼ mile (400m) until you reach Burthallan Lane.

❼ Right along Burthallan Lane for ¼ mile (400m), then just past the house named Bryward follow signs for Zennor, left, over a stone stile and along a narrow hedged path, to a stone stile into a field. Keep ahead, then cross the wall right. Reach a grassy area, go right to a hidden stile next to two metal gates. Follow right-hand field edge for ¾ mile (1.2km) through fields and over stiles to Trowan Farm.

❽ Cross a stile into the lane; turn left, then right, through a farmyard. Go left over a stile at the next cottage, and right over another stile. Follow the field path to pass behind Trevalgan Farm. Go over a stile alongside a gate beside the final buildings. Go straight across the field to a stile and continue through small fields and over stiles to a surfaced lane. Turn left and reach the end of Point ❶ in 200yds (183m). Retrace your steps across Little Trevalgan Hill to the car park.

Hell's Mouth and the North Cornwall Coast

On the rollercoaster of headlands and clifftops around Godrevy Point

Distance: 5½ miles (8.8km)
Total ascent: 700ft (213m)
Paths: mostly good but can be muddy; short stretch of metalled road
Terrain: cliff top, open grassland
Gradients: two steep ascents on cliff path
Refreshments: café and Sand Sifters Hotel, Godrevy car park; Hell's Mouth café
Park: Godrevy National Trust car park, reached from the B3301, 2½ miles (4km) north of Hayle. Do not park next to café
Difficulty: 2

1 Turn left out of the car park and walk up the road to the coast of St Ives Bay.

2 Follow the cliff-top road for ½ mile (800m), passing Godrevy Farm. St Ives is visible on the opposite side of the bay. Just before the toilets (seasonal only) on your right, bear left across open, springy turf to a stile.

9 Take the B3301 right, back past Hell's Mouth, up the hill to the North Cliff National Trust car park. Descend into the Red River valley with St Ives Bay ahead. At the stone bridge turn right and back to the car park.

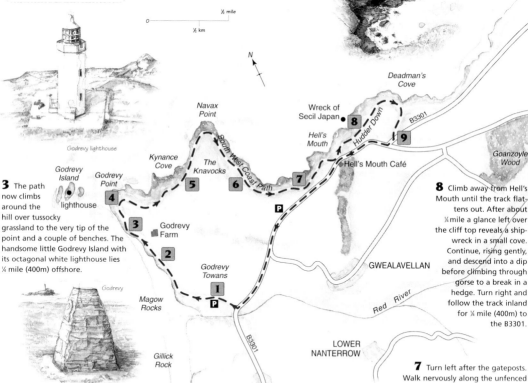

Hell's Mouth

Godrevy lighthouse

½ mile

0

½ km

N

Godrevy

Godrevy Island

Godrevy Point

lighthouse

Magow Rocks

Godrevy Towans

Godrevy Farm

Gillick Rock

Navax Point

Kynance Cove

The Knavocks

South West Coast Path

Deadman's Cove

Wreck of Secil Japan

Hell's Mouth

Hudder Down

B3301

Hell's Mouth Café

Goanzoyle Wood

GWEALAVELLAN

Red River

LOWER NANTERROW

GWITHIAN

HAYLE

St Ives Bay

B3301

3 The path now climbs around the hill over tussocky grassland to the very tip of the point and a couple of benches. The handsome little Godrevy Island with its octagonal white lighthouse lies ¼ mile (400m) offshore.

8 Climb away from Hell's Mouth until the track flattens out. After about ¼ mile a glance left over the cliff top reveals a shipwreck in a small cove. Continue, rising gently, and descend into a dip before climbing through gorse to a break in a hedge. Turn right and follow the track inland for ¼ mile (400m) to the B3301.

4 Continue round the cliff top, with magnificent views up the coast. On a clear day you can see the faint outline of Trevose Head, nearly 30 miles (48km) up the coast. Follow the path over some very impressive (unfenced) cliffs for ¾ mile (1.2km), to a kissing gate.

5 Take the track, rising gently, over the downland of The Knavocks to the highest point of the bleak headland and a tiny point. Continue, descending slightly, through an area of gorse to two stiles.

6 Cross a field to another stile and turn left along the lane, which becomes a narrow path after 100yds (91m). Follow the path through thickets to two granite gateposts.

7 Turn left after the gateposts. Walk nervously along the unfenced cliff top and heave a sigh of relief when the path veers slightly inland. Continue over Hudder Down, above impressive cliffs, to descend to Hell's Mouth and the B3301.

Smugglers' Tales from the Helford River

Following the tracks of excise men and 'free traders' around this idyllic Cornish inlet

WALK
5

Distance: 7 miles (11km)
Total ascent: 900ft (275m)
Paths: can be very muddy in places, particularly in winter
Terrain: fields, farm tracks, coast path
Gradients: undulating; several steep sections
Refreshments: Shipwright's, Helford
Park: by the church in St Anthony-in-Meneage, 8 miles (12.9km) from Helston
Difficulty: 2

9 Opposite the church turn left, and after 100yds (91m) take the footpath on the right (signed Carne), which eventually descends through woods to the road beside Gillan Creek. Turn left and after 140yds (128m) turn left again for St Anthony.

8 Turn left and cross the road. After 15yds (14m), take the path on the right to some houses. Continue to the main road, turn right, then immediately left, downhill to Manaccan church.

1 From the front of the church, facing the water, turn left up the hill, bearing right at a pebbly wall, to a lane and kissing gate. Walk to a stile where the field narrows and cross it to take the path around the headland and returning to the stile.

2 Follow the right side of the field through a kissing gate. After 3 stiles go through another kissing gate on the right, and continue along the wooded path above the estuary, past several coves, to a cottage and stables.

7 Cross into the cottage's farmyard and at the bottom take the right gate. Turn right and follow the edge of the field to a gate. Turn left through this and descend to a stile. Cross the stile, bear right and cross two streams, continuing uphill through woods, across two stiles until the path opens out into a field. Bear right diagonally uphill across the field to a stile between two trees.

6 Follow signs for Frenchman's Creek, to a stile on the left by a gateway. Cross the stile and take the path above the creek to a small car park. Turn left up the lane to the road opposite Kestle Cottage.

3 Bear right between the ruins and the cottage and then left up a track. Fork downhill at the top of the track and turn left up some steps just before a white cottage. Continue past the sailing club and a kissing gate on the right and go through another one straight ahead.

4 Turn left, then immediately right, to follow the road down through the village to a footbridge. Cross this, turn right and continue to the Shipwright's pub. Go left up the hill out of the pub car park, ignoring the path on the right to the ferry, and after 100yds (91m), turn right at a footpath sign.

5 Take the footpath to Penarvon Cove. Cross the beach and take the track left and uphill, away from the cottages. Join the road and after another 120yds (110m) turn right at a cattle grid.

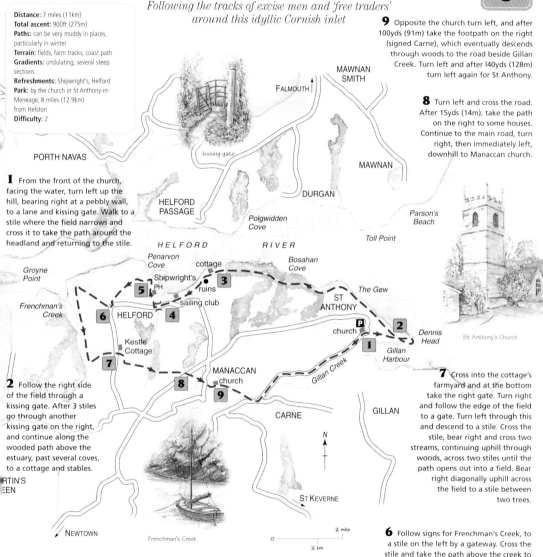

St Anthony's Church

Frenchman's Creek

WALK 6

ABOUT • THE EDEN PROJECT

The Eden Project, completed in 2001, is a spectacular theatre which tells the story of human dependence on plants. The huge biomes are able to produce a range of world climates and house a wide variety of plants from arid desert cactii to mature rainforest trees.

Southwest England

DISTANCE • 3 miles (4.8km)

TOTAL ASCENT • 361ft (110m)

PATHS • country lanes and well-maintained bridlepaths (some muddy after wet weather)

TERRAIN • undulating farmland, wooded valleys and old china clay workings

GRADIENTS • one short steep ascent near the start; a long downhill run at the end

REFRESHMENTS • café and restaurant at the Eden Project; The Britannia Arms on the A390 opposite Tregehan Gardens; Cornish Arms at St Blazey Gate

PARK • by the roadside near the Methodist Church in Tregrehan village, signposted off the A390 St Blazey Gate to St Austell

DIFFICULTY • 2

Eden, Eighth Wonder of the World

❶ Walk up the lane from your car, leaving the church on the left and the metal-railed stream on the right. Keep on uphill through a wooded area, with evidence of old mine workings.

❷ After ½ mile (800m), where the lane bends sharp left, turn right up the track signed bridlepath/footpath/cycle route 3 to pass Restineas Cottage, left.

❸ About 200yds (182m) further on you pass a signed path, right, that enters the project. Just beyond this, turn left along a new signed bridlepath created by the building of Eden, which has removed the original path that ran a little to the south. The path runs steeply uphill then veers left to reach a small wooden gate. (For a picnic spot with good views of the coast to the south, turn right just before the gate, walk through the grassy area, then turn right through the shelter belt to reach a second field.) To

continue on the main route walk through the gate; the path runs into a large level area, part of the old china clay workings.

❹ Turn right, unsigned, and continue for 766yds (700m); the broad path runs slightly uphill, then downhill along a field edge, before ascending again to reach one of the entrance roads into Eden. Turn right and within 400yds (364m) you will be able to see the biomes.

❺ If you don't want to visit the Eden Project at this point of this walk cross the road and follow the bridlepath, which runs along a green lane to reach the road at Quarry Park.

❻ Turn right down the busy road to pass another way into the Eden Project on the right; you can see the site through the hedge here.

❼ At the next staggered crossroads turn right down a quiet country lane, signed Tregrehan and St Austell. This lane runs steeply downhill to meet a crossroads in Tregrehan; turn right here and walk past the children's playground and the church to the start of the walk.

• DON'T MISS •

*If you want a clearer picture of what working life was like in a Cornish china clay quarry, visit the **Wheal Martyn China Clay Heritage Centre** (open Easter–end October), 3 miles (5km) to the northwest at Carthew. This, the nearest working quarry to Bodelva, will give you a good insight into the industrial history of this unique area. There are woodland walks as well as a visitor centre with exhibitions, gift shop and café.*

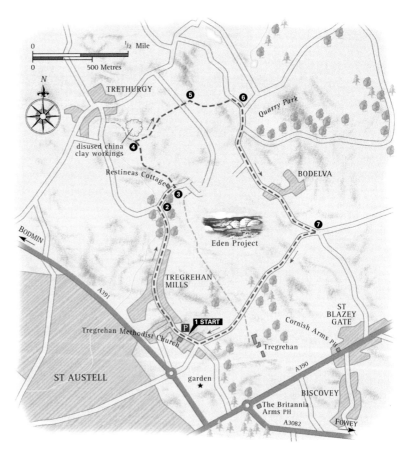

WALK

7

ABOUT • ST CATHERINE'S CASTLE

This walk starts from the old pilchard-fishing hamlet of Polkerris and leads you along the cliffs to the lovely St Catherine's Castle, which is actually more of a fort. It was built by the town's residents in 1510 to protect them from attacks from France.

Southwest England

DISTANCE • 6 miles (9.6km)

TOTAL ASCENT • 246ft (75m)

PATHS • coast path, woodland and field tracks (some muddy after wet weather), and country lanes

TERRAIN • cliffs, farmland, wooded valleys

GRADIENTS • some short, steep ascents/descents on coast path and inland valleys

REFRESHMENTS • Rashleigh Arms, Polkerris; café at Readymoney Cove; pubs, cafés and restaurants in Fowey

PARK • free parking in Polkerris; unsurfaced, unmarked car park on right, before village, descending lane signed off the A3082 Fowey to St Austell road just east of Polmear

DIFFICULTY • 2

Henry VIII's Coastal Fort at Fowey

1 From the car park entrance turn right and head for the Rashleigh Arms by the beach. Turn left (signed public toilets), and follow the coast path signs up concrete steps, and zigzag steeply up through woodland. At the T-junction turn left away from the sea to reach a coast path post at the field edge.

2 Turn right; follow the coast path along the field and through a gate. Pass through another gate, then climb for 2 miles (3.2km) up to a gate/stile. Just past the

National Trust sign for The Gribbin the path divides; keep right to reach the daymark.

3 Follow the coast path downhill for ¾ mile (1.2km) to reach Polridmouth. Ignore the footpath left (to Menabilly); follow the path behind the beach past the house and lake, to cross the weir on stepping-stones.

4 Continue up steep steps on to Lankelly Cliff (NT). Pass through the next gate, go round the field

edge, and drop down steeply to a stile. Walk up the next field. Descend through a gate to Coombe Haven. Continue over a stile to enter Alldays Fields, then through a small gate into Covington Wood.

5 Turn sharp right to reach St Catherine's Point; take the next path, right, to the castle. Retrace your steps and turn right to rejoin the coast path, descending to a T-junction behind Readymoney Cove.

6 Turn left, uphill, for ½ mile (800m) following the deeply banked Saints' Way (signed with a cross), to meet a lane. Turn left to reach Coombe Lane. Turn right to to lead into Prickly Post Lane.

7 Follow signs left through a drive and down a narrow footpath. Go through a gate and downhill over a stream, under a bridge and uphill over a stone stile. Continue downhill, over a stile, to reach Trenant; cross the drive and the stone stile. Go through the next gate, then downhill and over a stream on a railed footbridge. The path continues over a stile by a ruined cottage, then uphill through a gate into Tregaminion farmyard. Walk through the farmyard, turn right, then left at the farmhouse to reach a T-junction.

8 Turn right along the lane; after 200yds (183m) turn left on a footpath to rejoin the coast path post at Point 1. Go ahead and retrace your steps downhill to Polkerris.

• DON'T MISS •

Daphne du Maurier fell in love with Cornwall while on holiday in Fowey in her early 20s. She lived for several years at Ferryside, next to the Bodinnick Ferry, and based many of her best-known novels on the area. Every May the town hosts the du Maurier Festival of Arts and Literature.

ST AUSTELL

B3269

NEWTOWN

River Fowey

BODINNICK

POLKERRIS

1 START

Tregaminion

Trenant

B3269

Ferryside

ferry

Rashleigh
Arms PH

2

Saints' Way

8

A3082

7

FOWEY

MENABILLY

Saints Way

6

castle

ferry

St Catherine's
Castle

Readymoney
Cove

castle

POLRUAN

5

St Catherine's Point

4

Lankelly Cliff

Coombe
Haven

Polridmouth

Little
Gribbin

The Gribbin

3

Gribbin
Head

A3082

N

0   1 Mile

0   1 Kilometre

WALK 8

ABOUT • LOSTWITHIEL

The extensive dry-moated ruins of Restormel Castle are wonderfully atmospheric. During the 13th century the castle served as the seat of feudal government in the area and is the best-preserved examples of a motte-and-bailey construction in Cornwall.

Southwest England

DISTANCE • 4½ miles (7.2km)

TOTAL ASCENT • 410ft (125m)

PATHS • woodland tracks and fields

TERRAIN • mixed woodland and farmland; short stretch of pavements through the town

GRADIENTS • gradual; one short steep ascent from Restormel Farm to Hillhead

REFRESHMENTS • café at Lanhydrock House; The River pub and Duchy Coffee Shop both in Fore Street, Lostwithiel

PARK • National Trust car park by Respryn Bridge (honesty box) for Lanhydrock House (signed off the A38 just east of Bodmin, and off the A390 west of Lostwithiel)

DIFFICULTY • 2

Restormel Castle at Lostwithiel

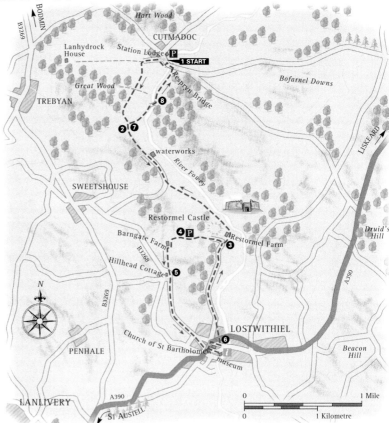

❶ Leave the car park via the exit and turn right. Take the first lane left by Station Lodge, signed Lanhydrock. At the Lodge and gates to The Avenue, turn left down Newton Lane, signed permitted footpath only. Continue to a wooded track which descends for ¾ mile (1.2km); veer left to meet two dark red gates, ahead and right.

❷ Turn right through the gate, signed footpath to Restormel Castle, and cross the field. Go through the next gate, and then another by the waterworks to join a lane then continue for 1¼ miles (2km). Where the lane bends right, keep straight on along the farm lane (dead end), with views to the castle ahead. The lane runs through Restormel Farm to meet another lane.

❸ Turn right uphill (in summer the gates are open; in winter climb over the stile) to reach the car park; turn right for the castle.

❹ On leaving the castle go through the car park, over a stile in the far left corner, and up the field, keeping the hedge on your left. Cross the wooden ladder stile and pass through a gap in the hedge. Continue uphill, keeping the hedge on your right. The path veers left, ignoring the first stile on the right. At the top, turn right over a stile, then left at the footpath post near Barngate Farm. Cross the next ladder stile and pass through a gate to meet the road opposite Hillhead Cottage.

❺ Turn left; descend Bodmin Hill for ¾ mile (1.2km) to meet the A390 in the centre of Lostwithiel.

Cross the road and continue down Fore Street to the museum, St Bartholomew's Church and the River Fowey. Retrace your steps to the A390 and turn right to pass the Royal Talbot, on your left, and Tourist Information Centre, on your right.

❻ Turn left along Restormel Road (unmarked), following the brown tourist signs to the castle. At the entrance to Restormel Farm keep straight on to retrace your steps past the waterworks and through the fields to reach the red gate at Point 2 of the walk.

❼ Go through the gate and turn right to pass almost immediately through another red gate. Follow the woodland path to meet the River Fowey; the path bends left to meet a wooden footbridge.

❽ Cross the footbridge and turn left to walk along the river bank. The path ends at a kissing gate; turn left to cross Respryn Bridge, then turn right into the car park.

DON'T MISS

The 18th-century Restormel House, just below the castle, has superb battlements in the Gothic style.

WALK

9

ABOUT • TINTAGEL

Steeped in Arthurian legend and lore, it's not surprising that Tintagel remains so popular. But this walk offers a different perpective on this famous landmark as it explores 'Din Tagell', part of the Dumnonia kingdom, the stronghold of a Celtic king.

Southwest England

DISTANCE • 4 miles (6.4km)	**REFRESHMENTS** • Castle Beach Café at the entrance to Tintagel (April to end October); pubs and cafés in Tintagel
TOTAL ASCENT • 262ft (80m)	
PATHS • undulating, sometimes rocky coast path; quiet lanes and fields, some muddy after wet weather	**PARK** • lay-by on the right at the bottom of the hill on the B3263 Tintagel to Boscastle road, just past Willapark Manor Hotel
TERRAIN • rugged cliffs, coastal farmland	**DIFFICULTY** • 2
GRADIENTS • some steep ascents and descents on coast path	

Around Tintagel

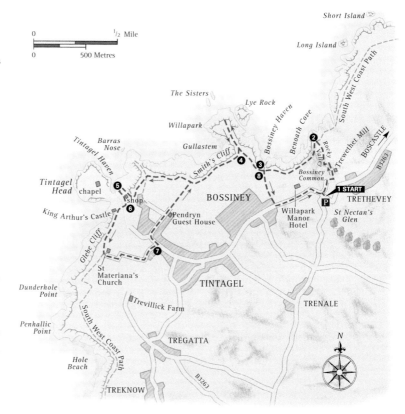

❶ Cross the road and follow the sign to the coast path, which leads down a tarmac drive to pass Trout Leap restaurant and right over the stream on a railed footbridge. Follow the rocky path through the ruins of Trewethet Mill (Celtic Trust) and cross the stream to enter Rocky Valley (NT). By the next bridge keep straight on to join the coast path.

❷ The path veers left and continues up a long flight of steps to cross Bossiney Common above Benoath Cove, then drops steeply down concrete steps to a gritty track by Bossiney Haven.

❸ Walk straight on up concrete steps and over a stile, then down steps to cross the stream via a stile/wooden-railed footbridge and on to Willapark (NT). Follow the path up steps and through a wooden gate; keep straight ahead (herringbone wall, left) to reach the top. Turn right and walk to the end of the headland to enjoy the views ahead. Retrace your steps to the coast path.

❹ Continue right as the path undulates along Smith's Cliff, and through a kissing gate above Gullastem. The path leads on to Barras Nose (NT) via a stile and gate; follow the path to descend over craggy terrain to Tintagel Haven and the castle entrance via a footbridge over the stream.

❺ Turn left and walk inland past the English Heritage shop.

❻ Just past the toilets follow the coast path signs steeply right and uphill to pass another entrance to the castle, then left along Glebe

Cliff to reach St Materiana's Church. Turn left and follow the lane inland to Tintagel village.

❼ Turn left; follow the road to a sharp left bend, with Pendryn Guest House on the right. Go straight ahead on the track, signed to the coast path. Cross the kissing stile and the next field, then cross a wooden stile and go straight on, keeping the wall on your right. Go

through the gate/stile and follow the wall round to the right to rejoin the coast path on Smith's Cliff. Retrace your steps to meet the gritty track by Bossiney Haven (Point 3).

❽ Turn right and walk inland to the edge of Bossiney via a kissing gate; toilets on the right. Cross the B3263; turn left and follow the pavement back to your car.

WALK 10

Bolt Head's Wartime Secrets

From prehistoric times to the Cold War this South Devon headland has kept watch over the sea

Distance: 7 miles (11.3km)
Total ascent: 700ft (215m)
Paths: cliff and field paths, farm tracks, short stretch of metalled road; mostly good but occasionally muddy
Terrain: cliff top, open grassland
Gradients: two steep ascents on cliff path
Refreshments: Port Light Hotel, Bolberry Down (limited winter opening)
Park: Bolberry Down car park, seaward of the Port Light Hotel and reached by following signs from the A381 at Malborough
Difficulty: 2

1 From the boulders at the end of the car park, follow the coast path with the sea on your right for about ½ mile (800m) to where the track drops down and then cuts back inland to the floor of a steep valley.

2 Continue down the valley and over a footbridge spanning a stream. Ascend steeply along the path right, skirting the pinnacled ridge to seaward. After a stile, descend into a small valley, cross a footbridge and ascend straight to just before the ridge. Turn inland onto the plateau of The Warren.

3 Follow the clifftop for 1 mile (1.6km) to a wall and stile. At the next wall take the right-hand stile, signed for Bolt Head. Continue up over the open top of Bolt Head, bearing right to a wall and stile.

4 Descend rightwards via a small valley to the headland with its ruined lookout.

5 Return to the stile and continue downhill with the wall on your left. Turn left over a stile (signed Soar Mill Cove) and just before the next wall turn right (signed South Sands) down to a stile.

6 Cross the stream and take the lane to a stone barn. Go through the gate, uphill for 50yds (46m) and right, through another gate, to a fingerpost. Turn left, up the valley to East Soar Farm, left through a gate, then through the farm gate to follow the farm track past the farmhouse and the nuclear bunker with its radio mast, to East Soar car park.

7 Follow the road to the white cottages, going straight on to where the Soar Mill road joins from the left. 100yds (91m) on, at Rew Cross, take the footpath which strikes left over fields to Southdown Farm.

8 Cross the road via two stiles and bear right, then left around the barn to take a path beside a bramble hedge for ¼ mile (400m) to a stile in the corner of the field. Cross this, turn left along the tree-lined Jacob's Lane for ½ mile (800m) to the road and follow this left past radio masts to the car park.

Bolt Tail

Hope Cove

HOPE

GALMPTON

coastguard lookout

SW Coast Path

Slippery Point

Bolberry Down

Portlight Hotel

West Cliff

BOLBERRY

radio masts

KINGSBRIDGE

A381

Lantern Rock

Southdown Farm

MALBOROUGH

Soar Mill Cove

Rew Cross

SOAR

COLLATON

REW

Steeple Cove

Lloyds Signal Station

COMBE

BATSON

The Warren

bunker

East Soar Farm

radio mast

caravan park

SALCOMBE

A381

Off Cove

Overbecks (NT Museum & Gardens)

North Sands

South Sands

Kingsbridge Estuary

ferry

Starehole Bay

Bolt Head

gate and stile

SW Coast Path

WALK 11

ABOUT • SLAPTON SANDS

Slapton Sands serves as a reminder of the lives that were both lost and saved in World War II. In 1943, the US army trained here for the D-Day landings but during a rehearsal a convoy of vessels was torpedoed by German craft, killing 1,000 soldiers.

Southwest England

DISTANCE • 5 miles (8km)

TOTAL ASCENT • 328ft (100m)

PATHS • narrow, quiet country lanes and paths; some muddy after wet weather

TERRAIN • shingle beach, rolling farmland and freshwater ley

GRADIENTS • level on beach and round ley; some short steep ascents/descents inland

REFRESHMENTS • the Start Bay Inn at Torcross, also cafés and fish and chips; pubs at Stokenham and Slapton

PARK • memorial car park on Slapton Sands off A379, just below Slapton Bridge

DIFFICULTY • 2

A Memorable Stroll along Slapton Sands

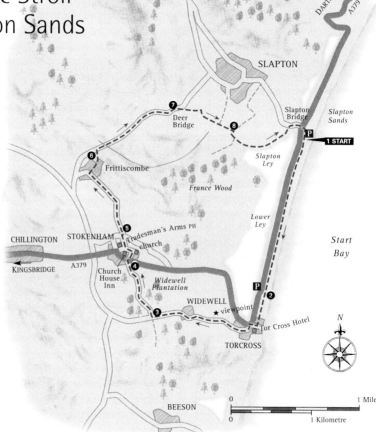

❶ Walk along the back of the beach, keeping the toilets and road on your right, and the sea on your left, to reach the edge of Torcross. The Sherman tank memorial is across the road in the car park.

❷ Follow the concrete walkway between the houses and sea. At the end, turn right before the old Tor Cross Hotel (holiday apartments), then left before the post office up a steep narrow lane (toilets, right). Pass Torcross viewpoint, a butterfly garden. Continue up the lane to pass through the hamlet of Widewell.

❸ After 400yds (366m) turn right down a narrow unsigned lane, opposite a footpath to Beeson and a post-box. Walk steeply downhill past Widewell Plantation to reach the A379 opposite the Church House Inn at Stokenham.

❹ Cross the road and go up the lane between the pub and the Church of St Michael and All Angels. The lane veers left; when you can see the Tradesman's Arms ahead turn right by Sunnyside up a narrow lane to meet Kiln Lane. Turn right.

❺ Almost immediately, turn left up another quiet lane. Leave the houses and descend to ancient Frittiscombe. Pass the farmhouse on your right and an old barn on your left. When the lane veers left and uphill, turn right along the track signed Scrubs Lane to Deer Bridge Lane. Follow this as it veers left uphill to meet the lane.

❻ Turn right and proceed downhill, with views of the ley to your right, to cross Deer Bridge.

❼ Turn right along a small wooded path signed Marsh Lane. The route follows the marsh edge to reach a junction of paths; Slapton village is signed to the left. Walk straight ahead along the boardwalk, signed permissive route to nature reserve, passing through an area of willows. Ascend wooden steps to a T-junction and follow another footpath, left, which leads to the village.

❽ Turn right, signed Slapton Sands via nature trail, and follow the narrow, undulating path as it weaves along the ley edge. There are four dog-friendly stiles and occasional wooden steps along this section, but nothing difficult. As the road comes into view note the pillbox below the path, right. The path meets the road via a gate; turn right towards the sea, then right to reach your car.

• DON'T MISS •

*The remains of **Hallsands**, just to the south of Torcross, provides another example of how this part of the coast has suffered over the years. This small fishing village was almost completely destroyed during a huge storm on the night of 16 January 1917.*

Among the Tors of Dartmoor

A spectactular walk among the granite tors of this last southern wilderness

WALK 12

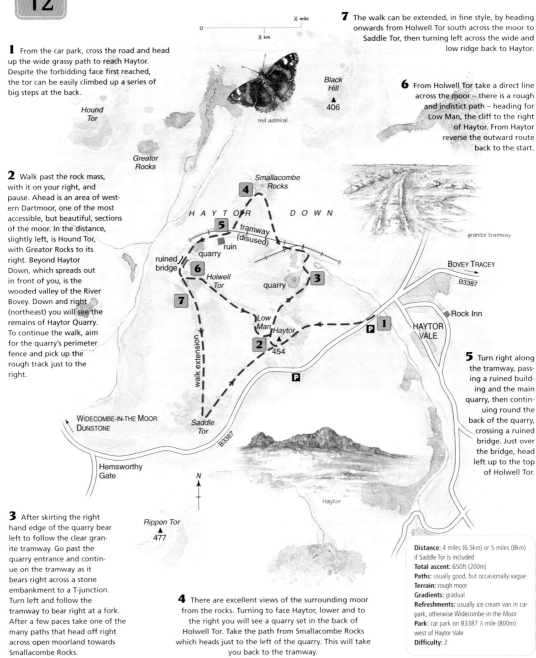

½ mile

0

½ km

red admiral

Black Hill ▲ 406

Hound Tor

Greator Rocks

H A Y T O R   **D O W N**

Smallacombe Rocks

4

tramway (disused)

5

ruin

ruined bridge

quarry

6

Holwell Tor

quarry

3

7

Low Man Haytor

2

454

walk extension

P

P

1

BOVEY TRACEY

B3387

● Rock Inn

HAYTOR VALE

P

granite tramway

WIDECOMBE-IN-THE MOOR
DUNSTONE

Saddle Tor

B3387

Hemsworthy Gate

N

Rippon Tor ▲ 477

Haytor

1 From the car park, cross the road and head up the wide grassy path to reach Haytor. Despite the forbidding face first reached, the tor can be easily climbed up a series of big steps at the back.

2 Walk past the rock mass, with it on your right, and pause. Ahead is an area of western Dartmoor, one of the most accessible, but beautiful, sections of the moor. In the distance, slightly left, is Hound Tor, with Greator Rocks to its right. Beyond Haytor Down, which spreads out in front of you, is the wooded valley of the River Bovey. Down and right (northeast) you will see the remains of Haytor Quarry. To continue the walk, aim for the quarry's perimeter fence and pick up the rough track just to the right.

3 After skirting the right hand edge of the quarry bear left to follow the clear granite tramway. Go past the quarry entrance and continue on the tramway as it bears right across a stone embankment to a T-junction. Turn left and follow the tramway to bear right at a fork. After a few paces take one of the many paths that head off right across open moorland towards Smallacombe Rocks.

4 There are excellent views of the surrounding moor from the rocks. Turning to face Haytor, lower and to the right you will see a quarry set in the back of Holwell Tor. Take the path from Smallacombe Rocks which heads just to the left of the quarry. This will take you back to the tramway.

5 Turn right along the tramway, passing a ruined building and the main quarry, then continuing round the back of the quarry, crossing a ruined bridge. Just over the bridge, head left up to the top of Holwell Tor.

6 From Holwell Tor take a direct line across the moor – there is a rough and indistict path – heading for Low Man, the cliff to the right of Haytor. From Haytor reverse the outward route back to the start.

7 The walk can be extended, in fine style, by heading onwards from Holwell Tor south across the moor to Saddle Tor, then turning left across the wide and low ridge back to Haytor.

Distance: 4 miles (6.5km) or 5 miles (8km) if Saddle Tor is included
Total ascent: 650ft (200m)
Paths: usually good, but occasionally vague
Terrain: rough moor
Gradients: gradual
Refreshments: usually ice cream van in car park, otherwise Widecombe-in-the-Moor
Park: car park on B3387 ½ mile (800m) west of Haytor Vale
Difficulty: 2

WALK 13

ABOUT • CASTLE DROGO

Castle Drogo, built in 1930, is now owned by the National Trust. Built of local granite, it was the result of a partnership between the architect Sir Edwin Lutyens, one of the foremost architects of the Edwardian era, and millionaire, Julius Drewe.

Southwest England

DISTANCE • 4½ miles (7.2km)

TOTAL ASCENT • 395ft (120m)

PATHS • good field and woodland tracks; some muddy after wet weather

TERRAIN • steep-sided river gorge, mixed deciduous woodland and open moorland

GRADIENTS • one long, steep climb from Fingle Bridge

REFRESHMENTS • The Angler's Rest at Fingle Bridge; the Sandy Park Inn, Sandy Park

PARK • Roadside parking at Dogmarsh Bridge, just south of Sandy Park on the A382 Whiddon Down to Moretonhampstead road

DIFFICULTY • 2

Castle Drogo, Lutyens' Masterpiece

❶ Walk from your car towards the bridge. Turn left through the kissing gate, following the footpath signed Two Moors Way, to enter the Castle Drogo Estate. Walk along the river, passing through two kissing gates. Go over a footbridge to enter oak woodland then negotiate a stile/small gate.

❷ Turn right to cross the river on a suspension bridge*, ascend steps to cross the big granite wall. Turn left along the track, which leads through a five-bar gate. Continue along this undulating track, soon passing a pumping station on your left, part of the castle's hydro-electric scheme. Continue along the track through Hannicombe Wood to reach Fingle Bridge.

❸ Turn left to cross the old packhorse bridge and take a break at The Angler's Rest. To continue the walk turn right from the pub and up the lane through the parking area.

❹ After 100yds (91m) turn left, following a footpath signed Hunter's path. This narrow wooded path climbs steeply up to reach open moorland above the gorge and joins the Hunter's path (which comes in from the right); keep left and pass through granite gateposts towards the castle, which can be seen ahead.

❺ At the next signpost (Drewsteignton) turn right up wooden steps; do not cross the stile ahead, but almost immediately turn left across Piddledown Common following the signs for Castle Drogo. The next sign directs you along the Gorse Blossom Walk to reach the castle drive.

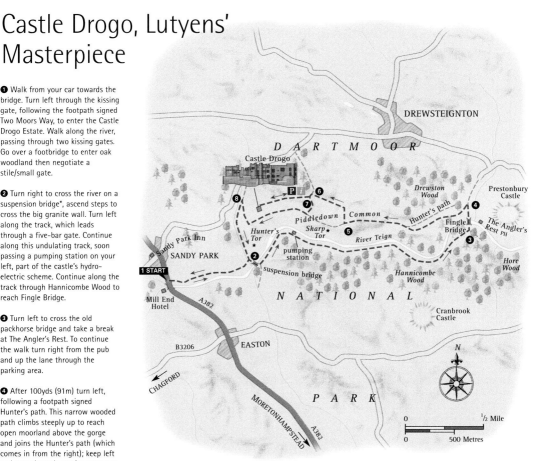

❻ Turn left; at the car park sign turn right to reach the entrance to the castle and gardens. After your visit, retrace your steps out of the car park and turn left down the drive to continue the walk.

❼ Almost immediately turn right, signed Hunter's Path. Keep straight on downhill, and descend wooden steps, to meet the path along the edge of the gorge. Turn right and

follow the path below the castle, veering right to meet a lane through two wooden gates.

❽ Turn left downhill, signed Fisherman's Path. Cross the cattle grid and follow footpath signs to pass to the left of the thatched Gibhouse and down the wooded path to the river. Turn right over the footbridge and stile, and

retrace your steps across the meadows to your car.

* At the time of going to press the suspension bridge was closed due to flood damage. If it has not reopened, continue on Fisherman's Path close to the north bank, to Fingle Bridge and pick up the directions part way through Point ❸.

ABOUT • HARTLAND

The coastal scenery off Hartland Point is spectacular but to the sailors and smugglers of the 18th century it must have offered a cruel welcome. The jagged cliffs were responsible for a number of shipwrecks and, inevitably, the lives of many sailors.

Southwest England

DISTANCE • 3½ miles (5.6km)

TOTAL ASCENT • 360ft (110m)

PATHS • fields, grassy coast path, quiet country lanes and farm tracks

TERRAIN • dramatic and rugged coastal scenery, rolling farmland

GRADIENTS • some short but steep climbs on the coast path

REFRESHMENTS • Wreckers' Retreat pub at Hartland Quay; cream teas available in Stoke in the summer; The Hart Inn, The Anchor and the King's Arms pubs in Hartland village

PARK • west of St Nectan's Church in Stoke, signed from Hartland

DIFFICULTY • 2

Shipwrecks and Smugglers at Hartland

❶ With the church on your right, follow the wall round to meet a footpath sign pointing left. Follow the path between the cottages and the lane, over a stile, through a kissing gate and over a stile into a field. Turn right, downhill, with views of the sea at Blackpool Mill. Walk along the lower edge of the field to enter the woods above the Abbey River, right, to reach the coast path.

❷ Turn left through a gate; follow the path uphill to Dyer's Lookout, and across Warren Cliff past the ruined tower, left. Leave the field by a stile by the Rocket House.

❸ Turn right; follow coast path posts along the cliff edge and down steps to join the lane leading to Hartland Quay.

❹ From the car park follow coast path signs on and up steps to pass along the cliff edge round the back of Well Beach. Go through a kissing gate and follow the coast path to the right passing through a five-bar gate to avoid mighty

St Catherine's Tor. Cross the stream, cross the next field and pass through a gate. The path now continues uphill, towards the coast, and over a stile before dropping down to Speke's Mill Mouth. Pause for a moment to enjoy its impressive run of waterfalls, totalling 160ft (49m).

❺ Turn left up the track, following coast path signs inland, then turn right at the next post to cross the stream on a footbridge. Turn left at the next post, signed coast path valley route. Keep straight on at the next two signposts, signed Milford. Leave the heathland over a stile into a field; walk straight to the top and out through a gate, to join a farm track that meets the lane at Milford.

❻ Turn left downhill, pass Docton Mill to reach the crossroads at Lymebridge.

❼ Turn left and continue uphill through Lymebride to reach Kernstone Cross. At the crossroads continue straight ahead along the green lane, signed unsuitable for motors. At the entrance to Wargery Farm turn left downhill and follow the track to the edge of Stoke, where it veers right. Go straight on to reach the village centre.

❽ Turn left and walk through the churchyard, turning left at the church door to return to the start of the walk.

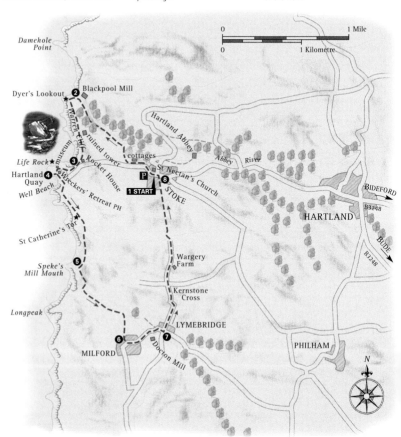

The Rocky Coast beyond Woolacombe

The North Devon coast becomes spikier as the sands give way to clifftop paths

WALK

15

1 From either car park turn left, following the South West Coast Path alongside the road to Mortehoe. It's possible to walk nearer to the sea in places but you must return to the road before the bend at the foot of the hill up to Mortehoe.

2 Follow the coast path signs to cut out the bend in the road and follow the road a short distance up the hill towards Mortehoe. About 300yds (273m) up the hill turn left. Follow the coast path signs for the next 3 miles (4.8km). The path keeps close to the coast all around Morte Point, down into a little valley below Mortehoe and another behind the beach at Rockham and up to Bull Point lighthouse.

3 At the entrance to the lighthouse compound turn right up the tarmac drive. However, it's worth continuing on the coast path to the seat on the hillock above the lighthouse for the view along the coast to Ilfracombe and returning to the drive. The drive ascends 1 mile (1.6km) to the edge of the village at Mortehoe.

4 Pass through the signed gateway at the end of the drive and take the second footpath signposted to the left, passing through a thicket alongside a house. Take the stile into the field, carrying straight on across the middle of the field and coming out by a stile onto a bend in a tarmac drive. Keep right, going up the drive past the golf course and from the bend onto a road at the top.

5 Turn right down the road towards Mortehoe and take the first field gateway on the left. Keep straight ahead with the bank on your right and cross a stile onto a drive in a caravan site. Turn left, following the drive to a footpath by a stream. Cross the stream at the bottom and go up to the junction with a footpath. Bear right along the path and take the first turning left. Keep straight ahead between the caravans.

6 At the end of the caravan site drive, find a path descending through the trees and crossing the stream at the bottom. Ascend to the path junction and turn right and over a stile by a National Trust sign. The path descends the valley side for nearly a mile (1.6km). Just before the bottom there is a small gate at a sharp bend in the path. Take the gate and follow the road straight down to the coast road. Turn left to return to the start.

Distance: 6 miles (9.6km)
Total ascent: 650ft (200m)
Paths: generally good; grass slippery when wet
Terrain: coastal grass and heathland, fields
Gradients: gradual and fairly short
Refreshments: Woolacombe
Park: either of two car parks by beach in Woolacombe village; can be busy in summer, but there is plenty of other parking
Difficulty: 2

Map labels:
Rockham Bay
Bull Point
lighthouse
Lee Bay
ILFRACOMBE
South West Coast Path
combe
combe
Morte Point
HIGHER WARCOMBE
Borough Valley
MORTEHOE
Ship Aground PH
golf course
caravan park
ILFRACOMBE
tourist information centre
war memorial, Woolacombe
WOOLACOMBE
Fortescue Arms PH
Morte Bay
Red Barn PH
B3343
B3343
Woolacombe Sand
BRAUNTON
South West Coast Path
Woolacombe
N
0   ½ mile
     ½ km

High Moors above the River Exe

*Never tamed by human industry, The Chains retain the
wildness that impressed Exmoor's earliest settlers*

WALK 16

1 From the lay-by walk along road towards Simonsbath for 350yds (319m). Turn right down drive signed to Mole's Chamber (follow blue waymarked signs all the way to Wood Barrow). Follow bridleway off the drive at point where it becomes private, and go through gate at bend after bridge. After next gate take smaller path straight ahead, keeping slightly right and following top of steep valley side, gradually descending to stream. Follow path through gate at Mole's Chamber.

6 Take gate signed to B3358 or detour 300yds (273m) for view from Chains Barrow and return. Follow line of posts all the way to bottom of field. Go through gate and follow bank on left down to road and start.

5 Go through gate and follow bank over dam and upwards 1 mile (1.6km).

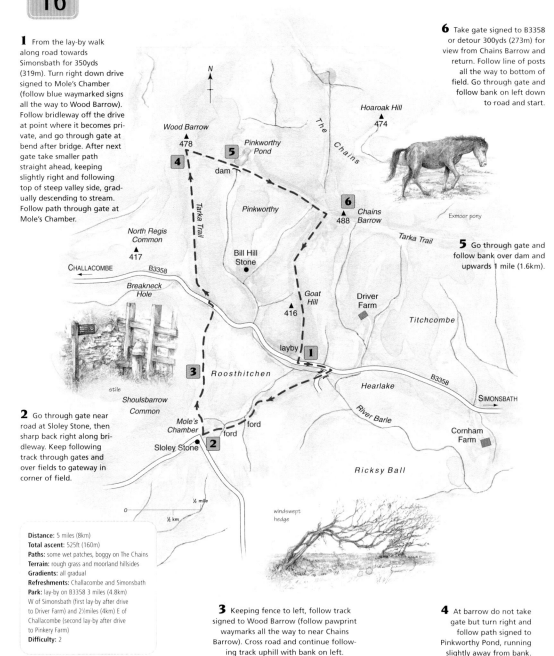

Exmoor pony

2 Go through gate near road at Sloley Stone, then sharp back right along bridleway. Keep following track through gates and over fields to gateway in corner of field.

Distance: 5 miles (8km)
Total ascent: 525ft (160m)
Paths: some wet patches, boggy on The Chains
Terrain: rough grass and moorland hillsides
Gradients: all gradual
Refreshments: Challacombe and Simonsbath
Park: lay-by on B3358 3 miles (4.8km) W of Simonsbath (first lay-by after drive to Driver Farm) and 2½miles (4km) E of Challacombe (second lay-by after drive to Pinkery Farm)
Difficulty: 2

3 Keeping fence to left, follow track signed to Wood Barrow (follow pawprint waymarks all the way to near Chains Barrow). Cross road and continue following track uphill with bank on left.

4 At barrow do not take gate but turn right and follow path signed to Pinkworthy Pond, running slightly away from bank.

In Search of Lorna Doone on Exmoor

R D Blackmore's heroine lived among these charming combes and peaceful moors

WALK

17

1 Cross the road from the car park entrance and take the bridleway along the heath, signed to Broomstreet Farm.

2 Turn right up the drive past Yenworthy Lodge. Cross the road, take the stile and follow a yellow waymarked path down to Oare. Skirt through trees around a farm at Oare House then turn left onto a road, over a bridge and up to Oare church. Turn left, then take the gate to left of churchyard, signed to Larkbarrow. Follow the blue waymarks straight up over fields, keeping the field perimeter on your right.

3 At a bend leave the track and follow the Larkbarrow bridleway sign up over a field, bearing slightly right. Turn left through a gate and follow blue waymarks along the fence and banks for 1½ miles (2.4km) to a waymark at the end of the straight line of the bank. Cross the middle of the field, bearing slightly left to a gate in the fence.

Distance: 9 miles (14.5km)
Total ascent: 920ft (280m)
Paths: vary from wide tracks to open moor; boggy in patches
Terrain: valley, fields, moor and heath
Gradients: mostly easy with short steep parts
Refreshments: teas at Cloud Farm and Malmsmead, cold drinks at County Gate (all seasonal)
Park: National Park car park, toilets and visitor centre at County Gate, 7miles (11.3km) west of Porlock on A39
Difficulty: 2

Bristol Channel

N

Old Barrow Hill
▲ 346

Embelle Wood

LYNTON

A39

County Gate

Yenworthy Farm

Yenworthy Lodge

Yenworthy Common

Broomstreet Farm

East Lyn River

Southern Wood

A39

PORLOCK

Oare House

MALMSMEAD

Cloud Farm

Oare Water

North Common

FELLINGSCOTT

OARE church

OAREFORD

Malmsmead Hill
▲ 388

Blackmore Memorial

Oare Common

Chalk Water

Badgworthy Wood

Oare church

Deer Park

South Common

Badgworthy Water

ford

Larkbarrow

Badgworthy Water

Trout Hill

Malmsmead

6 Go through a gate and down the road to Malmsmead. Turn right at the road junction and cross the bridge by the ford. Continue up the road for 400yds (364m) and turn left down a bridleway to pass Parsonage Farm. Cross a bridge, turn right and follow the bridleway up the steep hill to County Gate.

5 Through the gate, keep the bank on your left down to a track and gateway with a signpost. Turn right and follow the track signed to Doone Valley. The track passes through a small gate signed to Malmsmead, goes down to ford a stream, then up and down to a sturdy wooden bridge following a well defined track. Turn right and follow the same side of the river for 3 miles (4.8km), all the way down to Malmsmead. The track crosses a plank bridge in the Doone settlement and goes uphill and right to Malmsmead. Cross a bridge by the water slide at Lank Combe and, after Badgworthy Wood, pass the Blackmore Memorial.

4 Go through the gate and keep straight upwards across the middle of the next field and over the top to a gate through a low bank onto the moor, still following Larkbarrow bridleway signs. Cross the moor straight ahead and bearing slightly left. Keep straight on and do not be misled by numerous tracks. In ½ mile (800m) you should have rounded the head of a small combe and come to a gate in a bank with a bridleway sign.

½ mile

0   ½ km

Spectacular Views from the Quantock Hills

Last of the southwest moorlands, the Quantocks boast fine views over Somerset and the Bristol Channel

WALK

18

Distance: 7 miles (11.3km)
Total ascent: 820ft (250m)
Paths: mostly good but muddy after rain; shallow stream to ford in Holford Combe
Terrain: open heath or wooded valley
Gradients: gradual, but one short, steep downhill section
Refreshments: Plough Inn, Holford, and teas in village in season
Park: car park in old quarry by bowling green at Holford, on minor road between Holford village and Alfoxton Park
Difficulty: 2

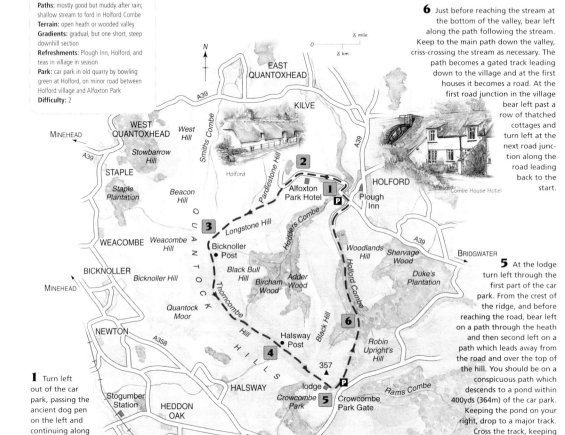

ponies, Quantock Hills

6 Just before reaching the stream at the bottom of the valley, bear left along the path following the stream. Keep to the main path down the valley, criss-crossing the stream as necessary. The path becomes a gated track leading down to the village and at the first houses it becomes a road. At the first road junction in the village bear left past a row of thatched cottages and turn left at the next road junction along the road leading back to the start.

5 At the lodge turn left through the first part of the car park. From the crest of the ridge, and before reaching the road, bear left on a path through the heath and then second left on a path which leads away from the road and over the top of the hill. You should be on a conspicuous path which descends to a pond within 400yds (364m) of the car park. Keeping the pond on your right, drop to a major track. Cross the track, keeping downhill towards the bottom of the wooded valley ahead. The path steepens at the edge of the wood and becomes stony.

1 Turn left out of the car park, passing the ancient dog pen on the left and continuing along the road. Keep on the road, which becomes a hotel drive, past Alfoxton Park Hotel, following the youth hostel signs.

2 Ascend steeply to a hairpin bend in the woods. Leave the road and continue straight ahead, following the path up the bottom of the valley. Emerging from the trees at a crossing of tracks on the heath, keep straight ahead, bearing slightly right and gradually uphill, following the sign for West Quantoxhead. Keep uphill on the main track. At the top of the hill turn left, descending slightly.

3 Soon you will meet the main track along the Quantock ridge at Bicknoller Post. Bear left along this track. You can follow the higher track over Thorncombe Hill or the lower one along the left-hand side of it, but continue ahead along the ridge. Keep slightly to the left along the top of the hill to join the main track, which drops to a tall post and crossing of tracks at Halsway Post.

4 Go straight ahead up the ridge with a fence on your right. Keep on the main track over the hill and down to a dip in the ridge and lodge at Crowcombe Park Gate.

WALK 19

ABOUT • PILSDON PEN

Pilsdon Pen, territory of the Durotriges tribe, commands a superb defensive position. By 600–400 bc the hill fort was a busy trading centre and the farmland you cross on this walk would have been familiar to generations of Iron-Age farmers.

Southwest England

DISTANCE • 6 miles (9.6km)	**GRADIENTS** • one short, steep climb and descent; otherwise gradual
TOTAL ASCENT • 450ft (137m)	
PATHS • well-marked; tracks may be muddy and difficult after prolonged rain (boots essential); otherwise firm; some road walking	**REFRESHMENTS** • pub at Birdsmoorgate
	PARK • lay-by on south side of B3164 at junction with minor road to Pilsdon village, 2 miles (3.2km) west of Broadwindsor
TERRAIN • grassland, fields, scrub, woodland	**DIFFICULTY** • 2

The Iron Age Farmers of Pilsdon Pen

❶ Cross the road and climb for 437yds (400m) to the top of Pilsdon Pen. Take the path in the far right corner, through three ramparts. At the fence, turn right to the National Trust notice board.

❷ Go through a gate, turn right with a plantation of young, broad-leaved trees on the left. Where the planting ends, turn downhill, diagonally right to a gateway. Follow the track to a lane. Cross and continue for ¼ mile (400m) to Lower Newnham Farm.

❸ At the farm, turn right, then left between barns. Keep ahead on the permissive path around the edge of field (can be muddy) to a bridge in a gap in the hedge. Cross the bridge and follow the track uphill. Before the track ends turn right over a stile and go along the field edge for 273yds (250m). Cross stiles and head diagonally right up the field to go through a gate.

❹ Turn right, down lane between high hedges. At a farm drive, keep ahead to the B3164. Turn left on to the road for 273yds (250m).

❺ Leave the road at the sign for Wall Farm. Immediately turn left uphill on a narrow track between banks with trees on top. As you enter woodland, keep ahead on a ridge, to the right of waymarked tree. Continue close to the ridge following the line of low-spreading beech trees to right.

❻ As the beech bank curves right before a clearing, walk straight ahead to the brow of the hill. Here, turn left on a crossing path and

head up to the line of trees on the horizon. Aim for the National Trust Lewesdon Hill sign, a third of the way along from the right.

❼ Enter beech woods and follow a

broad path. Over the rise, keep ahead on the grass, soon curving right, with steep beech hangers either side. At the end of the flat top, take the obvious, narrow path ahead, passing the NT sign. Beech trees crown the banks on either side. Keep near to the right bank and follow path into a gulley. Meet a track and turn right.

❽ Go through a gate and turn right on to a lane. Pass Higher

Brimley Coombe Farm and Lower Brimley Coombe Cottages. Keep straight ahead on the track. Drop down round a wooded gulley, and climb to a gate. Don't go through the gate, but follow the track uphill to the right, along the side of the hill. Where the main track swings right, turn left on to a narrow path between hedges. Go through a gate, then follow the blue waymarker uphill. Meet the B3164 and turn left to return to your car.

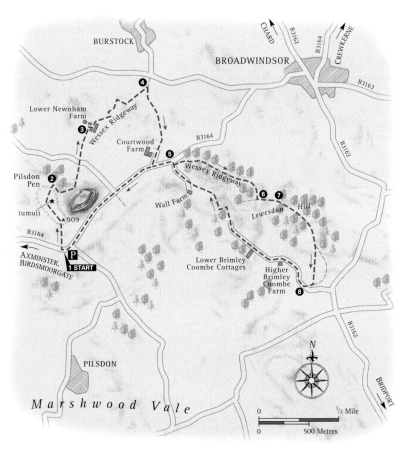

WALK 20

The Benedictine monastery at Abbotsbury was founded in 1044 and demolished during the Dissolution of Monasteries, ordered by Henry VIII. The tithe barn is all that remains but serves as a reminder of the power once wielded by this gentle order of monks.

Southwest England

DISTANCE • 6½ miles (10.4km)	**GRADIENTS** • gradual climb to St Catherine's Chapel, short steep climb to Abbotsbury hill fort
TOTAL ASCENT • 650ft (198m)	
PATHS • well-marked throughout; ascent to Abbotsbury hill fort and some paths can be muddy and difficult after prolonged rain; otherwise firm; road-walking in village	**REFRESHMENTS** • choice in Abbotsbury
	PARK • village car park
TERRAIN • village roads, grassland, short stretch of shingle, tarmac track and fields	**DIFFICULTY** • 2

Around Abbotsbury's Monastic Complex

❶ With your back to the entrance to the village car park, take the path in the far right corner of the car park. Turn left at a ruined gable wall, part of an abbey outbuilding, turn right at the pond, and then left on to the lane. The tithe barn is ahead of you. Continue to a fork. Take the right-hand road, signed Swannery Pedestrians.

❷ At a low stone waymarker, turn right on to a track to St Catherine's Chapel. Keep ahead over a footbridge and skirt the hill. Join the track that climbs 437yds (400m) to the chapel.

❸ From the stile behind the chapel, walk to the brow of the hill and then go downhill, aiming right and following the line of a copse. At the foot of the slope, reach a stone waymarker. To visit the Swannery (Mar-Oct), keep straight ahead for just over ½ mile (800m). Retrace your steps to this point.

❹ From the waymarker, follow signs for the Sub-Tropical Gardens, skirting the hill with the sea on your left. Turn left along the coast path (may be muddy), signed Chesil Beach, for ½ a mile (800m).

A short stretch (800ft/250m) on shingle brings you back to the beach car park.

❺ Continue on the tarmac path, with Chesil Bank on your left. Pass the drive to Lawrence's Cottage, and at a low stone waymarker turn right uphill, for the hill fort. Go round the back of East Bexington Farm and diagonally right uphill towards a cottage in trees. Over a stile turn immediately right, with the hedge on your right. Enter an area of scrub and trees and follow the sign to the hill fort. The path is steep and can be muddy and slippery. At the top, follow the stone wall to the right. Reach the road and, across it, the double-bank Iron Age hill fort.

❻ Walk along the southern rampart with superb views over the Fleet, Chesil Beach and Portland. Past the trig point, drop down to a stile and cross a lane. Continue along Wears Hill.

❼ Just beyond a gate, reach a signpost. Following directions for Abbotsbury village, walk diagonally right downhill for 328yds (300m), through old stone quarries, and continue for 875yds (800m) to join Blind Lane. Turn right into Back Street and left on to the main road through the village for village car park. If you used beach car park, continue from Point ❶.

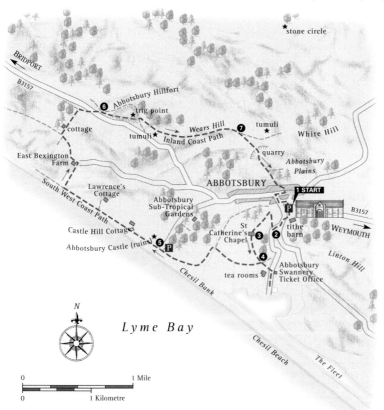

Lyme Bay

0 — 1 Mile
0 — 1 Kilometre

Purbeck's Ghost Village

*Lost in time, the Dorset village of Tyneham is preserved
amid the army ranges*

WALK

21

1 Turn right from the car park, towards Tyneham village. The town trail is short but interesting. Each of the buildings has a marker and a leaflet available from the church explains what they were. The church and schoolroom contain an exhibition of the village history.

7 Return to the path and, following the yellow markers, ascend Gad Cliff and proceed along the coastal path. Cross a stile and, at the sign pointing left to Tyneham, head downhill following the markers. This will return you to the car park.

2 From the water fountain in front of the church take the road to the right past a marker pointing to Flower's Barrow and Whiteway car park. Follow the yellow waymarkers, passing behind the church and going through a kissing gate, and continue uphill.

6 Continue over the wooden bridge and turn left up a stone track, going right at the yellow marker, up the steps to arrive at a cairn. From here take the track up Worbarrow Tout for a superb view over the bay and the switchback cliffs.

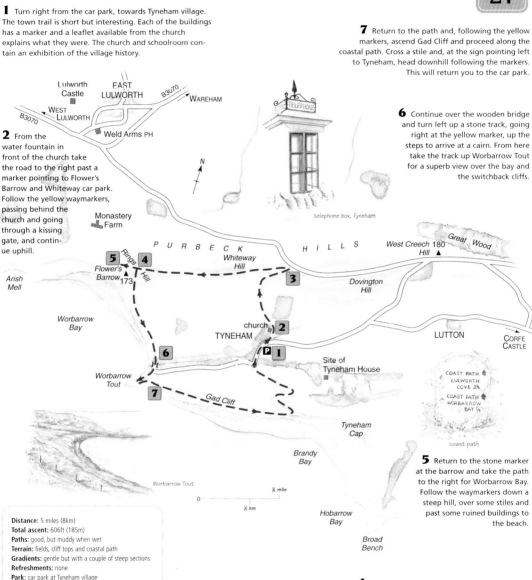

telephone box, Tyneham

5 Return to the stone marker at the barrow and take the path to the right for Worbarrow Bay. Follow the waymarkers down a steep hill, over some stiles and past some ruined buildings to the beach.

Distance: 5 miles (8km)
Total ascent: 606ft (185m)
Paths: good, but muddy when wet
Terrain: fields, cliff tops and coastal path
Gradients: gentle but with a couple of steep sections
Refreshments: none
Park: car park at Tyneham village
Note: this walk is on the Lulworth Army Ranges and access is strictly controlled. They are open most weekends and in holiday periods, but for up-to-date information, call the MOD Range Office on 01929 462721 ext. 4819
Difficulty: 2

3 At the flagpole at the top take the path to the left, cross a stile and head uphill past a trig point. Continue on the path downhill, until the road curves to the right. Veer left onto a track at the yellow marker.

4 Continue along the track, over a stile, following yellow waymarkers. When you reach an area with picnic tables, you are in the middle of Flower's Barrow. A stone marker points the way to Lulworth Cove. Continue on this path to the outer rings of this prehistoric fortification for a superb view along the coast.

Dorset Heaths of Thomas Hardy

Explore the rolling, varied landscape which the writer knew and loved

Distance: 9 miles (14.4km)
Total ascent: 165ft (50m)
Paths: good but muddy in wet weather
Terrain: heathland, woodland, open roads and fields
Ascents: very few and gradual
Refreshments: Wise Man Inn, West Stafford (half way round the walk)
Park: Hardy's Cottage car park (National Trust), Higher Bockhampton
Difficulty: 2

1 From the car park head for Hardy's Cottage, signed via a woodland path. From there take the path, signposted Puddletown, to a path junction. Continue to the next junction and turn right, continuing until the path descends steeply. The Rainbarrow is through a break in the hedge to the right.

2 Continue down the steep path, ignoring all other paths, until it turns left to the bottom of the hill. Take the small track through the bushes, ignoring the stile to the right, continuing over two stiles then left across the field. Cross the road to the track opposite.

8 Go through the farmyard and follow the footpath sign. Cross 3 fields, over stiles, through gates and past a house, turning left onto a farm track. Continue across a minor road, eventually turning left at a crossroads. The path forks right, then turns left and leads down to the car park.

7 Over a bridge turn right, following the waymarkers, through a kissing-gate, across a field and a bridge. Continue over another bridge, turn left and then right to Stinsford. Retrace your steps to the river and continue to Lower Bockhampton. Cross the bridge and turn left, signposted Thorncombe Wood.

6 Cross to Max Gate. Continue across the bridge, turning right before the roundabout and right again towards a gate marked Louds. Turn left before this, into Smokey Hole Lane. Cross a railway bridge down to a road. Turn right, right again then left for Stinsford.

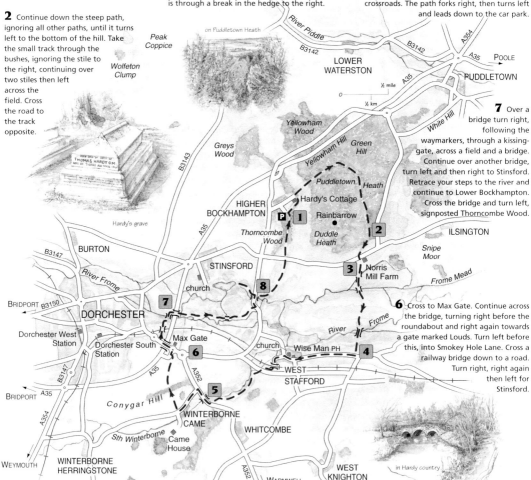

3 Continue along the farm track until a junction; bear left then right following the blue waymarkers. Follow this track across the field and cross the bridge over the river. Follow the blue waymarker through a gate and continue to the end of the track. Turn right at the gate, then go over the field to cross the wooden bridge and stile. Walk with the fence to the left, over another stile, across the field and through the gate to reach the end of the track.

4 Continue to the junction with the road, then turn right to West Stafford. Turn left at the church along Rectory Lane. Follow the blue waymarkers, under the railway bridge, across the road and over a stile. Continue through several gates until you reach a gate to the main road.

5 Turn right and then left through gates beside a lodge. Continue to the crossroads at Came and turn right towards Dorchester. At the top, where the road curves, go straight ahead. Cross the stile, following signs for Max Gate, exiting at a roundabout.

The Mystery of the Cerne Abbas Giant

High on a Dorset hillside a strange figure is carved in the chalk

WALK
23

1 In Cerne Abbas, make your way to the church, which stands in Abbey Street and walk along the street with the church to your right. To your left is an elegant row of timbered houses complete with overhangs.

2 Go past the village pond, to the right. Ahead now is beautiful Abbey Farm.

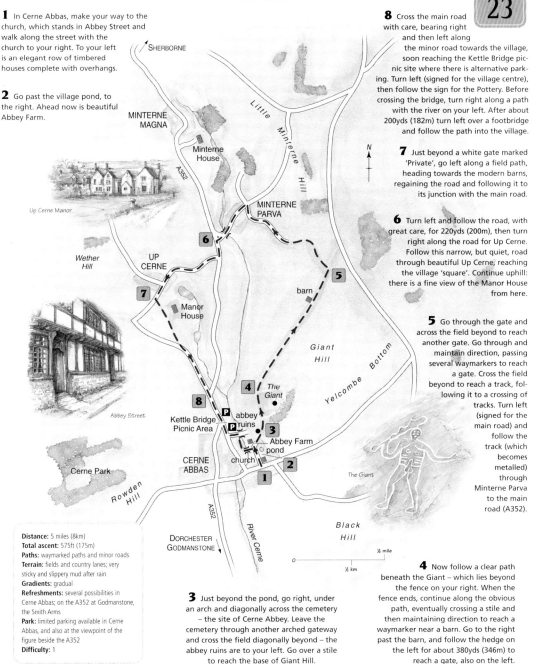

8 Cross the main road with care, bearing right and then left along the minor road towards the village, soon reaching the Kettle Bridge picnic site where there is alternative parking. Turn left (signed for the village centre), then follow the sign for the Pottery. Before crossing the bridge, turn right along a path with the river on your left. After about 200yds (182m) turn left over a footbridge and follow the path into the village.

7 Just beyond a white gate marked 'Private', go left along a field path, heading towards the modern barns, regaining the road and following it to its junction with the main road.

6 Turn left and follow the road, with great care, for 220yds (200m), then turn right along the road for Up Cerne. Follow this narrow, but quiet, road through beautiful Up Cerne, reaching the village 'square'. Continue uphill: there is a fine view of the Manor House from here.

5 Go through the gate and across the field beyond to reach another gate. Go through and maintain direction, passing several waymarkers to reach a gate. Cross the field beyond to reach a track, following it to a crossing of tracks. Turn left (signed for the main road) and follow the track (which becomes metalled) through Minterne Parva to the main road (A352).

4 Now follow a clear path beneath the Giant – which lies beyond the fence on your right. When the fence ends, continue along the obvious path, eventually crossing a stile and then maintaining direction to reach a waymarker near a barn. Go to the right past the barn, and follow the hedge on the left for about 380yds (346m) to reach a gate, also on the left.

3 Just beyond the pond, go right, under an arch and diagonally across the cemetery – the site of Cerne Abbey. Leave the cemetery through another arched gateway and cross the field diagonally beyond – the abbey ruins are to your left. Go over a stile to reach the base of Giant Hill.

Distance: 5 miles (8km)
Total ascent: 575ft (175m)
Paths: waymarked paths and minor roads
Terrain: fields and country lanes; very sticky and slippery mud after rain
Gradients: gradual
Refreshments: several possibilities in Cerne Abbas; on the A352 at Godmanstone, the Smith Arms
Park: limited parking available in Cerne Abbas, and also at the viewpoint of the figure beside the A352
Difficulty: 1

ABOUT • SHERBORNE

Founded by the Saxons and set amid green valleys and wooded hills, Sherborne is a lovely, mellow-stoned town. It was also home to one of the most famous figures of the Elizabethan court, Sir Walter Raleigh, who lived here from 1592 until his death in 1618.

Southwest England

DISTANCE • 5½ miles (8.8km)	**REFRESHMENTS** • choice of pubs and cafés in Sherborne; tea room in Sherborne Castle
TOTAL ASCENT • 400ft (121m)	
PATHS • good, but field paths can be waterlogged after heavy rain	**PARKING** • main long-stay car park accessed off Long Street or Ludbourne Road (close to Sainsbury's). Alternative parking at station
TERRAIN • parkland, farmland, town streets	
GRADIENTS • gradual; one steep ascent	**DIFFICULTY** • 2

Sir Walter's Refuge

❶ With your back to the abbey, turn left along Half Moon Street, then right down South Street. Fork left past Sainsbury's and cross the railway to a T-junction. Cross over and take the waymarked path left, diagonally uphill. Bear left beside railings down to a turnstile gate and right along the drive to visit Sherborne New Castle.

❷ Return along the drive to the turnstile gate and go uphill. Bear left and beyond the gate take the grassy path between fields to a gate. Bear right on a track to a gate and go uphill towards a thatched building in trees. Go through a gate and go steeply uphill into the deer park. Bear right at the top to a gate into woodland.

❸ Shortly, follow the path left, and disregarding the concrete path right, keep ahead to farm buildings. Turn right along the access road to a drive. Turn left, then right with a yellow marker down a track along the field edge. At a junction of paths, cross the stile on your left and walk beside woodland to a gate (house left).

❹ Enter the deer park and proceed straight ahead, downhill along the line of telegraph poles, towards a farmhouse. Keep ahead beyond a gate to cross a bridge over the River Yeo. Continue along the right-hand field edge to a gate beside Pinford Farm.

❺ Turn left along the drive, then just beyond a gate, turn right through a gate into a field. Head uphill towards an ornate drive entrance and a gate. Turn right through the gateway and take the second path left. In a few paces, bear right following yellow markers along a path through a copse, eventually reaching a stile.

❻ Head straight across the field to a gate, then bear half-left to double stiles in the hedge. Proceed diagonally right to a gate and pass beneath the railway bridge. Just beyond, bear off right to a stone stile and walk to the A30, beside St Cuthbert's Old Church.

❼ Cross and follow the lane to Oborne. Cross the small bridge on your left, pass the church and keep ahead, uphill along a cobbled path. Remain on the path to the A30.

❽ Follow the bridleway opposite, beside Four Acres, to a stile and descend to a gate. Keep ahead to a gate and go through the farmyard to a lane. Turn left, then right at the T-junction into Sherborne. For the Old Castle take the first road left; otherwise, keep ahead along Long Street into the town.

• DON'T MISS •

St Cuthbert's Old Church in Sherborne, is an enchanting small stone building between the A30 and the railway station. Only the chancel survives of the 1553 church. Note the 14th-century slip-tiles, the rustic, 17th-century communion rails, and the medieval pillar piscina.

Map

0 — 1 Mile
0 — 1 Kilometre

N

B3145
SHAFTESBURY
A30
OBORNE
❼
❻
St Cuthbert's Old Church
❽
SHERBORNE
B3148
❺ Pinford Farm
YEOVIL
A30
Old Castle
Sherborne Lake
abbey
P
1 START
station
Sherborne New Castle
❷
thatched building
❸
HAYDON
house
❹
River Yeo
Honeycomb Wood
DORCHESTER
A3030
A352
NORTH WOOTTON
ALWESTON

The Other Sides to Cheddar Gorge

A fine circuit of nature proves there is more to Cheddar than cheese and tourists

WALK

25

1 From car park turn right towards the Gorge. Cross the bridge and take the next road on the right, keeping uphill. Just before the brow of the hill turn left up behind cottages. At the end of the lane follow the bridleway up to the left. Keep following the Gorge Walk waymarks along the edge of the gorge for 1¼ miles (2km). The path ascends to the top of a ridge and descends through woodland to the road at the head of the Gorge.

2 Cross the road and take the gate and track ahead into Black Rock reserve. Follow the main track up the bottom of the valley for ⅔ mile (1km). After the National Trust sign turn right over a wall and follow the waymarks up the bottom of the valley for another mile (1.6km).

6 Cross a stile from fields into a scrubby area. Bear left, then right, to pick up the Gorge Walk waymarks. Keep dowhill with the Gorge on your left. It is worth the detour down a steep flight of steps to a viewpoint. Returning, the path steepens to descend through woods to a track. Turn left down the track, then right and down the road through the Gorge to return to the start.

5 Turn right along the road and take the next turn to the left, down a farm drive. Keep right of Charterhouse and Piney Sleight Farms, then follow the yellow waymarks ahead across fields, keeping close to the walls on your right.

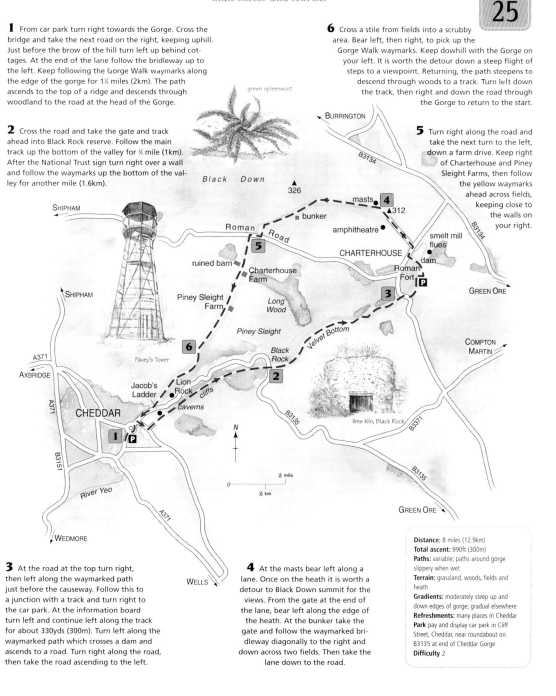

green spleenwort

BURRINGTON

Black Down

▲ 326

SHIPHAM

Roman Road

masts **4**
▲312

bunker

amphitheatre ●

smelt mill flues

CHARTERHOUSE

dam

ruined barn

5

Charterhouse Farm

Roman Fort 🅿

GREEN ORE

SHIPHAM

Piney Sleight Farm

Long Wood

Piney Sleight

3

Velvet Bottom

COMPTON MARTIN

A371

6

Pavey's Tower

Black Rock

AXBRIDGE

Lion Rock

Jacob's Ladder

cliffs

Caverns

2

B3135

lime kiln, Black Rock

B3371

CHEDDAR

1 🅿

N

B3151

½ mile

River Yeo

0   ½ km

B3135

A371

GREEN ORE

WEDMORE

3 At the road at the top turn right, then left along the waymarked path just before the causeway. Follow this to a junction with a track and turn right to the car park. At the information board turn left and continue left along the track for about 330yds (300m). Turn left along the waymarked path which crosses a dam and ascends to a road. Turn right along the road, then take the road ascending to the left.

WELLS

4 At the masts bear left along a lane. Once on the heath it is worth a detour to Black Down summit for the views. From the gate at the end of the lane, bear left along the edge of the heath. At the bunker take the gate and follow the waymarked bridleway diagonally to the right and down across two fields. Then take the lane down to the road.

Distance: 8 miles (12.9km)
Total ascent: 990ft (300m)
Paths: variable; paths around gorge slippery when wet
Terrain: grassland, woods, fields and heath
Gradients: moderately steep up and down edges of gorge; gradual elsewhere
Refreshments: many places in Cheddar
Park pay and display car park in Cliff Street, Cheddar, near roundabout on B3135 at end of Cheddar Gorge
Difficulty 2

WALK

26

In 1685, Wells was the centre of strife as a rebel army arrived looking for new recruits to overthrow the papist King. After the Battle of Sedgemoor, Lord Chief Justice Jeffreys arrived in Wells and condemned hundreds of rebels to death or transportation.

Southwest England

DISTANCE • 9½ miles (15.3km)

TOTAL ASCENT • 1,000ft (305m)

PATHS • streets then field tracks and farm lanes, a little road walking

TERRAIN • town, pastureland and woodland

GRADIENTS • a steep ascent up the Mendip escarpment out of Wookey Hole

REFRESHMENTS • several pubs and tea shops in Wells and Wookey Hole, none on rest of route

PARK • by the old Tythe Barn in Silver Street

DIFFICULTY • 3

Wells and the Pitchfork Rebellion

❶ Walk up Silver Street to the Bishop's Palace. Turn left by the moat, go under arch into Market Square. Turn right at the far right corner up Sadler Street. Go right on to New Street and follow it round to the left. Turn left, signed West Mendip Way, and follow the alley around to a left turn, down Lover's Walk. At the back of the sports' pitches fork right, and right over the footbridge. Go through the school grounds to a gate on the far side. Continue up the hill towards houses. Cross the road and at the top of the footpath opposite, cross to another footpath. Go through a gate to emerge on a track.

❷ In 50yds (46m) turn left on a road, uphill past a quarry. Turn left (workings on your left). Bear right through the woods at a stile just before the road bends right. By lime kilns, turn left down a lane. In 400yds (366m), as lane veers left, go through gate, right, to a fenced path, left. Go down the left edge of a field, turn right on the road into Wookey Hole, pass the pub, bear left in front of the paper mill. Turn right towards the caves.

❸ Walk up the lane until it bends round right. Cross the fields, following signs for Monarch's Way. Go half right up the field, aiming for a fence into some woods. Continue up the hill to a junction of hedges. Beyond this, turn left to meet the top of Green Lane, coming up from the other side of the Coomb. Turn right and continue up the hill.

❹ At top go right, in front of wall. Cross three fields; in fourth, aim for hedge in front of buildings. Turn right down to a gate on left. Go through and follow hedge, carry on half-left to a track. Over

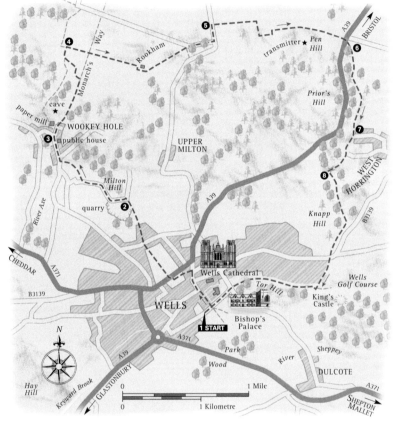

cattle grid go left past a bungalow and right at junction with Durston Drove. At T-junction, go left along Old Bristol Road for 200yds/183m.

❺ Turn right, signed Pen Hill, cross two fields, a stile and tuen right. Follow field edge to stile on far side. Turn right, to transmitter support. Through gate to follow a track round to the right, emerging on road in front of a white house.

❻ Go through a gate opposite to join a bridleway to the right of a field. Go through a gate in the corner and descend to the stream. Continue down through the woods then through a gate and stile on the left. Bear right with the stream and stay with the rising track.

❼ In a clearing by a white house turn right and follow the track left to a stile. Cross and follow the

left-hand field edge to a stile in the next field. Immediately beyond, turn right down to a stile. Descend steps to cross a bridge, turn left.

❽ Follow the path to Wells Golf Club. Cross the road, go through the gate to the path between the golf course and houses. Continue on this streamside path to a road. Cross, go through gate opposite and return to Silver Street.

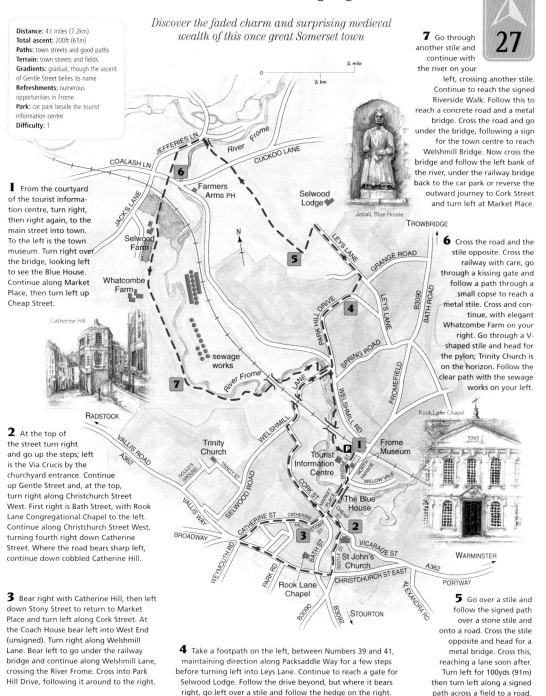

Frome's Medieval Highlights

WALK

27

Discover the faded charm and surprising medieval
wealth of this once great Somerset town

Distance: 4½ miles (7.2km)
Total ascent: 200ft (61m)
Paths: town streets and good paths
Terrain: town streets and fields
Gradients: gradual, though the ascent of Gentle Street belies its name
Refreshments: numerous opportunities in Frome
Park: car park beside the tourist information centre
Difficulty: 1

detail, Blue House

1 From the courtyard of the tourist information centre, turn right, then right again, to the main street into town. To the left is the town museum. Turn right over the bridge, looking left to see the Blue House. Continue along Market Place, then turn left up Cheap Street.

Catherine Hill

2 At the top of the street turn right and go up the steps; left is the Via Crucis by the churchyard entrance. Continue up Gentle Street and, at the top, turn right along Christchurch Street West. First right is Bath Street, with Rook Lane Congregational Chapel to the left. Continue along Christchurch Street West, turning fourth right down Catherine Street. Where the road bears sharp left, continue down cobbled Catherine Hill.

3 Bear right with Catherine Hill, then left down Stony Street to return to Market Place and turn left along Cork Street. At the Coach House bear left into West End (unsigned). Turn right along Welshmill Lane. Bear left to go under the railway bridge and continue along Welshmill Lane, crossing the River Frome. Cross into Park Hill Drive, following it around to the right.

4 Take a footpath on the left, between Numbers 39 and 41, maintaining direction along Packsaddle Way for a few steps before turning left into Leys Lane. Continue to reach a gate for Selwood Lodge. Follow the drive beyond, but where it bears right, go left over a stile and follow the hedge on the right.

5 Go over a stile and follow the signed path over a stone stile and onto a road. Cross the stile opposite and head for a metal bridge. Cross this, reaching a lane soon after. Turn left for 100yds (91m) then turn left along a signed path across a field to a road.

6 Cross the road and the stile opposite. Cross the railway with care, go through a kissing gate and follow a path through a small copse to reach a metal stile. Cross and continue, with elegant Whatcombe Farm on your right. Go through a V-shaped stile and head for the pylon; Trinity Church is on the horizon. Follow the clear path with the sewage works on your left.

7 Go through another stile and continue with the river on your left, crossing another stile. Continue to reach the signed Riverside Walk. Follow this to reach a concrete road and a metal bridge. Cross the road and go under the bridge, following a sign for the town centre to reach Welshmill Bridge. Now cross the bridge and follow the left bank of the river, under the railway bridge back to the car park or reverse the outward journey to Cork Street and turn left at Market Place.

ABOUT • FOSSE WAY

Shortly after the Roman invasion military roads were laid across Britain to enable speedy movement of troops. As well as being straight, you can often identify them by the agger, the raised platform between two ditches, which makes for their distinctive profile.

Southwest England

DISTANCE • 5 miles (8km)

TOTAL ASCENT • 390ft (119m)

PATHS • field tracks, country lanes and a converted railway track bed

TERRAIN • pastureland and edge of town

GRADIENTS • steep ascent from Welton Hollow and Clandown Bottom

REFRESHMENTS • none on the route but several pubs in Radstock, Welton and Midsomer Norton

PARK • 100yds (91m) up Millards Hill or carefully down the lane towards Welton Manor Farm

DIFFICULTY • 2

A Roman Highway through the Mendips

❶ Walk down the lane towards Welton Manor Farm, go through the left-hand gate and follow the right-hand field edge to a stile. Cross and continue for 300yds (274m) to another stile on the right. Walk diagonally across the field, heading for a railway bridge. Cross the stile and climb the steps to the Norton–Radstock Greenway. Turn left and follow the former railway for 500yds (457m) to some bollards across the track.

❷ Turn left and cross the stile into the field. Keep the hedge on your left and follow the rising path to a gate into an enclosed lane. Follow this section of Roman road (the Fosse Way) between hedges and up on to the top of the hill. Continue as it dips back down between hedgerows to Clandown Bottom. Cross a stream and turn left as you emerge in housing.

❸ Turn left at the T-junction along Springfield Place. Pass the old chapel (converted into housing) and go through an arch in the row of cottages ahead to a gate and field beyond. Follow the streamside path up the valley. At the end of the field cross the stile and continue on a better track with the stream on your left. Cross a stile by a gate and bear right to join a farm track coming down the hill. Turn immediately left and continue through a gate on to a road.

❹ Cross, go through the gate opposite and walk up the track with the stream on your left. Near the head of the valley, aim for the top left-hand corner by a pond. Cross the stream, go through a gate and follow the left-hand field edge up to a stile in the corner. Stay with the hedge to the next stile. Cross, turn half-right aiming for a stile diagonally opposite.

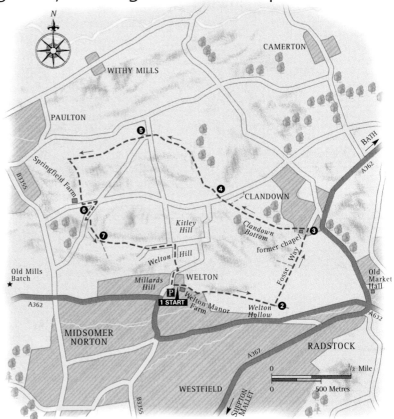

❺ Emerge on a road and take the lane directly opposite. After 100yds (91m), as the lane swings left, take the footpath on the right along the edge of a field. Cross a stile at the far corner and continue with the hedge on your right, then go across the opening to a side field. Turn left at the end on an enclosed lane; turn right. Cross the stile and turn left into a field. Follow the left-hand edge until it becomes an enclosed lane. Go through the gate and go down the hill to join a farm track. Turn left by Springfield Farm.

❻ Turn right at the junction. In 200 yds (183m) turn left through a stile, then turn right beyond a gap in the hedge. Follow the hedge through two fields and, 50yds (46m) into a third field, turn left to join a crossing path over a stile on the far eastern side.

❼ Follow the enclosed Binces Lodge Lane, past a white house on the left, until it becomes surfaced and joins a minor road on a bend. Go straight ahead to another junction on the right. Turn right past a row of houses. At the end of the road keep straight on down the snicket (narrow alley between houses) to emerge on the bend in Millards Hill, 100yds (91m) above the start.

Lansdown – a Civil War Battle for Bath

Where Sir Beville Grenville led his Cornishmen in a heroic charge

1 From lay-by cross road and follow well-waymarked Cotswold Way, joining private road to fire brigade building.

2 Turn right with Way just before brigade complex, then, soon, left along field path. Follow Way to trig point on Hanging Hill, seen over wall. Turn left over stile and step left to walk past trig point, continuing with hedge on right. Cross stile to reach golf course, bearing left to follow bridleway along left edge. Turn right, as signed, to follow Cotswold Way across course and then left along bridleway between wood on right, and course's northern edge, on left.

3 Leave course through gate, soon turning left off descending track, with Cotswold Way to stile. Walk parallel with fence on left, and follow it sharp left then on, across Little Down hill fort, exiting across section of ditch. Turn right and follow edge of hill, with race course starting stalls on left, to panorama dial at Prospect Stile.

8 Eventually, Cotswold Way joins from right. Carry on through gate and after 100yds (91m) go right, uphill to wall and Cotswold Way signpost. Go over stile and walk with wall on right to scarp edge where much of the Battle of Lansdown was fought, before bearing left to monument. Lay-by is 100yds (91m) further along track.

7 Continue past church, passing house on right, to Tynings Cottage (on left). Turn left just before cottage, climbing steep lane. Go over crest and descend to barn on right. Turn left up signed bridleway, maintaining direction where it narrows.

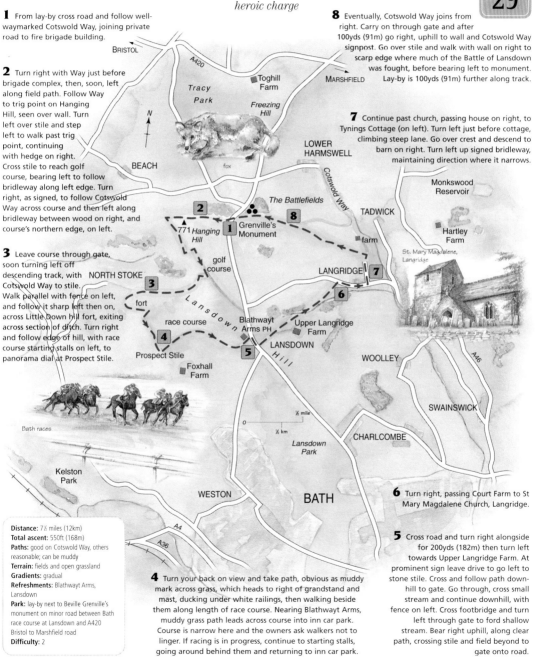

6 Turn right, passing Court Farm to St Mary Magdalene Church, Langridge.

5 Cross road and turn right alongside for 200yds (182m) then turn left towards Upper Langridge Farm. At prominent sign leave drive to go left to stone stile. Cross and follow path down-hill to gate. Go through, cross small stream and continue downhill, with fence on left. Cross footbridge and turn left through gate to ford shallow stream. Bear right uphill, along clear path, crossing stile and field beyond to gate onto road.

4 Turn your back on view and take path, obvious as muddy mark across grass, which heads to right of grandstand and mast, ducking under white railings, then walking beside them along length of race course. Nearing Blathwayt Arms, muddy grass path leads across course to inn car park. Course is narrow here and the owners ask walkers not to linger. If racing is in progress, continue to starting stalls, going around behind them and returning to inn car park.

Distance: 7½ miles (12km)
Total ascent: 550ft (168m)
Paths: good on Cotswold Way, others reasonable; can be muddy
Terrain: fields and open grassland
Gradients: gradual
Refreshments: Blathwayt Arms, Lansdown
Park: lay-by next to Beville Grenville's monument on minor road between Bath race course at Lansdown and A420 Bristol to Marshfield road
Difficulty: 2

WALK

30

ABOUT • BRISTOL

A walk around Bristol will reveal the city's role in the 18th-century slaving triangle. It is worth picking up a booklet on the Slave Trade Trail, from the Tourist Information Centre, as it makes a valuable companion as you tour the city.

Southwest England

DISTANCE • 4½ miles (7.2km)	**REFRESHMENTS** • a huge range throughout route
TOTAL ASCENT • 215ft (66m)	
PATHS • pavements throughout	**PARK** • Bristol Industrial Museum pay-and-display (maximum three hours)
TERRAIN • city centre, parkland, quayside and residential streets	**DIFFICULTY** • 1
GRADIENTS • very steep ascent of Constitution Hill	

On the Slave Trade Trail

❶ From the museum turn left over Wapping Bridge. Turn left on the quayside and walk around the Arnolfini Gallery, to cross Pero's Bridge. Go ahead towards the TIC then veer right by Explore@Bristol. Turn right in front of the museum and cross the road to go up some steps. Pass the cathedral on your left to emerge on College Green and turn left.

❷ Continue to Deanery Road and take the second right up York Place, opposite the Three Tuns. Cross into Brandon Hill Park up some steps and take the left-hand path. Walk through the park and emerge on Jacob's Well Road by the Wildlife Trust. Cross and walk up Constitution Hill.

❸ At the top cross Lower Clifton Hill and Clifton Road. Bear left, on the level, to Regent Street and turn right up Merchant's Road. Turn left and walk round Victoria Square. At the end of the second side, turn right in front of Lansdown Place, then left down Queen's Road. Take the first left down Richmond Park Road to Pembroke Road.

❹ Turn right and cross Queen's Road down Richmond Hill. At the bottom, turn left down Queen's Road and cross the Triangle. Turn left down Park Street and second left on Great George Street to see the Georgian House. From here the walk follows the Slave Trade Trail.

❺ Return to Park Street and turn right. Cross and take next left along Unity Street then right down Denmark Street . At the bottom, turn left on St Augustine's Parade. Go along Colston Avenue under the Centregate arch to the Three Loaves of Sugar. Continue under the arches of modern buildings to Lewin's Mead Sugar House on the left.

❻ Turn right and cross through the arch opposite to Broad Street. Take the third alley on the left to see Taylor's Court, then return to Broad Street, past the Guildhall and turn right to look at Corn Street. Turn round at the Commercial Rooms and return towards Broad Street but turn right in front of No 56, down All Saint's Lane by All Saint's Church.

Go straight ahead through the covered market and across two roads. Descend steps by St Nicholas's Church and cross to the waterfront along Welsh Back.

❼ Take the second right up King Street, past the Llandoger Trow and the Theatre Royal. At the bottom, turn left and follow the pavement round into Queen Square. From the Custom House, cross the park, turn left to the Hole in the Wall, cross the road and then the bridge on Redcliffe Way.

❽ Go right, round roundabout past the Quaker Burial Ground (left) and St Mary Redcliffe (right) on to Redcliffe Hill. Take the second right on Guinea Street, and right down Alfred and Jubilee Places. Turn right on to Redcliffe Parade East, and cross to descend a ramp to the quayside by Redcliffe Caves.

❾ Follow the quayside round to the left and cross the footbridge in front of the Ostrich. Turn right to Merchant's Wharf, Wapping Bridge and the Industrial Museum.

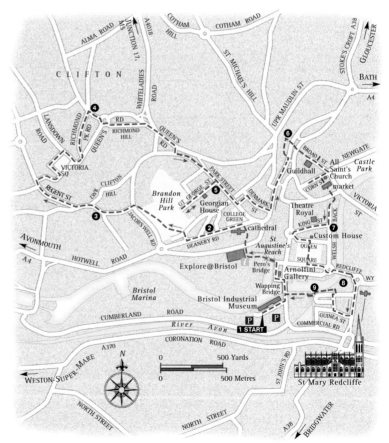

WALK 31

The opening of the Severn Bridge in 1966 was a remarkable event. It was then one of the world's longest spanning bridges and still remains a remarkable landmark. During your walk it is worth pausing at the viewing platform to enjoy the views.

Southwest England

DISTANCE • 5½ miles (8.8km)	**REFRESHMENTS** • Boars Head, Aust; White Hart, Littleton-upon-Severn
TOTAL ASCENT • 262ft (80m)	**PARK** • roadside parking in Aust
PATHS • field and riverside paths and tracks	**DIFFICULTY** • 2
TERRAIN • gentle farmland on the eastern shore of the Severn	
GRADIENTS • one steep climb near the end of the walk	

Views Over the Severn Estuary

❶ With Aust church behind you, walk through the village and turn left just before the Boars Head into Sandy Lane. Bear right by cottages and modern houses and pass beneath the motorway. Go straight over at the next junction towards Manor Farm offices and keep to the left of the farmhouse.

❷ When the track swings right to a house, continue ahead through a galvanised gate. Head up the right-hand boundary of the field to a waymark by the hedge corner. Veer diagonally right across the field and make for a gate in the bottom corner. Follow the field edge for a few paces to reach a galvanised gate and stile. Turn left here and follow the track to Cote Farm. Just beyond the farm buildings, veer off to the right to a gate and stile.

❸ Pass under power lines and make for a stile in the field corner. Keep ahead, following the field boundary round to the left and right. Head for a gate, cross a stream and then join a clear track which runs all the way to the village of Littleton-upon-Severn. Turn left at Salmon Lodge and follow the road to the White Hart

Inn. Head out of the village to a green and turn left at the junction.

❹ Follow the lane through countryside, passing cottages on the left. Oldbury Nuclear Power Station is in the distance, over to the right. Pass a footpath on the left and a bridleway on the right and follow the lane to the entrance to a cottage on the right. Bear left over a stile and join the Severn Way, following the path up the embankment.

❺ Walk along the old sea wall towards the Severn Bridge. When you reach an electricity substation on the left, look for a gate and stile. Cross over and head up the steep hillside to the remains of an old look-out. Keep right and cross two stiles into the grounds of the

Severn View service station. Walk along to the Severn Bridge viewing area and follow the path to a sign for Aust.

❻ Go down the steps and across the top of the motorway toll booth. Bear left on the far side and walk down to the next junction. Keep right and pass the Severn River Crossing maintenance unit before reaching the next junction. Turn left and cross the A403, following the road back to Aust and the start of the walk.

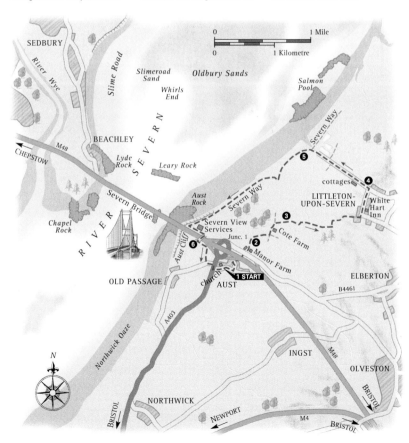

WALK 32

Uley Bury and Hetty Pegler's Tump

*Strange earthworks abound on this walk through
the Cotswold fringe*

1 In Uley take the path to the right of the church; before the churchyard wall ends, bear right up a path which leads to a stile into a steeply rising grassy field.

2 Climb the slope, aiming diagonally left, up to a stile into the woods. Follow the path up through the woods to another stile. Cross the stile and bear left to walk around the ramparts of Uley Bury hill fort, a 1-mile (1.6km) circuit. Keep high up when you get to the second side of the fort.

3 After completing three sides of the circuit, keep ahead through the trees for 200yds (182m) to join the well-waymarked Cotswold Way below a lay-by on the B4066. Follow the Cotswold Way through Coaley Wood for 1 mile (1.6km) and on reaching a junction of path, bridleway and road end, take a sharp right, ascending to meet the B4066.

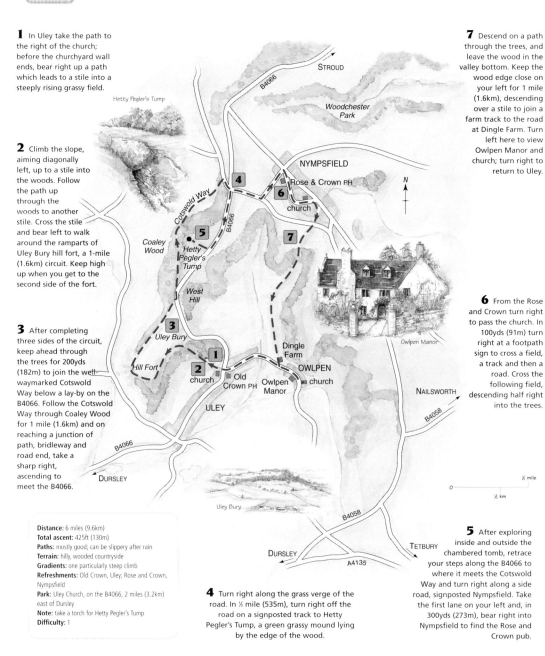

7 Descend on a path through the trees, and leave the wood in the valley bottom. Keep the wood edge close on your left for 1 mile (1.6km), descending over a stile to join a farm track to the road at Dingle Farm. Turn left here to view Owlpen Manor and church; turn right to return to Uley.

6 From the Rose and Crown turn right to pass the church. In 100yds (91m) turn right at a footpath sign to cross a field, a track and then a road. Cross the following field, descending half right into the trees.

5 After exploring inside and outside the chambered tomb, retrace your steps along the B4066 to where it meets the Cotswold Way and turn right along a side road, signposted Nympsfield. Take the first lane on your left and, in 300yds (273m), bear right into Nympsfield to find the Rose and Crown pub.

4 Turn right along the grass verge of the road. In ⅓ mile (535m), turn right off the road on a signposted track to Hetty Pegler's Tump, a green grassy mound lying by the edge of the wood.

Distance: 6 miles (9.6km)
Total ascent: 425ft (130m)
Paths: mostly good; can be slippery after rain
Terrain: hilly, wooded countryside
Gradients: one particularly steep climb
Refreshments: Old Crown, Uley; Rose and Crown, Nympsfield
Park: Uley Church, on the B4066, 2 miles (3.2km) east of Dursley
Note: take a torch for Hetty Pegler's Tump
Difficulty: 1

ABOUT • GREAT WITCOMBE

The setting alone, reminiscent of a Mediterranean landscape, makes this walk worthwhile. The villa commands superb views across the valley and the remains, which show the original floor plan, leave you in no doubt that this was once a sumptuous country house.

Southwest England

DISTANCE • 7½ miles (12km)

TOTAL ASCENT • 700ft (213m)

PATHS • good; slippery in places

TERRAIN • bridleways, tracks, field paths, stiles, tarmac roads

GRADIENTS • mostly gradual; climbs are steep but short

REFRESHMENTS • seasonal tea-shop near start; Air Balloon pub, Brockworth and Gloucester near by

PARK • Roman villa car park, 1½ miles (2.4km) from Brockworth turn-off A417

DIFFICULTY • 2

Great Witcombe's Grand Roman Villa

❶ Take the path downhill from the car park for 33yds (30m). Follow waymarkers to a gate and the Cotswold Way; turn left. Soon pass The Haven Tea Garden on the left and continue to a big junction; here conifers have infiltrated the indigenous beeches. Turn left.

❷ Soon pass a dilapidated ornamental gateway. After 137yds (400m) turn right at a T-junction (left is a private drive). Continue for 328yds (300m), to a clear fork of tracks. Go right, slightly uphill, for 186yds (170m).

❸ Turn sharply right and back to leave the Cotswold Way and follow a bridleway signed Horse Trail to Brimpsfield, which goes uphill, then left to the B4070. Turn right and in 22yds (20m) cross the road and continue ahead signed Brimpsfield 1½ miles (2.4km). At a T-junction turn left. Keep the fence/wall on your right. The path, initially enclosed by tree-lined walls, opens on to a bend in the road. Continue ahead along the road to reach a T-junction of minor roads.

❹ Cross the road and continue ahead on a bridleway. Join a farm track and in 22yds (20m) turn left over a stile to Birdlip. Turn left at the road. Take a path beside a school; walk on cricket field side of a football pitch fence. Beyond a flagpole turn half-left. At a B-road turn right, then take the old road, left, to Barrow Rake Viewpoint plaque.

❺ Take the obvious path (Cotswold Way) on the escarpment. Later, in woodland, the track descends to a road. Go straight over and down through trees; soon turn right to

rejoin the road. Just after a sharp bend take the public bridleway to the right.

❻ Continue straight ahead, keeping the fence on your left. Go to end of barns being converted. Cross a stile, turn partially left, downslope, to another stile then a gap in trees. Follow right-hand edge of a field down to a house. Follow the path beside the house and down a long drive. Take the second footpath on left (shortly after footpath beside green-surfaced tennis court), climb stile and diagonally cross two small fields to another road. Go straight across into fields.

❼ Take field paths, turning half-left across the third field towards houses. Follow a path between houses leading to a minor road. Turn left; in 44yds (40m) turn right (waymarked), and after 22yds (20m), at end of a garden, take

the stile on the right to cross diagonally to the reservoir road. Cross the causeway.

❽ Skirt Witcombe Reservoir on a good track (ignore a footpath on the right, beside buildings) which later rises with a stream on the left (ignore left turn signed Private). The track later deteriorates. Keep straight ahead uphill (do not cross the stream) through pastures. To enter the Roman villa proceed uphill and around it through farmyard. The car park is 328yds (300m) ahead.

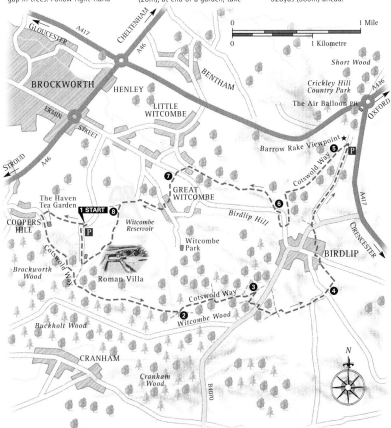

Turmoil at Tewkesbury

A walk across the Bloody Meadow from Tewkesbury recalls its bitter role in the Wars of the Roses

1 From the Abbey Lawns car park go through the gate, along the north of the abbey and leave by the main gateway, turning left. Pass the long-stay car park then turn right along Lower Lode Lane. Go left at the Battle Trail sign (crossed swords).

2 Go over a stile to the right and follow the hedge to a plinth commemorating the battle. Turn right along the lane, through the golf club gates and along the drive, veering left along the signed footpath, and following further waymarks to reach a stile.

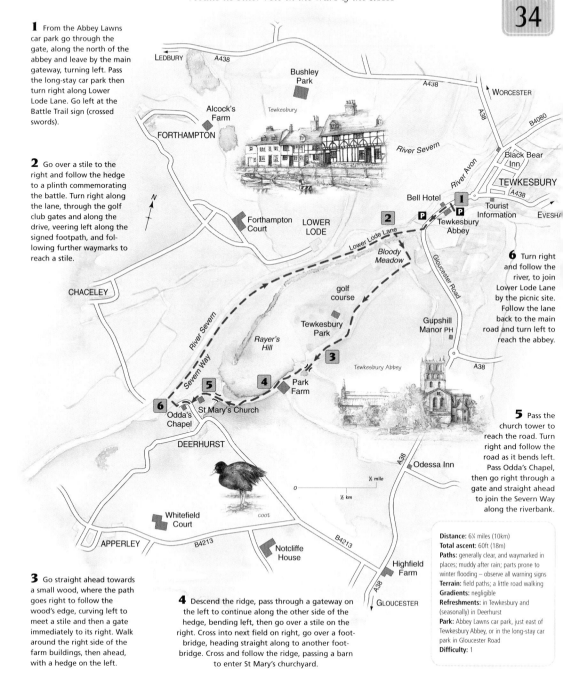

6 Turn right and follow the river, to join Lower Lode Lane by the picnic site. Follow the lane back to the main road and turn left to reach the abbey.

5 Pass the church tower to reach the road. Turn right and follow the road as it bends left. Pass Odda's Chapel, then go right through a gate and straight ahead to join the Severn Way along the riverbank.

3 Go straight ahead towards a small wood, where the path goes right to follow the wood's edge, curving left to meet a stile and then a gate immediately to its right. Walk around the right side of the farm buildings, then ahead, with a hedge on the left.

4 Descend the ridge, pass through a gateway on the left to continue along the other side of the hedge, bending left, then go over a stile on the right. Cross into next field on right, go over a footbridge, heading straight along to another footbridge. Cross and follow the ridge, passing a barn to enter St Mary's churchyard.

Distance: 6¼ miles (10km)
Total ascent: 60ft (18m)
Paths: generally clear, and waymarked in places; muddy after rain; parts prone to winter flooding – observe all warning signs
Terrain: field paths; a little road walking
Gradients: negligible
Refreshments: in Tewkesbury and (seasonally) in Deerhurst
Park: Abbey Lawns car park, just east of Tewkesbury Abbey, or in the long-stay car park in Gloucester Road
Difficulty: 1

WALK

35

ABOUT • AVEBURY

Avebury is the largest stone circle in the British Isles and part of the village is located in this mysterious henge, built between 2600–2100 bc. Starting at the Alexander Keiller Museum, the walk takes you to the Sanctuary, West Kennet Long Barrow, and Silbury Hill.

Southwest England

DISTANCE • 6½ miles (10.4km)

TOTAL ASCENT • 250ft (76m)

PATHS • well-marked; low-lying sections (especially path between Silbury Hill and car park) may be muddy after prolonged rain, otherwise firm

TERRAIN • downland tracks, field paths, stiles, woods.

GRADIENTS • gradual climbs to the Ridgeway and to West Kennet Long Barrow

REFRESHMENTS • in village

PARK • designated car and coach park, well signed on north side of A4361

DIFFICULTY • 2

Avebury's Ancient Monuments

❶ With the entrance to the car park behind you, take the path in the right-hand corner, passing information boards. The bank, ditch and standing stones of the south-western corner of the henge are ahead of you. At the road (High Street), turn left and cross into the churchyard. Visit the museum beyond the church. Continue past the Great Barn and the National Trust tea-shop.

❷ Climb steps ahead, just beyond the National Trust shop, and enter the henge. Walk around the perimeter of the henge with the bank on your left. Turn right on to the fenced footpath beside the road, by one of the largest stones in Avebury – the Swindon Stone. Cross the road to see the two impressive stones of the Cove, then continue to the gap in the bank in the right-hand corner.

❸ Through a gate and turn left on to a track (Green Street). Passing farm buildings the track becomes wider and climbs gradually.

❹ Meet the Ridgeway. Before turning right along this track, detour ahead to see the 25,000 sarsen stones on Fyfield Down (some are visible from The Ridgeway). Return to the Ridgeway and continue south for 1¾ miles (2.8km) to meet the A4.

❺ Cross this fast, busy road with extreme care. Before continuing down the track opposite, visit the Sanctuary. The route continues down the right-hand edge of a field. In the bottom corner, turn right through a blue waymarked gate, along the edge of fields with the River Kennet on your left.

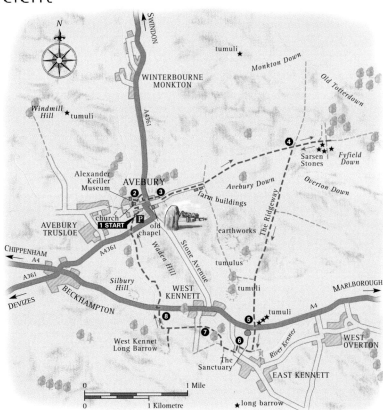

❻ Meet a road and turn left on to it, crossing a bridge. Turn right on to a signed byway on the the far side of a pumping station. When you reach a junction of paths, continue ahead following the footpath sign and almost immediately turn right (yellow waymark on tree) into a narrow tunnel of trees. Cross a stile and keep left round the edge of a field to meet a lane.

❼ Cross the lane and continue ahead. At the end of the second field, detour left to visit West Kennet Long Barrow. Return to the route and continue westwards and over the river to the A4.

❽ Cross the road, go through the gate almost opposite. Follow the sign for Avebury, passing close to Silbury Hill. Continue on the river bank to the A4361 and car park.

• DON'T MISS •

Windmill Hill is an early neolithic causeway enclosure thought to have been in use between 3700 and 2500 bc. It lies 1½ miles (2.4km) north of Avebury and can be reached on footpaths from Avebury High Street (or roadside parking at Avebury Truslow).

Old Ways on the Wiltshire Downs

Prehistoric pathways, Saxon defences and a Georgian canal towpath span this quiet corner of Wiltshire

WALK

36

Distance: 8 miles (12.9km)
Total ascent: 519ft (158m)
Paths: mainly good; lower paths and towpath can be very wet
Terrain: downland, linear earthwork, gentle farmland, canal towpath
Gradients: one lengthy climb, though not steep
Refreshments: Kings Arms, All Cannings; Barge Inn, Honey Street
Park: on roadside by Alton Barnes church, in Vale of Pewsey between Devizes and Marlborough
Difficulty: 2

1 From Alton Barnes church, go through the turnstile to follow the paved path towards Alton Priors church. Keep left of the tower, go through a kissing gate and turnstile and follow the road between houses. Cross over at the next road junction, follow the Ridgeway up to the next road and turn right. Turn left through a gate into Pewsey Downs National Nature Reserve, up the grassy track parallel to the road. Approaching a fence, bear left up to the summit of Walker's Hill.

6 Continue past the next bridge at Stanton St Bernard, and the Barge Inn at Honey Street, to the next bridge. Go up to the road and follow it into Alton Barnes. The turning for the church is on the right.

5 Cross to All Cannings Cross Farm and continue, keeping a fence on the left. Keep in line with power cables and follow the track to meet a bridleway. Turn left and walk to the canal. Drop down to the towpath and, keeping the waterway on the left, follow it to the next road bridge.

2 With round barrows on left, go down to cross the ditch and follow the path towards the White Horse. Continue above the chalk carving, through a gate and on to a fence on the right. Follow the fence, making for a gate round the far side of the woodland. Follow the track across open downland to a gate. Continue ahead with a fence on the right to the next gate. Go through it and, with a fence on the right, drop down the field to a gate and stile.

3 Turn left and follow the track down to the Wansdyke at the foot of the hill. Keep the ditch on the right and follow the linear earthwork in a westerly direction for about 1½ miles (2.4km).

4 At a fence by a gate and bridleway sign turn left, with the fence on the right and head south over Tan Hill. At the summit make for a stile in the field corner. Head down to the next stile and gate, then turn left and drop down to the field corner. Cross a stile and turn immediately right. Keep the fence on your right and follow the path to the next gate and stile. Don't cross it, but turn left and follow the path along the foot of the escarpment. Turn right at the fence corner and follow the path to a stile in the right-hand boundary; step over and join a path south through trees. Follow it to a grassy track running to the road.

Pewsey Downs

Horton Down

Allington Down

Wansdyke

All Cannings Down

Thorn Hill

MARLBOROUGH

Furze Hill

Wansdyke

Ridgeway

Wansdyke

St Ann's Hill

Tan Hill

293

Mille Hill

294

white horse

Knap Hill

261

Rybury Camp

Clifford's Hill

Walker's Hill

round barrows

DEVIZES

White Horse, Walker's Hill

ALLINGTON

All Cannings Cross Farm

STANTON ST BERNARD

Pewsey Downs Nature Reserve

PEWSEY

ALL CANNINGS

All Cannings Bridge

Kennet & Avon Canal

ALTON BARNES

church

ALTON PRIORS

church

Woodborough Hill

204

Tawsmead Copse

Kings Arms PH

Stanton Bridge

HONEY STREET

Barge Inn

Picked Hill

193

Kennet & Avon canal

WOODBOROUGH

VALE OF PEWSEY

Sarum's Cathedrals

Follow the Avon from New Sarum's majestic cathedral to fortified Old Sarum, Salisbury's medieval forerunner

Iron Age Hill Fort to Medieval City

Set on a bleak hill overlooking Salisbury stands the deserted ramparts and earthworks of the original settlement of Old Sarum. People lived on this windswept hilltop for some 5,000 years: the outer banks and ditches were part of an Iron Age hill fort, and several Roman roads converge on the site. The Saxons followed and developed a town within the prehistoric ramparts.

Normans built the inner earthworks and, within them, a royal castle and two palaces. In 1075 Bishop Osmund, William the Conqueror's nephew, constructed the first cathedral. Old Sarum rapidly developed and for 150 years it was a thriving medieval city, well placed at a major crossroads. However, lack of space, shortage of water, tensions between clergy and royals and the exposed site led to a gradual decline during the late 12th century, and a new cathedral was built at New Sarum in 1220.

The Rise of Christianity

Norman rule had a profound effect on English society, in particular upon the Church, remodelling its structure, giving a new impetus to the building or reconstruction of parish churches. The Normans' policy towards religion differed radically from that of the Anglo-Saxons.

Bishops were ordered to transfer their headquarters from Saxon rural minsters to more populous centres, part of a centralisation that enabled the Normans to control the population. The rapid growth of Old Sarum from 1070 led to the transference of the rural see of Sherborne to the emerging city in 1075. Old Sarum was closer to the geographical centre of the huge diocese and, more importantly, the new bishop was Osmund, William the Conqueror's nephew and former chancellor.

Bishop Osmund built a fine cathedral close to the castle and palace. It set new standards, which were widely adopted in cathedrals throughout England. Instead of being run on monastic lines, it was served by 36 canons under the direction of four officers. Architecture was Romanesque and characterised by its lavish scale and rich library. Following Osmund's death in 1099, Bishop Roger was responsible for building elaborate palaces and the rebuilding of the cathedral.

As the cathedral grew more powerful, friction developed between the clergy and the military governor at Old Sarum. This eventually led to the removal of the cathedral to a new city, Salisbury, in the early 13th century. Building began in 1220 and was largely completed by 1250. Set within a spacious close, this new building provided a model for parish churches throughout the area.

ALONG THE AVON TO OLD SARUM

Southwest England

❶ Enter the shopping area close to Sainsbury's and turn left to follow the Riverside Walk sign before the covered walkway. Walk beside the Avon, cross the car park access road and continue beneath two bridges. Cross a road and keep to the tarmac path beside a green. Ignore the footbridge on the right, cross a bridge over a side channel and bear right along the raised riverside path.

❷ Keep to the river bank along a boardwalk to a metal gate. Continue beside the river. Soon, bear half-left away from the river to a gate. Turn right between a hedge and fencing to reach a pitted tarmac path. Turn right, cross a footbridge over the Avon

and soon bear right along a metalled track to the road in Stratford-sub-Castle.

❸ Turn right along the pavement, then just beyond Old Forge Cottage, cross the road to join a wide path beside Dairy Cottage, that gradually climbs to Old Sarum. At a T-junction of paths, keep left along the base of the hill fort; then, at a fork, bear right and ascend on to the outer rampart. Bear left around the fortifications, eventually descending to a stile by the access road. Follow the road right to tour the earth fortifications and to visit the inner bailey.

❹ Retrace your steps through the outer earthwork and go right to

pass through a gate. Go through another gate and, just before the road, turn right, signed Stratford, by the hedge. Go through a gate and keep left, downhill to another gate by the Parliamentary Tree memorial. Turn right and enter Stratford-sub-Castle. Keep ahead and, shortly, cross by the right-hand bend to follow the path beside houses, signed City Centre.

❺ Reach a wide track and in a few paces cross the tiny footbridge on your right. Keep right along a gravel path through the grounds of the Sports Centre, the path bearing left alongside the river. Soon cross the footbridge to join the outward route back to the city centre and your car.

Distance: 5 miles (8km)

Total ascent: 230ft (70m)

Paths: mostly good; metalled close to the city centre; can be wet and muddy beside the Avon

Terrain: water meadow, city centre and farmland

Gradients: mainly flat; one gradual climb to Old Sarum

Refreshments: plenty of choice of tea rooms and restaurants in Salisbury; The Old Castle opposite entrance to Old Sarum

Parking: main car park close to Sainsbury's; signed off Ring Road, west of city centre

Difficulty: 2

Southeast England

There is an air of busy industriousness in the southeast of England. Road and rail routes hum with activity, and even the sky is seldom free from aircraft. All the conurbations, and especially London, are in a constant state of motion. Amid the hustle and bustle there are green oases of peace and calm to discover, an immensely long and complex history to unravel, ancient ways to travel, mysteries to ponder – and the best way to see it all is on foot. It's a gentle, rolling landscape with no towering heights, essentially agricultural but well wooded in places, threaded by a fine assortment of paths and tracks. As you tread in the footsteps of packmen and pilgrims, warriors and wayfarers, you glimpse a landscape that has altered little, despite centuries of change.

The white cliffs of Dover, the Seven Sisters and other chalk cliffs form England's southern bulwark. The eastern coast is altogether gentler and lower-lying, often crumbling into the sea. Sand and shingle are constantly on the move, and the region is rich in maritime history.

Between the Thames and the English Channel the landscape rises and falls according to the underlying geology, forming ridges such as the North Downs, Weald and South Downs. Away from the high downs you could enjoy a tour of little towns and villages. By the time you reach the ancient royal capital of Winchester you are in Hampshire and within easy reach of the bountiful walking opportunities of the New Forest.

North of the Thames and London the only high ground is formed by the chalk escarpment of the Chilterns, famous for their well-established beech woods. You can traverse a stretch of the ancient Icknield Way along their foot or climb to Ivinghoe Beacon, Combe Hill or other notable heights to enjoy the view.

It's possible to drive across Suffolk and Norfolk and be aware only of the vast prairie-like fields, but take a walk through the landscape and you will be astounded by its variety and complexity. The ancient underground warren of Grime's Graves and the lingering remains of huge, isolated airfields are just two intriguing stories waiting to be told.

Best of the Rest

Westerham It's not surprising that Winston Churchill purchased his country retreat, Chartwell, here. It might be in the heart of the Kentish commuter belt, but there's something timeless and deliciously rural about Westerham. It would be easy to imagine that the village had slept peacefully for centuries, undisturbed by the outside world but during World War II, fighter planes frequently darkened the skies above, as pilots from nearby Biggin Hill airfield battled overhead to save Britain from invasion.

Beacon Hill North Hampshire's landscape of gently rolling hills and crystal clear rivers tops out in a fine ridge of downland, mirroring the Ridgeway on the opposite side of the Kennet Valley. At Beacon Hill, above Highclere near Newbury, the views are far reaching and spectacular. The strategic vantage point was not lost on the local Iron-Age population, who built a mighty hill fort here.

Thames Path From the Thames Barrier to its Cotswold source, the Thames Path follows England's greatest river. Around Kew and Richmond, London's more opulent suburbs show their back-garden style and hundreds of pleasure craft line the banks.

Essex marshes This small corner of Essex from Burnham to Bradwell-on-Sea is closer in spirit to the deserted shores of Suffolk than the brashness of Southend-on-Sea. Bradwell has an intriguing history – an ancient barn near by was found to be a Saxon church, part of what must have been impressive fortifications built on the edge of the sea.

Norfolk Coast Lashed by the North Sea and prey to ungovernable tides, the Norfolk coastline seems wilder and more remote than most – and a birdwatcher's paradise. The perfect way to explore it is on the Norfolk Coast Path, from Hunstanton to Cromer, which threads its way through dunes and salt-marshes, and takes in stately Holkham.

Suffolk Coast Cut off from the rest of the country by the road and rail lines running 5 miles (8km) inland, this is one of the most isolated and unspoilt stretches of coast in the country. The variety of habitats means that you can see a great diversity of wildlife, and seaside towns like Southwold and Aldeburgh are good start and end points for walks.

Epping Forest The 6,000 surviving acres of this once mighty forest make a great day out for the family, only a Tube ride away from central London. Pick up a hiking leaflet at the visitors centre and choose a walk through stands of ancient pollarded oak, beech and hornbeam, or picnic on a grassy heath.

Coast to Coast on the Isle of Wight

Connecting tidal and fresh water nature reserves on the western side of this lovely island

WALK

38

1 From The Square in Yarmouth head towards the church and walk along St James Street to cross the A3054 into Mill Road. At the sharp left bend, follow the arrowed path ahead (signed Freshwater) towards the old tide mill. Ignore the footpath left, walk beside the mudflats and turn right along the old railway. Remain on this path for 1½ miles (2.4km) to the causeway at Freshwater.

2 Turn left, away from the river, and follow the lane to the B3399. Turn left and cross almost immediately into Manor Road. In a few paces bear left (Freshwater Way) and gently ascend across grassland towards Afton Down. Go straight at a junction beside the golf course, soon to follow the gravel track right to the clubhouse. Go through the gate, pass in front of the building and walk down the access track, keeping left, to the A3055. Turn right, downhill, into Freshwater Bay.

3 Walk past the car park and turn right into Coastguard Lane, opposite Albion Tavern. Keep ahead at the end, along a path skirting the edge of marsh and eventually reaching a road. Turn right, then, just before the river bridge, turn left into Afton Marshes Nature Reserve.

6 Climb the stile to the right of the metal gate, pass through a copse to a stile and bear left, uphill, along the field edge. Enter the field on your left and keep to the path along the right-hand edge to a stile on the edge of woodland. Soon drop down through the wood to a track and turn left, following it to the A3054. Turn right along the pavement, back into Yarmouth.

5 Take the waymarked path (Freshwater Way) between a cottage and the churchyard. Cross a stile and proceed along the farm road. At the farmyard entrance cross the double stile on the left and bear right along the field edge, skirting a barn to a stile. On reaching a track and the main entrance to Kings Manor Farm, cross the stile ahead beside double gates and follow a wide track to a gate and junction of paths.

4 Cross the footbridge, bear right towards Yarmouth and join the nature trail, following the left-hand path beside the stream, through the reserve to the A3055. Turn left and almost immediately cross over to join footpath F61 along the old railway. In ½ mile, (800m) reach The Causeway and turn left, following the lane to Freshwater church and the Red Lion.

Distance: 6 miles (9.7km)
Total ascent: 240ft (73m)
Paths: good; very wet and boggy in winter
Terrain: marsh, open grassland, woodland
Gradients: one gentle climb
Refreshments: tearooms and Albion Tavern, Freshwater Bay; Red Lion, Freshwater; pubs and tearooms, Yarmouth
Park: car park by A3054, near Lymington to Yarmouth ferry terminal, or park at Lymington Pier and take the ferry to Yarmouth
Difficulty: 1

½ mile

0

½ km

Sconce
Point

ferry
terminal

castle YARMOUTH

church

old tide
mill

A3054

marsh mallow

Tide Mill, Yarmouth

THORLEY

THORLEY
STREET

B3401

CARISBROOKE

River Yar

NORTON

6

N

Kings
Manor
Farm

NORTON
GREEN

A3054

Red Lion PH   church

5

2

CARISBROOKE

B3399

B3399

FRESHWATER

A3055

Afton Marshes
Nat. Res.

4

EASTON

Albion
Tavern PH

AFTON

golf club

East Afton
Down

BRIGHSTONE

A3055

3

*Freshwater
Bay*

All Saints, Freshwater

*Compton
Bay*

WALK 39

ABOUT • THE NEW FOREST

From Brockenhurst explore the once-exclusive royal hunting preserve of William the Conqueror. Established by William in 1079, the New Forest is still a magical place and the natural habitat for a wide variety of flora and fauna.

Southeast England

DISTANCE • 6 miles (9.6km)

TOTAL ASCENT • 33ft (10m)

PATHS • paths and tracks, well-defined in places. Can be wet in winter

TERRAIN • village streets, heath and woodland. Keep dogs on leads at all times

GRADIENTS • one very gentle climb

REFRESHMENTS • Brockenhurst has a choice of inns and hotels

PARK • free car park in Brookley Road, Brockenhurst

DIFFICULTY • 2

The New Forest: King among Deer Parks

❶ From the car park turn right and follow Brookley Road to the Watersplash, a local landmark. Bear right and pass railings. On the right are the entrances to Overbrook and Brocket Green, beyond them take a kissing gate by the entrance to Brookway and join a footpath alongside a stream.

❷ Pass a row of houses and gardens. Go through two kissing gates and turn left at the next road. Follow Butts Lawn and head for the next junction by a telephone box. Bear left for a few paces, then swing right on a track signed access to allotments.

❸ Approaching the allotments, veer a little to the right, continuing across heathland known as Black Knowl, keeping woodland to your right. Continue between gorse bushes and at a clear path, turn right towards trees. When the path ends, keep left to a wide track, turn right and head for Bolderford Bridge.

❹ Cross the bridge and swing left in front of the gate by the sign for Lyndhurst. Keep right at the fork and follow the path to cross a footbridge, keeping the fence close to your right-hand side.

❺ Turn left at the next junction, by a bridge. Follow the track across open heath to a gate by silver birch trees. Continue for several hundred yards, turn sharp left at the junction. Follow the grassy track by pine trees to a stile.

❻ Head diagonally right, following the clear path through the heather, towards an opening in the trees. Cross the river at the bridge with

wooden handrails. Continue ahead using small footbridge (no handrails) then swing right towards Aldridgehill Cottage.

❼ Keep the cottage on your right and follow the drive for 50yds (46m). Take the left fork and

follow the woodland path down to the footbridge over Ober Water. Continue ahead following the path up the gentle slope to a bend in the road. Go straight on alongside a car park to the next junction.

❽ Turn right, then left by Ober Lodge. Follow the track towards the Burley road. As you approach it, veer left to a parallel track which joins the road. Continue along the path parallel to the road. Make for Brookley Road on the right and return to the car park.

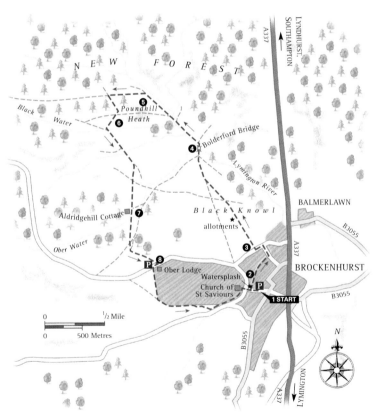

On the Trail of the Rufus Stone

In Hampshire's special Heritage Area a king once died

in mysterious circumstances

1 With Rufus Stone opposite, turn right and walk along to Sir Walter Tyrrell Inn. Veer left at 'Except for Access' sign and cross turf, keeping to right-hand half of open grassy area. Cross several little streams and make for obvious gap in trees. Negotiate shallow ford here and follow indistinct path ahead. Cross winter ford and simple water meadow bridge spanning gully. Keep left when path forks just beyond bridge and follow it through trees to join concrete track leading to Long Beech Caravan Park. Pass several barriers to reach water tower.

2 Pass concrete track immediately beyond tower and continue for about 50 yds (46m) to barrier. Veer right here and make for some wooden posts. Follow path between bracken and gorse bushes and head for corner of King's Garn Gutter Inclosure. Continue on path, keeping inclosure boundary fence on right. Avoid gate in fence and look for Janesmoor Pond up ahead. Make for next corner of inclosure and turn right.

3 Follow path down between inclosures descending gently into glade. Head for track, avoid gates on left and right and go straight on over track to wood. Cross over stream (King's Garn Gutter) and follow path through trees to emerge on edge of golf course. Keep to track beside greens and fairways and when it peters out, continue over grass, keeping tight to woodland on left. Walk behind two greens before heading out across open ground, dotted with gorse bushes and fringed by woodland on left, towards car park on far side.

4 Cricket ground is to right between trees. Cross grass, keeping building on right, and continue along wooded edge of golf course. Curve left to another green on right, and join clear track running up slope to left. Walk across car park and continue to road. Turn left and head for Brook. Follow road through village, pass The Bell Inn and The Green Dragon and avoid footpath on left just beyond.

5 Pass Canterton Lodge and veer right into Canterton Lane. Follow road over several streams and note large white house up on left bank. Continue ahead when lane becomes stony underfoot and pass bridleway on right. On left now is Bignell Wood. Follow track as it swings right to Greys Farm.

6 Pass between wooden posts and veer left off track, following path to gap in trees ahead. On reaching clearing immediately beyond them, turn right at junction by manhole cover and follow path across stream, up gentle slope and back to car park.

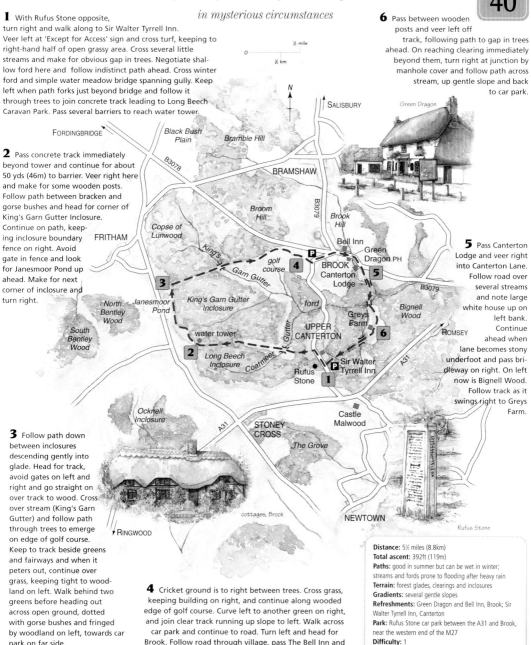

Green Dragon

SALISBURY

FORDINGBRIDGE

Black Bush Plain

Bramble Hill

B3078

BRAMSHAW

Broom Hill

B3079

Brook Hill

Bell Inn

Green Dragon PH

Copse of Lunwood

FRITHAM

King's Garn Gutter

golf course **4**

P

BROOK

Canterton Lodge **5**

3

North Bentley Wood

Janesmoor Pond

King's Garn Gutter Inclosure

ford

Greys Farm **6**

Bignell Wood

ROMSEY

South Bentley Wood

water tower

UPPER CANTERTON

Gutter

A31

2

Long Beech Inclosure

Coatmber

Rufus Stone

P Sir Walter Tyrrell Inn **1**

Ocknell Inclosure

A31

STONEY CROSS

Castle Malwood

The Grove

cottages, Brook

NEWTOWN

RINGWOOD

Rufus Stone

Distance: 5½ miles (8.8km)
Total ascent: 392ft (119m)
Paths: good in summer but can be wet in winter; streams and fords prone to flooding after heavy rain
Terrain: forest glades, clearings and inclosures
Gradients: several gentle slopes
Refreshments: Green Dragon and Bell Inn, Brook; Sir Walter Tyrrell Inn, Canterton
Park: Rufus Stone car park between the A31 and Brook, near the western end of the M27
Difficulty: 1

WALK 41

Even before the arrival of the Romans, Winchester was an important tribal centre, and under King Alfred's rule it became the capital of England. Winchester Cathedral was begun in 1079 and the library contains a 10th-century copy of Bede's history.

DISTANCE • 6 miles (9.6km)

TOTAL ASCENT • 220ft (67m)

PATHS • well-marked throughout; some mud after rain on water meadow paths

TERRAIN • street pavements, downland, water meadows

GRADIENTS • flat, except for ascent and descent of St Catherine's Hill

REFRESHMENTS • wide choice in town

PARK • Chesil Street long-stay car park, or (Mon–Fri, 07.30–18.30, Sat 07.30–1800) Park-and-Ride from Bar End (signed from M3 Junctions 9 and 10) to King Alfred Statue, Broadway

DIFFICULTY • 2

Winchester – King Alfred's Capital

❶ At King Alfred's Statue look, as he does, up the High Street, with Abbey Gardens, site of the Nunnaminster, to the left. A few yards up the street, turn left into Abbey Passage to see the excavations of the abbey church. Return to the High Street and turn right. At City Bridge, opposite City Mill, turn right into The Weirs for the Riverside Walk (look out for the remains of a Roman wall). At a signpost, turn left over the River Itchen, then right to join a road for 100yds (91m). Cross at the corner into a private road.

❷ In 50yds (46m), signed Itchen Way, turn right across the river. Continue through water meadows, with the river on your left, to a road bridge. Turn left over bridge, then right into a parking area.

❸ With the river on your right, take the path for St Catherine's Hill under the railway bridge. Where the path divides, take the left fork. Follow the clear path to a crossing of paths at the summit. Turn right to the miz-maze.

❹ Facing the maze at the point where you first reached it, turn right (the beech copse beyond the maze is now on your left). Walk to the edge of the hill for views of Winchester, right, and the Hospital of St Cross, left. Turn left and walk along the top of the hill, with the water meadows on your right. At a gap in the ramparts, take the long flight of wooden steps to the bottom of Plague Pits Valley.

❺ Turn left on to the path by the Itchen Navigation. Go under the railway bridge and at a junction turn right, signed St Cross. Cross the Itchen, then turn right on to a farm road. The footpath continues ahead through a stile.

❻ Continue straight ahead on the footpath past St Cross Hospital (detour left to visit). At the road, cross diagonally right and continue through the water meadows.

❼ At Winchester College buildings, turn right, then left into College Walk. Turn left into College Street (keep ahead for Wolvesey Palace). At the end of College Street, turn right, go through Kingsgate, then right for the Close and cathedral.

❽ With your back to the West Front and the site of Old and New Minsters, walk left of the war memorial, between trees, to the City Museum. Cross The Square for the High Street. Turn right for King Alfred's Statue.

(map)

FULFLOOD
site of Hyde Abbey Church
B3330
WINNALL
Winchester City Museum
1 START King Alfred Statue
City Mill
Chesil St
Wolvesey Castle
Abbey Gardens
Winchester Cathedral
Winchester College
BAR END
water meadows
park & ride
STANMORE
hospital
Junction 10
N
ST CROSS
water meadows
River Itchen
Itchen Navigation
farm
Miz-maze
St Catherine's Hill
Plague Pits Valley
Junction 11
SOUTHAMPTON
Twyford Down
B3040
B3335
B3404
A31
M3
NEWBURY
BASINGSTOKE
A3090
A2090

0 — 1/2 Mile
0 — 500 Metres

WALK
42

ABOUT • STEEP

This hilly walk in Steep introduces the landscape that inspired the poetry of Edward Thomas. The walks visits his two homes and Shoulder of Mutton Hill, his poetic inspiration, and the Sarsen Stone, laid in his memory by Walter de la Mare.

Southeast England

DISTANCE • 5 miles (8km)

TOTAL ASCENT • 545ft (166m)

PATHS • field, woodland paths and tracks

TERRAIN • rolling countryside at western end of the South Downs. Some tracks and paths are suitable for dogs off the lead

GRADIENTS • hilly on the outward leg; steep ascent to Shoulder of Mutton Hill

REFRESHMENTS • the Harrow Inn and the Cricketers Inn at Steep

PARK • roadside parking in the vicinity of All Saints' Church, Steep

DIFFICULTY • 2

The Poet of Steep

1 With All Saints' Church on your right, follow Church Road for 50yds (46m) to a sharp right-hand bend. Bear left into woodland and swing immediately right. Follow the clear path between trees and down to a galvanised kissing gate. Cross a stream and head towards Steep Farm, to cross two stiles.

2 Pass the farm and veer right at the end of the buildings. Keep left after a few paces and follow the track down to a stream. As the track curves right, go towards a stile at the foot of a steep bank. Don't cross it; instead turn left and follow the woodland path. Cross a stream and make for a cottage in trees. Cross over the drive and continue on a clearly defined path.

3 Keep to the left of silos and outbuildings and look for a finger post here. Swing left to a stile and gateway and follow the field edge to the corner. Head for a gap in the trees and take the path uphill, along the woodland edge. Make for a stile in the right-hand boundary and cross the field, parallel to power lines. Look for a stile by a metal gate and join a path which runs up above some woodland. Continue on the enclosed path to the lane.

4 Turn right and keep left after 400yds (366m) when the lane forks. Bear left after a few paces to a stile and follow the path between lines of trees, up the hillside to a stile in the woodland boundary. Turn left and follow the green lane as it climbs steeply through the trees. Ignore paths left and right, and eventually pass a green sign for Ashford Hangers, followed in 200yds (183m) by a barrier. Further on, the walk coincides with a section of the 21-mile (34km) Hangers Way.

5 To visit the Poet Stone, follow Hangers Way, left, 100yds (91m) after it joins the main path from the right. After a few paces it goes right, go straight on, steeply descending to the stone. Return to main track, turn left and follow lane until it leads between houses. Look for The Red House, before The Edward Barnsley Workshop, and continue to the road junction.

6 Bear left, then immediately left again on a sunken bridleway. Descend steeply for 500yds (457m), to a fork. Keep right and rejoin the Hangers Way. Follow it over a stream and between trees. After 600yds (549m), at the road by a barrier, turn left and pass Old Ashford Manor.

7 Walk along 200yds (183m) to Berryfield Cottage, right, followed by Ashford Chace. Continue for 50yds (46m), and turn right signed Hangers Way. Follow the track and as it bends right by a private sign, veer left to a woodland path. After a right and left bend, continue for 400yds (366m) then turn right down some steps to a waterfall.

8 At the road beyond, keep right and continue for 200yds (183m) to a right-hand turning. Bear left here, through a kissing gate. Turn right and skirt the field to a plank bridge and stile in the corner. Cross into woodland, follow the path to a playing field. Cross and emerge opposite All Saints' Church.

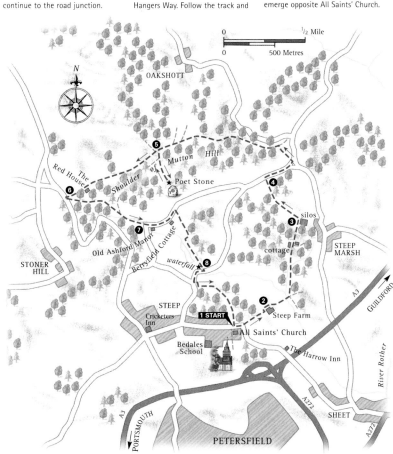

A stroll along a section of Roman road and the breezy South Downs leads you to Bignor Roman villa. The excavated remains at Bignor date from about the 4th century AD but suggest that the inhabitants enjoyed a lifestyle not so different from our own.

Southeast England

DISTANCE • 8 miles (13km). Short walk omitting Stane Street 5½ miles (8.8km)

TOTAL ASCENT • 262ft (80m)

PATHS • clearly waymarked, defined tracks, quiet country lanes; some muddy sections

TERRAIN • woodland and downland

GRADIENTS • gentle to moderate, with one steady climb

REFRESHMENTS • White Horse pub, Sutton; tea room at Bignor Roman Villa. Picnic benches along Stane Street at Point 5 (in the woods) and Point 6 (in the open)

PARK • roadside parking near the White Horse pub, Sutton

DIFFICULTY • 2

Roman Life at Bignor

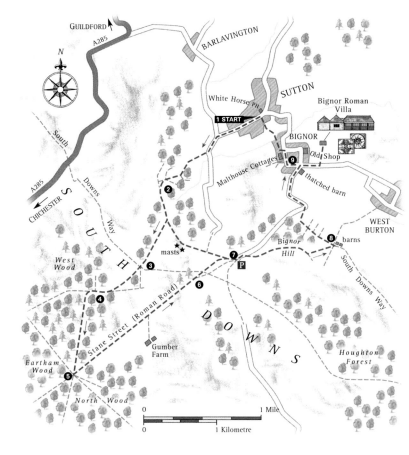

❶ Take the road left of the White Horse, signed Barlavington and Duncton. Beyond the edge of the village, bear left on to the road signed as a dead end, ignoring the right turn to Barlavington. After 250yds (229m), where the road bends left, bear right on to a bridleway. Continue and climb steadily up a wooded escarpment, ignoring a signed footpath, left.

❷ At staggered track junction at the top, continue ahead for 30yds (27m) then bear left following a blue waymark arrow up the hill and beyond the treeline towards two masts. At Bignor Hill NT sign fork left and in 50yds (46m) turn right. (For a shorter walk continue ahead, avoiding right turns, to the car park at Point ❼.)

❸ At a five-way junction (NT Slindon Estate sign, left), ignore South Downs Way (which crosses your path) and take next right turn on to a lesser path (fence on right, woodland on left). At next junction turn right towards forest.

❹ Soon after entering the forest, follow a blue waymark arrow left, downhill. The track is bordered on the left by an old boundary dyke. Follow the blue arrows.

❺ At the bottom, at a seven-way junction by a bench, turn left, signed Bignor, along the ridge of Stane Street. Avoid side turns. Continue through a gate, across open land.

❻ By a bench, ½ mile (800m) after a NT sign on the right for Gumber Farm, avoid the gate ahead and take a stile up on your left behind a bench, cross the track and continue along Stane Street. Keep forward at the junction on the South Downs Way (which joins from the left), turning right at the next signpost where the view opens out.

❼ At the car park (by a signpost with Roman names – *Londinium* etc), continue along the South Downs Way, which forks right on a track heading over the summit of Bignor Hill. Continue on the South Downs Way, bearing left where signed.

❽ At a junction by barns, turn left on to a bridleway, heading slightly uphill through woods. Ignore side turns. The track levels, then descends. Turn right at a road T-junction, downhill. At T-junction by a thatched barn, turn left (go right for Bignor Roman Villa).

❾ After a right bend, take the second signed path on the left, just after Malthouse Cottages. Pass through the garden below the house, then alongside a stream on the left. Ignore the first footbridge. The path soon crosses footbridges and comes out into an open field. Continue up the field to a stile left of the nearest telegraph post. Cross the next field via an uncultivated strip to Sutton.

A Wealth of Wildlife in the Arun Valley

A walk across the wetlands of the Arun Valley and up onto the Down reveals why this area is affectionately known as the Sussex Camargue

WALK

44

1 From the car park turn right across the bridge and over the stile (Wey-South Path) immediately right. Walk along the river bank, pass through a gate and bear right on reaching a track. Bear sharp left beyond Limekiln house and follow the track through farm buildings, ignoring the path right by metal barns. At a fork bear right and descend past Hayles Barn.

2 Turn left along the field edge to a gate in the corner. Turn right following Wey-South Path marker to go through a gate and across a bridge on the left. Turn right beside the ditch and soon cross the wooden bridge into Amberley Wild Brooks. Keep to the path, heading south through marshland, over a stile to open pasture and on to another stile, joining the track to Amberley village. Turn right at the lane then right again at the T-junction towards the church. Drop down to pass Rock Cottage and follow the track beneath the walls of Amberley Castle.

3 Bear right at a gate and follow the path to the railway line. Cross via stiles and remain on the path towards Bury Church. Climb a stile and bear left to cross a bridge over a dyke. Keep ahead, cross a further bridge and water meadow to join the raised path beside the River Arun. Turn left and follow the river bank, bearing left to a gate beyond the footbridge over the river. Now on the South Downs Way (SDW), soon follow the fenced path right to reach the B2139.

6 Turn left and continue to a T-junction at Greatham. Turn left and follow the road for just over ½ mile (800m) back to the car park.

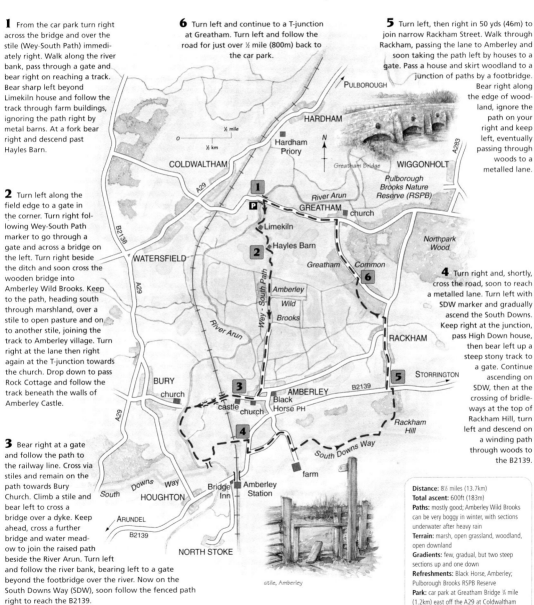

5 Turn left, then right in 50 yds (46m) to join narrow Rackham Street. Walk through Rackham, passing the lane to Amberley and soon taking the path left by houses to a gate. Pass a house and skirt woodland to a junction of paths by a footbridge. Bear right along the edge of woodland, ignore the path on your right and keep left, eventually passing through woods to a metalled lane.

4 Turn right and, shortly, cross the road, soon to reach a metalled lane. Turn left with SDW marker and gradually ascend the South Downs. Keep right at the junction, pass High Down house, then bear left up a steep stony track to a gate. Continue ascending on SDW, then at the crossing of bridleways at the top of Rackham Hill, turn left and descend on a winding path through woods to the B2139.

Distance: 8½ miles (13.7km)
Total ascent: 600ft (183m)
Paths: mostly good; Amberley Wild Brooks can be very boggy in winter, with sections underwater after heavy rain
Terrain: marsh, open grassland, woodland, open downland
Gradients: few, gradual, but two steep sections up and one down
Refreshments: Black Horse, Amberley; Pulborough Brooks RSPB Reserve
Park: car park at Greatham Bridge ¼ mile (1.2km) east off the A29 at Coldwaltham
Difficulty: 2

stile, Amberley

WALK 45

ABOUT • BURPHAM

King Alfred established over 30 burhs, or settlements, along the boundary of the Kingdom of Wessex to protect his citizens from the plundering Danes. Set near the lovely Arundel Castle, this walk explores the fortified Anglo-Saxon settlement at Burpham.

Southeast England

DISTANCE • 5 miles (8km)

TOTAL ASCENT • 500ft (152m)

PATHS • clearly waymarked tracks and quiet lanes; some muddy sections

TERRAIN • chalk downland and forest; three stiles

GRADIENTS • gentle main ascent; shorter, steeper descent and ascent near end

REFRESHMENTS • George and Dragon, Burpham; picnic bench above River Arun

PARK • free car park by George and Dragon (not part of pub) at Burpham; plenty of roadside parking in village

DIFFICULTY • 2

Burpham's Anglo-Saxon Settlement

❶ Cross the road from the car park entrance and take the path into the churchyard. Keep right of the church, and by a signpost cross steps over the churchyard wall. Follow the right edge of the field. At a road, turn right, then keep forward downhill at the next road junction.

❷ Take the next left, Coombe Lane; this becomes unsurfaced by a house and a pumping station. On emerging into a field, fork right at a waymark post, on a rising path marked with a yellow arrow, and soon climb a stile. Turn left at a junction of tracks at the top.

❸ After the track curves round to the right, keep right at the first junction and turn left at the second. Take the next bridleway off to the right, through a gate and uphill. After passing through a belt of trees and a gate, the track veers slightly right, passing to the left of the trig point (summit pillar).

❹ Do not pass through the next gate just before a major track junction, but turn sharp right keeping in the field with the trig point, along the left edge of the field. Where the fence on your left reaches a corner, turn left along a row of trees as waymarked.

❺ Beyond the next gate enter a small field surrounded by trees and keep forward at a junction as signed, picking up a woodland track alongside a fence on your right. Avoid the next signed footpath on the right, and keep to the bridleway.

❻ Turn right at a five-way junction, then immediately fork right. Soon reach another signed junction of bridleways and keep forward downhill, on a sunken path. At the foot of the wooded slope turn left and left again.

❼ Where the main track is about to rise, fork right through a gate and follow the valley floor. Turn right at a signpost, up through a gate. Just after, keep forward to ascend steeply where main track bends left. The path leads along a wooded strip between fields.

❽ Emerge by a gate into a field, and keep forward to a gate into woodland. Follow the woodland path downhill and turn right along the road. In Wepham village, turn left at the road junction.

❾ Where the road bends right, take the signed path rising diagonally, on the left, up the bank

• DON'T MISS •

St Mary's Church in Burpham has two fine 12th-century Norman arches, one with a zig-zag decoration, the other with grotesque carvings of human and ape-like heads.

of the Anglo-Saxon camp (or burh). Enter a recreation field via a stile, cross to the stile opposite (where a picnic bench just to the left gives a fine view of Arundel Castle and the river) and turn right to return to the car park.

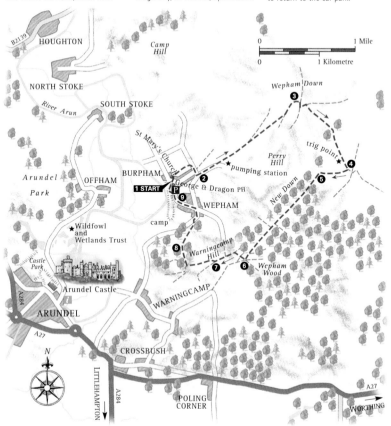

WALK 46

This walk in the South Downs offers superb views and a feast of ancient sites. These include the flint mines at Cissbury Ring, a scheduled ancient monument, mined between 4500–2300 BC, and an Iron Age hill fort, home to a large community in about 350 BC.

DISTANCE • 8 miles (13km)	**REFRESHMENTS** • none, but Cissbury Ring is a wonderful spot for picnics
TOTAL ASCENT • 700ft (213m)	
PATHS • clearly waymarked and defined tracks; some muddy sections	**PARK** • Chanctonbury car park and picnic site (signed Chanctonbury Ring), off A283 west of Steyning and east of the junction with A24
TERRAIN • woodland and downland	
GRADIENTS • some steep sections	**DIFFICULTY** • 2

The Flint Mines at Cissbury Ring

❶ Turn left out of the car park and continue to the end of the surfaced road. Keep forward on a bridleway by 'unsuitable for motors' sign. Follow the bridleway as it bends right along the bottom edge of the woodland until a blue waymarker points left, uphill; 70yds (64m) later fork right.

❷ Emerge into the open at the four-way junction of tracks at the top of the slope, with trees marking Chanctonbury Ring prominent away to your right. Turn left on the South Downs Way, and avoid side turnings.

❸ At a four-way crossing before a gate (with a stone memorial beyond), turn right to leave the South Downs Way on a cinder track signed 'public right of way' with a green waymarker.

❹ In ½ mile (800m), turn left at the bottom of a deep valley and take the path along the valley floor, following blue waymarkers, first between intermittent hedgerows, later alongside a fence on the right.

❺ At the end of the valley, turn right at a T-junction of tracks and, ignoring a left path just after barn on the left, continue to the car park at the end of the road.

❻ Detour left to Cissbury Ring by the National Trust sign; go through the gate and follow the yellow waymarker. Carry on to the next gate and take the steps up to the top. Turn right and walk around the ramparts, looking for the hummocky flint mine site. Return via the steps; take the track opposite through the car park.

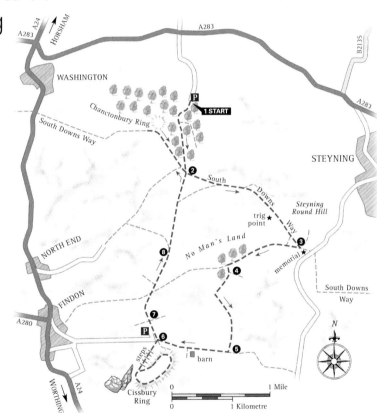

❼ Keep forward at the next major junction of tracks, following a green waymarker, and fork right 40yds (37m) further on. (Left is private property and is fenced off.) At the fork of tracks with a grass triangle in middle, keep forward following the green waymarker and avoid the immediate next right fork. Follow the green waymarker straight ahead, ignoring the path to the left.

❽ After passing trees on your right, continue straight ahead following the green waymarker. Pass trees on your left, ignoring a left turning. Continue to a junction passed earlier on the walk. Before descending ahead through woods, detour left along the South Downs Way to visit Chanctonbury Ring. Return to the junction of paths and follow the blue waymarked route to return to the car park.

WALK 47

ABOUT • LEWES

Lewes has a long and rich history. Shortly after the Battle of Hastings William de Warenne, brother to William I, built Lewes Castle. Close by is the Battle of Lewes site where Simon de Montfort's victory over Henry III eventually led to the first parliament.

Southeast England

DISTANCE • 7½ miles (12km)	**REFRESHMENTS •** plenty of pubs, cafés and restaurants in Lewes
TOTAL ASCENT • 900ft (274m)	**PARK •** Lewes rail station car park or pay-and-display car park on the other side of the rail line
PATHS • waymarked paths and defined tracks; sheep runs can be muddy	
TERRAIN • town and downland	
GRADIENTS • an initial steep ascent, two gentler climbs later	**DIFFICULTY •** 2

Lewes – Town of the Conquerors

❶ Leave the station car park by the way you entered. Turn right at immediate junction by the White Star Inn, then left before All Saints Centre (former church), up Church Twitten. At the top, turn right, down the High Street. Go forward at the traffic-lights through the precinct to the far end of town.

❷ Go forward at the road junction, up Chapel Hill (width restriction sign). Climb steeply and after a stone seat on your left and before a golf course sign, turn left. Before a gate with Cuilfail Estate sign, turn right, up the path. Emerge on to the golf course, go forward to tallest post (yellow arrow and 'take care' sign), with a memorial obelisk on the left, and continue ascending gently following posts.

❸ At far end of golf course, avoid descending but take a stile into pasture, over another stile and continue to a stile on the skyline where the view opens out ahead. Go forward towards trees as waymarked, to go down a track with a fence and woods on left.

❹ At the bottom, by a large concrete-based pond (usually dry), do not go through the gate but turn right, uphill (licensed path to Mount Caburn, landowner allows public use). Avoid two forks to the right, to follow a wide grassy path to view Mount Caburn that is soon joined by a fence on the left and head towards to the mound.

❺ Reach the gate and sign for Mount Caburn National Nature Reserve. Walk around the ramparts or climb the mound for a magnificent view and return to the

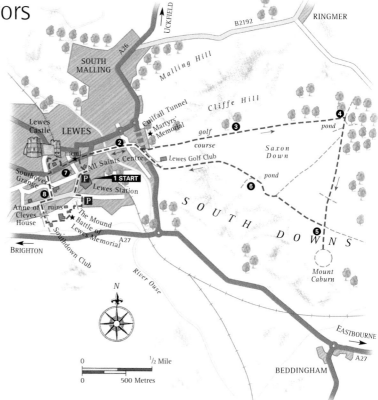

gate. Retrace 200yds (183m), then left over the stile and follow path downhill. At the bottom, cross a stile and follow the valley floor.

❻ Pass to the left of the concrete-based pond, cross two waymarked stiles (may be muddy) and in 75yds (70m) go diagonally right, up past marker post. Continue uphill to the golf course car park and turn left on the road to descend into Lewes.

Follow main route back through town and up the High Street.

❼ Beyond the war memorial and traffic lights, turn right into Castle Gate, passing under two castle archways. Go left at the viewpoint by the railings, down Castle Lane. At New Road, take steps up on the left (Pipe Passage). Turn right on High Street, then left down cobbled Keere Street (quite steep).

❽ Go forward at the road junction at the bottom (pass Southover Grange and gardens on the left), and right along Southover High Street. Turn left after the church into Cockshut Road. Turn left after the rail bridge on the path past the priory ruins and Battle of Lewes Memorial, left around the sports field and left on the path past the mound to road. Turn left, then right to the station car park.

The South Downs and the Bloomsbury Set

A fine downland walk introduces the landscape which inspired a Bohemian generation

WALK

48

1 From the main street walk past the Cricketers Arms to the end of the village and take the walled path signposted to the church. Continue past the church to a field where you turn right. Walk past a silage pit and at a T-junction turn left onto a farm track.

2 With a barn on your right, turn left into a tree-lined path. Continue up the hill, past a house, to meet a pebbled track. At crossroads, turn right towards Firle Beacon, about 4 miles (6.4km) away. At the end of this path, take the far left track with wonderful views over to Alfriston and the Cuckmere Valley, up to a ridge on the South Downs Way.

7 Continue past barn on right and brick and hung-tile cottages on left, until fork in the road. Turn left and take road back to Berwick's main street.

6 Climb stile and go straight on along the edge of a field (signposted for Berwick). Go through a break in the hedge on the right and turn left into next field. Continue along the edge of it, turning left at the end and walking alongside a hedge, then turn right, following path between two fields which leads to a farm track. Bear left.

5 Cross this road and follow the path between two houses. Take the first track on left down to Alciston. At the church turn right up public footpath to the porch door. Climb over stile on left and walk alongside flint wall on right to another stile.

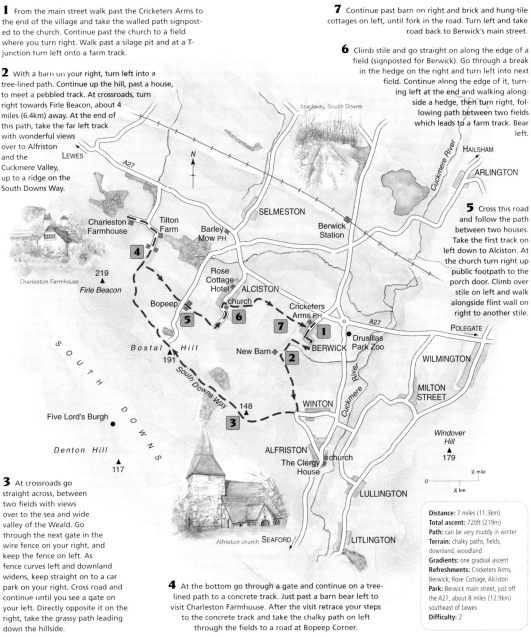

3 At crossroads go straight across, between two fields with views over to the sea and wide valley of the Weald. Go through the next gate in the wire fence on your right, and keep the fence on left. As fence curves left and downland widens, keep straight on to a car park on your right. Cross road and continue until you see a gate on your left. Directly opposite it on the right, take the grassy path leading down the hillside.

4 At the bottom go through a gate and continue on a tree-lined path to a concrete track. Just past a barn bear left to visit Charleston Farmhouse. After the visit retrace your steps to the concrete track and take the chalky path on left through the fields to a road at Bopeep Corner.

Distance: 7 miles (11.3km)
Total ascent: 720ft (219m)
Path: can be very muddy in winter
Terrain: chalky paths, fields, downland, woodland
Gradients: one gradual ascent
Refreshments: Cricketers Arms, Berwick; Rose Cottage, Alciston
Park: Berwick main street, just off the A27, about 8 miles (12.9km) southeast of Lewes
Difficulty: 2

Up and Down on the Seven Sisters

White cliffs epitomise the South Coast and there is no better place to walk on them than the Seven Sisters

WALK 49

1 From the car park cross the road, and with the visitor centre on your left, walk up the grassy hill, on the South Downs Way, to a flint wall at the top. Climb over the wall, turn slightly to the right and take the Friston Forest Forestry Commision signpost. The path soon leads steeply to steps down to Westdean Pond.

2 Take the road on the right of the pond, signposted Friston and Jevington, and continue on into Friston Forest. Follow the ride between the trees until it curves left. Do not follow this, but take the wide fork straight ahead and continue until this meets a narrow track.

Distance: 7 miles (11.3km)
Total ascent: 250ft (76m)
Path: wide forest rides; good field paths
Terrain: forest, fields, downland
Gradients: some steep sections on Seven Sisters
Refreshments: Seven Sisters Restaurant and Tea Rooms, Exceat
Park: car park at Exceat, on A259 opposite Seven Sisters Country Park Visitor Centre
Difficulty: 1

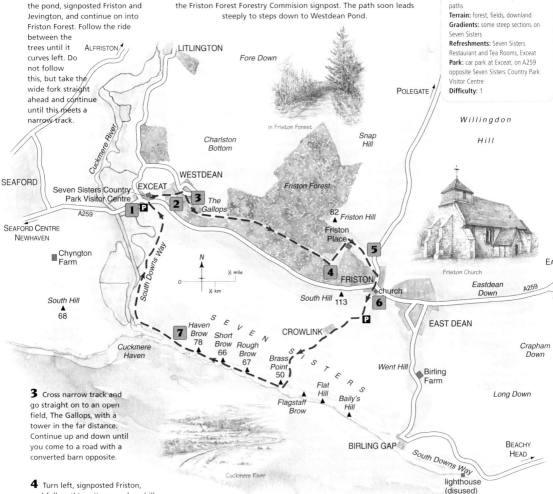

3 Cross narrow track and go straight on to an open field, The Gallops, with a tower in the far distance. Continue up and down until you come to a road with a converted barn opposite.

4 Turn left, signposted Friston, and follow this as it curves downhill to the right and uphill to a gate on the right. Go through this into a field, with an electric fence on your right, and walk to the gate at the far end.

5 Walk diagonally across the next field. Climb over the stile at the end, up some steps onto a minor road which leads to the A259 at Friston church and pond. Cross the road.

6 Follow the no-through road next to the church, past the National Trust car park, and down the tarmac path to the hamlet of Crowlink. Walk through a gate to a grassy path and follow this until the Downs open up. Bear right up the hillside to tackle Brass Point l60ft (50m), Rough Brow 216ft (67m), Short Brow, 2l4ft (66m), and the last Sister before Cuckmere Haven, Haven Brow (also, the highest at 253ft/78m).

7 At a signpost follow the South Downs Way down to Cuckmere Haven, with a wire fence on your left. Turn right along a concrete path which leads back alongside the river to Exceat car park.

WALK 50

ABOUT • THE CUCKOO TRAIL

The Cuckoo Trail, opened in 1990, runs along the track of a former railway and is part of the 9,000-mile (15,000km) Sustrans Cycle Network due to be completed in 2005, which aims to promote a traffic-free 'sustainable transport' network.

Southeast England

DISTANCE • 6 miles (9.6km)

TOTAL ASCENT • 300ft (91m)

PATHS • clearly waymarked tracks and field paths, mostly along Cuckoo Trail and Wealdway; lanes; some muddy sections

TERRAIN • disused railway track, quiet lanes, gently rolling farmland. Many stiles

GRADIENTS • gentle

REFRESHMENTS • pub, café, chip shop and food shops at Horam; Gun Inn, Gun Hill; picnic benches along trail

PARK • Cuckoo Trail car park at Horam: turn off A267 at village centre by Horam Inn on to B2203; first turn on right, Hillside Drive, signed car park and toilets

DIFFICULTY • 2

Along the Cuckoo Trail

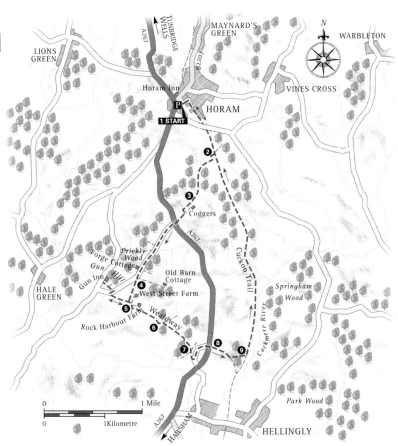

❶ Turn right out of the car park, then immediately left at a Cuckoo Trail sign, into a housing estate, bearing right as signed. Ignore the next right, signed Cuckoo Trail with horse-rider symbol, but keep ahead on the Cuckoo Trail (a former railway track), signed Hailsham/Polegate.

❷ After passing under a brick bridge and 130yds (119m) after a wedge-shaped bench on your left, turn right down steps to a stile and follow yellow arrows, first turning left along a field. The route continues along the left edge of three larger fields, then down through woodland and crosses over a footbridge.

❸ Emerge from woodland, continue forward to the top left corner of field, over a stile, then along the left edge of the next two fields (cross by stile). Cross another stile on the left. Turn right along the driveway, cross the A267 and take Swansbrook Lane opposite. Continue for 547yds (500m) to Forge Cottage on your right.

❹ In ¼ mile (400m) past the cottage take the right-hand path of two signed paths on your left (the left-hand path follows a driveway to Old Barn Cottage). Follow the left edges of three fields. At a farm track, turn left (or to detour to the Gun Inn, turn right, right at a T-junction, then left over a stile after 100yds (91m), and follow the field edge to the pub; return the same way).

❺ Keep right at the first junction (left goes to West Street Farm) and follow WW (Wealdway) waymarkers, almost immediately turning left as signed just after the entrance to Rock Harbour Farm. Follow the left edge of the field and continue forward across the middle of the next two fields.

❻ Beyond the third field go through a small wooded area, then turn right along field edges (avoiding a path branching to the left). Near the end of the second field take a stile on your right then turn left inside the edge of the wood, then go over a footbridge.

❼ Leave the wood and go up into the field, soon joining the left edge, then cross a stile to the right of houses. Continue in the next field, cross a driveway 15yds (14m) right of a cattle grid, and down to a stile. Turn left on the road (leaving the Wealdway), which bends right to the A267.

❽ Cross the A267 and cross the stile opposite, go down a bank and follow the left edges of two fields. Beyond the second field take a stile on your left and cross two fields diagonally to take a stile into trees – avoid a gate to the left of this.

❾ Turn left along the Cuckoo Trail for 2½ miles (4km) to Horam and the start of the walk.

'Mad Jack's' Brightling Follies

A tour of the charming landmarks built by
'Mad Jack' Fuller, a Sussex eccentric

WALK
51

1 From crossroads follow Willingford Lane (signed Burwash Weald) with Obelisk on left. Pass Barn Farm right and take bridleway left along concrete track. At junction, just beyond cottage, turn left over a stile and follow left-hand edge of field to another stile.

8 Ignore arrowed path right through trees and keep to ha-ha. Proceed at end through small copse and large gate into field. Turn left along field edge to gate and follow path signed The Sugar Loaf through woodland to forest drive. Bear right and keep right by Forestry Commission board to lane. Turn right, then left at junction (signed Burwash), and follow lane back to start.

2 Bear half-right downhill to bridge and stile. Head straight uphill, then down to stile and descend to cross bridge. Climb steps and stile, then head uphill to gate and turn right at junction, following hedge to stile. Proceed to stile on edge of woodland, turning left at fingerpost on path parallel with woodland. Shortly, turn right at junction.

3 Cross forest track and descend through gorse. Ignore path on left and continue down sunken bridleway to cross stream. Follow path left to track and turn sharp left on bridleway, passing two posts. Ascend for ¼ mile (400m), past two houses.

4 Follow lane uphill. Disregard first footpath left and take second arrowed path, beyond two houses. Go through gate, pass right of pond at fingerpost by hedge ahead. Keep straight on path towards Sugar Loaf. Cross double stile and bear half-left to gap in hedge near end of houses.

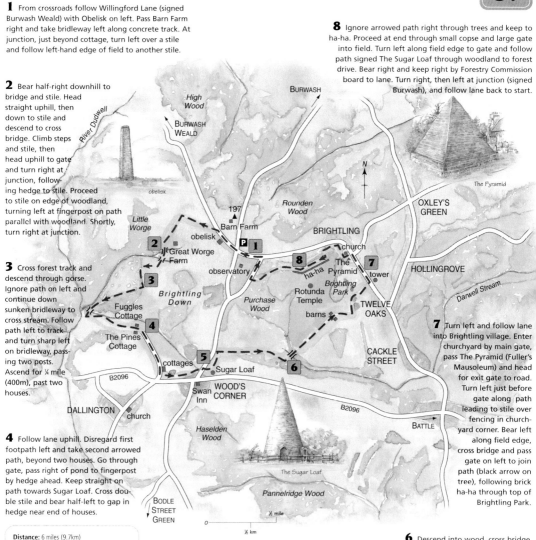

Distance: 6 miles (9.7km)
Total ascent: 650ft (198m)
Paths: good; muddy after rain
Terrain: fields, woodland, open parkland
Gradients: gradual
Refreshments: Swan Inn, Wood's Corner
Park: on verge near Fuller's Obelisk and Observatory on Brightling Down, between Wood's Corner and Burwash, 1 mile (1.6km) north of B2096 at Wood's Corner
Difficulty: 2

5 Turn left along road to entrance to salvage yard. To view Sugar Loaf, enter yard (yellow arrow), pass gates to first yard and follow markers uphill along fenced path to gate. Return to yard entrance and follow white arrows on right into Purchase Wood. Ignore path to Brightling, left, and keep ahead on path (signed The Tower), eventually merging with gravel track. ½ mile (800m) into woodland look for arrowed post left for The Tower.

7 Turn left and follow lane into Brightling village. Enter churchyard by main gate, pass The Pyramid (Fuller's Mausoleum) and head for exit gate to road. Turn left just before gate along path leading to stile over fencing in churchyard corner. Bear left along field edge, cross bridge and pass gate on left to join path (black arrow on tree), following brick ha-ha through top of Brightling Park.

6 Descend into wood, cross bridge and pass through gate into Brightling Park. Proceed through gate ahead and follow path through edge of woodland to gate. Keep left along field edge (The Temple clearly visible to left - no access), eventually reaching gate by barns. Turn right on track and keep left at junction to follow track to lane. Turn right to view The Tower.

WALK 52

ABOUT • DOVER

Since the first Roman invasion in 55 BC, Dover has borne the brunt of invading forces. This walk takes you along a historic stretch of the White Cliffs to Dover Castle, which was used as an underground nerve centre during World War II.

Southeast England

DISTANCE • 7 miles (11.3km)

TOTAL ASCENT • 498ft (152m)

PATHS • generally good, some field paths can be muddy

TERRAIN • clifftop, farmland and some pavements through the town

GRADIENTS • gentle climbing along cliff; otherwise fairly level

REFRESHMENTS • café at visitor centre; pub and tea room at St Margaret's Bay; pubs and a tea room in St Margaret's at Cliffe

PARK • NT car park (fee) at Gateway to the White Cliffs visitor centre on Langdon Cliff, follow signs to Dover Castle

DIFFICULTY • 2

Along the White Cliffs of Dover

❶ From the Gateway to the White Cliffs visitor centre walk away from Dover. Take the path at the end of the last parking area and fork right, signed Saxon Shore Way (SSW). Gently ascend to the top of the cliff to a stile. Follow concrete markers and descend beside fence to a track. Cross over with SSW marker and climb out of Langdon Hole (NT), passing the steep steps down to Langdon Bay, to a stile.

❷ Soon turn right with SSW marker and stay on the clifftop path towards South Foreland Lighthouse (NT). At the boundary by properties below the lighthouse, follow the path inland. Pass the gates to the lighthouse and turn right at a junction of paths (SSW). Keep right at a crossing of routes. Follow the track past the windmill to a gate on your right leading on to Lighthouse Down (NT).

❸ Follow the clifftop path to a gate by a house. Rejoin the track, descend to a crossing of tracks and turn right. Pass St Margaret's Museum and Pines Garden and bear right at a junction to reach the road at a sharp bend. Turn right to visit St Margaret's Bay.

❹ Climb the steps on your left by the footpath post. At the top, keep ahead on the pavement for ½ mile (800m) into St Margaret's at Cliffe. Walk through the village and take the road on the left, signed Dover.

❺ Keep to the left-hand verge and soon bear left to a waymarked stile. Walk through a narrow paddock to a stile, then proceed alongside the right-hand fence to a stile. Bear half-right along the defined field path to a stile and maintain

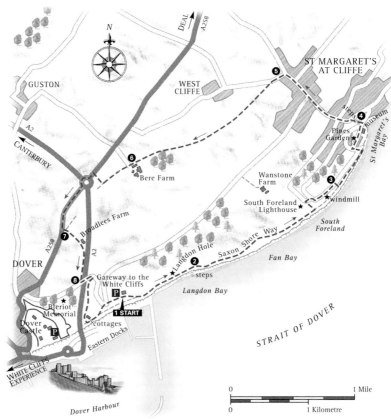

direction. Briefly walk by a copse, then follow the path half-right to reach a stile by trees.

❻ Pass to the right of a farm, cross the drive and a stile and walk along the left-hand field edge to a stile. Turn right to the A258. Turn left to the roundabout, cross Jubilee Way and keep to the pavement beside the road for Dover Castle.

❼ In ¼ mile (400m), cross the stile on your left and pass through Broadlees Farm. Descend the track to a gate and turn immediately right through another gate. Walk parallel with the A2 to a stile and ascend steps to a road.

❽ Turn left across the bridge, bear right with the road and shortly take the path right (unmarked). Follow the path left across scrubland,

parallel with the A2, and eventually pass in front of cottages to join the SSW. Turn left and climb to the road, turning immediately right back to the visitor centre.

• DON'T MISS •

*The great views of Dover at **South Foreland Lighthouse**, built in 1843 and used for early radio experiments.*

WALK 53

ABOUT • CANTERBURY

Birthplace of Christianity and mecca for pilgrims, Canterbury is famous for its association with the poet Geoffrey Chaucer, author of The Canterbury Tales. *After your walk, step back in time with a visit to the Canterbury Tales Visitor Attraction.*

Southeast England

DISTANCE • 3 miles (4.8km)	**REFRESHMENTS** • cafés, pubs and restaurants in the city centre
TOTAL ASCENT • 66ft (20m)	
PATHS • surfaced roads	**PARK** • long and short stay car parks (fee) around the city walls
TERRAIN • city streets	**DIFFICULTY** • 1
GRADIENTS • level; short ascent to city walls	

The Tale of Canterbury

❶ With your back to Westgate Archway and Museum, walk along the pedestrianised St Peter's Street towards the town centre. Cross the River Stour and pass Eastbridge Hospital (Pilgrims Hospital) on your right. Continue past the library and Guildhall Street, turn right along St Margaret's Street.

❷ Pass the Canterbury Tales visitor attraction and the Tourist Information Office, then turn right down Hawks Lane, signed to Canterbury Heritage. At Stour Street, turn left, pass the Canterbury Heritage Museum and at the end of the street, keep ahead along Church Lane to pass St Mildred's Church.

❸ Before the ring road, turn left between metal bollards and walk past the Norman castle. At Castle Street, turn right then left along the pavement by the ring road. In a few paces, bear left along Castle Row, then right by the toilets into Dane John Gardens. Keep right, climb on to the city walls.

❹ Climb the path to the monument on top of Dane John

• DON'T MISS •

Stroll beyond St Augustine's Abbey to visit St Martin's Church, the oldest parish church in England still in constant use. Believed to date back to Roman times, St Augustine worshipped here before he established his own monastery. Also you can walk through reconstructions of Roman buildings at the Roman Museum, set underground at the level of the Roman town.

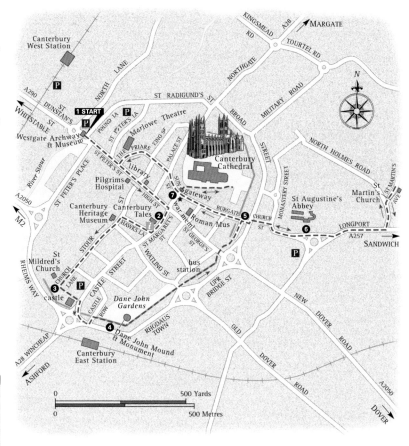

Mound for the fine city view. Continue along the walls above the bus station and descend to cross St George's Street. Continue to Burgate.

❺ Turn right, cross the pedestrian crossing over the ring road and walk along Church Street to the junction with Monastery Street.

Cross over to the fine gatehouse, turn right and follow Longport left to reach St Augustine's Abbey.

❻ To visit St Martin's Church, keep left at the roundabout, turn first left, then right into St Martin's Avenue. Retrace your steps back to the pedestrian crossing over the ring road and walk ahead along

Burgate to the war memorial and the cathedral gateway.

❼ Turn right through the gate to visit the cathedral. Go ahead along Sun Street, then over a junction into Orange Street. Continue along The Friars to pass the Marlowe Theatre. At St Peter's Street, turn right back to Westgate Archway.

Following the Pilgrims through Kent

*At Hollingbourne, medieval pilgrims bound for
Canterbury found hospitality in a pleasing village*

1 From the street opposite the manor house walk up the road by the house. Turn right where the path forks. You will pass a converted oast house. Follow the byway sign. At the electricity sub-station, go right and up to the Pilgrims' Way.

6 Cross Broad Street then go up steps following North Downs Way signs, over a stile, then down steps into a wood. At the T-junction, turn left then right and go through a metal barrier. Coming out onto open land, turn left and go through three gates and follow the path across fields and through trees back down to Hollingbourne.

5 Go up a steep hill, then down and over two stiles. Follow North Downs Way as it bends, left then right near the farm, then go over two more stiles and through the wood. In a field follow the path to the top corner and go over a stile then right to the road.

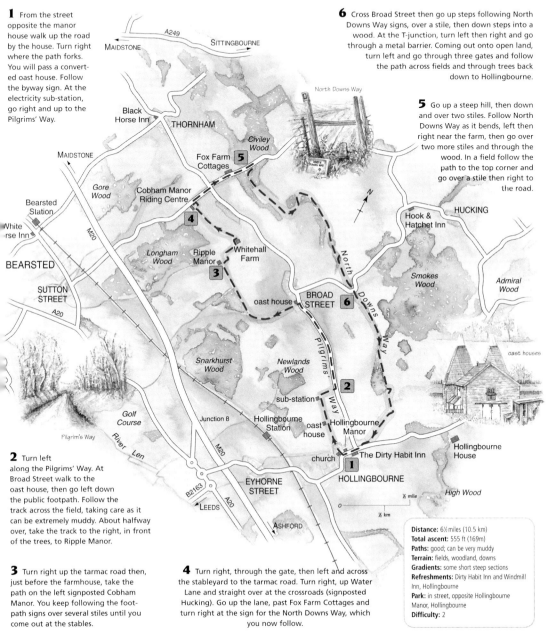

2 Turn left along the Pilgrims' Way. At Broad Street walk to the oast house, then go left down the public footpath. Follow the track across the field, taking care as it can be extremely muddy. About halfway over, take the track to the right, in front of the trees, to Ripple Manor.

3 Turn right up the tarmac road then, just before the farmhouse, take the path on the left signposted Cobham Manor. You keep following the footpath signs over several stiles until you come out at the stables.

4 Turn right, through the gate, then left and across the stableyard to the tarmac road. Turn right, up Water Lane and straight over at the crossroads (signposted Hucking). Go up the lane, past Fox Farm Cottages and turn right at the sign for the North Downs Way, which you now follow.

Distance: 6½ miles (10.5 km)
Total ascent: 555 ft (169m)
Paths: good; can be very muddy
Terrain: fields, woodland, downs
Gradients: some short steep sections
Refreshments: Dirty Habit Inn and Windmill Inn, Hollingbourne
Park: in street, opposite Hollingbourne Manor, Hollingbourne
Difficulty: 2

WALK

55

Historic Medway Towns

A rich and varied past is all around you on the historic streets of Rochester and Chatham

Distance: 5½ miles (8.8 km)
Total ascent: 100ft (30m)
Paths: good
Terrain: city streets
Gradients: gentle
Refreshments: available throughout
Park: Rochester Station
Difficulty: 1

1 From Rochester Station turn left, go under the rail bridge and walk right, down to the main road. Turn left along Medway Street, follow the road round, then turn left again up Dock Road, signposted to Historic Dockyard.

2 Keep walking up this busy road. Go straight on at the roundabout, then left into the Historic Dockyard. After exploring the dockyard come out and turn left. Go over the roundabout, then past the Medway Tunnel. Cross the road at the next roundabout and walk up to the submarine Ocelot.

3 Follow the road back into town. At the clock, cross over to the Pentagon Shopping Centre. Turn right up a pedestrianised street, then go right along a quiet part of Chatham High Street. Keep going straight ahead, back to Rochester Station.

4 Pass the station, walk up to the main road, cross over and walk down the pedestrianised High Street. Just after Eastgate House turn left, up Crow Lane. Cross over at Restoration House and follow the sign for Centenary Walk, which leads over a small park.

Rochester Castle

200m
0
200yds

N

5 Turn right at the end, go down the hill, then left at the bottom. Pass the cathedral, cross the road and turn left round the castle, following Centenary Walk signs. Pass Satis House, turn right at the river, then right again by the bridge.

6 Walk right along the High Street, exploring the small alleys and passageways. Cross the road at the end and walk back to the station.

St Mary's Island

3 HMS Ocelot

MARITIME WAY

Quayside (office development)

MEDWAY TUNNEL

SITTINGBOURNE

HMS Ocelot

Waterside (office devpt)

Pembroke (office development)

Historic Dockyard

Brompton Barracks

WOOD STREET

DOCK ROAD

WESTCOURT ST

NEW BROMPTON

STAIRS HILL

barracks

Kitchener Barracks

church (incl. Medway Heritage Centre)

Fort Amherst Heritage Park & Caverns

dockyard

Churchills PH

2

Town Hall

Gardens

CROSS STREET

Pentagon Shopping Centre

BROOK

GRAVESEND LONDON

A2

Reach

Norman Conquest PH

Guildhall Museum

visitor centre

Charles Dickens Centre

Eastgate House

Rochester Station

Chatham Ness

North Foreland PH

almshouses

HIGH STREET

BEST STREET

GILLINGHAM

A2

NEW ROAD

MEDWAY

RIVER

Limehouse Reach

Bridge

Satis House

gardens

ESPLANADE

ST MARGERETS ST

CASTLE

HILL church castle

HIGH

cathedral

Eagle Tavern

IN GATE

CORPORATION ST

CROW LN

VICTORIA ST

VINES LANE

EAST ROW

STAR HILL

5

6

1

4

Nag's Head PH

Restoration House

recreation ground

CITY WAY

A2

A229

MAIDSTONE

NEW ROAD

MANOR RD

MAIDSTONE

Chatham Station

A230

Victoria Gardens

TALBOT RD

GLOBE LN

A231

MEDWAY ST

Gashouse Point

WALK 56

ABOUT • DOWN HOUSE

Down House, Charles Darwin's home for 40 years, has been carefully recreated by English Heritage. This walk explores the countryside he knew, and passes the former estate of High Elms House, where his friend the naturalist, Sir John Lubbock, lived.

Southeast England

DISTANCE • 6½ miles (10.4km)

TOTAL ASCENT • 500ft (152m)

PATHS • clearly waymarked and defined tracks; mud; some roads

TERRAIN • woodland and downland

GRADIENTS • one fairly steep woodland descent; otherwise well-graded

REFRESHMENTS • bar, café, toilets at High Elms golf club house; pubs, tea room and shop in Downe; tea room at Down House

PARK • public car park for High Elms Golf Course between Downe and Farnborough; roadside parking in Downe

DIFFICULTY • 2

Darwin's Home at Downe

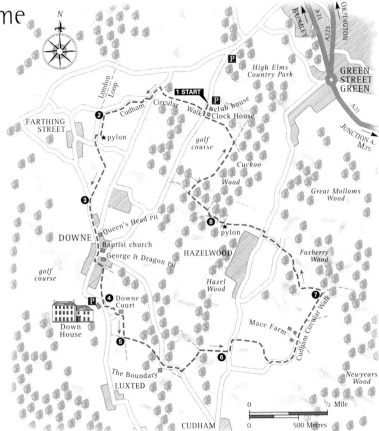

❶ Turn left out of the car park, on to the road. Opposite the Clock House, turn right on a path by a post-box, signed Cudham Circular Walk, follow this to Downe. Turn left on the road, then right on to a track, Bogey Lane. Soon ascend the steps on your left and go along the field edge.

❷ Avoid the London Loop which bears right, and continue to the far field corner by a pylon. Cross a stile and left on a track. Go ahead at the junction of tracks, signed Downe, across the fields (yellow waymarks). Continue to the road.

❸ Turn left on to the road. At Downe village centre, go forward along Luxted Road, past the Baptist church. Turn left before railings (signed Cudham with a red and white English Heritage sign denoting route to Down House), between the houses and along a field edge. In the second field keep right at a junction of paths and go forward into the next field to cross a stile on the right on to the road opposite Down House.

❹ After visiting Down House return to the field by the same stile opposite Down House. Turn right along the field edge, turn left in the field corner to a stile and go forward to take a waymarked path on the right (leaves Green Circular Walk). Pass Downe Court Farmhouse, go over a concrete drive and left along the field edge.

❺ Go left at the path crossing midway through the field; go along the next field edge, and down through the woods. Turn right on to the road, then left on a signed bridleway by Cudham

village sign. Ascend steps, ignore a left turning, and go forward by buildings to a road junction.

❻ Go left along the road. After 70yds (64m) turn right on a field path (Cudham Circular Walk, continues to the car park), which bends right at the end of the third field. Go left along a lane. Continue forward at a junction by some houses, on a track signed

Green Street Green. Later, ignore the path to your right.

❼ In woodland, turn left at the junction, to go out of the woods. Go forward at the next junction, along the road. At the main road, turn right and immediately left through a gate, along a field and into Cuckoo Wood near a pylon. Go uphill on the path and forward at two junctions.

❽ Ignore the path into the field but keep right, inside woods, and continue up to the track corner. Keep left uphill. Turn right at Cudham Circular Walk sign, then take the next right fork (near the edge of a golf course), along a broad path. Go left by a barrier and signpost, on to a fenced path which leads down through the golf course to the road. The car park is on the right.

In London's East End

History unfolds, street after street, in this exploration of a lesser-known London

WALK

57

1 From the Tower Thistle Hotel, by Tower Bridge, turn right and walk up St Katharine's Way. Cross the road and take the right fork which is Mansell Street. Go under the subway and take exit 14 marked Middlesex Street (Petticoat Lane).

6 Turn left and follow the signs for the Thames Path and Riverside Pubs. Follow the Thames Path signs all the way, taking the riverside links off left wherever possible. Not all are continuous and you'll need to return to the road on occasions. When you reach St Katherine's Dock, follow the signs through the dock and come out on the other side at Tower Bridge.

5 Turn right and follow pedestrian signs to Canary Wharf. At Ontario Way, on your left, is a spiral staircase at the corner of a new building. Go up the stairs and walk above the road to Westferry Circus. Walk down to Riverside Pier and Canary Wharf, then turn back, go down the steps again and back to Westferry Station.

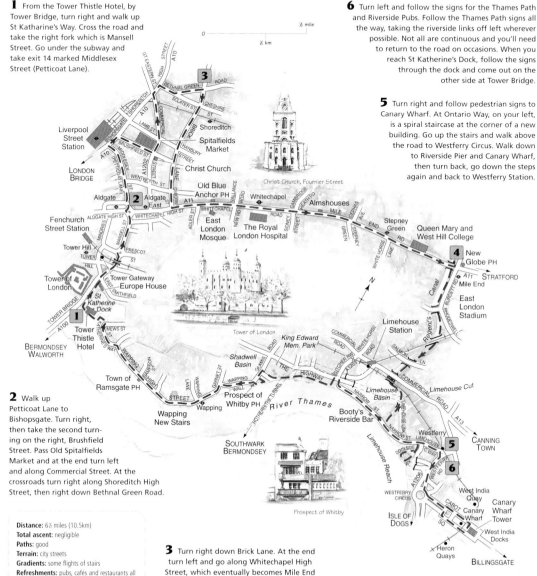

2 Walk up Petticoat Lane to Bishopsgate. Turn right, then take the second turning on the right, Brushfield Street. Pass Old Spitalfields Market and at the end turn left and along Commercial Street. At the crossroads turn right along Shoreditch High Street, then right down Bethnal Green Road.

Prospect of Whitby

Distance: 6½ miles (10.5km)
Total ascent: negligible
Paths: good
Terrain: city streets
Gradients: some flights of stairs
Refreshments: pubs, cafés and restaurants all along route
Park: NCP St Katharine's Way car park, next to Tower Thistle Hotel, by Tower Bridge
Difficulty: 1

3 Turn right down Brick Lane. At the end turn left and go along Whitechapel High Street, which eventually becomes Mile End Road. Keep walking ahead until you reach the bridge over the Regent's Canal. Go over the bridge and immediately turn left. Take the steps down to the canal and walk down to the left.

4 Walk down to Limehouse Basin, under the Docklands Light Railway, then turn left. Go over a bridge, through a play area then turn left at the converted wharves and walk along Barleycorn Way and Limehouse Causeway to Westferry Station.

WALK 58

Discover 17th-century London – the plague, the Great Fire and the beginning of banking and commerce. At this time, London was undergoing enormous changes, and mostly at the hands of one man, architect Sir Christopher Wren (1623–1723).

Southeast England

DISTANCE • 3 miles (4.8km)	**REFRESHMENTS** • numerous inns and coffee shops along the way
TOTAL ASCENT • nil	
PATHS • city streets	**PARK** • plenty of car parks in London, though it can be expensive and the streets are often congested. Nearest underground station – Monument
TERRAIN • pavements, cobbles, streets and alleyways	
GRADIENTS • level	**DIFFICULTY** • 1

Exploring Wren's London

❶ From The Monument walk along Monument Street. Approach the junction with Lower Thames Street, bear left into cobbled Lovat Lane. Pass The Walrus and Carpenter pub and look for Church of St Mary at Hill. Visit the church, leave by a different door and turn left to the junction with Eastcheap.

❷ Turn right and follow it into Great Tower Street. Pass St Dunstan's Hill, approach All Hallows-by-the-Tower, cross over into Mark Lane and turn right into Hart Street. Pass Seething Lane and continue into Crutched Friars. Pass under the railway and turn left into Lloyds Avenue. Bear right along Fenchurch Street towards St Botolph's Church.

❸ Keep left, go to the rear of the church, and take the subway to Houndsditch. Soon turn left into St Mary Axe. The Baltic Exchange is ahead. Turn right along Camomile Street, cross Bishopsgate and Old Broad Street to pass All Hallows London Wall Church. Pass Great Winchester Street, Blomfield Street and Finsbury Circus, and turn left into Copthall Avenue.

❹ When the road bends left, veer right down an alley to Telegraph Street. Turn left at Moorgate and walk along to the back of the Bank of England. Turn right and follow Lothbury to Gresham Street and continue to Guildhall Yard. See St Lawrence Jewry, and cross to turn left into Milk Street.

❺ Bear right at Cheapside and walk to St Paul's Cathedral. Retrace your steps briefly along Cheapside and look for flower beds and an arch on the right between

two banks. Through the arch turn immediately left to reach steps (gardens and fountains to the right), and cross Bread Street to a alley leading to St Mary-le-Bow.

❻ Keep to the right of the church, bear right at the junction and walk along the narrow pedestrianised street for a few paces, turning left into Well Court. Follow it round to the right. Cross Queen Street into Pancras Lane, then cross Queen Victoria Street to Bucklersby. Keep to the left of the Saxon church of St Stephen Walbrook and take the alley, St Stephen's Row, next to it.

❼ Look for the little churchyard, hemmed in by buildings, and turn right at the next junction. Bear right into St Swithins Lane. At Cannon Street, turn left and left again into Abchurch Lane. Pass St Mary Abchurch and, at King

William Street, bear left and walk to the Bank of England and the Royal Exchange.

❽ Keep right and follow Cornhill. Pass St Michael's Church, then turn right into Gracechurch Street. Swing left into Leadenhall Market and take the first right turning. Keep right at Lime Street and cross Fenchurch Street into Philpot Lane. Turn right at the next road junction, then left into Pudding Lane. Return to Monument. Monument Underground Station is on the right.

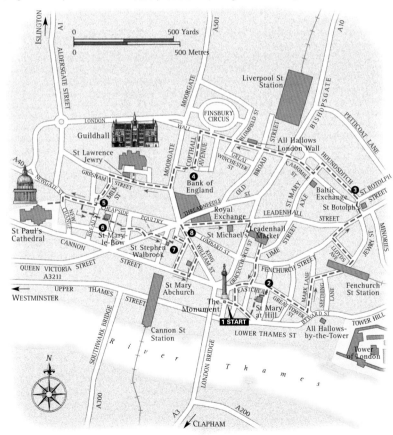

Chobham Common –
Last of the Surrey Heaths

The ever present gorse marks this heath apart from the sprawl of Surrey's commuterland

WALK

59

Distance: 7 miles (11.3km)
Total ascent: 245ft (75m)
Paths: mostly good; can become waterlogged after heavy rain
Terrain: heath, common, woodland, fields, several stretches of road
Gradients: gentle
Refreshments: Four Horseshoes and Cricketers Inn, Burrowhill
Park: Longcross car park, just off the B386, western end of Longcross
Difficulty: 1

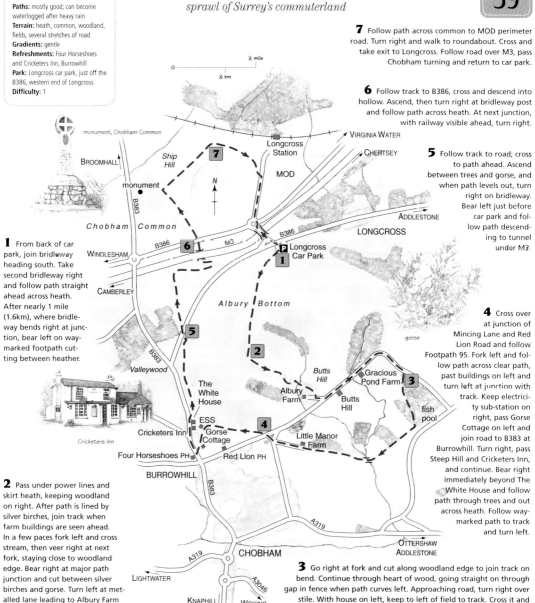

7 Follow path across common to MOD perimeter road. Turn right and walk to roundabout. Cross and take exit to Longcross. Follow road over M3, pass Chobham turning and return to car park.

6 Follow track to B386, cross and descend into hollow. Ascend, then turn right at bridleway post and follow path across heath. At next junction, with railway visible ahead, turn right.

5 Follow track to road; cross to path ahead. Ascend between trees and gorse, and when path levels out, turn right on bridleway. Bear left just before car park and follow path descending to tunnel under M3.

1 From back of car park, join bridleway heading south. Take second bridleway right and follow path straight ahead across heath. After nearly 1 mile (1.6km), where bridleway bends right at junction, bear left on waymarked footpath cutting between heather.

4 Cross over at junction of Mincing Lane and Red Lion Road and follow Footpath 95. Fork left and follow path across clear path, past buildings on left and turn left at junction with track. Keep electricity sub-station on right, pass Gorse Cottage on left and join road to B383 at Burrowhill. Turn right, pass Steep Hill and Cricketers Inn, and continue. Bear right immediately beyond The White House and follow path through trees and out across heath. Follow waymarked path to track and turn left.

2 Pass under power lines and skirt heath, keeping woodland on right. After path is lined by silver birches, join track when farm buildings are seen ahead. In a few paces fork left and cross stream, then veer right at next fork, staying close to woodland edge. Bear right at major path junction and cut between silver birches and gorse. Turn left at metalled lane leading to Albury Farm and follow it to junction. Bear left and follow road round sharp right bend. Pass bridleway on left and turn right to join path just before road curves left.

3 Go right at fork and cut along woodland edge to join track on bend. Continue through heart of wood, going straight on through gap in fence when path curves left. Approaching road, turn right over stile. With house on left, keep to left of field to track. Cross it and skirt wood, negotiating three stiles. Follow track towards houses ahead. Turn right at stile and swing left to cross stile and footbridge. Bear right to gate and follow path by stream to stile and trees. Cross into wood and follow path alongside fence. Eventually join tarmac drive straight ahead to road and turn right.

The Devil's Punch Bowl

A little bit of wilderness hides in the Surrey Hills

WALK

60

1 From car park follow track to left of café, heading away from A3. Keep left at path junction, walking to crossing of tracks by mast. Turn right towards height barrier and immediately bear down steep path to Highcombe Bottom. Keep left on merging with track. Leave woodland and take next path right, downhill to cross stream.

2 Pass youth hostel and turn left beyond gate. Pass Gnome Cottage and go straight ahead at bend to gate (by cattle grid). Cross open heath, ignoring tracks left and right before taking left path at fork (animal pens in field on right). Go through gate (by cattle grid) and continue to path junction by lane.

3 Turn right up steps, pass through Upper Highfield Farm, and pass tennis court to stile by gate. Follow concrete track down to silage storage area. Cross stile on left and ascend to cross A3. Bear left down to stile and descend through trees to another stile and driveway by house. Keep left, then, at crossing of tracks, turn right, around lake, to Blackhanger Farm driveway.

4 Bear right, cross stream and stile on left. Skirt house and garden to stile in field corner and pass through copse. Follow telegraph poles across next field to gate. At waymarker post bear right and follow track to Begley Farm. Go through gate on left and keep to right-hand edge of field to lane.

8 Walk down lane (eventually metalled) and take path (Greensand Way) right, just before post box. Disregard all paths left and right, cross edge of open heath and descend, going straight ahead at crossing of paths then forking left, steeply uphill. Keep right at house, keeping to track back to A3 and start.

7 Take second path right (ahead) for ⅔ mile (1km). Descend to crossing of trails and turn right. Cross next main path and descend steeply into wooded valley. Keep ahead at crossing of bridleways, cross stream then, just past gate on left, take unmarked path left. Ascend steeply to wide trackway by house and turn left.

6 Walk south from trig point, pass car park and take path ahead. Shortly, at crossing of paths, turn left and descend to staggered crossing of paths. Take second path right and gently climb, forking left at marker post to gate. Go round gate and shortly reach junction of five ways.

5 Turn left, then just before Boundless Farm (300m), take footpath right into Boundless Copse. Keep ahead, soon forking left, steeply uphill through coniferous trees and clearing. Continue ahead as paths cross and ascend steeply to waymarker post (Greensand Way) at top and summit of Gibbet Hill.

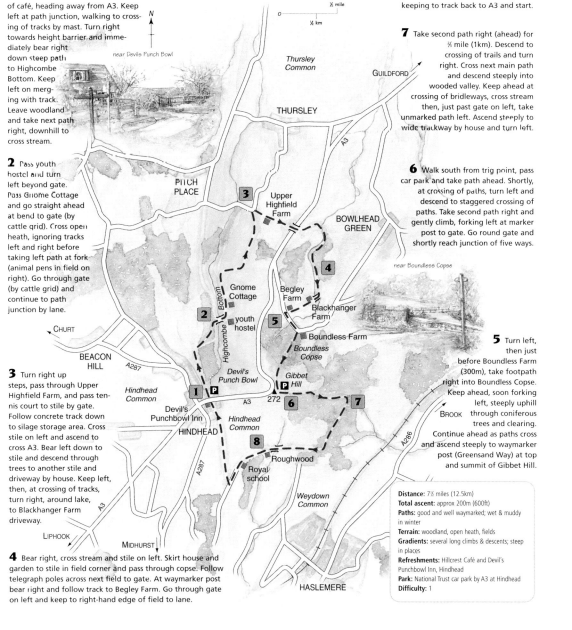

Distance: 7½ miles (12.5km)
Total ascent: approx 200m (600ft)
Paths: good and well waymarked; wet & muddy in winter
Terrain: woodland, open heath, fields
Gradients: several long climbs & descents; steep in places
Refreshments: Hillcrest Café and Devil's Punchbowl Inn, Hindhead
Park: National Trust car park by A3 at Hindhead
Difficulty: 1

WALK

61

Calleva Atrebatum, or Silchester, was built shortly after ad 43. Once a bustling town complete with streets, temple and amphitheatre, it was inexplicably abandoned in ad 400–500. Uniquely, a complete circuit of walls remains at the site.

DISTANCE • 5 miles (8km); optional circuit of walls, about 1 mile (1.6km)

TOTAL ASCENT • 98ft (30m)

PATHS • likely to be very muddy after rain

TERRAIN • fields, woodland, old lanes, some road walking

GRADIENTS • lots of stiles to negotiate, steep woodland paths

REFRESHMENTS • Calleva Arms pub, Silchester; Romans Hotel, Silchester

PARK • car park for Silchester Roman site on Wall Lane (free), on Mortimer side of modern Silchester

DIFFICULTY • 2

Roman Silchester

❶ Leave the car park via its entrance, cross the road, and take the old lane (fingerpost) directly opposite. Where the path rises, turn right at the fingerpost down a green tunnel of rhododendrons and holly. Cross a stile, keep left round the edge of the field and cross another stile. Cross a farm track and the stile opposite. Keep to the edge of the field, with the fence left, and cross the stile at the end.

❷ Ignore the track straight ahead, turn left along the old path at the field edge. Look right to see an ancient earthwork on the horizon. At the end, cross a stile and keep straight ahead along a line of oak trees. Continue downhill through the flinty field, following the hollow of an old field boundary, to a stream at the bottom.

❸ Cross a stile, footbridge and another stile, and keep straight up the hill. Half-way up, turn left and cross a stile into the woods. Cross the footbridge and continue up through birches (larch plantation on the left). At the top go through the gate and keep right along the field edge, to pass behind houses. After the last cottage (Rose Cottage), turn right over the stile and walk up the driveway.

❹ At the lane turn right, passing stables and an old farmhouse, right. Keep ahead down the old lane to the bottom of the hill. Where the track forks, keep right. After the bridge, turn left and go straight across the field towards a stile at the edge of the woods.

❺ Cross the stile and go ahead into trees. Cross a track, and a stile over a wire fence. Emerge from the woods and continue straight across the field towards a gate. Cross the stile and follow the path diagonally down to the right.

❻ At the bottom of the hollow, cross the bridge and stile and head diagonally left up the field. Before you reach the top corner, go through the squeeze gate on left, and turn right on to the gravel lane. This becomes a road by the thatched cottage (The Mount), and leads to a junction with a post-box. Turn right and through the squeeze gate for the Roman amphitheatre.

❼ Return to the road (Wall Lane) and turn right. Follow this past Manor Farm, into Church Lane. Stone walls can be seen on the right, and St Mary's Church. Keep heading downhill, and follow the path up on to the top of the wall.

❽ (Optional route: follow walls round for a complete circuit.) Retrace your route to this crossing point and stay inside the walls on a path along a fence. Turn right and go through the churchyard. Keep left, through a gate and along the path, with farm buildings on your right. Keep on this path, and bear left on to a track which runs for ½ mile (800m) across the Roman town. Pass excavation site (closed).

❾ At the opposite side, go left, then right through the gate. Follow the path for ¾ mile (1.2km) to the museum. (To reach modern village, cross the road and bear left, to take footpath through the trees.) Retract your steps to point ❾ and go left. Turn right just before the wooden gate to the car park.

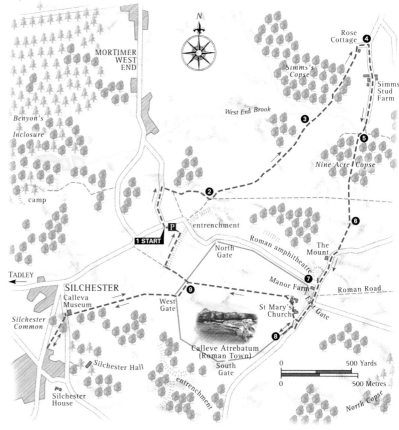

WALK

62

The White Horse was recorded in medieval records as 'a wonder', but its purpose remains a mystery. The walk also takes you to Wayland's Smithy, a 5000-year-old long barrow, along the Ridgeway, Britain's oldest road, and to Uffington Castle, an Iron-Age hill fort.

Southeast England

DISTANCE • 7 miles (11.3km)

TOTAL ASCENT • 415ft (126m)

PATHS • mixture of downland tracks, field paths and tarmac roads

TERRAIN • exposed downland and gentle farmland. Keep dogs on leads across the farmland of the Vale of the White Horse. Parts of the Ridgeway are suitable for dogs

GRADIENTS • one long, quite steep climb to the Ridgeway

REFRESHMENTS • The White Horse Inn at Woolstone

PARK • large free car park off B4507 signed Uffington White Horse & Waylands Smithy

DIFFICULTY • 2

The White Horse at Uffington

❶ From the car park go through the gate and follow the outline of the grassy path along the lower slopes towards the hill. Make for a gate and cross the lane to join a bridleway. Keep left at the fork, by a bridleway waymark, and walk along to the head of Uffington White Horse.

❷ Descend steeply on the path to the tarmac access road, keeping the chalk figure of the White Horse on your immediate left, or, if you wish to avoid the steep, grassy down slope, retrace your steps to the lane. Bear right and continue down to the junction with the B4507.

❸ Cross over and follow the road towards Uffington. Pass Sower Hill Farm and continue to a path on the left for Woolstone. Cross the stile and keep the hedge on your right. Make for two stiles in the field corner. Continue across the next field to a stile, cut through trees to the next stile. Keep ahead with the hedgerow on your left.

❹ Cross the stile, turn left at the road and walk through the picturesque village of Woolstone. Bear left by The White Horse Inn and follow the road left to All Saints Church. As you approach it, veer right across the churchyard to a stile and a gate. Cross a paddock to a further gate and stile.

❺ Turn left up the road and take the first right at the footpath sign. Follow the field edge, keeping hedge on your left, to eventually reach a stile.

❻ Turn right and walk through the trees to a footbridge. Cross it to a field, head diagonally left to a stile and turn right. Follow the field edge to a stile within sight of a thatched cottage. Cross and go ahead to a stile, the cottage is now level with you on the left.

❼ Cross the road and follow the D'Arcy Dalton Way. Make for a stile, cross a paddock and head for the road by the village sign for Compton Beauchamp. Cross over and take the drive to the church, next to the manor. Retrace your steps to the sign and walk up to the junction with the B4507.

❽ Cross over and climb quite steeply up to The Ridgeway. Turn right to visit Wayland's Smithy. Bear left to continue the walk. Follow the track to a crossroads signed Woolstone and continue on the Ridgeway uphill to reach the grassy ramparts of Uffington Castle on your left. Leave the track here, cut through the remains of the fort to the access road and return to the car park.

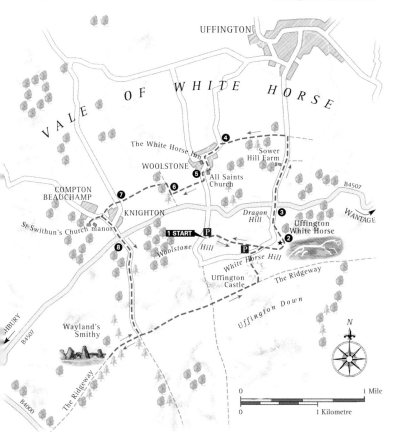

Riverbank Tales from the Thames at Cookham

*This section of the majestic Thames inspired poets,
artists and the author of 'The Wind in the Willows'*

WALK
63

Distance: 8 miles (12.9km)
Total ascent: 316ft (96m)
Paths: mostly good; can get very wet and muddy
Terrain: riverbank, meadow, escarpment, woodland, fields
Gradients: one short steep section
Refreshments: various in Cookham; The Jolly Farmer at Cookham Dean
Park: Cookham Moor car park, west of Cookham
Difficulty: 1

1 From car park walk across grass towards village. Ignore kissing gate left and follow Cookham High Street to junction with A4094. Turn left towards Wooburn and Bourne End, past Tarry Stone. Turn left through churchyard towards riverbank.

7 Keep left of September Grange and follow path to field corner. Turn right past golf course sign, keeping fence and hedge on right. Cross fairways, aim left of corrugated barns and make for railway bridge ahead. Cross it and turn right to follow grassy path by fence and hedge. Join track and follow it to road. Turn left by drive to 'Fiveways' and follow path to kissing gate. Bear right and return to Cookham Moor car park, crossing footbridge over Fleet Ditch just before it.

2 At Thames Path turn left, passing through two gates by sailing club. Continue upstream, crossing Marsh Meadow to kissing gate leading to Cock Marsh. Follow path by river, veering left under railway bridge.

3 With line of villas right, follow path back to riverbank. Pass through kissing gate and veer away from river at Ferry Cottage. Turn left at concrete drive and head towards Winter Hill. Follow track across field to pond. Pass through kissing gate to junction and turn right. Head diagonally up to gate and stile, then join road.

River Thames

Bourne End railway bridge

M40, HIGH WYCOMBE

A4155

BOURNE END

WELL END

A4094

CORES END

LITTLE MARLOW

Bourne End Station

Walnut Tree PH

Woolman's Wood

A4155

HEDSOR

3

Cock Marsh

Thames Path

Ferry Cottage

COOKHAM

Thames

golf course

7

Holy Trinity Church

2

Crown PH

Cliveden

River

MARLOW

4

Spencer Art Gallery

Hillgrove Farm

Winter Hill

Rivendell House

COOKHAM RISE

1

A4094

Marlow Station

HENLEY-ON-THAMES

A4155

A404

Inn on the Green

5

cricket pitch

Cookham Station

N

Strand Water

½ mile

0   ½ km

Jolly Farmer Inn

6

COOKHAM DEAN

MAIDENHEAD

B4447

MAIDENHEAD

4 Turn right past Stonehouse Lane and Gibraltar Lane, following road above river. Shortly, veer half-right to path running parallel with road. Walk past several parking areas to path into woods. Turn right after several steps and follow drive to 'Rivendell' entrance. Bear immediately right of gate and follow woodland path. Veer right at fork and follow path to road. Cross and head up steep bank to seat on right. Join path just beyond seat and follow for about 100yards (91m) through Quarry Wood. Turn sharp left then immediate right fork, making for woodland corner by road.

Tarry Stone

5 Bear right into Grubwood Lane and pass houses. Turn left immediately beyond and follow path parallel to wide drive. Make for bottom of slope, then head up on path beside fence towards farm buildings. In field corner join woodland path to left. At green at Cookham Dean follow lane to war memorial. Turn right into Church Road.

6 Bear left immediately beyond church and just before Jolly Farmer Inn, then left at next footpath sign. Follow road to Huntsman's Cottage and York House as it becomes a green lane, to gate, and continue to road. Bear left to road junction. Cross to Bradcutts Lane and follow for about ½ mile (800m). Turn right at Hillgrove Farm and follow path to right, over concrete stile. Fork left to lane and cross over to footpath opposite.

Historic Routes across the Chilterns

*Along the Ridgeway to Ivinghoe Beacon, then back through
beechwoods, this is a trail steeped in history*

WALK

64

1 From centre of village, facing Greyhound Inn, go right, up road for 300yds (273m), past footpath and sports ground on left, to bridleway on left, by Greenings Farm. Follow this gently uphill for 500yds (455m), ignoring path off left, to footpath on right. Cross stile and take this as it dog-legs up through golf course to sign visible in front of woodland at top of course.

2 Go through fence gap, cross over track and enter woodland through kissing gate. Go through woodland, turning right to join Ridgeway National Trail, continuing down to edge of wood to view Nature Reserve interpretative panel. Retrace steps 30yds (27m) and follow Ridgeway National Trail up to left. Follow this through woods, emerging at gate in open grassland above remains of Pitstone Quarry on left.

Distance: 7½ miles (12km)
Total ascent: 1,100ft (335m)
Paths: good; can be muddy
Terrain: farmland, downland and woodland
Gradients: moderate, two steeper sections
Refreshments: two pubs and a shop in Aldbury
Park: in the centre of Aldbury, by the pond
Difficulty: 2

7 As path levels out, take right fork above cottage, then bear left into clearing by Bridgewater monument. Facing front of monument turn left and leave clearing on descending track to right of cottages. Descend quite steeply down sunken lane, staying right at any junctions, to emerge in village. Turn right on metalled road to return to village centre.

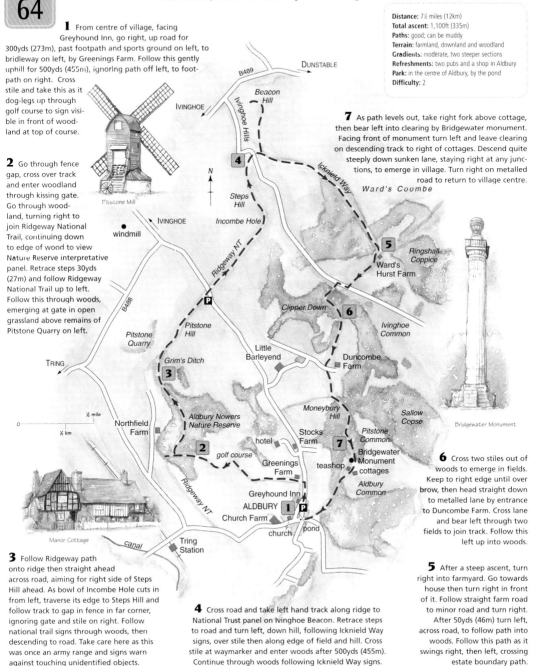

Pitstone Mill

windmill

Bridgewater Monument

Manor Cottage

6 Cross two stiles out of woods to emerge in fields. Keep to right edge until over brow, then head straight down to metalled lane by entrance to Duncombe Farm. Cross lane and bear left through two fields to join track. Follow this left up into woods.

3 Follow Ridgeway path onto ridge then straight ahead across road, aiming for right side of Steps Hill ahead. As bowl of Incombe Hole cuts in from left, traverse its edge to Steps Hill and follow track to gap in fence in far corner, ignoring gate and stile on right. Follow national trail signs through woods, then descending to road. Take care here as this was once an army range and signs warn against touching unidentified objects.

4 Cross road and take left hand track along ridge to National Trust panel on Ivinghoe Beacon. Retrace steps to road and turn left, down hill, following Icknield Way signs, over stile then along edge of field and hill. Cross stile at waymarker and enter woods after 500yds (455m). Continue through woods following Icknield Way signs.

5 After a steep ascent, turn right into farmyard. Go towards house then turn right in front of it. Follow straight farm road to minor road and turn right. After 50yds (46m) turn left, across road, to follow path into woods. Follow this path as it swings right, then left, crossing estate boundary path.

WALK 65

ABOUT • LETCHWORTH

The Garden City of Letchworth pioneered the idea of conscious town planning. Inspired by a pamphlet written by Ebenezer Howard in 1908, Letchworth aimed to resolve the problem of unhealthy slum dwellings and overcrowded terraces.

Southeast England

DISTANCE • 6 miles (9.6km)

TOTAL ASCENT • negligible

PATHS • pavements, with a short stretch through a park

TERRAIN • town, parkland

GRADIENTS • some gentle ascents

REFRESHMENTS • plenty of choice in the town

PARK • Station Place West long stay car park next to the station; multi-storey car park behind the cinema

DIFFICULTY • 1

Around Letchworth

❶ In Station Place, with the war memorial on the right, head west out of the square, noting leafy Broadway down to the left, and the Broadway Hotel. Turn right over the railway bridge. Admire the Spirella underwear factory, left.

❷ Turn right into Nevells Road. Pass houses dated 1914 to more individual, small houses, built as experimental low-cost homes in 1950, with different building materials, such as the rock-like tin cladding at No 212. The Settlement, built as a temperance pub, is now a community centre. Retrace your steps and turn right up Cross Street.

❸ Turn left at the end on to Icknield Way, and near the unusual brown timber-clad house at the entrance to The Quadrant, cross the main road and take the tarmac path straight across the park of Norton Common.

❹ Where the path emerges on Willbury Road, cross over and turn right. Pass the crescent of Westholm, on the left, the epitome of Garden City design, with its white rendered and gable houses grouped around a tree-filled green. Eastholm is a corresponding arc on the next corner. Cross Willbury Road again, and descend, right, into Norton Way North. Note the bigger houses, set back from the road with trees and hedges.

❺ At the modern St George's Church, turn left into Common View. The further you walk up here, the more interesting the little terraced groups become, with each distinctive row of four proclaiming its designers. Keep right along here to the end, then retrace your steps to Cromwell Green, a lower-scale contrast to Westholm.

❻ Turn down here between the houses, and right on to Glebe Road, back towards the town centre. The factories are only a row away, but this is still very pleasant. At the junction, go left down Norton Way North and pass under the railway bridge.

❼ Bear left, cross at the bollards, and enter Rushby Mead, a long

and delightful breath of country in the town. Stay on this road across two junctions, and at the end, turn right and cross at the crossing.

❽ Continue to the next traffic-lights, turning left into Willian Way, a beautiful avenue of bigger individual houses. Turn right into Barrington Road to pass the extraordinary Cloisters (private), and turn right again into Cloisters Road, past modern, much less individual housing. Cross the main road and the little green (note the thatched kiosk, right) and bear left into Sollershott East. Pass Sollershott Hall, left, and turn right up the main avenue of Broadway.

❾ At Souberie Avenue, turn right and follow this curve to its junction with Meadow Way. Turn left here, and right into the big Broadway square. Pass the museum on your right, turn right, and bear immediately left at the cinema into the main shopping area of East Cheap. Follow this back down to Station Place.

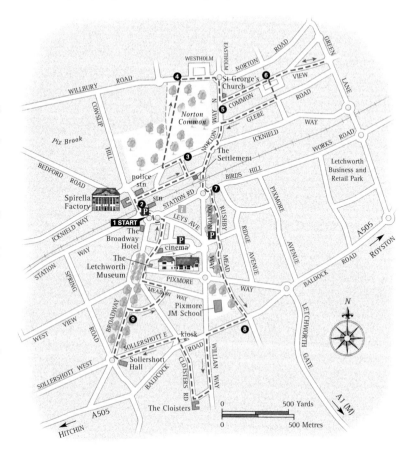

Southeast England

Village Ways in Coggeshall

*Exploring an Essex village which has retained
its medieval charm*

1 Leave the car park by the clock tower. Cross the road diagonally and turn left into Church Street. Continue to Woolpack Inn and church on the left. Cross road opposite the end of the church and take marked Essex Way path on the right.

2 Continue past the school into the recreation ground to the left-hand corner and turn left into East Street. Follow a footpath then cross over and take the Essex Way to right at the end of houses. Follow hedge to a stile and continue by fence following Essex Way towards farmyard.

3 Turn right and pass a mill on the left, through the farmyard with abbey ruins on right. Continue past the chapel to T-junction (Grange Barn opposite). Turn right down the hill. Beyond a bridge, turn left then shortly left again into West Street. (Paycocke's is on left). Cross over, taking the path by an old school.

4 Follow the path to a gap in far right of field, continue, then go left by a little bridge. Go ½ mile (800m) up lane, approaching the busy A120. Cross over, taking no-through road. Continue ¾ mile (1.2km) to Bungate Wood.

5 Continue through the wood and after 300yds (274m) follow the yellow waymark left, diagonally across the field. Cross a lane and go straight over field by pylon. Follow to waymark and go along hedge. Turn left, then right into lane, passing the Compasses pub.

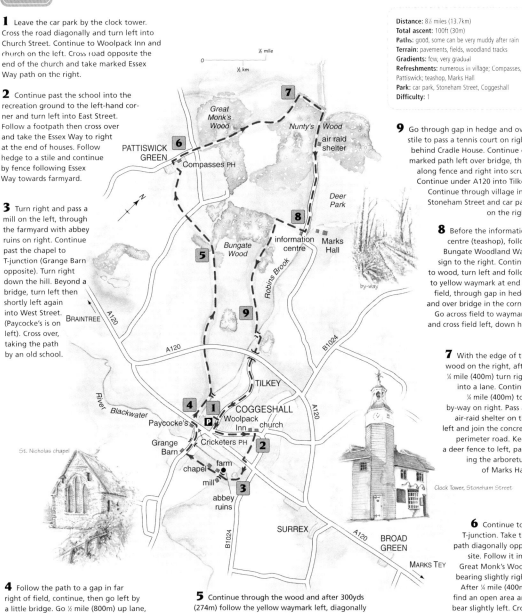

½ mile

0

½ km

Great Monk's Wood

PATTISWICK GREEN

Compasses PH

Nunty's Wood

air raid shelter

Deer Park

Bungate Wood

information centre

Marks Hall

Robins Brook

by-way

BRAINTREE

A120

A120

River Blackwater

St. Nicholas chapel

Paycocke's

Woolpack Inn

church

COGGESHALL

Cricketers PH

Grange Barn

chapel

farm

mill

abbey ruins

TILKEY

SURREX

BROAD GREEN

MARKS TEY

B1024

A120

B1024

A120

Clock Tower, Stoneham Street

Distance: 8½ miles (13.7km)
Total ascent: 100ft (30m)
Paths: good, some can be very muddy after rain
Terrain: pavements, fields, woodland tracks
Gradients: few, very gradual
Refreshments: numerous in village; Compasses, Pattiswick; teashop, Marks Hall
Park: car park, Stoneham Street, Coggeshall
Difficulty: 1

9 Go through gap in hedge and over stile to pass a tennis court on right, behind Cradle House. Continue on marked path left over bridge, then along fence and right into scrub. Continue under A120 into Tilkey. Continue through village into Stoneham Street and car park on the right.

8 Before the information centre (teashop), follow Bungate Woodland Walk sign to the right. Continue to wood, turn left and follow to yellow waymark at end of field, through gap in hedge and over bridge in the corner. Go across field to waymark, and cross field left, down hill.

7 With the edge of the wood on the right, after ¼ mile (400m) turn right into a lane. Continue ¼ mile (400m) to a by-way on right. Pass an air-raid shelter on the left and join the concrete perimeter road. Keep a deer fence to left, passing the arboretum of Marks Hall.

6 Continue to a T-junction. Take the path diagonally opposite. Follow it into Great Monk's Wood, bearing slightly right. After ¼ mile (400m), find an open area and bear slightly left. Cross a stile and go over the field towards Nunty's Wood.

Constable's Suffolk Landscapes

*From 'Dedham Vale' to 'The Haywain', the Suffolk
countryside was a constant theme in the artist's work*

WALK

67

8 After 75yds (68m) take right fork, signed to Dedham. Follow a narrow path to a gate and cross a field with the river to left. Follow the path across a field to a road. Turn left, over the bridge, past the mill and back to the car park on the left.

1 Turn left out of the car park and up to T-junction. The church and old grammar school are opposite. Turn left and where the road bends sharp right, take the path signed Flatford, diagonally to the left. Keep right at the farm.

7 Retrace your steps to the war memorial opposite the church. Take the no through road right. After 300yds (273m) take a footpath to right, signed private road. Continue down the track, past a cottage, keeping left, then right to a bridge. Go over bridge.

6 Turn left at the crossroads and follow the road for ¾ mile (1.2km) to the church, turning right. Continue past the Constable birthplace plaque on the fence to the right. Turn left at the no-through road by a shop to see his studio, on the left.

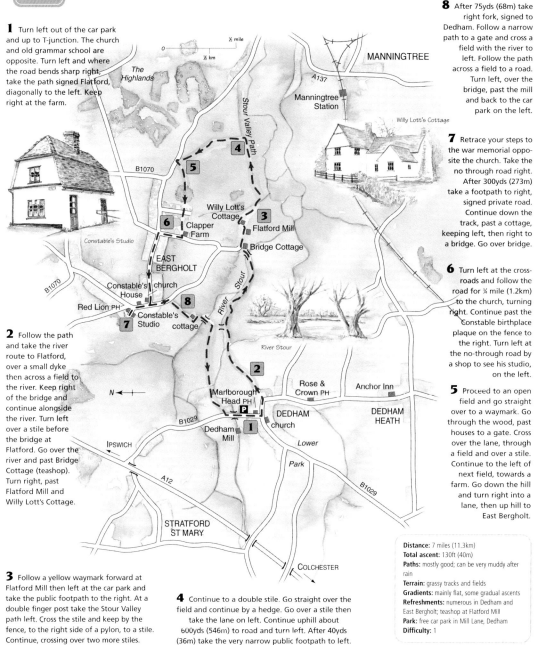

2 Follow the path and take the river route to Flatford, over a small dyke then across a field to the river. Keep right of the bridge and continue alongside the river. Turn left over a stile before the bridge at Flatford. Go over the river and past Bridge Cottage (teashop). Turn right, past Flatford Mill and Willy Lott's Cottage.

5 Proceed to an open field and go straight over to a waymark. Go through the wood, past houses to a gate. Cross over the lane, through a field and over a stile. Continue to the left of next field, towards a farm. Go down the hill and turn right into a lane, then up hill to East Bergholt.

3 Follow a yellow waymark forward at Flatford Mill then left at the car park and take the public footpath to the right. At a double finger post take the Stour Valley path left. Cross the stile and keep by the fence, to the right side of a pylon, to a stile. Continue, crossing over two more stiles.

4 Continue to a double stile. Go straight over the field and continue by a hedge. Go over a stile then take the lane on left. Continue uphill about 600yds (546m) to road and turn left. After 40yds (36m) take the very narrow public footpath to left.

Distance: 7 miles (11.3km)
Total ascent: 130ft (40m)
Paths: mostly good; can be very muddy after rain
Terrain: grassy tracks and fields
Gradients: mainly flat, some gradual ascents
Refreshments: numerous in Dedham and East Bergholt; teashop at Flatford Mill
Park: free car park in Mill Lane, Dedham
Difficulty: 1

WALK

68

The timbered façade of Lavenham offers the perfect image of a Tudor wool town, at its peak during the reign of Henry VIII. Lavenham offers some superb 16th-century architecture including the Guildhall of Corpus Christi and the Swan Inn.

Southeast England

DISTANCE • 5 miles (8km)

PATHS • mostly firm, but sections can be muddy; keep dogs under strict control in the town and through farmyard and fields

Terrain • town, former railway, open farmland, quiet lanes

GRADIENTS • some gentle slopes, but mostly fairly level

REFRESHMENTS • Swan Inn, Lavenham; National Trust tea rooms in Guildhall, Market Square

PARK • in the car park, Lavenham, signed near the church; other parking available in the town

DIFFICULTY • 1

Lavenham – a Timbered Treasure

❶ Turn right out of the car park and head down hill into the town centre. Turn right just before the timbered Swan Inn into Water Street. Turn into the bottom of Lady Street to admire the old guildhall, now part of the inn but once one of four guildhalls around the town. Continue down Water Street. Pass the bottom of Barn Street, pause to admire its houses.

❷ Turn left up Shilling Street, passing Shilling Grange and other splendid timbered and plastered houses. Nos 22-24 are particularly fine. Turn left at the top into Bolton Street, and bear right into Market Square, passing a memorial to US airmen of World War II.

❸ After exploring the square, with its magnificent timbered Guildhall, little houses, butter cross and Angel Hotel, leave via Market Lane and turn right on the High Street. Continue over the brow of the hill, admiring the lovely old row of houses, Nos 61-63.

❹ At the bottom, just before the railway bridge, take the muddy path down to the left, signed Lavenham Walk. This bends left to join the route of the old railway line (which can be followed all the way to Long Melford), a lovely walk with occasional benches. Continue along this for about a mile (1.6km), with the big square tower of Lavenham church looming to your left, and trees forming a natural arch overhead.

❺ Cross the road via two metal gates and continue along the railway path for about a mile (1.6km). Go through the banks of a cutting, and through a squeeze gate under a brick road bridge. Stay on the line, to pass a Site of Special Scientific Interest with

unusual chalk downland vegetation. After another area of woodland the path deteriorates, emerging on to an open field. Keep straight ahead along the lower edge of the field to meet a junction of tracks.

❻ Turn left up the farm track, back over the hill. Stay on this track and follow the yellow waymarkers as it bends right, towards the farm, then left

between two old black barns. Follow the road round to the right, and at the junction with the track, keep left down the main drive towards Lavenham.

❼ At the end, turn right along the road for a short distance. A fingerpost indicates the path left. Follow it straight across the field towards the barred wooden gate. Cross the stile and keep straight on, with the hedge on your right.

Cross another stile, and go straight on to meet the lane.

❽ Turn right here towards the church, and turn left up the stone steps below the tower. Walk round three sides of the church, keeping it on your left, and take the little path in the bottom corner through the old wooden kissing gate.

❾ Head down the grassy path towards the pond. Go through the gate and over the bridge, and at the end of the lane turn right into Hall Road. Where this meets High Street, turn right to return to the car park.

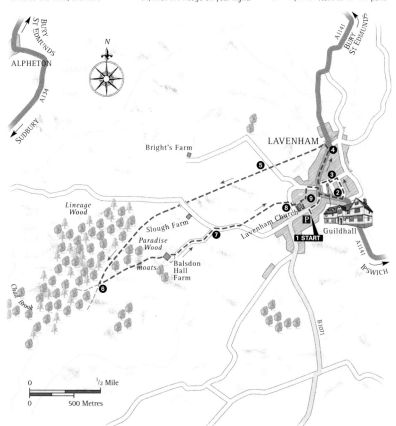

Atomic Secrets of Orford Ness

*This remote shingle spit on the Suffolk coast was once
the scene of historic military experiments*

WALK

69

1 From Orford Quay take the National Trust ferry to Orford Ness jetty. The Red Trail leads off up the road for ½ mile (800m) to a T-junction. Immediately on your right is the Old Telephone Exchange display building.

2 Leaving the display, turn right to pass the NT offices and workshops. In ½ mile (800m) bear right across a Bailey bridge over Stony Ditch. Bear immediately left, aiming for the lighthouse, to reach the Bomb Ballistic Building (display).

6 From Lab 1 return to the Black Beacon, and bear left to reach the Bailey bridge and the road back to the jetty.

5 The Blue Trail leaves the Red Trail at the Black Beacon and heads out south-west along the shingle for ⅓ mile (535m) to reach Lab 1 where non-fissile experiments were carried out on Britain's first nuclear weaponry.

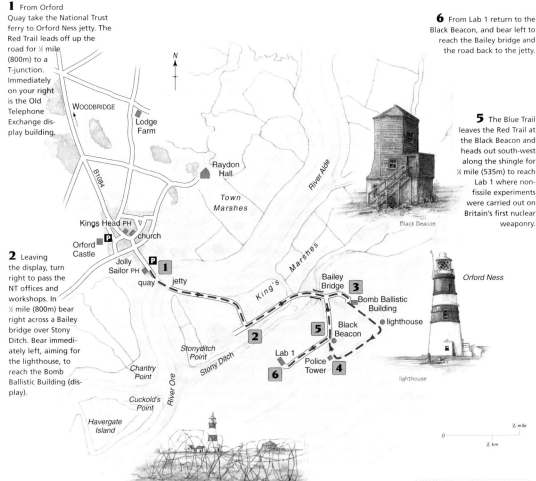

3 From the Bomb Ballistic Building, walk forward along the clear path through the shingle ridges to reach the lighthouse. Turn right and follow the path across the shingle and parallel with the shore, to the skeletal-looking Police Tower.

4 At the Police Tower turn right and walk inland to arrive at the Black Beacon (displays and upper-storey viewpoint over the entire shingle spit and surrounding countryside).

Distance: 5 miles (8km)
Total ascent: negligible
Paths: tarmac roads, shingle, tracks
Terrain: windswept shingle spit
Gradients: none
Refreshments: Jolly Sailor, Orford Quay
Park: Orford Quay
Note: passenger ferry from Orford Quay every 20 minutes, Thurs, Fri, Sat, Easter-end Oct. To visit in winter, call (01394) 450900. This is National Trust land and an entrance fee is payable
Difficulty: 1

Southeast England

The Huntingdon Home of Oliver Cromwell

On the banks of the Great Ouse in search of the Lord Protector

2 Go straight on at the traffic lights. When the road bends to the right, turn left along a footpath to Mill Common. Go diagonally left to a road and turn right, past Castle Hill, under the A14 and over a brook to join the Ouse Valley Way in Port Holme Meadow.

3 Walk straight across to a footbridge at Godmanchester Lock. Having crossed, turn left to reach Chinese Bridge. Cross into Godmanchester, leaving the Ouse Valley Way. Cross the B1043 to Cambridge Street then left into Chadley Lane to St Mary's Church.

1 From Princess Street, follow Literary Walk to High Street and turn left to All Saints' Church, the Falcon Tavern and the Cromwell Museum. Continue past the church and turn left into George Street.

Distance: 8 miles (13km)
Total ascent: negligible
Paths: good, but very muddy after rain; flooding possible in winter
Terrain: meadows, riverside, some streets
Gradients: none
Refreshments: good choice in Huntingdon and Godmanchester; pubs at Hemingford Abbots and Houghton
Park: car park in Malthouse Close off Princess Street, opposite bus station
Difficulty: 1

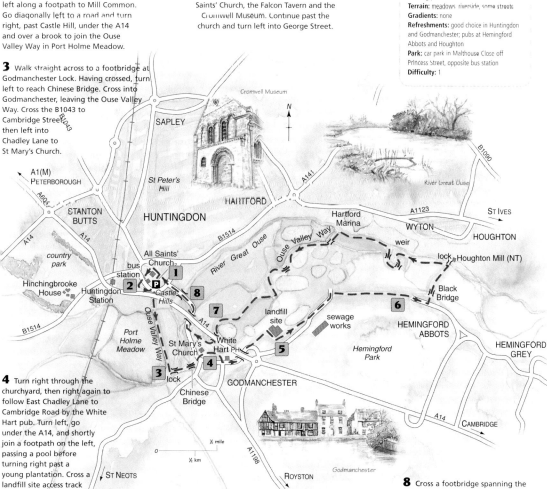

4 Turn right through the churchyard, then right again to follow East Chadley Lane to Cambridge Road by the White Hart pub. Turn left, go under the A14, and shortly join a footpath on the left, passing a pool before turning right past a young plantation. Cross a landfill site access track and continue beside a fence.

5 Ignore access to Cow Lane and carry straight on, climbing onto an embankment to walk along the top. At the far end descend to Cow Lane. Turn left, then join the second path on the right, a bridleway running beside a dismantled railway across a common.

6 After passing a pond, the bridleway veers slightly right to join Common Lane at Hemingford Abbots. Go straight on to reach Meadow Lane and turn left. Cross Black Bridge and Hemingford Meadow to Houghton Lock. Turn left beside the River Great Ouse, rejoining the Ouse Valley Way. Just follow the frequent waymarks now as the route explores the river, a tributary and flooded gravel pits.

7 Take an underpass beneath the A14 and head towards Godmanchester. Pass a housing estate to intercept a footpath/cycleway and turn right to the B1043. Turn right towards Huntingdon, crossing at the lights.

8 Cross a footbridge spanning the Great Ouse. Follow the road to the left, then walk through Castle Hills and along a passageway to Castle Hill. Proceed to Mill Common and turn right to Princess Street.

WALK 71

From the village of Nordelph, you explore the man-made landscape of the Fens, which caused deep controversy in the 17th century. With the permission of Charles I, Dutch engineers drained huge tracts of bog land to create a fertile landscape.

DISTANCE • 5 miles (8km)

PATHS • mostly good, but field path can be very muddy; some road walking

TERRAIN • village, fields, river bank

GRADIENTS • mostly level walking; a climb up the bank, and two awkward stiles and bridges to negotiate

REFRESHMENTS • Chequers Inn, Nordelph

PARK • car park by phone box, just over bridge off A1122, signed Welney.

DIFFICULTY • 2

The Wide Skies of a Fenland Landscape

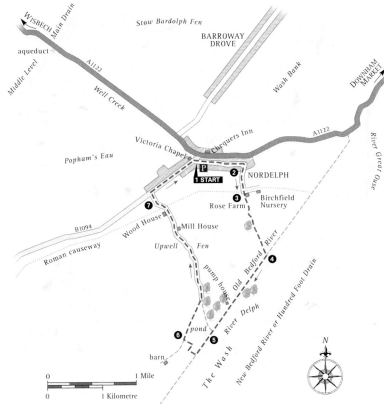

❶ From the car park and picnic area by the landing stage opposite the Chequers Inn, turn away from the bridge and walk down the High Street, parallel with Well Creek, which is on your left. Pass a row of terraced cottages, and the church (due for demolition at time of writing). Pass the village hall and war memorial on your right. Continue past a squat pepper-pot house, and a row of modern housing.

❷ Follow the main road as it bends sharp right and continues as Birchfield Road, away from Well Creek. A ditch, or lode, on your right separates you from the expansive fields.

❸ Where the road bends left, follow the footpath sign straight ahead along a grassy path by the lode. Stay along the field edge, following the course of the lode, heading for a lone poplar tree. At the tree, where the lode disappears underground, keep straight on, following the line of concrete fence posts.

❹ At the end of the field, cross the reedy drain via a footbridge. Cross the stile, climb up the river bank and turn right. Walk along the grassy river path of the Old Bedford River for about a mile (1.6km), with excellent views over the flat fen landscape. Note the flood meadow between the river and the parallel line of the New Bedford River.

❺ Descend near the oblong artificial fish pond on to the lower path, continuing through a gate. Shortly after passing under the pylons, look for a stile and

footbridge with a handrail down to your right – stepped access may be slippery. Cross over, and turn right on the opposite bank, bearing left with the field edge along the lode.

❻ At the concrete bridge, turn right on to the farm track. This becomes a tarmac road, passing through farm buildings and scattered houses. Just past Wood House farmhouse, look out for the

track off to the right (private) – this is the line of an old Roman causeway. Stay on the road, to reach a junction.

❼ At the junction, turn right and walk on the verge back towards the village. Where Coronation Avenue opens up on the left, cross over and continue into the village on the footpath. Turn right by the Victoria Chapel to the car park.

• DON'T MISS •

For a rare glimpse of what the Fens were like before they were drained, visit the nature reserve at Wicken Fen. Also worth a visit is The Wildfowl & Wetlands Trust, at Welney, which attracts thousands of whooper and Bewick swans in winter.

Grimes Graves and Brooding Breckland

*The heathlands of central Norfolk hide a
prehistoric flint mining site*

WALK

72

1 Turn left out of the Forestry Commission office car park. Cross an iron bridge over the Little Ouse river, then up the metalled road and over the level crossing. Continue along the road for about 1½ miles (2.4km), passing a house on your right along the way.

Distance: 6½ miles (10km)
Total Ascent: 100ft (30m)
Paths: good; grassy tracks, metalled roads
Terrain: forest and heathland
Gradients: mainly flat, some gradual ascents
Refreshments: shop in Santon Downham
Park: Forestry Commission car park in Santon Downham, off B1107 between Brandon and Thetford
Difficulty: 1

Grimes Graves visitor centre

MUNDFORD

2 Turn left along the main road, keeping to the wide verge. After about 300yds (275m), just before the 'Hidden dip' road sign, take a wide grassy track to the left. Carry straight on to the fence with a 'sheep grazing' sign. The track goes right, then immediately left by the fence, so that the grazing area is on your left.

West Tofts Mere

8 Take the second left track, signposted 'conservation ride', and walk along with the railway line on your right. After 600yds (546m), go under the railway bridge and turn left. Continue to the road, then turn right over the iron bridge and return to the car park.

3 Keep on the path until you reach the entrance to Grimes Graves. Turn right up the metalled road until you reach a gate by a house. Go through the gate and walk left along the wide verge.

Snake Wood

house

4

3

Grimes Graves visitor centre

5

Emily's Wood

6

2

West Tofts Heath

CROXTON

7

house

Santon Square

Santon Warren

BRANDON

8

SANTON DOWNHAM

1

level crossing

Stone Curlew

THETFORD

Thetford Forest

The Square

church

Little Ouse River

7 After 200yds (182m) the path bears right and then after about 40yds (37m) left. Continue downhill, past two black and yellow poles until you reach the railway line.

BRANDON

B1107

THETFORD

Warren Wood

4 Continue along the verge past a white metal gate and a public footpath sign to the left. After ¾ mile (1.2km), the road bends right and there is another white gate on your left. Take the next immediate left along a wide grassy track. Follow this straight path until another wide track crosses it. Here, turn left to follow a yellow arrow waymark.

5 Go straight on past two more yellow arrows. At the next yellow marker, turn right. After about 550yds (500m), at a clearing, five paths converge.

6 Take the path directly opposite which bears only slightly to the left, not the one by the white signpost. After 300yds (275m), the path bears diagonally right and then, very shortly, to the left. Continue, following the yellow signs.

WALK

73

Hethel Airfield and Norfolk's American Invasion

On the trail of American airmen in a tiny Norfolk village

1 From lane by Hethel church continue to T-junction and turn right. Turn left to view air-raid shelters. Retrace steps to lane and T-junction.

2 Cross stile by gate on left and go diagonally across field towards left of White Cottage. Cross stile near pond in front of cottage, then bear left towards Hethel Thorn. Cross stile in corner then walk diagonally across field to stile in corner by trees. Walk with field left and trees right to track.

3 Turn right and follow track past farm buildings to lane. Turn right and, after 150yds (137m), take footpath left. Cross stile and continue through woods. At gate path crosses ditch to right. Cross another ditch and follow right-hand ditch past small pond to corner of wood.

4 At gate turn right along edge of field, with ditch and hedge left. Turn left at road down to church on right. Cross churchyard left of church, to stile. Cross field diagonally right to stile, then over another field to telephone box.

5 Turn right on B1113. After 75yds (68m), turn right into Poorhouse Lane. At end bear left between hedges. At fields, bear left and continue left of ditch and hedge towards farm buildings. Cross lane to stile and path.

6 Continue by field edge to footbridge. Cross to next field and stile ahead. Cross to road, turn left then right, over stile to path under B1113. Continue with fence on left for 400yds (364m) to cottage. Bear right over footbridge.

Distance: 7 miles (11.2m)
Total ascent: 120ft (37m)
Paths: mostly good; can be muddy; some roads
Terrain: farmland and villages
Gradients: mainly flat; some gentle ascents
Refreshments: Bird in Hand, Wreningham
Park: on verge just past Hethel church, ¾ mile (1.2km) from B1113 at Bracon Ash
Difficulty: 1

½ mile

½ km

White Cottage, Hethel

US war memorial

NORWICH

EAST CARLETON

N

moat house

ruins of air raid shelters

3 farm

Hethel Thorn

old airfield

Lotus Car Works

Brunel House

Old Entertainment Hall

2 white cottage church

4 Bracon Hall

church

WYMONDHAM

10

Corporation Farmhouse

Church Farm **1** HETHEL

old school

5 BRACON ASH

B1135

6 farm buildings

10 Walk along track with Brunel House on left as it bears right and becomes grassy. Cross double stile into field with pond. Old Entertainment Hall is through hedge on left. Pass through gateway to track. Bear left, go through gate, turn left and walk past Church Farm. Pass through two gates and turn right to Hethel church.

Hethel Bridge

B1113

9

WRENINGHAM

church

Bird in Hand PH

7 ruined cottage

8

9 Walk along road for 400yds (364m), then take footpath on right towards farm buildings. Keep left of farm and go through gap in hedge to road. Turn left and take next right into Potash Lane, signposted East Carleton. End of old runway is to left. Turn right at Brunel House.

Wreningham church

TOPROW

FLORDON

BUNWELL

7 Turn right, then immediately left with hedge and ditch left. Follow to road and cross to lane past Bird in Hand to Wreningham church. Take path opposite, along field edge to end. Turn right towards wood.

8 Don't cross stile, but turn right and after 60yds (55m) turn left over bridge. Take path to road and turn right. Where road bends right, take footpath left. After 50yds (46m) bear left over stile and bridge. Go right again, keeping ditch and hedge on right, to kissing-gate. Pass through and turn left on road.

WALK

74

ABOUT • SANDRINGHAM

Sandringham offers the epitome of an Edwardian royal country house. It was designed to be a large, comfortable home, suitable for entertaining large parties. Opened in 1968 as a country park, this part of the estate offers free access for walkers.

Southeast England

DISTANCE • gardens 1½miles (2.4km); country park 3½ miles (5.6km)

TERRAIN • landscaped, formal gardens with wheelchair access throughout; woodland

PATHS • gardens: mainly firm, gravel paths; country park: mostly firm, but sections in woods can be muddy

GRADIENTS • gardens: level, easy walking; country park: some slopes and steps

REFRESHMENTS • tea room and restaurant at visitor centre; tea room by museum

PARK • car park by the visitor centre

CONTACT • the Estate Office (01553) 772675 for details of opening times

DIFFICULTY • 2

A Very Royal Estate

❶ From the visitor centre, cross the main road, pass the war memorial on your right, and bear left, via the ticket office, into the gardens. Turn left on a gravel path, and follow it through the woods.

❷ Leave the path to see a wall, with memorials to Sandringham's working dogs. Keep along the main path and through an area of rhododendrons. Go under the arch and turn left to see Norwich Gates.

❸ Retrace your steps and turn left through another rhododendron arch, following the main path. Note the *Wellingtonia gigantica*, right, before you bear left on to the main drive. Follow this round to the yew hedges in front of the house, turning right to the main entrance.

❹ Leaving the house via the ballroom, turn left and right through the hedge, and take the path diagonally right to rejoin the main drive. Keep straight here, and take the small path, left, to visit the museum and tea room (and toilets) in the old stable block.

❺ Walk out of the courtyard, turn left on the drive and right at a grass triangle, downhill. Leave the path and turn right along the stream, with York Cottage up to the left. Turn right on the path,

and keep left, passing the lake on your right. At the gates, follow the path right for views of the house.

❻ At the intersection of paths, turn right and go up to the house, exploring the terrace. Bear left through the formal North Garden, and at the Old Father Time statue turn left and join the path, passing memorials to the Queen's corgis.

❼ Turn right and pass through the turnstile to the church (or exit via the entrance). Leave the church and go left to the car park.

❽ With the visitor centre behind you, face the adventure playground and take the woodland path to the left, following yellow spots on the trees. At the sign turn right, following the yellow trail, and pass through a squeeze gate. Cross the estate road, follow the path across the grass and go through the wooden arch.

❾ Descend shallow steps, passing a pond and hide on the right, and through another squeeze gate. Continue through the woods and follow the yellow marks left. After about ¼ mile (400m), ignore the path on the left and keep straight on. Follow the yellow arrow up the steep path and steps to the left, to emerge on heathland.

❿ Turn right on the estate road and follow it to meet the main road. Cross over and descend the sandy track through woods.

⓫ At the bottom, follow the yellow arrow left up a straight grassy sward through trees, parallel with the road (right). Continue past the Donkey Pond, follow the yellow spots into the trees at the top, and turn right on to a broad grassy ride. At the triangular junction, cross the road to the left and pick up the yellow arrow, right, into the trees. Follow this path back to the visitor centre.

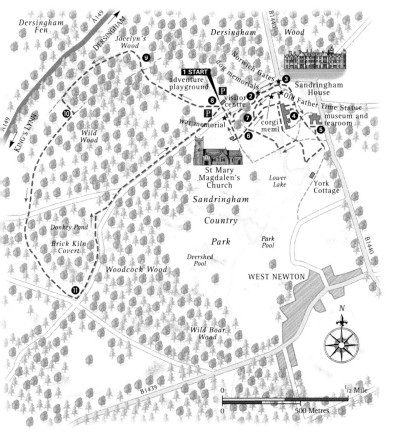

Wales

This is a most beautiful and varied country, one where there is still resistance to cultural change and a strong desire to retain an identity quite uninfluenced by external forces. Here in Wales are craggy heights, rock-strewn, heather-clad hillsides, barren moors, bright green valleys, silver rivers, mountain lakes, rocky, storm-tossed coastlines and sublime golden beaches. And over it all lies a complex mantle of history and mystery.

Much of walkers' North Wales is contained within the Snowdonia National Park, from time immemorial known to its inhabitants as Eryri, the 'Place of Eagles'. The popularity of Snowdon, the Carneddau, the Glyderau, the Rhinogs and the other mountains of Eryri has scarcely abated since the first recorded ascent of Snowdon in 1639 by botanist Thomas Johnson.

The eastern moorlands of Denbighshire flow westwards to the great natural barrier that is the River Conwy below the eastern fringes of the Carneddau. North and west, the isle of Anglesey, the 'Mother of Wales', and the delectable Lleyn Peninsula boast renowned landscapes to make your heart ache and your spirit rejoice.

A hundred years after the Domesday Book, Archbishop Baldwin of Canterbury began his mission to preach the Crusades in Wales in the quiet heartlands of Mid-Wales, at New Radnor, part of the great hunting Forest of Radnor.

Further south, the Rhinogs are rugged and rough, and certain to exact perspiration by the bucketful, as they no doubt did when traders first constructed their route through Cwm Bychan.

In the south, the borderland Black Mountains (Mynyddoedd Duon) are a paradise for walkers who revel in long, lofty ridges separated by valleys of quiet calm. To the west rise the distinctive, flat-topped summits of the Brecon Beacons, another Black Mountain (Mynydd Du) and the Fforest Fawr, names that speak of wilderness and desolation, and all contained within the Brecon Beacons National Park. The further west you go, the greater the feeling of isolation, but never in an over-powering way, for here the seclusion works as a panacea for workaday ills.

Best of the Rest

The Monmouthshire and Brecon Canal The only canal through a national park, the Monmouthshire and Brecon Canal offers easy walking amidst spectacular scenery. The ridges of the Brecon Beacons loom above, but the way along the towpath remains completely level, all the way into the centre of Brecon itself.

The Valleys The harsh edges of South Wales' industrial heartlands were always softened by the proximity of steeply wooded hillsides and liberating open moorlands. Now the industry has departed and the walker can return to the valleys, making good use of disused railway lines and the network of paths and tracks that kept workers and materials moving throughout the Industrial Revolution. The head of the Rhondda valley is particularly worth exploring.

Mid-Wales To the south of Strata Florida Abbey the wilds of Mid-Wales are often overlooked by walkers aiming for the mountains of Snowdonia or the high hills of the Brecon Beacons. And yet here is a landscape of intricate upland valleys, not at all spoiled by its forestation or reservoir developments. In fact it is these corporate utility invaders which have opened up the place for walkers, with car parks and nature trails. The serene upper reaches of the Afon Tywi, in particular, support a fine network of paths and trails for the walker in search of solitude.

Gower The beautiful sweeps of sand which characterise the handful of beaches on the Gower Peninsula attract thousands of holidaymakers in the summer months. Less well known is the fine stretch of cliff path which connects them – as dramatic as anything in Cornwall or Pembrokeshire. If you have a few days, the coast can be walked as a continuous path, otherwise extensive inland links allow each section to be done as a circular walk.

Betws-y-coed In the shadow of the great mountain mass of the Carneddau in Snowdonia a series of pretty valleys spreads like fingers to that of the much larger Afon Conwy. The environment here, though remote and sometimes inhospitable, has been much utilised, by early farmers, miners, reservoir-builders and foresters. The resulting landscape, around Llyn Crafnant and Llyn Geirionydd is a delightful tangle of lanes and paths amid small lakes, intriguingly overgrown old workings and ancient hill farms.

Wales

Dale – a Pembroke Peninsula

At the entrance to Milford Haven, the Dale Peninsula has always played a strategic role in maritime history

1 From the National Trust car park return to the road and go left where the road bends right towards Dale. Turn left to follow a concrete track which bears left to a stile beside a gate. Cross this, turn right and take another stile to reach the coast path.

2 Go left to walk with the sea on your right (leaving the islands of Skokholm and Skomer behind you). Follow the coast path to the road as it approaches St Ann's Head.

3 Go right along the road to pass the old High Lighthouse on your right, then turn left through a gate and turn right immediately to take a signposted path towards the Low Lighthouse. Turn sharply left, as signposted, to follow the coast path towards Mill Bay, still walking with the sea on your right.

4 Descend steps to cross a footbridge and climb up the other side. Continue with the sea on your right around West Blockhouse Point (with it's three transit marks – navigational aids). Follow the coast path around Watwick Point (where there is a single transit mark), cross a footbridge above Castle Beach and climb to join a road on Dale Point.

5 Turn left to follow the road downhill into Dale. Ignore a turning on your left and reach the Griffin Inn. Take a footpath on your left immediately after the pub and just before a boathouse. This leads to a road. Cross this and go ahead over a stile beside a gate and turn right to cross a stone stile and reach another road.

6 Go left along the road to pass St James' Church on your left. When the road turns left, leave it by going straight ahead on a track which passes Dale Castle on your right. When this track bends left, take the signposted footpath ahead to Westdale Bay.

7 Turn left with the signposted coast path to walk with the sea on your right. After crossing a series of stiles, take a kissing gate and look out for the stile beside a gate on your left, which you used on your outward journey. Turn left, inland, to cross this and retrace your steps to the car park.

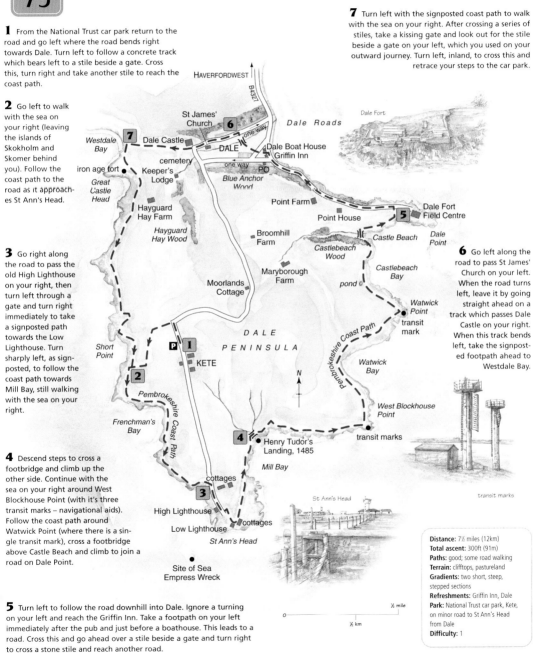

HAVERFORDWEST

B4327

Dale Fort

St James' Church **6**

Dale Roads

7 Westdale Bay Dale Castle

one way

DALE Dale Boat House Griffin Inn

cemetery

iron age fort Keeper's Lodge

one way PO

Great Castle Head

Blue Anchor Wood

Point Farm

Point House **5** Dale Fort Field Centre

Hayguard Hay Farm

Dale Point

Hayguard Hay Wood

Broomhill Farm

Castle Beach

Castlebeach Wood

Castlebeach Bay

Maryborough Farm

pond

Moorlands Cottage

Watwick Point

transit mark

D A L E

P E N I N S U L A

Pembrokeshire Coast Path

Watwick Bay

Short Point

P **1**

KETE

2

N

Pembrokeshire Coast Path

West Blockhouse Point

Frenchman's Bay

4 Henry Tudor's Landing, 1485

transit marks

Mill Bay

cottages

3

St Ann's Head

High Lighthouse

Low Lighthouse

cottages

St Ann's Head

transit marks

Site of Sea Empress Wreck

½ mile

0

½ km

Distance: 7½ miles (12km)
Total ascent: 300ft (91m)
Paths: good; some road walking
Terrain: clifftops, pastureland
Gradients: two short, steep, stepped sections
Refreshments: Griffin Inn, Dale
Park: National Trust car park, Kete, on minor road to St Ann's Head from Dale
Difficulty: 1

Strumble Head and the French Invasion

A memorial stone on this spectacular coastal walk marks the point where a Napoleonic army invaded Britain

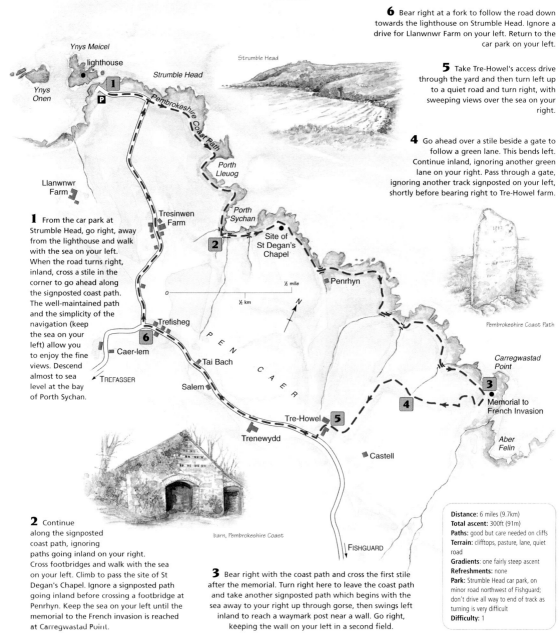

6 Bear right at a fork to follow the road down towards the lighthouse on Strumble Head. Ignore a drive for Llanwnwr Farm on your left. Return to the car park on your left.

5 Take Tre-Howel's access drive through the yard and then turn left up to a quiet road and turn right, with sweeping views over the sea on your right.

4 Go ahead over a stile beside a gate to follow a green lane. This bends left. Continue inland, ignoring another green lane on your right. Pass through a gate, ignoring another track signposted on your left, shortly before bearing right to Tre-Howel farm.

Pembrokeshire Coast Path

1 From the car park at Strumble Head, go right, away from the lighthouse and walk with the sea on your left. When the road turns right, inland, cross a stile in the corner to go ahead along the signposted coast path. The well-maintained path and the simplicity of the navigation (keep the sea on your left) allow you to enjoy the fine views. Descend almost to sea level at the bay of Porth Sychan.

2 Continue along the signposted coast path, ignoring paths going inland on your right. Cross footbridges and walk with the sea on your left. Climb to pass the site of St Degan's Chapel. Ignore a signposted path going inland before crossing a footbridge at Penrhyn. Keep the sea on your left until the memorial to the French invasion is reached at Carregwastad Point.

barn, Pembrokeshire Coast

3 Bear right with the coast path and cross the first stile after the memorial. Turn right here to leave the coast path and take another signposted path which begins with the sea away to your right up through gorse, then swings left inland to reach a waymark post near a wall. Go right, keeping the wall on your left in a second field.

Distance: 6 miles (9.7km)
Total ascent: 300ft (91m)
Paths: good but care needed on cliffs
Terrain: clifftops, pasture, lane, quiet road
Gradients: one fairly steep ascent
Refreshments: none
Park: Strumble Head car park, on minor road northwest of Fishguard; don't drive all way to end of track as turning is very difficult
Difficulty: 1

WALK 77

Hillwalkers know the delights of tramping this prehistoric highway. Dotted among the Bronze and Iron Age sites are blue rhyolite stones, relics of the Ice Age, believed to have been transported to and used to build Stonehenge, 150 miles (241km) away.

Wales

DISTANCE • 10 miles (16km)

TOTAL ASCENT • 1,607ft (490m)

PATHS • some tracks; indistinct or pathless

TERRAIN • grassy; also rough (tussocky and boggy); occasionally rocky. **Note: this route is for experienced hillwalkers. It should not be attempted in poor weather conditions. Keep dogs on lead at all times on this walk**

GRADIENTS • moderate

REFRESHMENTS • limited in Crymych

PARK • in lay-by on the Mynachlog-ddu road, approximately 1 mile (1.6km) off the A478 at Crymych

DIFFICULTY • 3

A Prehistoric Puzzle in the Preseli Hills

❶ Take the track opposite the lay-by. When in open countryside, resist the temptation to climb the fine summit of Foel Trigarn; instead take a virtually level line, just above the boundary with the pasture below. Continue following the clear track ahead for 1 mile (1.6km).

❷ When the field boundary – a broad drystone wall topped with hedgerow – drops away to the right for the second time, you must follow it. (This avoids some extremely boggy ground designated a Site of Special Scientific Interest.)

❸ Follow the wall closely when it goes right then left. Descend gently, avoiding prickly gorse, to join a track from an untidy farmyard. Keep ahead on the main track, ignoring the fork to a farm on the right after 250yds (229m). Pass the elaborate post-box for Geulan Goch, and eventually reach a minor road and telephone box after ¾ mile (1.2km).

❹ Turn left, and left again within 100yds (91m); shortly take the left fork, which leads to Mirianog, a house; do not take the right-hand fork signed Tŷ Coch. Pass to the left of Mirianog, out into open country. (The hostile notice to dog owners echoes the difficulty of farming life here.)

❺ When the path forks take the left-hand option to visit the clustered slabs of Carn Alw. (Apart from its Stonehenge bluestones, this historic site was once a very small fort; aerial photographs reveal some evidence of field systems around it.)

❻ Aim right of another outcrop, Carn Breseb, on an indistinct path, eventually rejoining the path from Mirianog. On the ridge turn right, following this prehistoric highway, waymarked for some of its length by wooden posts, to the cairn and Bronze Age barrow atop Foel Feddau.

❼ (If time and energy permit, the Preseli's summit, Foel Cwm-cerwyn, is a good mile/1.6km ahead and to the left.) Retrace your steps, then go further east along the ridge, over Carn Pica to Bwlch Ungwr.

❽ Veer right of the obvious path to visit the frost-shattered rocks of Carn Meini. Continue eastwards, picking up a farm track to the far end of a block of planted conifers.

❾ Turn left on a sinuous but clear path to Foel Trigarn. After viewing this impressive earthwork take a path which soon sweeps to the right, rejoining the outward route some distance before it enters the lane to return to the lay-by.

• DON'T MISS •

Pentre Ifan (off the A487, east of Newport) is a splendid burial chamber believed to be associated with Irish colonists, and dates from 3000 BC. The huge upright stones carry a massive, 17-ton capstone.

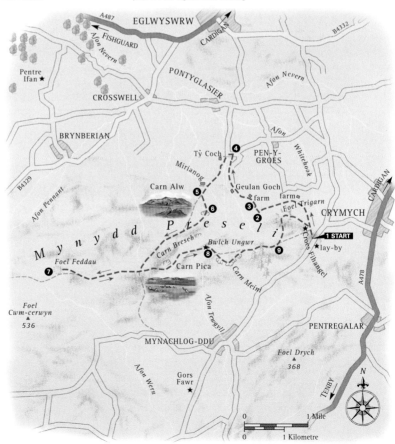

WALK 78

ABOUT • LAUGHARNE

The Boat House Museum at Laugharne was home to Dylan Thomas and where he wrote much of his poetry. Perfect for Dylan fans, this walk will also appeal to birdwatchers, and the 12th-century Laugharne Castle is definitely worth a visit.

Wales

DISTANCE • 6 miles (9.6km)

TOTAL ASCENT • 490ft (149m)

PATHS • good; slippery in places

TERRAIN • tracks, field paths, stiles, tarmac roads; **take care on the short stretch of road just after the caravan park, it can be busy**

GRADIENTS • mostly gradual

REFRESHMENTS • abundant in Laugharne

PARK • in Laugharne, just past the town square on the left-hand side. This is a tidal area, so check that it won't flood in your absence!

DIFFICULTY• 2

Dylan's Laugharne

❶ Turn along the shore, away from the castle. Shortly after a modern kissing gate ascend a signed footpath into woodland, emerging on cliffs overlooking the Taf estuary. Take the left, descending fork at information board. After steps, follow a track for 328yds (300m), past Salt House Kennels. Continue to the quarry road (Causeway Cottage).

❷ Turn right, up to the A-road. Turn right, following the road for 191yds (175m); take care here. Just after a caravan park, go left. Soon a set-back finger-post points to a stile at the back of a lay-by. Cross stile, go right and cross a field with telegraph poles, parallel to stream.

❸ On the other side of the field find a sunken track on the right, just around the left corner of a hedge which juts out. After 109yds (100m) pass a rusty gate. Further along pass a white house to join a dirt track to a tarmac road.

❹ Turn right and continue for 109yds (100m). Just after the 30mph sign take the left fork. The Lacques Water Pump is next to the fork on the right-hand side. Where the road bends sharply right and down, go straight ahead along Holloway Road (dead end sign). Beyond a row of cottages take a sunken lane and cross two fields to a minor road.

❺ Turn right, over the bridge and soon turn right on to the A-road. Continue for 22yds (20m) then turn left (dead end sign) and right through gates into the churchyard. Pass in front of the church, to cross a footbridge into a second churchyard. Dylan and Caitlin share a simple wooden cross, on the left. Leave through a kissing gate at the top of the churchyard. Turn right to a T-junction.

❻ Turn left up a waymarked sunken lane; if wet take care over slabby rocks. Continue for 328yds (300m). When in pasture, near a farm, move right, over stiles by an ash tree. In the field take a vague green track, right. Descend to a small wooded area. The path, later a sunken lane, emerges near a farmhouse.

❼ Turn right, away from the house, following waymarkers into a field above a vegetable garden. Cross the field and go over a stile by a large tree. The pasture deteriorates into a field of gorse, thistle and scrub, then rises gently to a good waymarked path through woodland to a hairpin bend on a tarmac road.

❽ Cross and follow a small lane. Soon steps on the left descend to Dylan Thomas's house, the Boat House, now a museum. Further along this path (Dylan's Walk), is Dylan's writing shed (a small garage with a blue door). Soon there is a choice of routes.

❾ Either take steps down to the shore, and follow a flagged causeway skirting the castle, or continue on Dylan's Walk. Turn left, then follow the road round to King Street. Near by is Brown's, and, opposite, the Pelican (where Dylan's parents lived). Turn left, passing Castle House, where Dylan and Caitlin often stayed, and pass the castle entrance down to the car park.

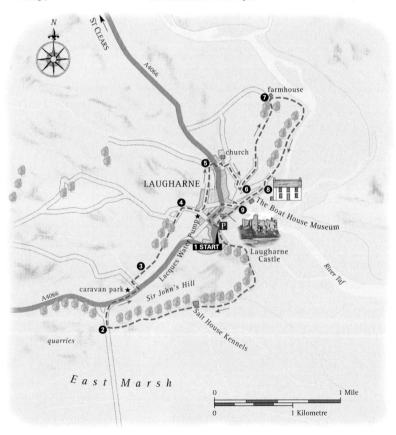

WALK 79

Welsh gold is still highly prized today and it's probable that the promise of rare metals such as lead and gold was a factor in the Roman invasion in AD 43. The mines are open from April to September and out of season there is a self-guided tour leaflet available.

DISTANCE • 4 miles (6.4km)

TOTAL ASCENT • 459ft (140m)

PATHS • good; slippery in places

TERRAIN • tracks, field paths, stiles and tarmac roads

GRADIENTS • some quite steep but not long

REFRESHMENTS • café at the gold mines, a pub in the village or take a picnic to have the trig point

PARK • National Trust Visitor Centre car park in Pumsaint village

DIFFICULTY • 2

The Roman Gold Mines at Dolaucothi

❶ Turn left on to the main road for 44yds (40m); then left into a beech avenue. Just beyond a right turn, signed Dolaucothi Farm B&B, climb a stile (red waymarker).

❷ Ascend diagonally on a grassy sunken lane to enter a well-established conifer plantation through a gate. Go uphill (pasture on your left), soon bearing slightly right, deeper into the forest. In about 328yds (300m), after a gate, turn half-right, staying within the forest. Walk a further 164–219yds (150–200m).

❸ Here the path turns downhill, into thick dark forest. Within 109yds (100m) reach a clear T-junction. Turn left, uphill, through further dense woodland. Soon emerge from the woods on to a lovely curving track to reach a modern gate.

❹ Turn sharp left on to a new farm track; immediately go through a second gate. Soon, after 27yds (25m), turn sharply up to the right (no track) to a ridge and a hedge inside a new double fence.

❺ Follow this for 44yds (40m) beyond the Pen Lan-dolau trig point. Cross the fence and turn left. Follow red marker post over a stile through a felled area (hazardous tree stumps). Turn left to re-enter standing forest ahead. Soon reach a gravel track.

❻ Turn left. After about 328yds (300m) turn abruptly right (marker post) for a sharp descent on a forestry track. As soon as you see a gate 109yds (100m) ahead and, beyond it, a footbridge, stop.

❼ Turn right (marker post), on a narrow path into, initially, felled forestry. Soon this path forms a dark dense corridor and joins an old, narrow-gauge railway track. One field before the Dolaucothi Farm buildings, reach a corner with two gateways.

❽ Turn through the gate on the left. In 44yds (40m) turn right, and proceed through stiles to the dilapidated walled garden. Turn left on to a track; after 329yds (300m) cross a stone bridge. Just after the shady picnic site turn right over a stile, on to a delightful elevated riverside path, to a T-junction.

❾ Turn left here to visit the gold mine. Otherwise, turn right, go down steps, cross a stile into a meadow and follow the riverside to the road bridge. Turn right, soon passing the beech avenue taken earlier, to return to the start.

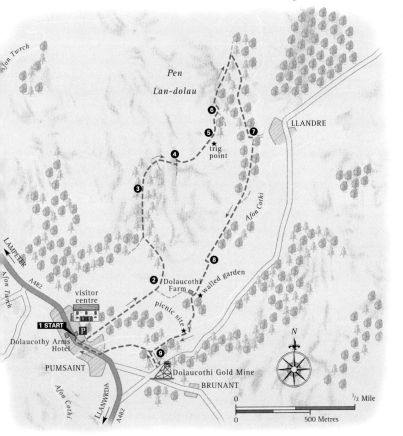

WALK 80

A Fairy Lake and the Black Mountain

A fine mountain walk in the backwaters of the Brecon Beacons National Park

1 From the car park at Blaenau, follow the stony reservoir supply track by the Sawdde stream up to the shores of Llyn y Fan Fach, taking the right fork just before the reservoir.

6 Turn left on a path descending above the north banks of the stream. The path comes down the sides of Bryn Mawr, towards a bridge conveying the outward track across the stream. It then swings right to avoid some squat cliffs. Look out for a little path on the left which makes the final descent to the car park at Blaenau.

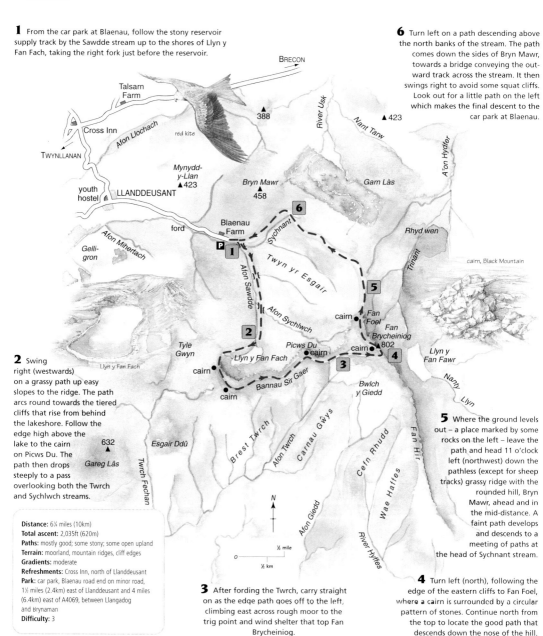

2 Swing right (westwards) on a grassy path up easy slopes to the ridge. The path arcs round towards the tiered cliffs that rise from behind the lakeshore. Follow the edge high above the lake to the cairn on Picws Du. The path then drops steeply to a pass overlooking both the Twrch and Sychlwch streams.

5 Where the ground levels out – a place marked by some rocks on the left – leave the path and head 11 o'clock left (northwest) down the pathless (except for sheep tracks) grassy ridge with the rounded hill, Bryn Mawr, ahead and in the mid-distance. A faint path develops and descends to a meeting of paths at the head of Sychnant stream.

4 Turn left (north), following the edge of the eastern cliffs to Fan Foel, where a cairn is surrounded by a circular pattern of stones. Continue north from the top to locate the good path that descends down the nose of the hill.

Distance: 6¼ miles (10km)
Total ascent: 2,035ft (620m)
Paths: mostly good; some stony; some open upland
Terrain: moorland, mountain ridges, cliff edges
Gradients: moderate
Refreshments: Cross Inn, north of Llanddeusant
Park: car park, Blaenau road end on minor road, 1½ miles (2.4km) east of Llanddeusant and 4 miles (6.4km) east of A4069, between Llangadog and Brynaman
Difficulty: 3

3 After fording the Twrch, carry straight on as the edge path goes off to the left, climbing east across rough moor to the trig point and wind shelter that top Fan Brycheiniog.

WALK

81

ABOUT • LLANGORSE LAKE

The crannog (artificial island) in Llangorse Lake is thought to be the ancient seat of the kings of the kingdom of Brycheiniog. This walk circumnavigates the lake before an ascent offers stiking views of the lake and the Brecon Beacons.

Wales

DISTANCE • 8 miles (13km)

TOTAL ASCENT • 900ft (274m)

PATHS • good; slippery in places. Lakeside paths may be underwater after prolonged heavy rain in winter months

TERRAIN • tracks, field paths, stiles, tarmac roads; roots in forest

GRADIENTS • some steep sections

REFRESHMENTS • caravan park shop at start; pubs and a shop/post office in Llangorse village

PARK • car park beside public lavatories, between caravan park and sailing club

DIFFICULTY • 3

The Sunken Island at Llangorse

❶ Aim for a concrete footbridge, left of the caravan park on Llangorse Common. Go diagonally left, soon observe the crannog, cross more fields, circumnavigating the lake (partly fringed with woodland), to reach St Gastyn Church at Llangasty-Tal-y-llyn.

❷ Turn right. After Llan (a house) take a waymarked footpath, left. Soon walk with the hedge on your right. Turn right, cross two fields diagonally, to a sunken lane, left of a farm. Turn right to a minor road.

❸ Go left. Take the first left turn, signed Cathedine half a mile. Turn right, beside Rectory Cottage. Take stiles through three fields; cross the fourth field diagonally to the B4560 (fast road). Turn right for 55yds (50m). Take a rough track to the right of farm buildings.

❹ Take a less distinct track (blue waymarker) before the ford, ascending along the left side of a lightly wooded stream. In an eroded gully find a gate up to the left. Follow this sunken lane until it peters out.

❺ Turn left, above a fence and broken wall, then soon go through an old gate (blue waymarker) to pass a farmhouse ruin. Continue on a path, now through bracken, until 55yds (50m) before the track descends to a gate.

❻ Turn sharp right, uphill, on a zigzagging green path. Turn left at a fence, then left again at fence corner. Descend to a converted barn. Continue to find a sheep track along field's left edge, go down to a gate among larches, beside overgrown, broken wall.

❼ Walk through the forest, back into bracken. About 100yds (91m) beyond a stream crossing, descend beside a farm track. At the next gate cross the farm track, taking the line of greatest slope down the field to the riding and climbing centre below.

❽ Turn right, then right again towards Cae-cottrel (farm). Take a stile on the left. Skirt this field to the left. Pass into the next field by a gap in the hedgerow (tiny stream), skirting left again, to farm buildings and a track.

❾ Turn right, following the lanes to Llangorse village. At a blind corner, immediately before St Paulinus's churchyard, take a narrow signed footpath beside a house. Cross fields to return to the start of the walk.

• DON'T MISS •

St Gastyn Church at Llangasty-Tal-y-llyn is impressive for the simple beauty of its location and architecture (inside and out). The Brecknock Museum in Brecon is also worth a visit, as is Y Gaer (also called Brecon Gaer), about a mile (1.6km) from Brecon – a Roman fort, dated c. AD 80, and occupied well into the 4th century.

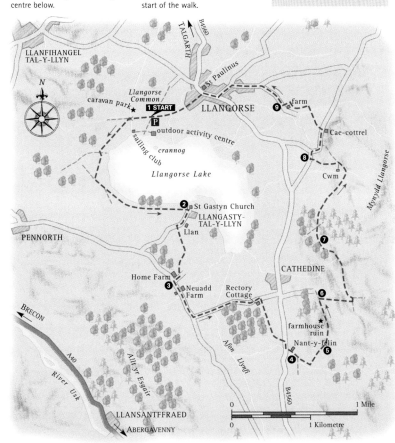

The Tracks of Industry

Following the course of a disused railway line in the county of Cardiff through the former industrial heartland of Wales

Transforming a Landscape

The mineral-rich valleys that run from the Brecon Beacons to the major urban centres of Cardiff and Swansea have teemed with industrial activity for centuries. This walk traces a route that, until relatively recently, was a major artery for the transportation of goods and people. Since the decline of the coal industry, the South Wales slagheaps have changed from black to grassy green, railways have become country tracks, and – ironically – as mining communities struggle to maintain their existence, the scenery has regained some of its pre-industrial beauty.

The Taff Trail runs, in its entirety, from Brecon to Cardiff; this section of the trail leads along part of the former Barry and Rhymney railway lines, skirting the hillside above the River Taff, the original means of moving cargoes from the Rhondda Valley mines to the southern shipping ports, and from there to all over the world.

Mines and Railways

South Wales was already a target for industrial speculators by the late 18th century. At first, iron was the main resource, but coal was needed to smelt it, and soon furnaces and pits were mushrooming all along the river valleys south of the Brecon mountains. Canals, river barges and horse-drawn trams shifted the produce at first, but the

quicker, cheaper steam engine came hot on the heels of the industrial boom. It was in Merthyr, further up the Taff, that steam-driven transport had an early breakthrough, when Richard Trevithick's locomotive train made its first brief trip on an old tramroad in 1804. This was the first steam-powered journey along iron rails. From then on, the 19th century was destined to be the age of steam. Railways appeared all over Britain, providing fast links between centres of industry and ports, improving communications and sparking off a craze for seaside holidays, as quick jaunts to the coast became a possibility even for people of modest means.

In South Wales the emphasis was on King Coal, as mines churned out millions of tons of the 'black gold', to fuel the engines and furnaces of the world. Around each pit, a mining town appeared, with rows of terraced houses clinging to the hillsides. People poured in to this once rural area; farm labourers abandoned the land, and workers arrived from abroad looking for employment. Mining families lived and worked in appalling conditions, while the industrial barons reaped huge profits. The Valleys became hotbeds of radicalism, and the whole shape of Welsh political, cultural and social life changed beyond recognition. Having passed the estates and factories of the Taff Vale towns, the route ends up at Castell Coch, a folly built for the coal magnate Lord Bute in the 1870s.

DOWN THE VALLEY LINE   Wales

❶ Start at the Treforest Park and Ride, at the railway station, and near the University of Glamorgan, originally founded as the South Wales and Monmouthshire School of Mines. To reach the old railway bed, cross the footbridge and go down the slope. Cross into Castle Street; at the end of the street, cross Forest Road and the pedestrian bridge over the Taff. Bear left to go under the road bridge and follow the pavement under the motorway bridge. Cross the road with care. Go round to the left and into Cemetery Road.

❷ Turn right and pass the cemetery and crematorium. Cremation was made legal in

1884, after local man Dr William Price had been prosecuted for cremating his baby son Iesu. Follow the Taff Trail sign to the right. The track passes between the houses of Ryhdyfelin, whose name probably derives from *rhyd felen*, 'yellow ford': iron in the clay turned the water here a distinct yellow.

❸ Presently the trail moves into oak woodland and passes the remains of an old colliery on the hill to the left. Above the trees, glimpses of sheep grazing on the mountain recall the pre-steam, pre-industrial era, when travellers admired the natural drama of the 'Glamorgan Alps'. At Nantgarw

the trail twists down into another estate and across the road on the valley floor, before climbing to the top of the opposite ridge.

❹ As the trail approaches the beech woods of Fforest Fawr, it passes Tŷ Rhiw Farm, built before the railways and the coal boom. You can leave the trail here, following the sign left past the farm, to descend to Taff's Well station for the train back to Treforest. But it is worth continuing to Castell Coch, the fairytale 'red castle' designed by William Burges. It's a 1½ miles (2.4km) on foot or by bus from Tongwynlais to Taff's Well station.

Distance: 6 miles (9.6km) to Taff's Well; 1 mile (1.6km) to Castell Coch

Total ascent: 250ft (76m)

Paths: surfaced paths, tracks: can be muddy and waterlogged in poor weather

Terrain: streets, paths, tracks

Gradients: one steep stretch

Refreshments: cafés, pubs in Treforest, café in superstore at Upper Boat (access from trail)

Park: Treforest Park and Ride

Difficulty: 2

Raglan's Civil War Fortress

During the Civil War Charles I retreated to this imposing castle in the beautiful Welsh Marches

Distance: 5 miles (8km)
Total ascent: 250ft (76m)
Paths: good; can be muddy after rain
Terrain: fields, enclosed bridleway
Gradients: few ascents and very gradual
Refreshments: various in Raglan
Park: Castle Street, Raglan or by Raglan Castle
Difficulty: 1

1 From Castle Street, take Chepstow Road, past St Cadoc's Church, towards Chepstow. Ignore the footpath on the left after the school and health centre.

2 Ahead, stay on left-hand side of road and, opposite Brooklands Farm B&B sign, enter gate with path leading towards sewage works to right. Before sewage works continue over concrete bridge, go straight across field and cross next field diagonally to far left corner. Cross stile and sleeper bridge and bear slightly left, following edge of sports field to gate onto lane.

3 Cross lane, go through gate and bear left, uphill, towards stile behind railway wagon shed. Cross to lane and go over stile opposite into cattle field. Follow hedge to right and cross stile into another field. Keep to right of field to reach stile onto road. Turn right and walk towards A40.

4 Turn left and cross to far side of A40. Walk along verge to steps down to signed footpath and stile into field. Cross field uphill to reach gate onto lane leading to Raglan Castle car park.

5 Turn right towards Castle Farm. Where lane bears left cross stile on right and with field edge on your left walk to another stile. Cross and follow left edge, crossing stile in it and bearing right to stile. Cross and turn left through gate. Cross track, go over stile and turn half-right across field beyond, passing small hillock.

6 At bottom of field cross stile and turn right, leaving hedge to go through left-hand gate ahead. Follow hedge on right, maintaining direction when it bears away. Cross ditch and continue to stile. Follow hedge on right, crossing stile over it and turn left uphill. Where field widens, turn left to cross stile.

7 Turn left along enclosed bridleway. Follow this downhill, then uphill, to reach road opposite Lower House. Turn left.

8 When road turns sharp right, cross stile on left into field and walk to right, round edge of field to stile in wire fence. Cross field, bearing left but aiming well to right of castle and church tower. Cross stile in far hedge and bear left, aiming for large hedge gap.

9 Go through gap and bear away from left field edge to reach hedge elbow across field. Bear left to walk with hedge to stile on to A40.

10 Then, cross and turn left along a verge about 330yds (300m), to reach gap in stone wall on the right.

11 Go through and turn right, crossing bridge into Castle Street.

TREGARE

Lower House

trackway

Pen-y-parc

ABERGAVENNY

A40

Castle Farm

Raglan Castle

Castle Farm

Raglan Castle

Beaufort Arms Hotel

Crown PH

RAGLAN

Brooklands Farm

Broom House

Raglan Castle

The Elms

A40

MONMOUTH

church

A449

golf course

border sheep

A449

USK
NEWPORT

N

0   ½ mile

0   ½ km

Monmouthshire's White Castle

*The gentle Monmouthshire countryside hides a grim
castle with a dark past*

1 From the Hostry Inn turn right down the lane. In 300yds (275m), on a left bend, keep ahead to St Teilo's Church.

2 Walk down the stone steps from the west end of the graveyard and take the signed footpath between a wire fence and the churchyard wall. Go through a kissing gate and over a field to the B4233. Across the road is the moated site of Hen Cwrt, the Old Court.

3 Turn left along the B4233. In 90yds (82m) turn right over a stile, and follow Offa's Dyke Path signs across five fields to a farm track at Great Treadam. Turn left to the road, and right for 150yds (137m), to turn right into a lane.

4 Follow the lane northwards for ¾ mile (1.2km) to a road by a large white house. Keep forward for 250yds (229m) to White Castle.

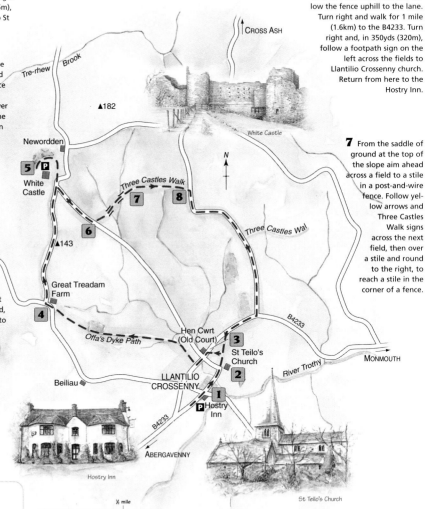

8 Don't cross this stile, but follow the fence uphill to the lane. Turn right and walk for 1 mile (1.6km) to the B4233. Turn right and, in 350yds (320m), follow a footpath sign on the left across the fields to Llantilio Crossenny church. Return from here to the Hostry Inn.

7 From the saddle of ground at the top of the slope aim ahead across a field to a stile in a post-and-wire fence. Follow yellow arrows and Three Castles Walk signs across the next field, then over a stile and round to the right, to reach a stile in the corner of a fence.

Distance: 5 miles (8km)
Total ascent: 425ft (130m)
Paths: lanes and grassy field paths
Terrain: gently rolling pastoral countryside
Gradients: one short, steep ascent
Refreshments: Hostry Inn, Llantilio Crossenny
Park: by Hostry Inn, Llantilio Crossenny, signposted from the B4233, 8 miles (12.9km) west of Monmouth
Difficulty: 1

5 From White Castle entrance kiosk retrace your steps to the head of the lane from Treadam but bear left here, downhill, on the road. In 450yds (412m) turn left up the steps at a Three Castles Walk sign, over a stile into a field.

6 Continue across three fields and down to cross a stream by a footbridge. Head diagonally left across the next field and, in 200yds (182m), bear right over a stream. Follow the hedge ahead, diagonally left up the slope.

Eric Gill in the Black Mountains

In this high valley in theBlack Mountains, the artist and sculptor Eric Gill settled into an eccentric lifestyle with his extended family

WALK

85

1 Take the lane between the chapel and the telephone box, climbing the hill. After 800 yards (730m), by a sign to the youth hostel, go right through a gate, down the track, over the river and up to a second gate.

6 When the path reaches the lane, turn left down the hill, go over a ford and pass The Monastery back to the village.

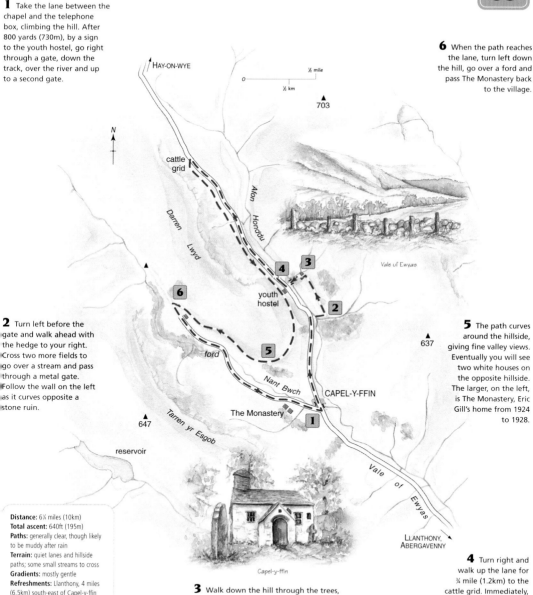

2 Turn left before the gate and walk ahead with the hedge to your right. Cross two more fields to go over a stream and pass through a metal gate. Follow the wall on the left as it curves opposite a stone ruin.

5 The path curves around the hillside, giving fine valley views. Eventually you will see two white houses on the opposite hillside. The larger, on the left, is The Monastery, Eric Gill's home from 1924 to 1928.

Distance: 6¼ miles (10km)
Total ascent: 640ft (195m)
Paths: generally clear, though likely to be muddy after rain
Terrain: quiet lanes and hillside paths; some small streams to cross
Gradients: mostly gentle
Refreshments: Llanthony, 4 miles (6.5km) south-east of Capel-y-ffin
Park: roadside parking in Capel-y-ffin, 14 miles (22.5km) north of Abergavenny
Difficulty: 2

4 Turn right and walk up the lane for ¾ mile (1.2km) to the cattle grid. Immediately, turn sharp left along the hillside. The path follows the hill's contours, keeping beside or parallel with a ruined stone wall.

3 Walk down the hill through the trees, crossing the stream, going through a metal gate. Continue downhill, with the stream recrossing your path, to go over a foot-bridge. Walk uphill to meet the lane at a stile to the left of a farm building.

WALK

86

ABOUT • LLANDRINDOD WELLS

The promise of health-giving waters at Llandrindod Wells brought Victorians here in their thousands. The walk takes you past the Pump Room and Temple Gardens before heading out of the town to the open countryside and views of the town.

Wales

DISTANCE • 7 miles (11km)

TOTAL ASCENT • 443ft (135m)

PATHS • good; can be muddy in places

TERRAIN • town streets, woodland, heathland

GRADIENTS • gradual; one short steep descent

REFRESHMENTS • selection of cafés in Llandrindod Wells

PARK • lakeside picnic area, at the top of Princes Avenue

DIFFICULTY • 2

A Welsh Spa Town

❶ Follow Princes Avenue towards town, turn left at the end and cross the road on to Spa Road. Follow this, bearing left before and after the railway bridge, to a roundabout. Go through Rock Park Spa gate and descend the main path. Cross the wooden footbridge towards the pump house.

❷ Turn sharp left to the stone bridge and chalybeate spring in the wall. Over the bridge, take the steep path (left, right) up the hill ahead. Continue under the railway arch and keep to the main path, lined with street lights.

❸ At the main road, cross, turning left and immediately right into a side street leading to a path through the park, back up Princes Avenue. In 109yds (100m) beyond the picnic area is Lake Cottage; go 82yds (75m) beyond this and turn left through a signposted gate.

❹ Follow the tarmac path for 55yds (50m); when the route swings left go ahead on the main path through the woods, for about 328yds (300m), to a clearing. On returning to the trees bear left (keep the boundary fence on your right). Cross the stile and go down towards a sign at the bottom of the field. Through the gate here, by the new houses, turn right, then immediately left between gardens, following the waymark arrow.

❺ Turn right on to the street; after 273yds (250m) take waymarked footpath to the right between numbers 9 and 10. Cross the stile and follow the path up through the woods, for 273yds (250m).

❻ Through the gate, follow the path between the gorse bushes to an open field; bear right towards a stile bisecting a conifer plantation.

Cross a stile and immediately take the small path, left, cross another stile to leave the plantation.

❼ Bear right, with waymarker. In 164yds (150m) cross a farm track; recross it 55yds (50m) further on. Continue for 219yds (200m), skirting a small hill. When this green track curves left, cross a stile ahead. Go through the gateway, right, in 11yds (10m), then cross the stile, left, following path with further stiles and gates down to Bailey Einon farm and the minor road.

❽ Turn right, then right again after 219yds (200m). Descend for 273yds (250m), cross stile, left, heading diagonally, and steeply, down the field to a stile at the bottom. Cross this, turn right to tarmac road, then left to a picnic area.

❾ Take the path opposite, ascending through the woods, emerging from conifers after 109yds (100m). At a lane, turn right and continue to a stile on the right opposite a plantation at the brow of the hill.

❿ Cross the stile and follow the path to the trig point. Bear slightly left to a stile and cross two fields. Bear down, right towards gorse bushes, behind which is a signpost and a stile. Cross the stile and head towards the woods, keeping right where the path forks near a pond. Continue for 328yds (300m) to another stile. Cross and turn left, to another stile in 44yds (40m). Cross to rejoin the outward route.

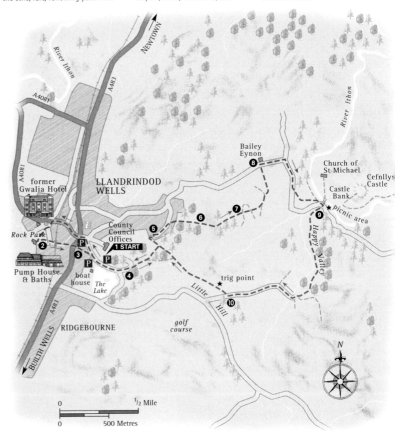

WALK

87

This walk takes you along a drovers' road before visiting the cave of the 16th-century outlaw Twm Sion Catti, thief, highwayman and master of disguise. He was a popular figure of the day and often protected from the king's officers in return for an evening's entertainment.

Wales

DISTANCE • 6 miles (9.6km)

TOTAL ASCENT • 300ft (91m)

PATHS • minor roads and forest trails. Paths very muddy and slippery in wet weather

TERRAIN • woodland, farmland

GRADIENTS • undulating roads. Tarmac tracks mostly flat or slightly uphill. Paths can be steep in places

REFRESHMENTS • Rhadirmwyn Bridge and Rhandirmwyn (nearest villages to the walk)

PARK • ample car parking spaces at start point by the dam

DIFFICULTY • 2

Along a Drovers' Road to the Cave of Twm

❶ Facing Llyn Brianne, bear left down a road, and at a T-junction turn right. Further on where the road forks branch left and after about 1/2 mile (800m) turn right into a car park serving the RSPB Dinas Reserve just entered.

❷ Head for a wooden kissing gate at the left-hand side of the car park. Follow a raised wooden pathway leading through woodland. When the boardwalk forks, branch right and follow a nature trail which runs parallel to the river.

❸ Taking care, follow the path through an ancient oak woodland and pass the cave and sometime home of Twm Sion Catti. (A path does lead from the nature trail to the cave, but it is not obvious and may be dangerous in wet weather.)

*The **drovers' roads** which you walk along this route have played an important part in history. Welsh drovers were the cowboys of their day, driving vast herds of cattle, sheep, pigs and flocks of geese to English markets in the hope of a good sale. They also acted as bankers, delivering and returning the locals' investments, and as an unofficial postal service. Their regular routes through Wales were punctuated with resting places and inns; one of the most remote and spectacular is the road over the hills from Tregaron to Llandovery.*

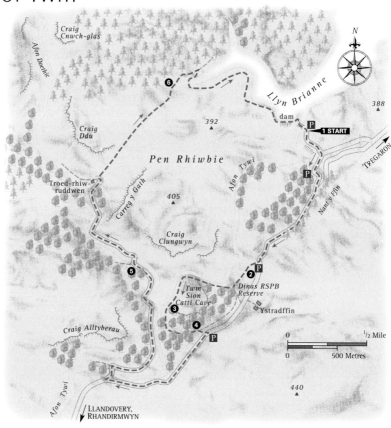

❹ Branch right when the woodland path forks and pass through a large wooden gate. Turn right on to a tarmac road and follow this for about a mile (1.6km). Then turn right on to a single-track road heading for Troedyrhiw and, passing over a bridge, press on, climbing gently.

❺ Cross a metal bridge and then continue until the surfaced road ends in front of a farm and bears sharply right, gently climbing a rough-surfaced vehicle track leading up a narrowing valley.

❻ Near the top of the valley, the path runs through a forest and,

beyond its high point, emerges on the other side, bearing sharp right. A short way on, climb gently to the left on a broad track parallel with the shore of Llyn Brianne, and eventually return to the dam. Cross and walk back to the car park and your car.

Abbey in the Wilderness

In the heart of Wales, Strata Florida Abbey was an important oasis amidst wild but beautiful uplands

WALK

88

1 From lay-by at south end of village, continue south along road towards Tregaron, going gently uphill to stile and ancient wooden foot-path sign on left.

2 Cross stile and follow track beyond towards caravans. Go on to cara-van site road and bear left, between vans. As road bears right, bear left past last caravan to stile in corner.

10 At farm lane bear left to road. Turn left, crossing hump-backed bridge and passing road, on left, for Strata Florida, to return to start.

9 As road turns sharp left, go right past tele-phone box and, soon, cross waymarked stile on left. Cross footbridge and bear left towards way-marked stile by gate. The path now follows Afon Teifi (left) all the way to Pontrhydfendigaid, with occasional waymarkers, stiles and gates.

Distance: 5½ miles (9km)
Total ascent: 500 ft (152m)
Paths: mainly obvious paths and lanes
Terrain: fields, country lanes and forestry
Gradients: gradual
Refreshments: Red Lion and Black Lion, Pontrhydfendigaid
Park: along main street or in lay-by at southern entrance to village, Pontrhydfendigaid
Difficulty: 2

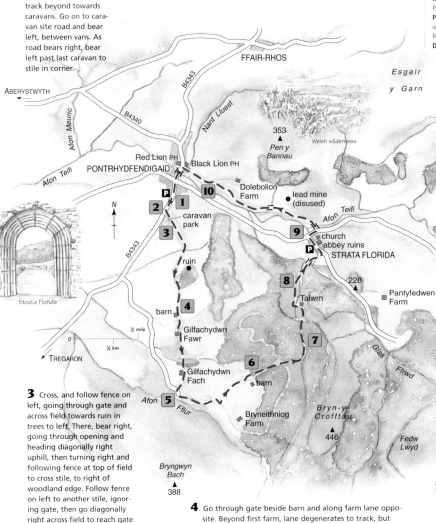

tile, Strata Florida

Strata Florida

8 An occasionally indistinct path follows stream down, crossing it once, to foot-bridge. Cross and follow stream bank to gate. Keep ahead along road beyond. Strata Florida car park is to left, ruins and church to right.

7 Follow track to gate and continue along lane beyond to ruin (Talwrn). Go left along ruin's top, near wall, to follow another lane to end. Go through gate and turn right, following stream. Soon bear left to gate, bearing left beyond to regain stream.

6 Follow bridleway through forest to forestry road. After 50 yds (46m), as it goes sharp right between trees, bear left along another bridleway. Follow to path coming down from right. Bear left with waymarker.

5 Turn left. When road ends, go through gate and follow lane beyond. As farm comes into view about ¼ mile (400m) ahead, take lane coming in from left, following it uphill. Approaching barn, go through gate on left and turn right along fence to gate into forest.

3 Cross, and follow fence on left, going through gate and across field towards ruin in trees to left. There, bear right, going through opening and heading diagonally right uphill, then turning right and following fence at top of field to cross stile, to right of woodland edge. Follow fence on left to another stile, ignor-ing gate, then go diagonally right across field to reach gate in top right corner. Go through and turn left immediately through another gate. Go diago-nally right towards barn.

4 Go through gate beside barn and along farm lane oppo-site. Beyond first farm, lane degenerates to track, but remains obvious. Beyond farmyard keep to left of hut and take lower, right-hand track into trees. Ford stream, go through gate and follow track uphill to second farm. Go through gate and ahead along farm lane to road.

Sarn Helen – the Roman Highway through Wales

A stretch of Roman Road leads to the legendary burial place of a great Welsh bard

WALK
89

1 Start at the Wildfowler Inn in Tre'r-ddôl. On the village street, face the pub, go right, past the garage, shop and café, to join the A487. Turn right towards Machynlleth, and, after passing the last house, turn right through a wooden gate into a forestry plantation. Climb with an attractive, narrow, path.

2 Bear left when the path forks. Ignore paths descending from your right. Go ahead across clear-felled hillside. The path becomes a firm track before reaching a lane. Go right uphill, passing a number of houses and, eventually, farm buildings at Cefngweirlog.

3 Reach the junction with Sarn Helen, coming as a track through a gate on your left. Turn right to walk along this quiet lane. Follow this section of Sarn Helen for over 1 mile (1.6km), ignoring a lane descending on your right. Cross a bridge over the Afon Clettwr and climb towards Gwar-cwm-uchaf farm. Turn left before you reach it, onto a rising track and ignore all branching paths.

7 Take a gate ahead to descend on a tree-lined hollow way towards Tre'r-ddôl. Emerge on the road, with a chapel on your left, and turn right across a bridge over the Afon Clettwr to return to the start.

6 Enter woodland at a bridleway waymark post and soon turn sharp right to descend a rough path which zigzags steeply down between oak trees. Go ahead through a gate into a plantation of conifers.

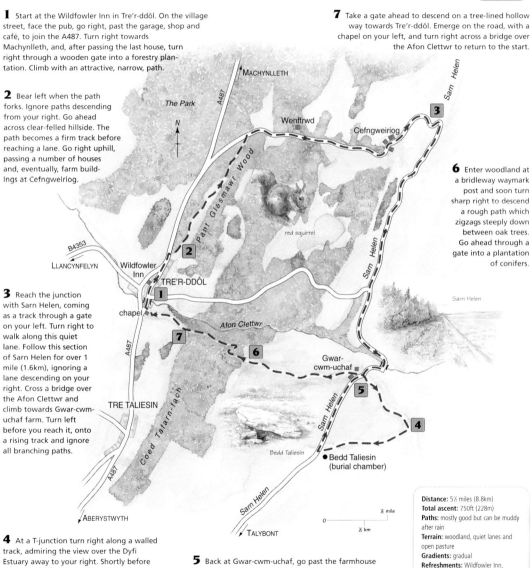

MACHYNLLETH

The Park

A487

N

Wenffrwd

Cefngweirlog

Sarn Helen

3

Pant Glasmawr Wood

red squirrel

Sarn Helen

Sarn Helen

B4353

LLANCYNFELYN

2

Wildfowler Inn

TRE'R-DDÔL

1

chapel

A487

Afon Clettwr

7

6

Gwar-cwm-uchaf

5

TRE TALIESIN

Coed Tafarn-fach

Sarn Helen

4

Bedd Taliesin

● Bedd Taliesin (burial chamber)

A487

Sarn Helen

ABERYSTWYTH

TALYBONT

½ mile

0

½ km

4 At a T-junction turn right along a walled track, admiring the view over the Dyfi Estuary away to your right. Shortly before returning to the lane which forms the route of Sarn Helen, notice the remains of the prehistoric burial chamber known as Bedd Taliesin on your left. Go through a gate to turn right along Sarn Helen, with fine views towards Aberdyfi over the stone wall on your left.

5 Back at Gwar-cwm-uchaf, go past the farmhouse then turn left through a gate and follow a path along the top edge of a sloping pasture. Keep on along the remains of a green lane. After passing a small group of trees, go forward to pass through a gate then proceed first by a stream and then beside a line of tree stumps. Keep on in the same direction along a hedged section and then along a rutted path.

Distance: 5½ miles (8.8km)
Total ascent: 750ft (228m)
Paths: mostly good but can be muddy after rain
Terrain: woodland, quiet lanes and open pasture
Gradients: gradual
Refreshments: Wildfowler Inn, Tre'r-ddôl
Park: considerate roadside parking in Tre'r-ddôl, just off the A487 between Aberystwyth and Machynlleth, 2 miles (3.2km) north of Tal-y-bont
Difficulty: 2

WALK 90

ABOUT • MACHYNLLETH

This walk around Machynlleth celebrates the town's long history: from the foundation of the first Welsh Parliament by Owain Glyndŵr in 1404 to the Celtica Centre founded in 1995 which offers a superb exhibition of Welsh culture and language.

Wales

DISTANCE • 5 miles (8km)	**REFRESHMENTS** • various pubs and cafés in Machynlleth
TOTAL ASCENT • 675ft (206m)	
PATHS • pavements, tracks and paths	**PARK** • main car park, off Heol Maengwyn, Machynlleth
TERRAIN • town, river meadows, moorland	
GRADIENTS • one fairly steep climb; one moderate descent	**DIFFICULTY** • 2

Machynlleth's Long History

❶ From the clock tower at the end of the main street, Heol Maengwyn, take the road to the north for 328yds (300m), towards the station. Pass the station and Dyfi Eco Park, and just before the Dyfi Bridge, take the surfaced footpath to the right along the river bank.

❷ Keep ahead, leaving the surfaced path where it goes over the new footbridge, and carry on along the river bank, crossing a low barbed wire fence. Follow the river through the meadows for 547yds (500m), crossing a stile.

❸ As the route nears the railway and the river swings left, climb the stile to the right and cross the railway with care. Bear left up the hill. On leaving the trees, bear right across the field towards a stile uphill from the gate; cross and turn right on to the track.

❹ Where the houses start, join the road and continue straight on for 656yds (600m), past Maes-y-Garth; at the T-junction by the cemetery, turn right. After the side turning, (Maes Dyfi, on the left, before the 'no entry' signs), turn left down the one-way street. At the end turn left on to the main street then right, up the road signed Llyn Clywedog/Llanidloes.

❺ Past Treowain Enterprise Park, opposite where the houses finish, take the signed footpath to the right. Follow the waymarkers, and after 219yds (200m) follow the wall for 328yds (300m), then bear right at the corner of the wall before zigzagging up a fairly steep hill. At the top of the hill, bear right to the corner of the forest.

❻ On reaching the trees, take the path to the right, away from the trees, passing between boulders 22yds (20m) ahead. In 328yds (300m), go through a gate and follow the track downhill for 109yds (100m). Go through the gate at a T-junction with a track, continue downhill, past the shale track on the left, through the woods, and past the farm Brynglas.

❼ In 437yds (400m) at the road, turn right. After 219yds (200m) turn right on to the path signed Glyndŵr's Way, cross the drive to the cottages and follow the path to the road. At the bottom, turn right into the grounds of the Celtica Centre.

❽ Cross the car park; go round to the front of the Plas (mansion) and entrance to the Celtica Centre. Follow the drive round to the left in front of the leisure centre, turning right at the roundabout to return to the clock tower.

• DON'T MISS •

From the hills above Machynlleth you will see one of the windmills belonging to the Centre for Alternative Technology (CAT), about 2 miles (3.2km) to the north of the town. This innovative centre, researches and practices sustainable forms of energy.

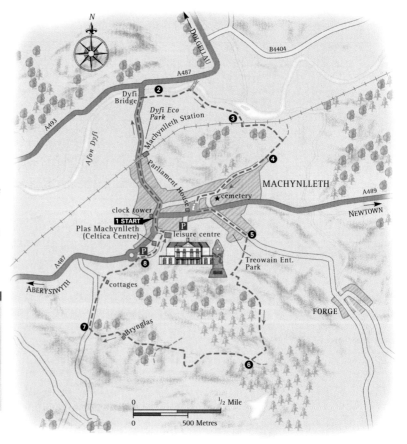

Mary Jones in the Dysynni Valley

In the footsteps of a remarkable woman, whose exploits were commemorated by Victorian missionaries

WALK 91

1 Walk north up the lane between the church and the cottage. As it bends left on the approach to a farm, go right, over a ladder stile or through the gate and along a track. Having passed through a gate behind the farm, fork right, climbing steadily on a stony track, and continue past an old quarry and a small larch plantation. Soon after a stream crosses the track, climb a stile on the left.

Distance: 6¼ miles (10km)
Total ascent: 330ft (100m)
Paths: clear tracks and quiet lanes; muddy stretch between Tyn-y-ddôl and Pen-y-meini
Terrain: hillside pasture and valley floor
Gradients: gentle
Refreshments: at Abergynolwyn, south of Llanfihangel-y-pennant
Park: opposite the church in Llanfihangel-y-pennant
Difficulty: 1

2 Descend to cross a footbridge over the Afon Cadair, then climb diagonally left to a stile onto a bridleway. Turn left and follow the track to reach Tyn-y-ddôl, where Mary Jones lived.

3 Just beyond the remains of her cottage go straight ahead at a footpath sign. The path runs beside the river, passing two farms, until it meets a stone wall. Keep on in the same direction, but just to the right of the wall. A series of stiles leads you on to pass a third farm, after which you turn left by a stream to a stile beside a chapel.

4 Turn left along the lane, then right over a small bridge and along a track, which runs between fields before entering them. Continue along field edges, soon with the Afon Dysynni on your left. At a junction with another path, continue forwards. The track soon curves left then right, crossing two bridges to reach a caravan site. Walk beyond the caravan site and farm to reach a lane.

5 Turn left and follow the lane for 1 mile (1.6km). Shortly, after crossing a bridge by Rhiwlas, turn right at the crossroads, signed Abergynolwyn. After 100yds (91m) turn left through the gateway at Caerberllan, then straight ahead to a gate.

6 Follow a track which contours along the lower slopes of a hill. Opposite the beginning of the rock in the valley, on which Castell y Bere stands, go through a green-painted iron gate on the left and head diagonally right across a field to cross a stile onto the lane.

7 Turn right soon passing the entrance to Castell y Bere, and follow the lane back to Llanfihangel-y-pennant.

Graig Lŵyd
Dysynni Valley
Cwm Llŵyd
Rhydcriw
Afon Dyffryn
Esgair Berfa
Mynydd Pennant ▲ 463
323 Craig Ysgiog
Mary Jones' Cottage
Mynydd Tyn-y-fach
TYN-Y-DDÔL
Mynydd Pen-rhiw ▲ 230
PEN-Y-MEINI
Afon Cadair
LLANFIHANGEL-Y-PENNANT
Castell y Bere
Foel Caer berllan ▲ 375
Mary Jones memorial
Afon Dysynni
caravan site
Llanllwyda Farm
Afon Dysynni
B4405
CORRIS DOLGELLAU
Craig yr Aderyn ▲ 233 (Birds' Rock)
Gamallt ▲ 294
Railway Inn
ABERGYNOLWYN
Nant Gwernol Station
Nant Gwernol
Abergynolwyn Station
Foel Fawr ▲ 344
cormorant
Mynydd Pentre
Talyllyn Railway
Tarren Fach
BRYNCRUG
B4405
Dolgoch Falls Station
Mynydd Tan-y-coed ▲ 491
N
½ mile
½ km

Cadair Idris –
the Mountain Nature Reserve

A challenging mountain walk around the bowl of
Cwm Cau in the Cadair Idris National Nature Reserve

WALK

92

Distance: 5½ miles (8.8km)
Total Ascent: 2,950ft (899m)
Paths: good; some rough; stream crossing difficult after heavy rain
Terrain: rocky, mountainous
Gradients: steep; occasionally very steep
Refreshments: none
Park: Minffordd car park at junction of A487 and B4405
Difficulty: 3

1 Walk to the back of the car park, where a well-signed path leaves through a gate. Follow a raised causeway to a kissing gate and visitor centre. Follow the path over a bridge to a gate into the nature reserve.

2 Follow the steep, mostly stepped path up through the woods, with the stream to your right.

3 Go through a gate to reach more open country, continuing to climb to a point where the plantation on your right swings away and the path runs very close to the stream. Note the path down to the water here. Take it to study the stream crossing. The stream must be crossed on the return route. In dry weather it can be crossed easily. **If not, you should reverse the route from Pen-y-gadair, rather than complete the circuit.**

4 Return to, and continue along, the path. High up to the right a ladder stile over a fence can be seen, the diagonal path descending to the stream is the return route. The outward path now takes you into Cwm Cau.

8 Descend on the path to Nant Cadair and carefully cross the stream to reach the outward path. Turn left downhill, and follow the outward route back to the start.

7 Continue downhill, close to the fence, to cross the ladder stile seen from the path to Cwm Cau. Look for the conifers below you to the right of the fence. If you reach these you have gone too far. You must cross the ladder stile to a clear path, descending initially diagonally, to the conifers at the stream.

6 From the summit, continue along a broad ridge (ENE). After about 15 minutes, at the low point of the ridge, before it rises to Mynydd Moel, a minor path forks right, terracing above Cwm Cau, then descending gently and later undulating past a number of springs to a fence and following it down to cross a ladder stile. If you miss this path, don't panic: the fence ahead rises almost to the top of Mynydd Moel so, wherever you meet it, cross it and follow it right downhill.

5 Just before a huge whale-back rock, bear left, climbing steeply to the top of the ridge. Turn right and continue along the ridge, always tending a little to the right, to the summit of Craig Cau, marked by a ladder stile and small cairn. Continue on the ridge, descending (NNE then N) past the top of a stone shoot, then swinging right uphill on rougher ground to the summit of Pen-y-gadair, marked by a trig point and a substantial stone shelter.

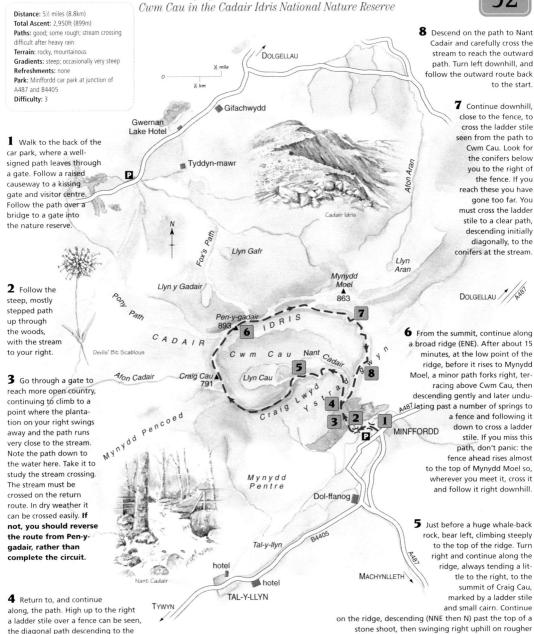

WALK 93

ABOUT • DOLGELLAU

This walk celebrates the Quakers or Friends who journeyed from this small Welsh town to Pennsylvania, USA, in the 1680s to escape persecution and give voice to their faith in a new land. Don't miss the Quakers' Heritage Centre, in Eldon Square.

Wales

DISTANCE • 6 miles (9.6km)

TOTAL ASCENT • 590ft (180m)

PATHS • some rocky and muddy tracks; can be slippery

TERRAIN • surfaced roads, tracks, fields

GRADIENTS • some steep ascents and descents

REFRESHMENTS • several pubs and cafés in Dolgellau; Fronoleu Country Hotel near top of first ascent

PARK • Marian car park, Dolgellau

DIFFICULTY • 3

Dolgellau's Quaker Trail

❶ From the Tourist Information Centre in Eldon Square, cross the square and take the left-hand road to Pont yr Aran/Aran Road. Cross the river and continue ahead, past the ambulance depot. Turn right, signed Tabor, to climb Fron Serth. Where the road forks, keep left.

❷ As the route descends, turn left in front of Tabor Cottage cottage. Shortly, turn left following public footpath sign. At the next junction pass Tyddyn Carreg farmhouse and through the metal bar gate, left. Follow the boundary wall across the field to the burial ground.

❸ Retrace your steps, pass the farmhouse and take the track to the right. Beyond Tŷ Newydd, go through the wooden gate keeping on the track ahead through *coed* (mixed woodland). Emerging from the wood, follow the track left and go through the gate.

❹ Cross the road and follow the public footpath opposite, up the drive past a house, through a farmyard and two further gates. At the top take the gate, right, and cross the field ahead. Go through the gap in the stone wall, a gate, and the next gap ahead. Bear right towards the ruined farm building.

❺ Turn right just before the cottage and follow the field boundary. Bear left to the metal gate and climb the wooden stile to its right. Follow the path between ferns, downhill.

❻ The route descends through woods bearing left above a farm. Cross two stiles, and follow the arrow to the left. Go through the metal gate (arrowed) and jump

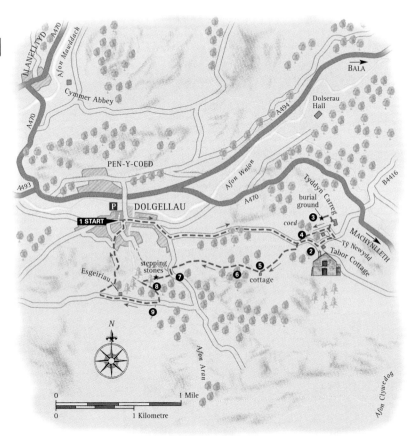

across the small brook. Continue ahead, with two houses on your right. Join the part-gravel track and cross the cattle grid; continue for 164yds (150m) to the lane.

❼ Follow the tarmac road left. Beyond the stream, take the footpath, right. At the wooden gate, follow the arrowed track, left, across a footbridge over the river. Go through the kissing gate and climb the track. Cross a stream

via stepping stones, then climb the stile into woods.

❽ Where the trail forks, take the left, ascending, path. At the T-junction, turn left and climb the steep, arrowed track. At the top, go through the wooden gate. Shortly, turn left along the stony track. Continue to the tarmac road.

❾ Turn right along the road, continuing through the gate across

the road and past Esgeiriau farmhouse after about ¼ mile (400m). Ignore footpath signed right. In ½ mile (800m) follow a bridleway sign, right. Take the main track round the hillside and downhill. Go through the metal gate just after a gap in the wall, left, to descend into town. At the first house, turn right. Continue ahead at the road, go straight across at the crossroads, then turn left for Eldon Square.

WALK 94

Rhaeadr Ddu – the Black Waterfall

*Deep forests cloak a lovely waterfall, where poets
and writers found inspiration*

1 From car park, follow main road left (south) for a few paces to black corrugated village hall and turn right between hall and river on gated lane. Climb gradually upstream with river away to left. Ignore drive to Ty-cerig on right.

2 About 200yds (182m) beyond drive, where lane bends right, look for waymark post in woodland ahead. Go to it and bear left along waymarked path towards footbridge over river. Just before footbridge, keep to path which leads directly to viewpoint of waterfall upstream from bridge. See lines of poetry carved on rock then retrace route a few paces and cross footbridge.

7 As track swings left, go ahead through small gate and descend with walled path. Pass buildings of Tyddyn-y-bwlch and through gate into woodland and, in 20yds (18m), after second gate, bear right at fork. Drop down to lane, go right (downhill) and follow it back to village and car park in Ganllwyd.

6 At track junction, turn right to follow track across river. Take track on right and, ignoring tracks through forest on left, bear right at two forks, keeping alongside river. At mountain bike waymark, take lesser track right, dropping downhill.

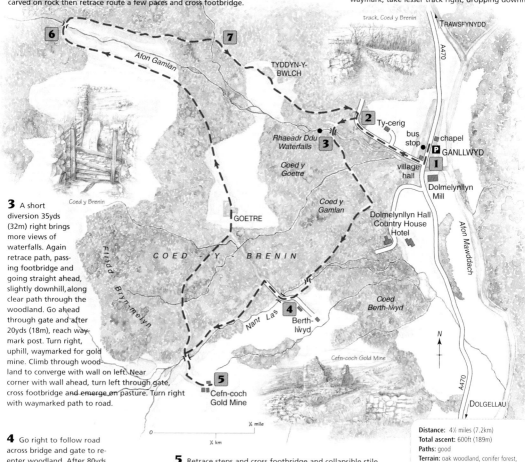

3 A short diversion 35yds (32m) right brings more views of waterfalls. Again retrace path, passing footbridge and going straight ahead, slightly downhill, along clear path through the woodland. Go ahead through gate and after 20yds (18m), reach waymark post. Turn right, uphill, waymarked for gold mine. Climb through woodland to converge with wall on left. Near corner with wall ahead, turn left through gate, cross footbridge and emerge on pasture. Turn right with waymarked path to road.

4 Go right to follow road across bridge and gate to re-enter woodland. After 80yds (73m), turn left along track between trees. Again converge with stream on left and ignore tracks on right. Turn left through narrow gap in wall, over collapsible stile and footbridge. Climb with paved way to ruins of Cefn-coch Gold Mine.

5 Retrace steps and cross footbridge and collapsible stile again. Go 35yds (32m) downhill on outward approach route to track junction and take track going ahead (ignoring track bearing left uphill and track used to reach here on right). Follow downhill to major track and go left through gate to pass buildings of Goetre. Continue along firm track through open space and back into forest. Then, back into open country, track rises to converge with river (Afon Gamlan) on right.

Distance: 4½ miles (7.2km)
Total ascent: 600ft (189m)
Paths: good
Terrain: oak woodland, conifer forest, pasture, quiet road
Gradients: some gradual climbs
Refreshments: none
Park: National Trust car park on eastern side of A470 in Ganllwyd, 5 miles (8km) north of Dolgellau
Difficulty: 2

On the Roman Steps through the Rhinogs

This ancient pathway through the heart of the Rhinog hills was one of many trade routes across the mountains

WALK
95

Clip
▲
590

1 Leave the car park through the gate at its top end and turn right. Cross the causeway over the stream, then a ladder stile, following the path rising through a wood.

Cwm-Mawr

little humped bridge

LLANBEDR

Distance: 4½ miles (7.2km)
Total ascent: 1,150 ft (350m)
Paths: excellent as far as the path to Llyn Du, rugged or poor thereafter
Terrain: heather clad and rocky mountains
Gradients: gradual, then steep and difficult
Refreshments: none
Park: car park at Llyn Cwm Bychan, 5 miles east of A496 in Harlech
Difficulty: 2

2 At the end of the woodland, cross another ladder stile and continue along the path to reach a little humped bridge. Beyond, the slabs of the Roman Steps appear.

Llyn Cwm Bychan

½ mile
0
½ km

3 300yds (274m) beyond the humped bridge, where a slab bridge crosses the stream, note a path forking right: this is the return route. For now, continue along the steps, following the stream and sometimes crossing it. Occasionally the steps disappear, but the way is always obvious, heading up towards a narrow, rocky cleft.

Carrig-y-Saeth
▲
439

Roman Steps

Craig
Wion

4 Go between round, wooden gateposts in a wall and continue along the steps. As the pass narrows, cross through another low wall. Some 600yds (546m) on, another wall crosses the route.

Gloyw
Llyn

Llyn
Morwynion

9 Follow the path downhill, briefly indistinct in boggy ground, but soon re-appearing. Pass a ruined sheepfold, then go through a gap in a wall. The path descends soon to the steps at the point noted on the outward route. Turn left to the little humped bridge and return to the start.

5 Go right immediately after this wall on a path climbing steeply beside the wall. Follow it, staying close to the wall to the crest of a ridge. Now descend, still following the wall, then climb again.

cairn

Bwlch Tyddiad

N

Llyn Du

6 On the final climb the path bears left, away from the wall, to a viewpoint above Llyn Du. Bear right from here to return to the wall and cross it by the stone stile. Follow the path beyond to pass through a wall gap. In a few minutes there is a view of Gloyw Llyn.

Llyn Du

Rhinog Fawr
▲
720

7 Be cautious now. Below you is a large boulder ruckle. Trace the line of a path which turns left under a cliff and skirts across the top of the rockfall, then makes its way down the left (as viewed) side. At the base of the ruckle, as you enter a small gully, break out, bearing right across boggy ground on a terrace above the lake. Pass through alternate boggy patches and areas of heather, and tend right towards the finger-like end of the lake.

8 Don't go down to the lake, but stay on the terrace to the far end of the lake. Bear right, away from the lake and from the network of paths select one which heads towards Clip. If you head directly for Llyn Cwm Bychan, you are too far left.

ROMAN STEPS

WALK

96

Built of local grey sandstone by Edward I in 1283–90, Harlech Castle has served as both a fortress and a refuge. In the Wars of the Roses it was besieged by Yorkists for nearly eight years, and the struggle is remembered in the song 'Men of Harlech'.

Wales

DISTANCE • 5 miles (8km)

TOTAL ASCENT • 200ft (61m)

PATHS • rocky track through woods – can be muddy; sandy track through dunes

TERRAIN • surfaced roads, steps, gravel track, sand dunes and beach, woodland track. **Make sure you complete the walk during low tide.**

GRADIENTS • steep steps to sea level; steep climb (rocky track and steps) to castle rock

REFRESHMENTS • cafés and pub in Harlech

PARK • castle forecourt; Upper Bron y Graig car park in town

DIFFICULTY • 2

Song of the Men of Harlech

❶ Start at the top castle entrance. With your back to the castle, turn right. Following the sign towards Harlech railway station, take the road that snakes downhill. Part way down, take the public footpath, left, down a flight of slate steps.

❷ Cross the road and follow the public footpath opposite. Cross the railway line with care and go through the metal gate. Follow the path, keeping the wire fence to your right. As you leave the golf course, ignore the track which forks right and take the sandy path between the dunes to the beach.

❸ Turn right and walk along the beach for about a mile (1.6km). From here you can enjoy magnificent sweeping views of the castle and bay. Then turn back and retrace your steps as far as the red-and-white striped pole (lifebelt point H7).

❹ Turn left along the marked sand path, which soon becomes a surfaced path. Go through the metal kissing gate and continue ahead to the main road.

❺ Cross the road. Turn left, then right (just past the Queen's Hotel) towards the railway station. Cross by the level crossing and turn left. Pass the turning to Woodlands Caravan Park and continue beyond the fire station to the public footpath sign.

❻ Turn right to go through the woods. Continue ahead, presently climbing quite steeply. Climb the gap in the stone wall and continue up a rocky slope to the more

clearly marked path. Turn right, uphill, and climb the steep steps.

❼ At the top of the steps climb over the metal bar. Turn right, and

follow the road back into town. At the crossroads, turn right, following the sign to return to the castle where it is worth leaving plenty of time to explore.

Barmouth, a popular beach resort about 12 miles (19km) south of Harlech, was the port used by Jasper Tudor and the other Lancastrian rebels. Jasper and his ally, Griffith Vaughan, plotted their assault on the throne in a house on the harbour, Ty Gwyn, now largely rebuilt.

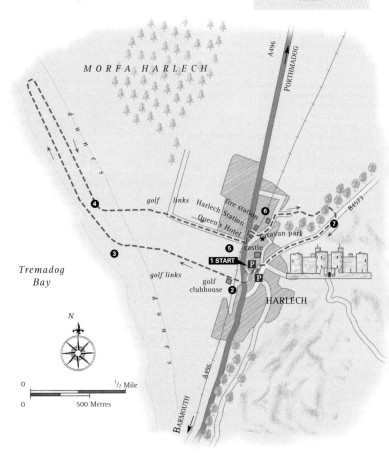

WALK 97

Born in the small town of Llanystumdwy, David Lloyd George, the 'Welsh Wizard', was one of the most charismatic politicians of the 20th century. He was elected Prime Minister in 1916 and was responsible for great social and political reforms.

Wales

DISTANCE • 5 miles (8km)

TOTAL ASCENT • 131ft (40m)

PATHS • some rough tracks; fields may be muddy

TERRAIN • surfaced roads, fields, stony tracks, pebble beach. **Make sure you complete the walk during low tide**

GRADIENTS • gradual

REFRESHMENTS • several pubs and cafés in Criccieth

PARK • Criccieth car park off Y Maes

DIFFICULTY • 2

In the Steps of the 'Welsh Wizard'

1 Start at the Memorial Hall, at the bottom end of Y Maes, the green at the centre of Criccieth. With your back to the hall, turn right, then right again, following the Caernarfon (B4411) sign. Climb the hill away from town.

2 At the Bron Eifion sign just beyond the former Baptist Chapel, now called Pen-y-Maes, turn left. Follow the single-track road past Bryn Awelon and bear right, into the countryside, where the road forks. Continue past the entrance to the Bron Eifion Fishery, right.

3 After visiting Lloyd George's memorial, right, turn back and retrace your steps as far as the entrance to Tŷ Newydd, now on your right. Take this turning, following the public footpath sign.

4 Continue past Tŷ Newydd and follow the public footpath arrow ahead, past a row of cottages. Go through the kissing gate and continue alongside the hedge.

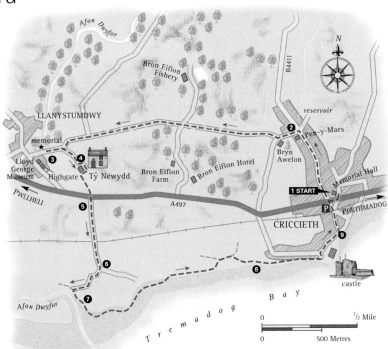

It's worth breaking your journey to visit the Lloyd George Museum and Highgate, two minutes' walk away, where the statesman's Victorian childhood home has been recreated, along with a 19th-century schoolroom, his uncle's shoe-making workshop and an immaculate cottage garden. You also pass Ty Newydd, the house which Lloyd George bought in 1943 and where he lived until his death in 1945.

Climb the stone stile and cross the field towards the road.

5 Cross the road and continue along the public footpath ahead. After crossing the railway bridge the track swings round to the left; fork right to the gate, signed footpath only, and climb the wooden stile.

6 Follow the path round to the right. Go through the wooden picket gate (alongside a wooden five-bar gate) and continue to

meet the river. Turn left to follow the river's course to the sea.

7 Continue on the track, which swings left and peters out into pebble beach: take care here and make sure the tide is out. Follow the beach round the headland. Climb to the path above and parallel to the beach, passing a National Trust marker on a boulder where the coast has eroded.

8 At the end of the track turn right towards Criccieth. Where the

track bends to the left, take the path along the cliff straight ahead, leading back into the town. Go through the kissing gate and continue ahead following the esplanade.

9 After passing the castle hill, just before the road begins to descend and with the pillar box on the corner, turn left up Tan-y-Grisiau Terrace. Continue to the end and cross the railway line. The Memorial Hall is diagonally ahead, to the right.

WALK 98

Pilgrims and Mysteries on Lleyn's Peninsula

A coastal walk through a landscape dominated by rituals

1 From car park, return to road junction and turn left, without crossing either bridge. Bear left uphill, ignoring turnings to right. When level with entrance to Dwyros camping site on right, turn left down signposted path. Pass houses and cross footbridge over Afon Saint to enter National Trust land.

6 On right is gate, stile and National Trust pillar, with track dropping down to Porth Meudwy valley. This is short cut described earlier. Continue past Cwrt (left) and go right at successive road junctions to retrace steps into Aberdaron, passing Dwyros on left.

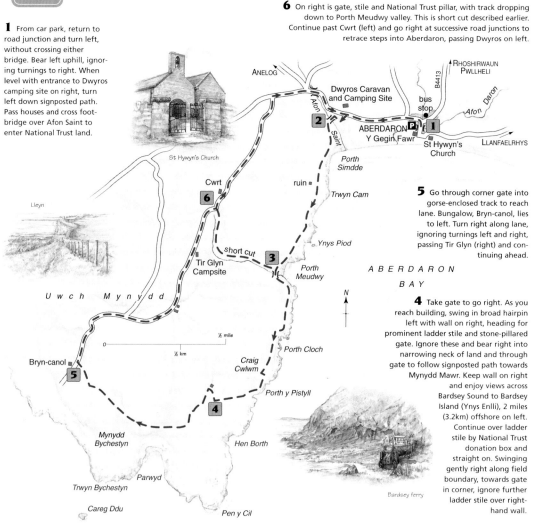

5 Go through corner gate into gorse-enclosed track to reach lane. Bungalow, Bryn-canol, lies to left. Turn right along lane, ignoring turnings left and right, passing Tir Glyn (right) and continuing ahead.

4 Take gate to go right. As you reach building, swing in broad hairpin left with wall on right, heading for prominent ladder stile and stone-pillared gate. Ignore these and bear right into narrowing neck of land and through gate to follow signposted path towards Mynydd Mawr. Keep wall on right and enjoy views across Bardsey Sound to Bardsey Island (Ynys Enlli), 2 miles (3.2km) offshore on left. Continue over ladder stile by National Trust donation box and straight on. Swinging gently right along field boundary, towards gate in corner, ignore further ladder stile over right-hand wall.

2 Follow coast path, keeping sea on left and ignoring path descending to beach at Porth Simdde. Continue past ruin (right) and through kissing-gate to log seat, then another kissing-gate before descending steps to inlet of Porth Meudwy. Track right offers short cut from here to stage 6 (near Cwrt). If you use this, keep to main track in valley bottom, ignoring side tracks.

3 Going ahead with signposted coast path, cross footbridge and climb steps up to stile. Ignore further stile, immediately on right skyline. Resume clifftop walk, keeping sea on left, passing Porth Cloch, then rising to pass Craig Cwlwm with its summit pond. Descend awkward outcrop to disused quarry. Ignore path and stile leading inland and continue on coast path, descending initially for 15 minutes to Porth y Pistyll. At its inland point, fork right, keeping to right-hand edge of field as you climb to gate in top right-hand corner.

Distance: 5½ miles (8.8km)
Total ascent: 350ft (107m)
Paths: good; some roads
Terrain: clifftop, pastureland
Gradients: some steep, stepped sections
Refreshments: many places in Aberdaron
Park: car park in Aberdaron, on B4413
16 miles (25.6km) west of Pwllheli
Difficulty: 1

WALK
99

The Menai Suspension Bridge (1826) was considered a feat of modern engineering. Started in 1819, Thomas Telford's design consisted of seven archways which supported the massive roadway, linking Anglesey to mainland Wales for the first time.

Wales

DISTANCE • 5 miles (8km)

TOTAL ASCENT • 104ft (32m)

PATHS • some minor roads; paths can become muddy and slippery in wet weather

TERRAIN • minor roads through village and farmland

GRADIENTS • roads mostly flat or slightly uphill; paths can be steep in places

REFRESHMENTS • Liverpool Arms Hotel and The Mostyn Arms public houses; tea rooms on Cadnant Road towards town centre

PARK • Coed Cyrnol car park, behind the Jade Cantonese restaurant in Menai Bridge; ample car parking

DIFFICULTY • 2

Crossing the Menai Bridge

❶ Leave the car park down a small flight of steps and turn right on to a tarmac path. Gently descending, this soon forks. Straight ahead is Church Island; to the left a broad promenade now runs parallel with the Straits. Continue along what is now a road through the arches of the Menai Suspension Bridge. Turn right immediately before the Liverpool Arms Hotel and walk on, bearing left into St George's Road. Pass The Mostyn Arms, go through the no entry signs and veer left.

❷ At the T-junction, turn right on Cadnant Road and, after 273yds (250m), cross to pass through a kissing gate. Ascend a waymarked path between the houses, cross the roadway part way up and follow the footpath sign carefully. An uneven path eventually leads to a stone stile. Turn left.

❸ After 22yds (20m) turn right on to a tarmac road, which later becomes a grassy, waymarked track. Go through a gate and continue along the right-hand field edge and through the hand gate. Go straight ahead towards the single tree and through the hand gate in the right-hand corner ahead. Follow the right-hand hedge, going through two more hand gates, then go down steps.

❹ Turn right along the roadside verge and take the next turning on the right (signed Llandegfan and Beaumaris). Follow a surfaced road and in ½ mile (800m) turn right on to a waymarked track.

❺ At the end of the track, just before the house, go through the gate on the left (waymark arrow on fence). After passing through

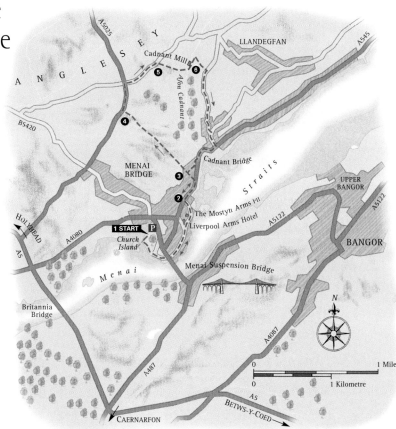

three small paddocks, head for a wooden stile on the left-hand side of the field. In the next field cross another stile half-way down the right-hand field edge. Descend a narrow path towards the left, cross a stream by a rock bridge and turn left through a wooden gate ahead.

❻ Pass Cadnant Mill on the left and, bearing right at the waymark sign, continue through the

farmyard to a T-junction. Bear right and continue for ½ mile (800m). At another T-junction, bear right to join the main road after 328yds (300m). Turn right, cross Cadnant Bridge, immediately turn right and 11yds (10m) along on the left, head along a waymarked path. The path gently rises, passing a large house on the right. Bear left here through a break in the hedge. Continue along

the path then, as the it veers right, turn left on to a narrower path. Go down to Cadnant Road again at the kissing gate and retrace your steps to the car park.

• DON'T MISS •

Near Menai Bridge is Church Island, the 6th-century home and refuge of Prince Tysilio, the son of Brochfael Ysgythrog.

Lost Civilisations on Tal y Fan

The hinterland of the North Wales coast is dotted with
mysterious stones and circles

Distance: 9½ miles (15.3km)
Total ascent: 1,725ft (526m)
Paths: mainly grassy and clear, but confusing in poor visibility
Terrain: mountain upland, hill pastures and rocky outcrops
Gradients: moderate
Refreshments: nothing near by; many places in Conwy.
Park: on roadside at the top of Sychnant Pass, the old hill road between Conwy and Penmaenmawr
Difficulty: 3

9 Retrace your outward journey for ½ mile (800m), then continue ahead on a good track descending to turn left onto a gravel track. Follow this to a car park and turn left again onto the road back to the start.

8 Pass around the hill fort and bear left to walk beside a collapsed wall, heading for Craig Celynin. A terraced track passes round the western side of Craig Celynin. From its north-western edge, cut across hill pasture to a wall gap in a corner. Through this, turn right, beside a wall, and follow it until you meet your outward route on the slopes of Cefn Maen Amor.

1 From the parking area, cross the road and go up to a gate. Beyond this, a track curves around the northern end of a broad ridge.

2 After 200yds (182m) take an obvious track turning sharply right onto higher ground and, at next waymarker, bear left on a green track. In 300yds (273m), at power lines, branch right and head across heather moorland to a wall and ladder stile.

3 Beyond the stile, descend a little (signposted North Wales Path) across the western slopes of Maen Esgob, and turn left above the white farmhouse through a pronounced pass between low hills (ignore a nearby waymark). Following a stony track, pass a small lake, and continue over the col on a grassy path to reach a substantial wall on your left.

4 Turn right and continue on a grassy track for 1 mile (1.6km) with the wall on your left and later veer right on the track across the flanks of Cefn Maen Amor. The track ascends to a massive standing stone below quarries. Go past this and, when the track forks, keep right, over the col.

5 Keep ahead, and in ¼ mile (400m), pass a ruin. The track continues across the northern slopes of Tal y Fan before turning and climbing south to a col between Tal y Fan and Foel Lwyd, where it meets a wall. Cross the ladder stile; the summit of Tal y Fan lies a few minutes up to the left. Return to the col.

6 Go down an obvious waymarked track with ladder stiles until you meet a lane near Cae Coch Farm. Turn left and, in 100yds (91m), branch left. In another 100yds (91m), turn left over a ladder stile and ascend towards the farm. In 50yds (45m), turn right to follow a track with a wall on your right.

7 This eventually leads to a ladder stile by a gate and continues above a wall. Follow this track to the hill fort of Caer Bach.

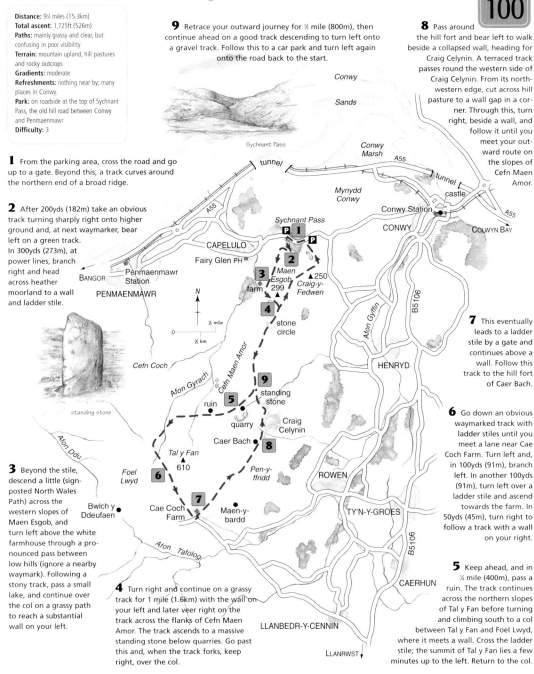

WALK
101

ABOUT • CONWY

This walk starts at Conwy Castle, built by Edward I after his conquest of Wales. The route then wanders along the estuary and up on to Conwy Mountain, a vantage point from where the tactical positioning of the castle is most evident.

Wales

DISTANCE • 7¼ miles (11.7km)

TOTAL ASCENT • 985ft (300m)

PATHS • minor roads, A-roads, rough tracks and paths

TERRAIN • remote farmland and hill country

GRADIENTS • road mostly flat; paths steep in places

REFRESHMENTS • Liverpool Arms in Conwy, many cafés and take-away food bars in town centre

PARK • Vicarage Gardens car park, inside the castle walls

DIFFICULTY • 3

In the Shadow of Conwy Castle

❶ From the car park turn right to reach the Guild Hall. Cross the road, turn right, then left, following signs for the Quay. Pass through a small archway and walk along the harbour front. Continue through another archway and bear right on to the signed North Wales Path (NWP).

❷ Continue alongside the Conwy estuary, parallel with Bodlondeb Woods. At a T-junction, turn left and walk to a main road. Go into the road opposite, and cross the railway by a footbridge. Continue past the drive to Beechwood Court, soon bearing right at the T-junction (waymarked). Just past the last houses on the right, branch right again at the fork to follow the NWP, and climb to a wooden stile giving access to Conwy Mountain. Ascend through bracken and gorse, eventually to follow a more level course across the flanks of the mountain.

❸ Continue for just over a mile (1.6km) to a waymark. Leave the NWP and bear left, descending to a more pronounced path beside a wall. Further on, rejoin the NWP and continue to a lateral farm track. Cross this and go forward on to a broad track to the parking area at Sychnant Pass.

❹ Cross the road and go up to a gate. After a short distance, take an obvious track turning sharp right on to higher ground. Shortly, bear left on a green track following waymarked NWP. Further on, as you pass under power lines for the third time, the track forks directly under them. Branch left here and continue along the track to a ladder stile over a wall.

❺ Beyond the stile, descend a little across the western slopes of Maen Esgob, and when the main track bears right, turn left through a pronounced pass between low hills, now leaving the NWP. Follow a track past a small lake (Llyn y Wrach), and shortly turn left, roughly parallel with a wall. Follow the track (which doesn't always stay by the wall and finally leaves it), to reach a group of walled enclosures. Bear right. Shortly the path descends quite steeply, and meets a surfaced road. Turn right.

❻ Soon, just before Y Bwthyn (The Cottage) and 109yds (100m) before the cattle grid, turn left through a gate on to an enclosed path to a field. Bear left across the field towards a stile, then follow an obvious route across two fields. In the next field, the route is less obvious but aims for the right-hand corner of a fence. From here, walk alongside a stream, aiming to

the right of a red-roofed house, near which you meet a road. Turn right and follow the road passing Oakwood Hall Park on the right. At a T-Junction turn right and soon turn left at a footpath sign. Continue through three fields, pass through a kissing gate then bear left along a field edge to meet another road. Turn right.

❼ Head towards Conwy and enter the town by passing through a pedestrian archway in the Town Walls. Turn right on to the main street to return to the start point of the walk.

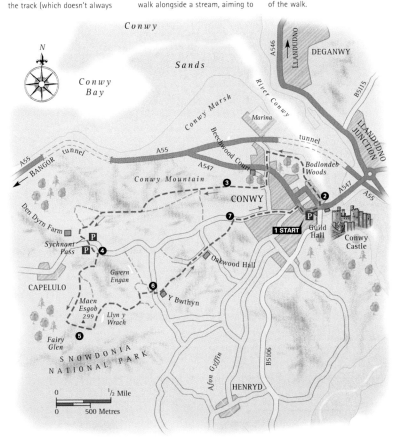

Wales

Watkin Path and the Heart of Snowdonia

Gentle walking in the heart of the Snowdon range, with a challenging option for greater views

1 From car park follow road towards Beddgelert for 50yds (46m), then cross to reach signed path. Cross cattle grid and follow tarmac lane away from main road, with river on right and woodland on left.

2 Leave tarmac lane at footpath sign, bearing left through gate on rough track, with wall on left and rhododendrons on right. Go ahead through gate and follow track curving right to reach kissing-gate, shortly after obvious incline up and down hillside.

3 Kissing-gate allows access to Snowdon National Nature Reserve. Within reserve track runs close to river. Cross bridge of massive sleepers over river and continue past ruined copper mines, and tall cypress tree looking distinctly out of place. Ahead now is bulky flat-topped rock outcrop of Gladstone Rock.

Distance: 4 miles (6.4km) or 6 miles (9.6km)
Total ascent: 1080ft (329m) or 2300 ft (701m)
Paths: excellent to Cwm Llan; poor or non-existent on Yr Aran
Terrain: mountainous
Gradients: gradual to Cwm Llan; steep and difficult on Yr Aran
Refreshments: none
Park: car park at Pont Bethania, on A498 between Capel Curig and Beddgelert
Difficulty: 3

4 Beyond rock track continues into Cwm Llan, eventually bearing right by old slate quarry buildings to offer superb view of Snowdon, to left, and Lliwedd, to right, with Bwlch y Saethau and Bwlch Ciliau between them. This walk terminates here and it is interesting to explore the old quarry buildings carefully.

5 As this is the walk's furthest point, it's now simple to reverse route back to start.

6 A fine, but arduous, extension follows rough path to right, just 70yds (64m) after recrossing sleeper bridge. Follow this diagonal path up to tramway track and turn right. Follow level tramway to where stream is crossed by slate slab bridge, with waterfall down to right. Just before crossing bridge, turn left off tramway and follow stream upwards. Path is very faint and intermittent. Where in doubt, head a little left of low point on ridge ahead, skirting bowl below and then swinging right, directly to pass of Bwlch-Cwm-Llan.

7 At pass, just before gap in wall, turn left and follow wall, using ladder stile to cross it and then keep wall on left, even when it drops slightly before rising again to ladder stile. Don't cross stile, but turn sharp right to follow stony track to summit of Yr Aran.

8 To descend, retrace path to ladder stile, cross it and follow to left of wall. Descent flattens, before low point of ridge. Carefully turn left and descend steeply heading cross-country, northeast. Aim just a little right of prominent waterfall in valley below, so as to avoid cliffs of Clogwyn Brith. When tramway is reached, a short detour right visits ruins of drumhouse at top of incline. Don't be tempted to climb down incline. Instead, return along tramway and descend to regain Watkin Path. Turn right and reverse route back to start.

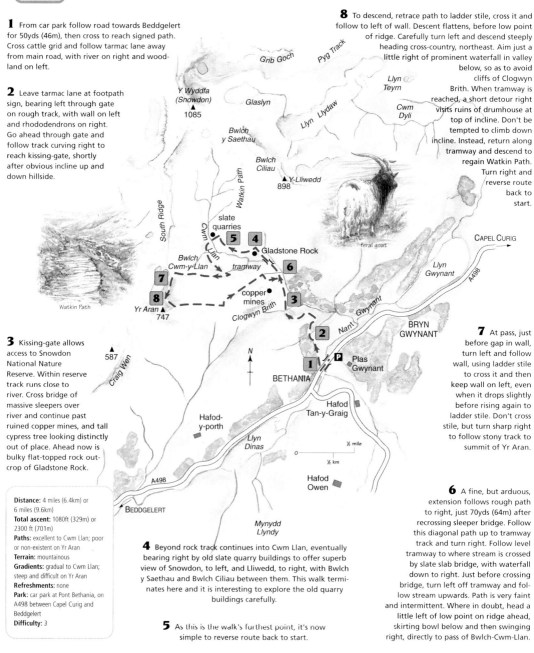

Wales

Quarrymen's Trails around Blaenau Ffestiniog

A fascinating mountain walk amidst the ruins of a once-thriving slate industry

Distance: 6 miles (9.7km)
Total ascent: 1,275ft (389m)
Paths: rough
Terrain: old quarry workings, rough moorland and bouldery mountainside
Gradients: fairly steep in places
Refreshments: café at power station **Park:** car park on minor road to power station visitor centre, Tanygrisiau, north of A496 between Blaenau Ffestiniog and Maentwrog
Difficulty: 3

1 From car park entrance turn right and, in a few paces, cross river bridge to top houses of Tanygrisiau. Turn left on slaty track, parallel to stream, to shores of Llyn Cwmorthin.

2 Cross slate footbridge beneath ruins of quarry barracks, then follow track round shore past derelict chapel. Continue on main track to right of more quarry buildings, and upward, climbing past further quarry buildings to Rhosydd Mines plateau.

3 From rear of rows of buildings (workers' barracks) and left og giant spoil heap, climb the slate incline to the top pulley house. Go straight ahead for 100yds (91m), but just before more derelict buildings, fork left on grassy track, passing right of spoil heap and buildings, then swinging half right to fence and ladder stile. Don't cross stile but follow fence and diversion markers skirting pit, eventually swinging back to re-join original path at metal gate. Follow grassy path to pass between Moel-yr-Hydd and Moelwyn Mawr.

7 Immediately before power station go left on waymarked path behind buildings and recross railway before climbing to metalled lane. Follow to junction just above visitor centre, then turn left on lane climbing back to car park.

6 Follow tramway for 100yds (91m). Remains of wall lead off at right angle right. Follow this down to north banks of Nant Ddu. Keep to faint path down left bank of stream, around isolated building and back towards stream, down to footbridge. Don't cross, but turn left through short tunnel to follow path swinging left, above shores of reservoir, before crossing Ffestiniog Railway to shoreline track towards power station.

5 On nearing high col beneath rockfaces of Moelwyn mawr, the track deteriorates as it crosses boulderfields. On reaching col, double back left for 50yds (46m), then descend on a faint path past Llyn Stwlan's southern shores. Path squeezes between the wall end of dam and a rocky bluff. Go down concrete steps and sharp left to main section of dam. Round end of low wall and return to buttress of dam. Keeping very close to buttresses, descend steeply on path to outlet stream at base. Don't cross fence, but go downhill with fence on left, aiming for top of tramway.

4 Go through gate, turn right for a few paces, then left to large cairn where quarry track traverses bouldery slopes beneath cliffs of Cragysgafn and high above Llyn Stwlan.

½ mile

0

½ km

Llyn Conglog

old chapel

Llyn Cwn Airsiog

waterfall

waterfall

Llyn Cwmorthin

Gareg Flaen-Llym

chapel

Rhosydd Mines

waterfall

Llyn Croesor

Moel-yr-Hydd
▲ 647

pits

Moelwyn Mawr
▲ 770

cairn

service road

Llyn Stwlan

dam

tramway

Moelwyn Bach
▲ 711

Nant Ddu

Llyn Stwlan dam

Nant Ystradau

tunnel

Gloddfa Ganol ● Slate Mine

Lechwedd Caverns

RHIWBRYFDIR

BLAENAU FFESTINIOG

Craig Nyth-y-gigfran

BETWS-Y-COED

A470

A470

BLAENAU FFESTINIOG STATION

Blaenau Ffestiniog Station

Tanygrisiau Station

The Slateman

waterfall

waterfall

TANYGRISIAU

power station visitor centre

dam

power station

Tanygrisiau Reservoir

Moel Ystradau
▲ 296

Afon Goedol

Ffestiniog Narrow Gauge Railway

TAN-Y-BWLCH MAENTWROG

A496

A496

N

ABOUT • CWM TRYWERYN

Beneath the tranquil waters of Llyn Celyn lies the small village of Capel Celyn. Despite the peaceful protests of villagers to save their town and their rural way of life it was flooded in the 1960s to provide Liverpool with a new water supply.

Wales

DISTANCE • 6 miles (9.6km)

TOTAL ASCENT • 300ft (91m)

PATHS • mainly clear tracks, paths and lanes; moorland can be marshy at times

TERRAIN • wild, open moorland

GRADIENTS • mainly gradual, one steeper ascent

REFRESHMENTS • none on route; picnic area by Llyn Celyn

PARK • lay-by on A4212, beyond the picnic area on the western edge of the lake

DIFFICULTY • 2

The Drowned Village of Capel Celyn

❶ From the large lay-by turn right on to the road. (If starting from the picnic area, turn left on to the road – this involves a longer walk on the verge of the main road.)

❷ Turn off the road at a small gate with public footpath sign on the right. Follow the path, crossing first the small bridge in the field, then the larger bridge over the Afon Tryweryn. Bear left, and soon see a waymark arrow on the telegraph pole before the hill.

❸ Head up the hill; at the post with the waymark arrow bear right and head towards the gate. Go through and follow the path downhill to the old railway.

❹ Turn left on to the old railway. Where the courtesy/permissive bridleway meets some houses and diverts on to the road, do not return to the railway, but stay on the road for about ¼ mile (400m).

❺ Reach a stile and clear track to the right. Follow this up to Llyn Arenig Fawr, climbing steeply in places. By the dam and the refuge hut, ignore the gate, continuing on the footpath towards the left over the shoulder of the hill.

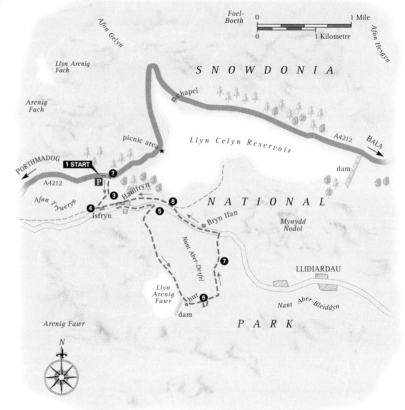

• DON'T MISS •

A lay-by towards the western end of the lake, where a modern chapel stands as a poignant memorial to Capel Celyn; behind it is a cemetery to which the graves were relocated when the original chapel was drowned. Open during the day in summer.

❻ In the valley, on reaching the stream, divert to the right to cross the footbridge then return to the path straight on up the hill. At the top of the hill, take the small indistinct path to the left which leads across to the far side of the hill to your left.

❼ Head for the right-hand corner of the stone wall, following the path along the side of this to the road. Turn left on to the road, pass the farmhouse Bryn Ifan and cross a bridge. Take the track to the right (signed) on to the courtesy path along the old railway.

❽ Follow the waymarks, keeping to the course of the old railway. Where the path meets a private garden and diverts on to the road, return to the path through the gate just after the house called Haulfryn, and retrace the route from Point ❹ back to the start.

Eastern Moorlands

*The exhilarating open moorlands of Ruabon Mountain
protect North Wales from the hubbub of English industry*

1 Leave the car park at its top corner by crossing a stile and turning left along the road. Cross the road and in a few strides turn right onto a signposted track, which curves right and rises onto heather moorland.

2 A number of tracks soon branch from the main track. Keep to the highest, and after ¼ mile (400m) go on past an isolated tree. A second isolated tree stands near a path junction, where the most prominent track turns right and descends. Ignore this, and go forward on a narrow and boggy path through heather.

3 At a waymark post, keep forward into a rising gully, beyond which you emerge onto the open top of Ruabon Mountain. Go forward, descending easily in a south-easterly direction towards a clump of trees at Mountain Lodge, about ¾ mile (1.2km) away.

8 Take an obvious path through a dip, and continue on the other side to join a good path parallel with a plantation boundary. Later, join the outward route just a few minutes from the start.

7 Beyond the plantation boundary, there is a steady haul on a narrow path across the heather moor, crossing the high point, veering right and descending to a waymark post at a path junction. Bear left and descend to another track. Turn right for 50yds (46m) passing a small pond, and then go left on a faint green path to pass around a circular bell pit after 100yds (91m).

6 Enter the plantation and follow the path with a stream on your right, to reach a clearing after ½ mile (800m). Cross the clearing to take the path on the right (now with a stream on your left). Shortly, at a fork, veer right uphill on a rocky path to the top of the plantation, ignoring the path from the left crossing the stream.

5 A few minutes further on leave the road for a bridleway on the right, going forward through a metal gate and along a delightful green track that soon rises to the left above a stream. As you near Newtown Mountain Plantation, watch for a path branching right, down to the stream, and taking you into the plantation.

4 The path later veers north of Mountain Lodge, and finally eases down via a kissing-gate to a road. Turn right and follow the road across a stream and, later, the inflow to a small reservoir.

Distance: 6 miles (9.7km)
Total ascent: 1,100ft (335m)
Paths: boggy but clear; potentially confusing in mist
Terrain: heather moorland and plantation
Gradients: two steady ascents
Refreshments: pubs in Minera
Park: car park on forest fringe, just north of World's End, on hill road between Minera and A542, north of Llangollen
Difficulty: 2

Map labels: WALK 105, rabbit, MINERA, memorial cross, Aber Sychnant, 562 ▲ Cyrn-y-Brain, MOUNTAIN, 460 ▲, 490 ▲, 492 ▲, 315 ▲, World's End, cross, pond, Craig Arthur, EGLWYSEG, 511 ▲, MOUNTAIN, Mountain Lodge, Newtown Mountain Plantation, 502 ▲, RUABON, Bryn Adda Flat, 364 ▲, PENYCAE, red grouse, Creigiau Eglwyseg, LLANGOLLEN, N, Trevor Rocks, Shropshire Union Canal, A539, GARTH, TREVOR, A539, RUABON, aqueduct, A5, LLANGOLLEN, River Dee, CHIRK, A5, ½ mile, ½ km, 0

WALK 106

ABOUT • LAKE VYRNWY

Lake Vyrnwy, a reservoir built in the 1880s, was created to give the expanding city of Liverpool a new water supply. It is now a renowned beauty spot and panoramic views of the dam and lake can be enjoyed just before the end of the walk.

Wales

DISTANCE • 4½ miles (7km)

TOTAL ASCENT • 400ft (122m)

PATHS • good; can be muddy in places

TERRAIN • dam road, lanes, forestry tracks

GRADIENTS • two moderate climbs

REFRESHMENTS • two cafés in Llanwddyn

PARK • village car park, entrance opposite workshops and Tourist Information Centre

DIFFICULTY • 2

Lake Vyrnwy

❶ Leave the village car park at the end nearer the village. Follow the path and steps up the side of the woods. On reaching the road follow the footpath past the visitor centre car park on the right. Turn right on to the dam and cross.

❷ At the far end of the dam turn right immediately down the steps. Follow the path to a footbridge, cross and keep along the side of the fence. On reaching the track follow it to the left, through the gate and along the river bank.

❸ Shortly go over a footbridge, cross the stile you see ahead, left. At the top of the path, cross another stile and turn left on to the lane. In 109yds (100m) take the right fork, (not Grwn Oer). In 219yds (200m) continue ahead, following a blue waymarker, and later round a right bend.

❹ When the tarmac lane bears down and left to a farm track, keep straight on, following the unmade track (blue marker). Enter forestry 328yds (300m) beyond. Follow the track, which later descends pleasantly, for 766yds (700m).

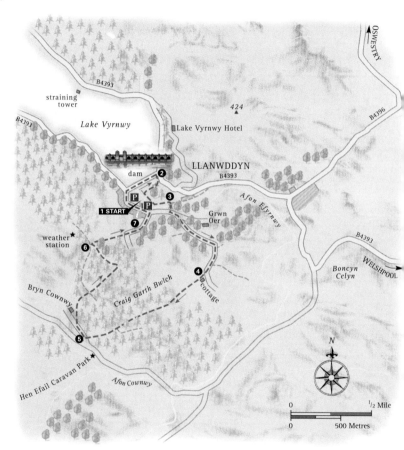

• DON'T MISS •

There is a lovely scenic drive right round Lake Vyrnwy. A Sculpture Trail has been established with natural wooden sculptures, which includes dolphins, otters, a giant dragonfly and the Pecking Order Totem Pole in the areas around the various visitor car parks. Details are available from the visitor centre in the village.

At the left hairpin bend, keep ahead, soon descending again.

❺ On meeting a T-junction with a lane, turn right. Just before Bryn Cownwy farmhouse, fork right and follow the forestry track steeply and steadily uphill. At a crossroads of forestry tracks keep straight on.

Keep on the main track, later following it round to the left.

❻ At a junction of tracks as you leave the trees, look for the waymarked gate straight ahead of you. Go through this and follow the waymarked path steeply descending by the side of the

fence to a stile in the far right-hand corner.

❼ Cross, turn right and go through stile and gate in 55yds (50m). Join a lane and follow it back down to the village. Cross the road, head left then right, and follow the access road back to the car park.

Breidden Hills – the Gateway to Wales

Long famed for their extensive views, the Breidden Hills hint at the great mountains beyond

1 From car park, walk up lane directly opposite Breidden Hotel. Ignore footpath left and follow lane towards Middleton Quarry. Fork right at junction, soon turning left on path uphill through gorse and bracken. Keep climbing through all path junctions to ridge at the top. Turn right on wide track to Middletown Hill.

2 Walk along ridge to summit then down to saddle. Descend left to lane and turn right. Pass Belleisle Farm and carry on to track on left, taking you past another farm, into pastureland. Maintain direction through first field, then follow left-hand hedge to woods. Cross stream and follow waymarked bridleway rising through woods. It crosses a flinty forestry road then continues to climb up to Rodneys Pillar, taking two left forks along the way. Beyond stile in fence, path traverses open hillside to another stile preceding steep climb to Rodney's Pillar.

7 At signpost by fence corner, near lower edge of wood, turn right. Two routes meet up by stile at edge of wood. Turn sharp left if you have just descended from higher route. Another stile leads to field. Turn left along its edge, past pig enclosure to farm track. Turn right to road, a little way out of Middletown, and follow it left, back into village.

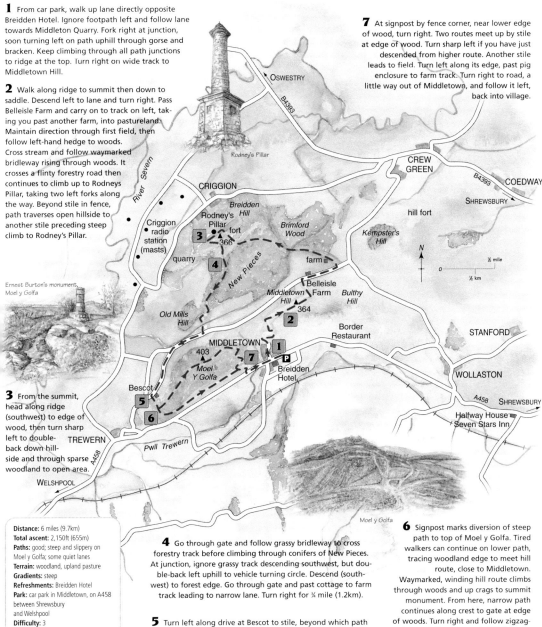

3 From the summit, head along ridge (southwest) to edge of wood, then turn sharp left to double-back down hillside and through sparse woodland to open area.

6 Signpost marks diversion of steep path to top of Moel y Golfa. Tired walkers can continue on lower path, tracing woodland edge to meet hill route, close to Middletown. Waymarked, winding hill route climbs through woods and up crags to summit monument. From here, narrow path continues along crest to gate at edge of woods. Turn right and follow zigzagging path down towards Middletown.

4 Go through gate and follow grassy bridleway to cross forestry track before climbing through conifers of New Pieces. At junction, ignore grassy track descending southwest, but double-back left uphill to vehicle turning circle. Descend (southwest) to forest edge. Go through gate and past cottage to farm track leading to narrow lane. Turn right for ¾ mile (1.2km).

5 Turn left along drive at Bescot to stile, beyond which path traverses afforested western slopes of Moel y Golfa.

Distance: 6 miles (9.7km)
Total ascent: 2,150ft (655m)
Paths: good; steep and slippery on Moel y Golfa; some quiet lanes
Terrain: woodland, upland pasture
Gradients: steep
Refreshments: Breidden Hotel
Park: car park in Middletown, on A458 between Shrewsbury and Welshpool
Difficulty: 3

Central England

Often regarded as a vague term for an amorphous region, the Midlands have always been at the centre of the country's developing communications. The area was first criss-crossed by a series of Roman roads – indeed Watling Street and the Foss Way are still important cross-country thoroughfares. Canals converged on the big city of Birmingham while the town of Crewe grew at a fortuitous intersection of roads and railways. Ironbridge was where the Industrial Revolution started. Moving eastwards across country, signs of industry diminish and there are vast, rolling fields and prosperous farmlands.

Yet there are also a few wonderful pockets of wilderness and a surprising amount of historical interest and heritage to discover in the midst of urbanisation and extensive farming acreage. The Malverns offer a taste of wilderness in an essentially agricultural region, and the huddled range of the Shropshire Hills also rises abruptly from fertile plains. The real upland wilderness though, is the Dark Peak – more specifically, the grough-riven blanket bogs of the Kinder plateau. The gentler White Peak is no less spectacular, but the landforms are altogether different and much influenced by the underlying carboniferous limestone.

It's a landscape well fought over through the centuries. During the Wars of the Roses one of the largest armies ever assembled descended on Bosworth Field so that rival claims to the throne could be settled. The same thing happened at Naseby, only this time it was full-blown civil war. In World War II the Midlands suffered mightily – not for nothing is this region known as the Battlefield of England.

You can walk in Shakespeare's footsteps in rural Warwickshire, and, if literary themes are to your liking, D H Lawrence's old haunts can also be investigated in Nottinghamshire. A variation on the theme could take you to Malvern, where Edward Elgar found musical inspiration.

Best of the Rest

Dovedale Dovedale has been one of the most popular beauty spots in the Peak District for centuries – Izaak Walton came here to fish and Lord Byron compared it to Greece and Switzerland. Late spring is the best time to explore the valley of the Dove, when the wildflowers are at their best, either on a continuous walk along the river through lush meadows and woodland or on any of the circular walks starting from nearby villages such as Hartington and Biggin.

Stiperstones The last outpost of the Shropshire Hills is a mysterious spread of rocks over a pocket of sweeping moorland. Close to the Welsh border, this is a strange, unpopulated land, with peculiar Anglo-Welsh placenames and a wealth of tracks and bridleways to tempt the explorer on foot. The Stiperstones themselves can form the basis for a variety of fine circular walks from Pennerley.

Rutland Water It is impressive enough that England's smallest county contains its biggest stretch of water, but in fact Rutland Water is one of the largest artificial lakes in the whole of western Europe. The nature reserve at the far western end of Rutland Water is managed by Leicestershire and Rutland Wildlife Trust, and you can obtain a permit to walk to the 15 different hides that dot the secluded bays and artificially created lagoons. Rutland Water is one of the most important centres for wildfowl in Britain – as many as 23,500 ducks and 250 different species have been seen since its creation in 1975.

Burton Dassetts The Dassett Hills and the lovely nearby Hamlets of Northend, Fenny Compton, Farnborough, Avon Dassett and Burton Dassett are the nearest you'll get to wild country in Warwickshire. The 100-acre (40ha) country park comprises a dramatic mix of rugged, grassy humps and bare hills reminiscent of the Peak District.

Monsal Trail The Peak District has an enviable network of relatively easy trails based around the former railway lines which criss-crossed its complex landscape. In Monsal Dale you can get a feel for how it must have been for passengers as the trail disappears and reappears in this tight little wooded valley, much loved by photographers.

WALK
108

Edward Elgar (1857–1934) is best remembered for his music, inspired by the dramatic backdrop of the Malvern Hills. It was here that he composed some of his greatest pieces and chose it to be the final resting place for himself and his beloved wife, Alice.

DISTANCE • 6 miles (9.6km)

TOTAL ASCENT • 750ft (228m)

PATHS • good; slippery in places

TERRAIN • tracks, field paths, stiles and tarmac roads

GRADIENTS • some quite steep but not long

REFRESHMENTS • kiosk (hot and cold drinks) and hotel near the end of route

PARK • Blackhill car park 328yds (300m) past Malvern Hills Hotel on B4232

DIFFICULTY • 2

Music in the Malverns

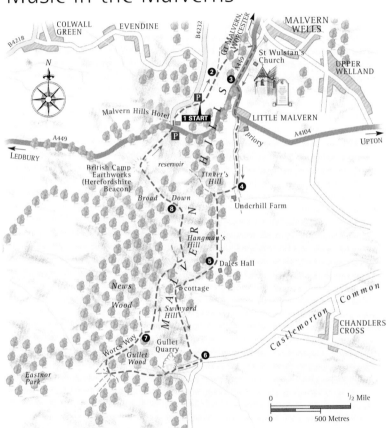

❶ Take a gently rising footpath from the far left-hand corner of Blackhill car park. Walk slightly to the left of the crest to a wooden seat dedicated to Florence Stuart and Harold Woodyatt Harvey.

❷ Take the right fork, soon descending steadily through woodland (ignore crossing path) to reach a tarmac road. Turn right, then right again at the main road,

to view St Wulstan's Church and Elgar's grave. Afterwards, continue to the road junction.

❸ Follow the road signed Upton A4104. At a sharp bend cross carefully to take a bridleway marked Little Malvern Estate Trust. Pass behind Little Malvern Priory, a former monastery, to admire the topiary in an extensive yew hedge. Reach a large solitary yew tree,

just as farm buildings become visible ahead.

❹ Turn right across a stile into a field. Walk diagonally left across the field to a rusty gate, well to the left of a modern grey gate. Continue to follow the path into dense woodland. At a T-junction turn sharply left. Come out of the woodland and continue until telephone wires supported on

double (not single) wooden poles are almost overhead.

❺ Turn two-thirds right, uphill through bracken. Ascend moderately, then later steeply, to eventually pass to the right of a faded-pink cottage. Here a farm track soon joins another. Descend steadily on this stony track to reach a road junction.

❻ At the road turn sharply back right along it to soon skirt Gullet Quarry and pool. Go straight ahead up a stony path to where seven tracks meet. Turn right, signed Worcs Way North, and continue for several hundred yards.

❼ At a clearing go up, right, to the ridge. Turn left. Look out for a low pointer (not obviously an arrow), marked Hangman's Hill, Broad Down, set in cement and stones at a junction. Take the right path to the indistinct top of Broad Down, continuing left along the ridge.

❽ Aim for a partly flagged stone path visible ahead to the left, to reach British Camp Earthworks (Herefordshire Beacon). Continue ahead, descend steps and gravel path, and, bearing right, take any of the clear paths leading down to a large car park opposite the Malvern Hills Hotel (kiosk and toilets nearby). Cross to take the B-road opposite (brief pavement then cross to a path) to return to the Blackhill car park.

• DON'T MISS •

Elgar's Birthplace Museum, in Broadheath, 3 miles (5km) west of Worcester, was established by his only child, Carice. Worcester Cathedral is a magnificent specimen in itself, and also pays homage to Elgar with a stained-glass window showing scenes from his Dream of Gerontius.

On Elgar's Malverns

*The town and shapely string of distinctive hills inspired
one of Britain's greatest composers*

WALK

109

1 From the car park go through the red gates towards the pool's entrance, but bear right to walk beside the building. Bear left around the back of the pool, then turn right across the footbridge over the pond. Follow the path through Priory Park, bearing left in front of the theatres building to reach a prominent lamp. Here, turn right to leave the park, bearing left, then right up a lane.

2 When the lane reaches Grange Road, turn left to a T-junction with Abbey Road.

3 Turn right along Abbey Road, passing the Abbey Hotel and going through the arch of the Abbey Gatehouse. Opposite the post office, bear left up the steps and turn right along Worcester Road. Just after The Unicorn, turn left up St Ann's Road. Go up the rising road, keeping straight ahead through the trees to reach a 'Turning Place Only' sign on the right. Here turn sharply back right on a path which rises through trees and rhododendrons.

4 Ignore a crossing path, continuing to join a wider path (from left) and following it to Ivy Scar Rocks, the largest Malvern rock outcrop. Immediately beyond the outcrop, bear left up a steep, narrow path, zig-zagging through gorse, broom and bracken.

5 At a T-junction with a wider path (Lady Howard de Walden Drive), turn right, soon reaching a seat. Turn left up a steep, but obvious, grassy path. Bear right at a junction, continuing to the top of North Hill with its splendid views.

6 Go downhill towards Table Hill ahead, bearing left at the col between the peaks and following a grassy path down to rejoin de Walden Drive. Turn right and follow the track towards Worcestershire Beacon, prominent ahead. At a panorama dial, bear right off the path for a steep short-cut to the summit.

7 Go downhill along the ridge top to reach a wide path at the base of a hillock. Follow the path around the hillock (on left) and past a covered reservoir, to reach the Gold Mine, a cylindrical stone signpost.

8 Turn sharply left along a path between trees. Just after the reservoir railings begin, fork left along a narrow, rising, grassy path passing above a quarry to the right, then zig-zagging to the quarry base. Continue ahead, with the quarry to the right, for a few paces, then turn left down a wide path.

9 Just as you reach a road, bear left, uphill, along a narrow path to another road. Bear left, following the road to signs for Foley Terrace and St Ann's Road. Soon bear sharply right along the drive to *Bello Squardo*. Go down the steps to the left of the gateway to Rose Bank Gardens. Continue to a road and bear left across it to a road down to the post office. Retrace your steps from point 3 to return to the start.

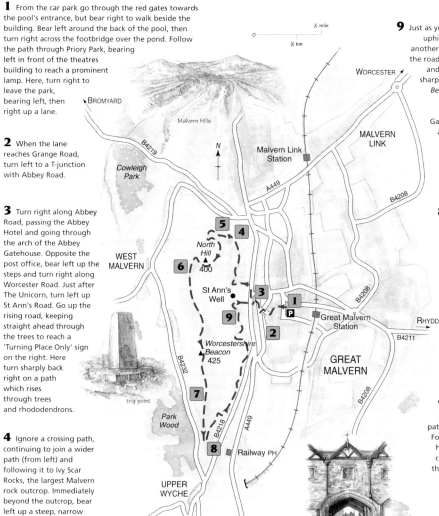

WORCESTER

BROMYARD

Malvern Hills

MALVERN LINK

½ mile
0
½ km

B4219

Cowleigh Park

Malvern Link Station

A449

B4208

MALVERN LINK

N

5 4

North Hill ▲ 400

WEST MALVERN

6

St Ann's Well

3

1
P

9

2

Great Malvern Station

RHYDD

B4208

B4211

Worcestershire Beacon ▲ 425

GREAT MALVERN

trig point

7

Park Wood

8   Railway PH

B4232

A449

B4218

B4208

UPPER WYCHE

B4232

LEDBURY

LEDBURY

Abbey Gatehouse

Distance: 5½ miles (8.8km)
Total ascent: 1300 ft (396m)
Paths: excellent
Terrain: grassy ridges and woodland; town walking at start and finish
Gradients: mostly gradual, but steep on ascent of North Hill
Refreshments: lots in Great Malvern
Park: car park opposite Splash swimming pool, Priory Road, Great Malvern
Difficulty: 2

WALK 110

ABOUT • LUDLOW

Ludlow found fame in A E Housman's A Shropshire Lad, but in the 15th century it was better known as a seat of power. In 1473 Edward IV sent his son to take control of the feudal marches and it marked the beginning of the end of Welsh independence.

Central England

DISTANCE • 5 miles (8km)

TOTAL ASCENT • 330ft (100m)

PATHS • mostly defined tracks; can be very muddy in wet weather. A little safe road walking

TERRAIN • some cultivated fields and forestry tracks

GRADIENTS • very gentle

REFRESHMENTS • numerous in Ludlow, but none on walk

PARK • car park off Castle Square, Ludlow. Larger car park behind Feathers hotel on Corve Street (follow signs to railway station)

DIFFICULTY • 2

The Marcher Lords of Ludlow

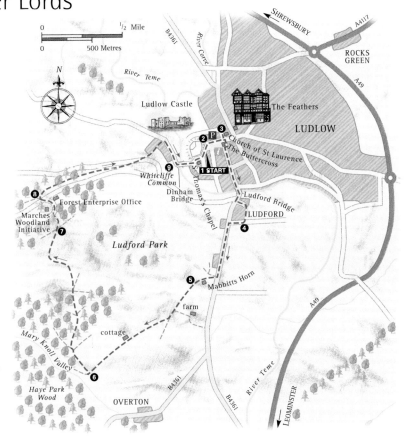

❶ Start at the Tourist Information Centre and museum, opposite the car park in Castle Square. Turn left out of the TIC and walk to Ludlow Castle at the end of the square. A full tour of the castle can take an hour

❷ From the castle walk back past the car park exit and down a cobbled arcade. Turn left when you see narrow College Street, then turn right to explore St Laurence's parish church, the largest in the county. The west window shows several of the Marcher Lords.

❸ Walk back down College Street, turn left and in 5yds (4.5m) turn right through the arches of The Buttercross (now Ludlow Town Council offices) and down Broad Street to Ludford Bridge. Beyond the bridge turn left into Park Road and follow it to the end. Cross the stile and walk ahead, keeping the wall/hedge on your right.

❹ At a driveway turn right, pass through a gate, and continue down to the main road (B4361). At the road turn left, continue for 383yds (350m) and, beyond three houses, take the driveway to Mabbitts Horn. Just beyond this house reach a stile.

❺ Cross the stile. After 219yds (200m) the path becomes a track with hedgerows on both sides. After a track marked 'Private', which leads to a farm on the left, take the right fork (waymarkers). Continue between hedges along this sunken lane for 437yds (400m). Pass through a gate into a field and in 109yds (100m) go through another gate in front of a cottage on to a track.

❻ After 383yds (350m) go through a tall gate before a hairpin bend on a gravel forestry road; turn right here, uphill, signed Mortimer Trail, permissive route. In 219yds (200m), at a bench, take a footpath at marker post 106. Follow these sequentially numbered marker posts carefully, later through a felled area, until, when in trees again, reach a rutted junction and post 119.

❼ Follow marker post 120, with a dense coniferous plantation on your left. At the main track turn right, pass the Forest Enterprise Office on your right, and reach the main road.

❽ Cross the road and take footpath signed Ludlow, which goes left then turns back to the right. This track has Mortimer Trail waymarks on it, follow these to a road. Turn right, then soon left, downhill, at a hairpin bend on the main road. Eventually continue round a right-hand bend to Dinham Bridge.

❾ Just before the bridge is Whitcliffe Common, on the right. Cross the bridge and walk uphill back to the castle, bearing left in front of St Thomas's Chapel, the oldest building in Ludlow.

Over the Long Mynd

Traversing the high moorland ridge above
Church Stretton

WALK
111

Distance: 8¾ miles (14km)
Total ascent: 1,150ft (350m)
Paths: mostly clear and firm, some boggy areas and some parts muddy when wet
Terrain: extensive heather moorlands buttressed by steep hill slopes
Gradients: fairly steep early on but much gentler ascent to the top
Refreshments: various in Church Stretton; Ragleth Inn and Mynd House Hotel at Little Stretton
Park: car parks on Easthope Road in the middle of Church Stretton
Difficulty: 2

1 From the car park leave town by walking along the Shrewsbury Road. Turn left into a road sign-posted for Carding Mill Valley and golf course. Fork right up a winding road at Trevor Hill, eventually turning left to reach the golf course and clubhouse.

2 Go through the gate to the right of the clubhouse marked 'Public Footpath to the Hills'. Turn right and walk alongside beeches, then turn left and follow marker posts up a valley and across the golf course. The path runs around the head of a valley and passes a shelter, then climbs a rise before heading off to the left. Keep following the marker posts, passing a black hut, until you overlook the Carding Mill Valley.

3 Go through a gate at the top of the golf course, bear right and follow a path gently uphill, around Haddon Hill. Use the most well-trodden path. Cross two boggy patches and step over a tiny stream a little further on. The path descends slightly and crosses a wider, fast flowing stream before continuing to contour round the hillside. After stepping over another stream, turn left uphill on a faint path to intercept a wide track.

4 Turn left and rise along the broad track over extensive heather moorlands. Ignore other paths, keeping to the broad track. At one junction there is a view down Carding Mill Valley to Church Stretton. Keep straight on, rising gently to reach a complex junction. Simply step to the right to follow a narrow track uphill.

5 The track leads finally to the top of the Long Mynd (1,696ft/517m). There is a trig point (small cement pillar) and a toposcope. Snowdon is named in the view, 63 miles (101km) away. Walk straight on down to a narrow road and turn right. After passing Pole Cottage (a black hut surrounded by trees) take a grassy path on the left.

6 The path curves right and, after about 440yds (400m), joins a broad, grassy track. In bad visibility you can follow the road for another 220yds (200m) and join this track where it leaves the road. Follow the track as it cuts through heather, bilberry and bracken, rising over Round Hill then descending to a saddle. The path rises to the right, then goes round a steep slope to reach another saddle. The gentle gradient eventually gives way to a steep descent to a gate by a stream. Ford the stream and cross a footbridge to reach a lane.

7 Turn right along the lane, then left and left again in Little Stretton. Note All Saints Church at the crossroads, with the Ragleth Inn opposite. Follow the road as it passes through fields to return to Church Stretton.

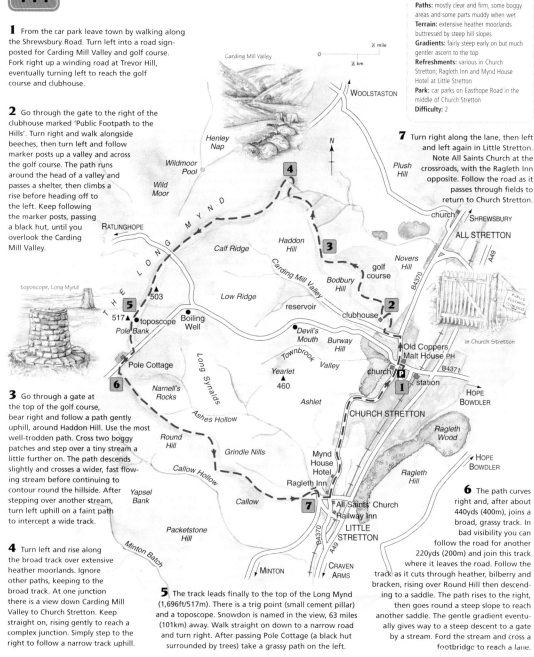

½ mile
0
½ km

Carding Mill Valley

WOOLSTASTON

Henley Nap

N

Plush Hill

Wildmoor Pool

Wild Moor

4

church

SHREWSBURY

ALL STRETTON

RATLINGHOPE

Calf Ridge

Haddon Hill

3

Novers Hill

golf course

B4370

A49

toposcope, Long Mynd

▲503

Low Ridge

Carding Mill Valley

Bodbury Hill

5
517▲ toposcope
Pole Bank

Boiling Well

reservoir

clubhouse

2

Old Coppers Malt House PH

PUBLIC FOOTPATH TO THE HILLS

In Church Stretton

Pole Cottage

Devil's Mouth

Burway Hill

Townbrook Valley

church

B4371

station

HOPE BOWDLER

6

Narnell's Rocks

Long Synalds

Yearlet ▲460

Ashlet

CHURCH STRETTON

P

1

Ashes Hollow

Round Hill

Grindle Nills

Mynd House Hotel

Ragleth Wood

Yapsel Bank

Callow Hollow

Callow

7

Ragleth Inn

All Saints' Church
Railway Inn

Ragleth Hill

HOPE BOWDLER

Packetstone Hill

Minton Batch

MINTON

LITTLE STRETTON

CRAVEN ARMS

A49

B4370

ABOUT • OFFA'S DYKE

In the 8th century Offa, King of Mercia ordered the construction of a dyke. It was to be both a physical border and emblematic of the division between Mercia and Welsh lands. This walk starts in Llanymynech, located in England and Wales.

Central England

DISTANCE • 6 miles (9.6km)

TOTAL ASCENT • 450ft (137m)

PATHS • clear paths, short section of road

TERRAIN • woodland, heathland, canal towpath

GRADIENTS • one steep ascent

REFRESHMENTS • tea rooms and pubs in Llanymynech

PARK • car park off B4398, behind Dolphin Inn and post office

DIFFICULTY • 2

From 'Sea to Sea' along Offa's Dyke

1 At the far end of the car park, take the towpath east for 55yds (50m). Pass under the bridge, ascend steps to the A483, cross the road and walk north for 164yds (150m). Take the lane ahead signed Offa's Dyke Path (don't bear right).

2 Just past The Coach House, take the right fork; 11yds (10m) beyond Peny Foel Cottages take the right fork. Go to the end of the tarmac (ignore Footpath 26 sign). Cross the stile that leads behind the end house, and in 109yds (100m) ascend steeply, left, signed Offa's Dyke Path. At the top turn left and cross the stile.

3 At the quarry turn left and follow the Offa's Dyke Path signs carefully for 656yds (600m) round the foot of the rocks, until you reach a gate to the golf course. Follow the path to the left round the edge of the green.

4 Follow Offa's Dyke Path in and out of the woods along the fourteenth hole. Beyond the green, at a waymarker, bear left and leave the golf course, without losing height, passing through scrub and woodland. In 437yds (400m) cross a stile into a coniferous plantation; 109yds (100m) beyond this, reach a redundant stile in a small gully. Do not follow Offa's Dyke Path left, but keep straight on ahead on a ridge to a stile beside a vegetable garden.

5 Do not turn right to tarmac, but go straight ahead (waymarker in undergrowth), through woods. In 55yds (50m) keep left, hugging the escarpment edge. In 219yds (200m) take the kissing gate into

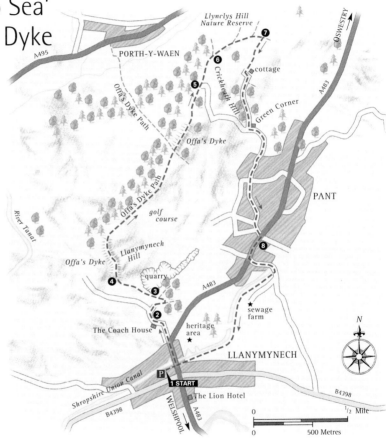

pasture. Continue, keeping the field boundary on your left, and ignore the second gate on the left in 11yds (10m).

6 In 164yds (150m) pass through a bigger gate and go straight ahead along a track (fence rejoins in 98yds/90m). Go through another gate in 77yds (70m) and continue along a narrow muddy path, ignoring the left fork. In 273yds

(250m) reach a gravel track (building 33yds/30m ahead) and turn right.

7 In 197yds (180m), where the track bends left to pass a dilapidated corrugated shed ahead, keep straight on up a muddy bridleway to a cream-painted stone-built cottage. Follow its access track for about 547yds (500m) to a T-junction at Green

Corner. Turn left and continue down the lane that becomes a road through a new estate, to the main road.

8 Turn right on to the main road for about 200yds (183m); just after the 40mph sign turn left down Rhiw Revel Lane. Across the bridge turn left and left again on to the towpath. Follow the towpath back to Llanymynech.

ABOUT • OLD OSWESTRY HILL FORT

Old Oswestry hill fort probably underwent at least three phases of building, starting around 600–400 bc. Once you get to the site, information boards offer a self-guided tour and it is a good place, on a fine day, to stop and enjoy the panoramic views.

Central England

DISTANCE • 7 miles (11km)

TOTAL ASCENT • 450ft (137m)

PATHS • good ; some sticky mud possible

TERRAIN • tracks, field paths, stiles, tarmac roads

GRADIENTS • gentle

REFRESHMENTS • near by in Oswestry

PARK • Gatacre recreation ground. Take the B4580 from the town centre. Where the B4579 forks right, turn sharp right into Oak Street, then first left into York Street, left into Gittin Street and right into Gatacre Avenue. The car park is at the top.

DIFFICULTY • 2

Old Oswestry

❶ Go down Gatacre Road, passing to the right of some allotments. Turn right into Liverpool Road, which later becomes York Street. Turn right into Oak Street, left into Willow Street, then first right into Welsh Walls. At a sharp left-hand bend turn right into Brynhafod Road, later Brynhafod Lane.

❷ Take the hedged bridleway beside 'Everglades'. Follow this for ½ mile (800m), continuing straight ahead where the path crosses the road. At a gate, turn right over a stile (waymarked). After two fields cross a fence beside a tiny brook. Turn left. Within 55yds (50m), before a large oak, go left through a gate, then follow the fence on your right.

❸ Go across a very narrow field, keeping the cream cottage (High Fawr Cottage) and wooded strip one field to your right. Go diagonally left across the next field to the gate. Maintain this direction through several gates and across a track from High Fawr Farm, aiming for the white cottage with a red chimney (Oerley Cottage).

❹ In the corner of the field, by the cottage, turn sharp right to follow the plantation boundary. At the end of the trees, carry straight on across the field, crossing a fence by a big holly bush. Bear left to the far field corner; turn left through the gate and cross the field to another gate.

❺ Turn right on to the bridleway and continue for 400yds (366m). Cross the B4580. After 328yds (300m) take the Brogyntyn Estate driveway and continue for 1 mile (1.6km) to the gatehouse and the B4579. Cross diagonally left, on to a waymarked lane. Fork right of Pentre-Pant on a track. Waymarked fields, a hedged lane,

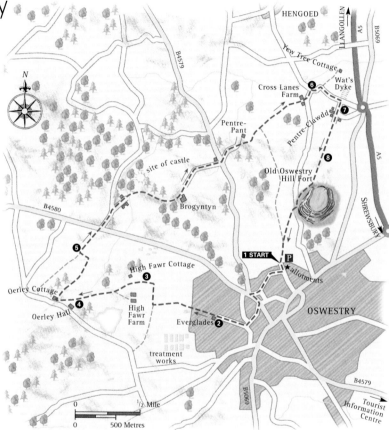

and several gates lead to Cross Lanes Farm. Go through the waymarked gate in the right-hand corner of the field and through the farmyard.

❻ Turn left on to the tarmac road. Soon turn right at a T-junction. Follow this winding lane (ignore Yew Tree Cottage driveway). At the first no through road sign turn

right, do not go ahead. Note Wat's Dyke on the left. Continue for 100yds (91m).

❼ At the second no through road sign keep straight ahead, not left. Shortly pass an enormous barn with traditional decorative brickwork. Go straight ahead to a waymarked stile, avoiding the farm.

❽ Follow a hedge aiming for Old Oswestry Hill Fort. At the fort turn right, and follow the boundary to reach a minor road. Turn left to the hill fort entrance. When you have finished exploring the site, go through the gate opposite and bear left across the field to the stile in the far corner and return to the car park.

Border Lines – on Offa's Dyke

*A walk along England's border with Wales reveals much
more than the great Saxon boundary marker*

WALK

114

1 Across the road from the Chirk Bank post office follow the canal towpath back towards Chirk, crossing the aqueduct to a tunnel at the end of it. A footpath now climbs to the Glyn Ceiriog road.

2 Turn left down the road for 100yds (91m) to a house named Pen-y-Waen, then follow a waymarked footpath on the right, across the cutting of the old Glyn Valley Tramway. Walk through woodland, returning to the road just short of Pont-Faen (bridge).

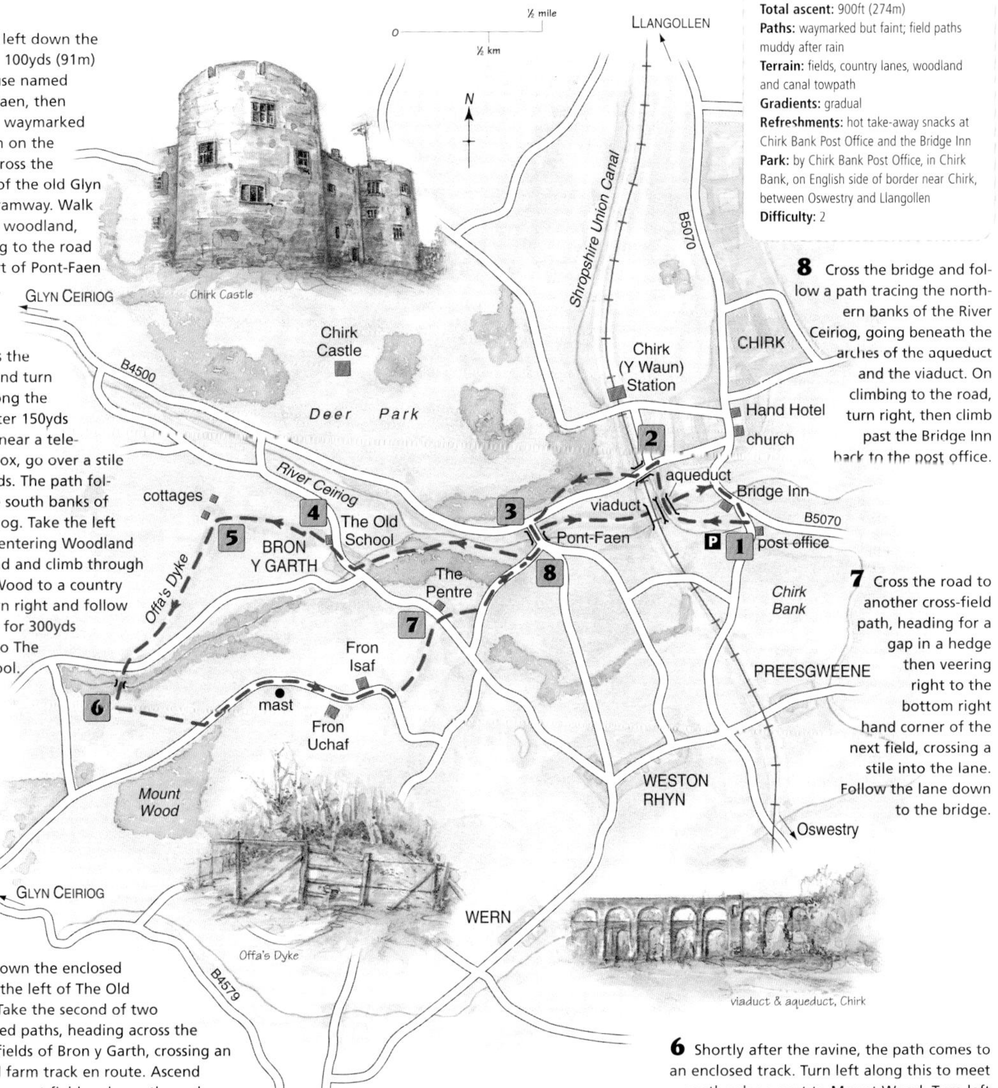

3 Cross the bridge and turn right along the lane. After 150yds (137m), near a telephone box, go over a stile into fields. The path follows the south banks of the Ceiriog. Take the left fork on entering Woodland Trust land and climb through Pentre Wood to a country lane. turn right and follow the lane for 300yds (274m) to The Old School.

4 Go down the enclosed track to the left of The Old School. Take the second of two signposted paths, heading across the sloping fields of Bron y Garth, crossing an enclosed farm track en route. Ascend across the next field and pass through a gate. In the next field follow a fence up on the right then cross a stile. On nearing some woods on the right, the path gets rather marshy, but the difficulties are short-lived. Past the woods, aim for the whitewashed cottage directly ahead.

5 Turn left, uphill by the cottage on a path that now keeps the earthworks of Offa's Dyke to the right. Beyond a narrow tarmac road the path drops into a wooded ravine, crossing the stream via a footbridge before climbing out on some steps.

6 Shortly after the ravine, the path comes to an enclosed track. Turn left along this to meet another lane next to Mount Wood. Turn left along the lane, which descends past two farms. At a sharp right-hand bend, leave the road for a field path tracing a hedge northeastwards and pass through a gate. Continue northeast across another field to emerge at the roadside by The Pentre.

7 Cross the road to another cross-field path, heading for a gap in a hedge then veering right to the bottom right hand corner of the next field, crossing a stile into the lane. Follow the lane down to the bridge.

8 Cross the bridge and follow a path tracing the northern banks of the River Ceiriog, going beneath the arches of the aqueduct and the viaduct. On climbing to the road, turn right, then climb past the Bridge Inn back to the post office.

Distance: 5¾ miles (9.3km)
Total ascent: 900ft (274m)
Paths: waymarked but faint; field paths muddy after rain
Terrain: fields, country lanes, woodland and canal towpath
Gradients: gradual
Refreshments: hot take-away snacks at Chirk Bank Post Office and the Bridge Inn
Park: by Chirk Bank Post Office, in Chirk Bank, on English side of border near Chirk, between Oswestry and Llangollen
Difficulty: 2

Map labels: LLANGOLLEN · Shropshire Union Canal · B5070 · Chirk Castle · CHIRK · Chirk (Y Waun) Station · Hand Hotel · church · Deer Park · aqueduct · Bridge Inn · B5070 · viaduct · Pont-Faen · post office · The Old School · BRON Y GARTH · The Pentre · Chirk Bank · PREESGWEENE · River Ceiriog · cottages · Offa's Dyke · Fron Isaf · mast · Fron Uchaf · Mount Wood · WESTON RHYN · Oswestry · GLYN CEIRIOG · B4500 · B4579 · Offa's Dyke · WERN · ½ mile · ½ km · N

Chirk Castle

viaduct & aqueduct, Chirk

Panorama from the Wrekin

*A walk up Shropshire's most prominent landmark
reveals enormous views*

WALK

115

Distance: 5 miles (8km)
Total ascent: 820ft (250m)
Paths: good, but muddy in places after rain
Terrain: roads, woodland, fields and steep ridge
Gradients: gentle, except for final very steep climb to the summit
Refreshments: Huntsman pub, Little Wenlock
Park: lay-by at Forest Glen, on minor road between Wellington and Little Wenlock, near a reservoir
Difficulty: 2

8 Continue across the summit ridge, soon descending through Heaven Gate and Hell Gate, and following a broad track as it curves past a semi-derelict cottage. After a little more descent, another bend, and a final fling with the woodland, the track ends directly opposite the start point.

7 Here, by a prominent yew tree, turn right and climb very steeply, finally breaking free of the tree cover as you approach a conspicuous rocky outcrop. The summit of the Wrekin rises just a short distance further on, and, on a clear day, is a good place to linger. A nearby toposcope iden-tifies distant hills and features.

1 Walk to the nearby road junction and turn right, heading for Little Wenlock. Continue (with care as there is no footway) until the road makes a pronounced bend to the right, where you leave it by branching left onto a shady green lane.

2 The green lane rises through trees to a track junction close to a group of ruined buildings. Beyond, the track – an old route to the hamlet of Huntington – descends gently, but you must leave it only a few strides after the ruined buildings by turning right onto an initially indistinct path into a narrow belt of woodland.

3 The path meanders through the woodland but eventually reaches a more direct, and slightly raised, path parallel with the woodland edge.

4 Leave the woodland at a stile and cross the field to another stile, before a short stretch of farm track leads you out to a road. Turn right and go down the road until, just before it bends sharply right, you can leave it at a stile on the left, to enter more light woodland.

5 A woodland path guides you down to a farm track. Cross this to a stile opposite, leading to open pasture. Turn left along the field edge and, after crossing an intermediate stile, continue up the field to another stile, beyond which is a broad forest track.

6 Turn left and follow the track for about ½ mile (800m) along the wooded base of the Wrekin until, just as it begins to descend, the track forks. Here, branch right into trees onto a path that also descends, as it rounds the southwestern edge of the hill. Continue with the track to an obvious path junction.

Valley of Revolution

*Coalbrookdale witnessed the birth of industry, but time
has healed the scars*

Distance: 5½ miles (8.8km)
Total ascent: 300ft (91m)
Paths: mostly good, riverside tracks are unsurfaced
and can be muddy; steps
Terrain: roads and pavements, unsurfaced river track
Gradients: steep climb to top of ridge
Refreshments: several cafés and pubs in Ironbridge
Park: in long-stay car park beyond roundabout from
visitor centre
Difficulty: 1

7 Facing the museum gates, turn left, following the road
under the railway bridge. Immediately after the bridge
turn left into Coach Road. At the end (now Station
Road) turn left to return to the visitor centre.

6 At the end of the road (now
Hodge Bower) turn right, then
after 50yds (46m) bear left
past the cottages. At the
White Horse pub turn left,
continuing to the top of the
hill before descending
down Church Road. At the
end of the road cross over
to the Museum
of Iron.

1 From the visitor
centre turn right,
towards the Iron
Bridge. Go under
the bridge and
keep ahead on the
riverside path to
the end, then
climb the steps
and turn right.

2 After about ½ mile
(800m), cross the suspension
bridge and turn left. From the
Tile Museum, follow Church
Road (left). Pass round the
wooden fence to the riverside
track. At the surfaced driveway take the
upper path to Maws Craft Centre.

3 A little further on bear left and take the lower track
to Ferry Road and on to the Boat Inn. Follow the unsurfaced
track ahead for views of the Coalport China Museum.

4 Retrace your steps to the Boat Inn and cross the War Memorial
Bridge. At the far side turn left. Follow the riverside track, then the
pavement. After 440yds (400m) keep left with the road (don't climb
to Blists Hill). In another 440yds (400m), where the road bears right,
branch left over a stile and along a meandering, wooded riverside
path. Eventually a waymarker points to the right. Ascend a flight of
narrow steps here to emerge at a junction with Wesley Road.

5 Follow Wesley Road
(opposite) then climb the
steep hill to the Golden Ball
Inn. From the inn go straight
ahead and, in 80yds (73m),
join the pedestrian path with the
railing. Cross the next road and
take Belmont Road, ahead.

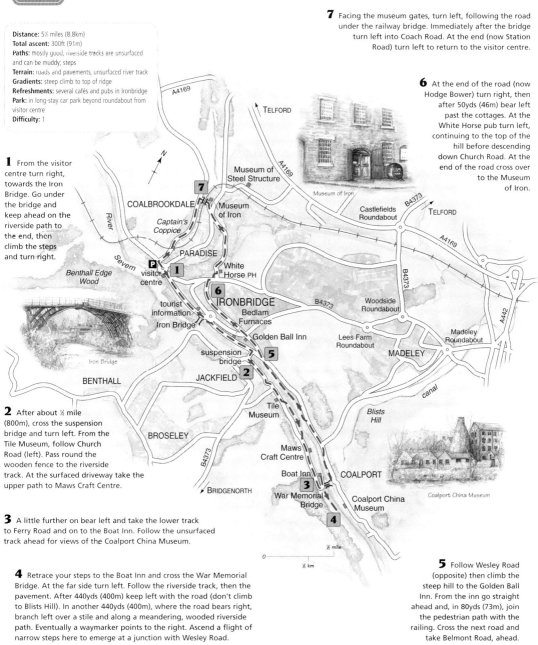

After defeat at the Battle of Worcester Charles II fled to Boscobel House. To avoid Cromwell's troops, who were searching the grounds, the King hid in an oak tree for 14 hours before fleeing to France where he stayed until the Restoration in 1660.

Central England

DISTANCE • 8 miles (13km)

TOTAL ASCENT • 135ft (41m)

PATHS • minor roads (one fairly busy but with wide verges), tracks and paths, some wet and muddy at times

TERRAIN • rolling countryside, arable fields, woodland

GRADIENTS • very gradual; mainly flat

REFRESHMENTS • two pubs passed on the route: The New Inns (sic) at Kiddemore Green and The Royal Oak at Bishop's Wood

PARK • at Boscobel House (English Heritage), open daily Apr–Oct 10–6, Nov 10–4; Dec Sat, Sun 10–4

DIFFICULTY • 2

The Royal Oak at Boscobel House

❶ Turn right out of the car park and right again at the T-junction. Ignore the left turn and follow the road for 1¼ miles (2km), keeping to the grass verge. About 250yds (229m) after a large, red-brick farmhouse, take the track signed bridle path, to the left.

❷ Continue, soon following a wall, and at the end turn right on to the lane. Take the track to the left to Chillington Farm. Follow the blue arrow waymarks through the yard, between two farm buildings. Follow the distinct path along the edge of a field, with a hedge on your left, then across another field.

❸ Turn right at a T-junction. Ignore drive to house with ponds on left, pass through the gate, leave the main track, taking the path to the left round the edge of the garden then across the field to a copse. Bear right to the wooden footbridge, follow the edge of the field, then a tree-lined path.

❹ At the end, turn left and follow the lane for ¾ mile (1.2km), passing Villa Farm, to reach a road, to the right, signed Black Ladies and Top Barn Farm. Follow track, curving left between The Black Ladies

(period house) and stables, bearing sharp left after the farm. Where the track forks, keep left.

❺ After Invicta Farm, follow the track to the left, ignoring bridleway signs to the right. Turn right on to the road; at the staggered crossroads go ahead into Old

Weston Road. Keep left into Royal Oak Drive and follow this to the right, then left, then left again at the T-junction.

❻ Take the signed footpath to the right, between fences, in front of the school at the end. Cross the stile, cross the field diagonally up to the left (or skirt round the field to the right if the field is in crop) to a stile, which becomes visible near the corner. Cross stile, turn right on to the road. Continue, and after about ½ mile (800m), beyond the woods, take the road, left.

❼ Bear left, then right to the farm. In front of the house, follow the faded arrows through the black gate to the left, round two sides of the stable yard, through another gate, round a shed, then through another gate into open country.

❽ Follow the path along the edge of a field (hedge/fence on left), down to a gate in the corner and on to a tree-lined path (can be muddy in places). Pass the ruins of White Ladies Priory; turn left on to a lane to return to the car park at Boscobel House.

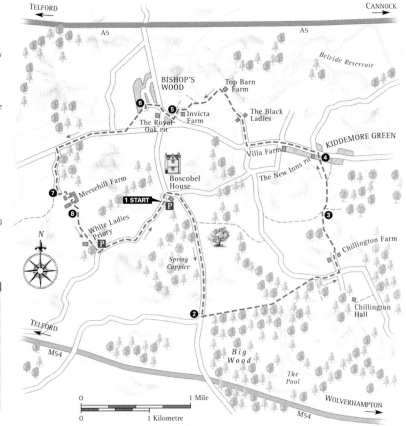

WALK 118

POW camps, a military hospital and training camps, Cannock Chase is rich in 20th-century history. Now designated an Area of Outstanding Natural Beauty, it is a place of remembrance to those who lost their lives in World Wars I and II.

Central England

DISTANCE • 7¼ miles (11.6km)

TOTAL ASCENT • 492ft (150m)

PATHS • generally good forest paths and tracks

TERRAIN • undulating commercial forest at various stages of maturity, broken by views across areas of natural heathland

REFRESHMENTS • café at Cannock Chase visitor centre

PARK • pay-and-display car park adjacent to visitor centre

DIFFICULTY • 2

The War Cemeteries of Cannock Chase

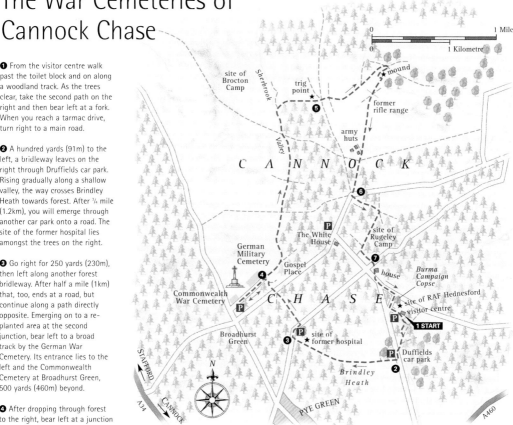

❶ From the visitor centre walk past the toilet block and on along a woodland track. As the trees clear, take the second path on the right and then bear left at a fork. When you reach a tarmac drive, turn right to a main road.

❷ A hundred yards (91m) to the left, a bridleway leaves on the right through Druffields car park. Rising gradually along a shallow valley, the way crosses Brindley Heath towards forest. After ¾ mile (1.2km), you will emerge through another car park onto a road. The site of the former hospital lies amongst the trees on the right.

❸ Go right for 250 yards (230m), then left along another forest bridleway. After half a mile (1km) that, too, ends at a road, but continue along a path directly opposite. Emerging on to a re-planted area at the second junction, bear left to a broad track by the German War Cemetery. Its entrance lies to the left and the Commonwealth Cemetery at Broadhurst Green, 500 yards (460m) beyond.

❹ After dropping through forest to the right, bear left at a junction marked Gospel Place. Beyond there, ignoring crossing tracks, follow the boundary between heath and forest for 1 mile (1.6km) into Sherbrook Valley. Eventually, where the track rises around a right-hand bend to a fork, bear right to climb the valley side, past a trig point to a main junction. Brocton Camp occupied the high ground to the west of the valley.

❺ Continue ahead, descending a quarter of a mile (0.4km) to a fork

above a valley and bear right, rising to a six-way junction a quarter of a mile (0.4km) beyond. Turn sharp right on to a narrower bridleway which, after bending below a high mound, rises beside a former rifle range. Part-way up, bear left along the main track and, after passing a group of huts, keep going to a road. The next section of the walk passes through the former Rugeley Camp.

❻ Go over to a bridleway opposite and follow it 300 yards (275m) to a crossing. Go sharp right along a grass track beside a forest camp site, and after ½ mile (1km), turn left along 'Heart of England Way'.

❼ At a road junction, walk ahead along Marquis Drive towards continue along a wide track to a barrier; the visitor centre is on the right.

• DON'T MISS •

Before beginning the walk, pop into the visitor centre, where there is an interesting display describing the history of the park and some of the plants and wildlife to look out for.

WALK

119

The Battle of Bosworth Field

The dramatic scene of Richard III's death is brought
alive by this walk through the Bosworth battlefield

1 From the car park entrance, turn right to cross the canal bridge; go down the steps (right) and follow the Ashby Canal footpath, straight ahead.

8 Just before the visitor centre, turn right and take the path signed to the Marsh and Sutton Cheney Wharf. This leads across the field, through the woods and along the canal to the car park.

7 Turn into Shenton Station, cross the railway and turn right, following the sign to Ambion Wood and back to King Richard's Well. At the well, go through the gate again, but now go straight ahead.

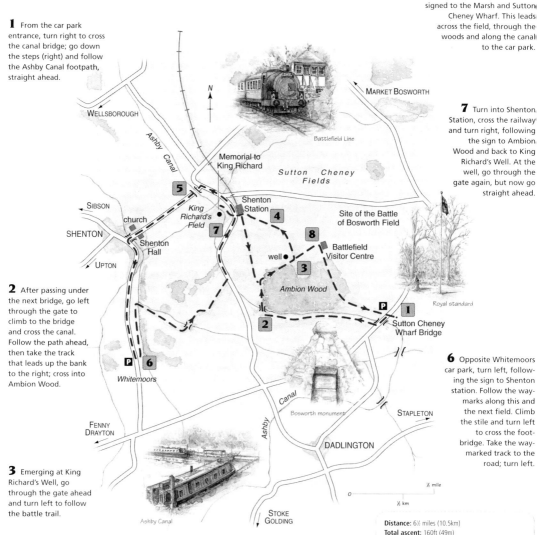

2 After passing under the next bridge, go left through the gate to climb to the bridge and cross the canal. Follow the path ahead, then take the track that leads up the bank to the right; cross into Ambion Wood.

6 Opposite Whitemoors car park, turn left, following the sign to Shenton station. Follow the waymarks along this and the next field. Climb the stile and turn left to cross the footbridge. Take the waymarked track to the road; turn left.

3 Emerging at King Richard's Well, go through the gate ahead and turn left to follow the battle trail.

4 Follow the trail to Shenton Station. Cross the railway (carefully: steam trains run regularly); cross the car park and turn right, then left onto the waymarked trail to King Richard's Field. Return to the road and continue towards Shenton.

5 Turn left under the aqueduct and walk through Shenton village. After crossing the river, turn left towards Whitemoors.

Distance: 6½ miles (10.5km)
Total ascent: 160ft (49m)
Paths: mostly good; can be very muddy
Terrain: woodland and fields
Gradients: short climb up banks
Refreshments: Bosworth Buttery at visitor centre; tea rooms at Whitemoors; The Almshouse at Sutton Cheney
Park: Sutton Cheney Wharf car park, southwest of Sutton Cheney along Wharf Lane
Difficulty: 1

Warwick's Medieval Castle

When not at war, England's 14th-century knights were stars of the country's favourite spectator sport: the tournament

An Impregnable Stronghold

After the 17th century, Warwick Castle evolved into a stately home, whose lavish house parties often included the monarch among the guests. Earlier, it had served more utilitarian purposes and, well before the Normans arrived, there had been a Saxon fort to defend against Viking raiders. Henry de Beaumont, one of William the Conqueror's vassals, built the first stone castle, but that was largely destroyed during the Barons Revolt in 1264. Today's castle dates mostly from 14th- and 15th-century rebuilding and was designed to be both imposing and impregnable. Seemingly both objectives were achieved, for the only assault on its formidable defences was an unsuccessful attack by Royalist forces during the Civil War.

Entertainment Medieval Style

Despite the disturbances of the 14th century, there was some comfort within the castle's spartan exterior and, for the nobility at least, life had many pleasurable diversions. Knights were the superstars of the day and, when not seeking honour on the battlefield, spent their time practising combat or competing in tournaments. These were great spectacles, the champions and their horses clad in shining armour and colourful liveries, which, besides adding glamour to the occasion they served a practical purpose on the battlefield by identifying the combatants. Jousting and single combat contests were popular, with prizes for the victor, the possible bonus of the loser's forfeited armour and horse, and favours from lady admirers. More unruly was the mêlée, a mock battle between opposing teams. Although the objective was victory through surrender, by unseating, knocking down or disarming opponents, things often got well out of hand.

Hunting parties were more civilised. These, too, gave an opportunity to demonstrate skills with horse, bow and sword, and to display favourite hunting birds and dogs. Many castles had menageries, with collections of hawks and dogs, but there were also more exotic animals, such as bears and lions. It is said that Richard the Lionheart had a crocodile, before it escaped into the Thames.

Little excuse was needed for a feast, and while the poor were lucky to have coarse bread, pottage and weak beer, the tables of the rich were a gastronomic delight. Beef, mutton, venison and boar were served, together with fish and game birds and such delicacies as peacock and heron. Rich and spicy sauces often flavoured the dishes, to disguise the taints of over-ripe food. Pastries, sweets and puddings were also popular, all washed down with imported wine. Jesters, jugglers and acrobats provided a floor show to a musical background from the minstrel gallery and, once the tables had been cleared, it was time to dance.

A WANDER AROUND WARWICK   Central England

❶ Walk through St Nicholas' Park to the river and turn left. Past a footbridge beyond the park, continue along a wooded riverside path. After a railway bridge and then the Grand Union Canal, carried high above on a three-arched aqueduct, turn left and climb steps to the canal's towpath. Instead of crossing the bridge, turn right and follow the canal around the town's northern edge, passing old warehouses and workshops that exploited the canal's cheap and relatively swift transport. After some 2 miles (3km), immediately before bridge number 51, leave the canal and climb on to the road above. Turn

left over the bridge and then go right into Budbrooke Road. Walk through a small car park on the left and carry on, following a short length of canal, the Saltisford Arm.

❷ Forced back to the road beyond its far end, pass beneath a railway bridge and immediately go right, crossing a redundant canal bridge. Over a gate/stile on the right, climb left up a tree-planted bank on to Warwick Racecourse and keep going between a driving range and golf course. Where the range ends, turn left past the club house and continue off the course.

❸ Carry on ahead up Linen Street and then turn right, down to the main road. At the main road, go left through West Gate, past the Lord Leycester Hospital and along the High Street. At Castle Street, turn right and then fork right beside Oken House. Cross the road at the bottom and enter a gate to the Warwick Castle. Its entrance is to the left.

❹ When you have visited the castle, leave the courtyard by the opposite gate and turn right down a flight of steps. Go left at the bottom and walk out to the main road. The car park is down to the right.

Distance: 5¼ miles (8.5km)

Total ascent: minimal

Paths: riverside and canal paths may be muddy; otherwise well surfaced-paths and tracks

Terrain: river and canalside paths; town paths in Warwick

Refreshments: plenty in Warwick and at the castle

Parking: car park off A41, by St Nicholas' Park and the River Avon

Difficulty: 1

WALK 121

ABOUT • EARLS BARTON

Earls Barton is one of the finest examples of Saxon architecture and building. Extensive church building in the 9th century marked the rise of Christianity in Britain and Earls Barton stands as testimony to the endurance of the church.

Central England

DISTANCE • 7½ miles (12km)

TOTAL ASCENT • 75m (246ft)

PATHS • outside the village the route follows good field paths (can be muddy) and well-surfaced tracks. Patches of nettles by the river

TERRAIN • open farmland

REFRESHMENTS • café in the village square, near the church

PARK • car park east of the village centre and street parking

DIFFICULTY • 2

The Architects of Earls Barton

❶ Leave the churchyard by the western gate and walk out of the village along West Street to a main road. Turn left, continue for 100yds (91m) and pass through a kissing gate on the right.

❷ Walk down the field, passing a power line post to a stile at the bottom. Continue along the edge of the next field, leaving over a stream. Keep the same direction up the next field to a gap in the top hedge, and carry on along a path across two fields towards Ecton, which can eventually be seen ahead. In pasture, cross to a gate in the far right-hand corner and walk out on to the main street.

❸ Turn left, continue for ½ mile (800m) beyond Ecton and cross a road bridge. Immediately after, go left on to a track descending beside the main road and turn right on to a farm track across the fields. At the far end, continue ahead (on the right fork) along a fenced path. Ignore the crossing track ahead and continue over a branch of the Nene by a packhorse bridge into a flood meadow beyond. Another bridge by a sluice lock leads into a caravan site at Cogenhoe Mill.

❹ Carry on across more arteries of the river to pass the mill and then immediately turn left through a gate into a field, signed The Nene Way. A riverside path leads downstream, past Whiston Lock to a bridge, ¼ mile (400m) beyond. Cross the river and continue down to White Mills Lock, where the path emerges on to a lane.

❺ Walk right, cross the river by three bridges, then turn left into a picnic area. Follow a riverside track past a gravel works and then

on beside a lake to reach Earls Barton Lock. Cross the river.

❻ Over the river, continue through a meadow, leaving by a stile by a mill cottage. From here a track climbs back up the hill and over the main road. Turn left at the top on to Doddington Road and return to Earls Barton.

Map showing the walking route around Earls Barton, Ecton, Cogenhoe, Whiston and Grendon, with the River Nene, Sywell Reservoir, and points 1-6 marked. Scale: 0 to 1 Mile / 0 to 1 Kilometre.

• DON'T MISS •

Ecton's church is another church worth a visit (keyholders are listed in the porch). As you walk through the village towards the church, note the the lovely mellow ironstone houses and the 18th-century village poor school, provided by John Palmer. Long before the Nene was improved by the installation of weirs and locks in the mid-18th century, it was an important transport route. Saxon builders brought the faced stone blocks for the tower of Earls Barton's church along it from quarries at Barnack located near Peterborough.

The New Model Army at Naseby

Across the battle site where Cromwell led his soldiers to change the course of British history

1 From the car park, walk into Naseby village to All Saints' Church and the Fitzgerald Arms. Follow the road signposted Sibbertoft, leaving the village and heading downhill. Turn right and follow a minor road, rising over a busy main road, crossing over Mill Hill and several gentle humps.

2 On the left is a stone monument, overlooking the countryside; an information board sketches out the salient points of the battle. You are now standing in Parliament's front line, facing the King's men on Dust Hill opposite.

3 Continue along the minor road, rising over Dust Hill, so that you can turn around and see things from the Royalists' point of view. When a road junction is reached, Sibbertoft is signposted to the left.

4 A bridleway is signposted at a gateway just to the left of the junction. If the fields have just been ploughed, then note that the signpost points exactly to the crucial gap in a hedge giving access to the next field. At that point, a gateway can be seen leading onto the next road. Turn left to walk into Sibbertoft.

5 To continue the walk, turn left without actually entering Sibbertoft, then left again following the signpost for Naseby. When this road suddenly bends left, walk straight on along another signposted bridleway, and turn right to follow a track past a brick building. The track runs alongside hedgerows bounding fields, so it twists left and right as it proceeds. When a junction of tracks is reached, turn right.

6 The track loses its firm surface and can be muddy. When a gate is reached on the left, go through it, then head off to the right to find a small gate leading into a woodland. There is a muddy track through the wood. When the track leaves the wood, it rises to a quiet minor road.

7 Turn left to follow the road back towards Naseby where the spire of All Saints' Church can be seen. There is a dip in the road, then later it rises over the main road and back into the village. Naseby Obelisk is in sight from the car park, and is easily visited by anyone wanting a short extension to the walk.

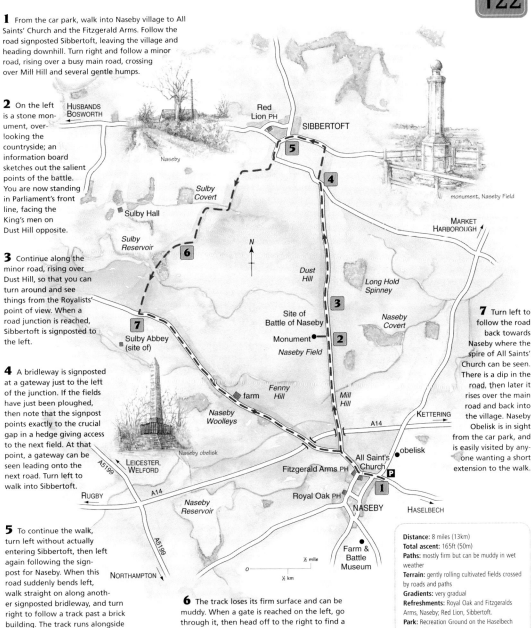

HUSBANDS BOSWORTH

Red Lion PH

SIBBERTOFT

Naseby

Sulby Covert

Sulby Hall

Sulby Reservoir

N

Dust Hill

Long Hold Spinney

MARKET HARBOROUGH

Site of Battle of Naseby

Monument

Naseby Field

Naseby Covert

Sulby Abbey (site of)

Fenny Hill

farm

Mill Hill

Naseby Woolleys

KETTERING

A14

LEICESTER, WELFORD

A5199

Naseby obelisk

obelisk

All Saint's Church

Fitzgerald Arms PH

RUGBY

A14

Royal Oak PH

NASEBY

HASELBECH

Naseby Reservoir

A5199

Farm & Battle Museum

NORTHAMPTON

½ mile

0

½ km

monument, Naseby Field

Distance: 8 miles (13km)
Total ascent: 165ft (50m)
Paths: mostly firm but can be muddy in wet weather
Terrain: gently rolling cultivated fields crossed by roads and paths
Gradients: very gradual
Refreshments: Royal Oak and Fitzgeralds Arms, Naseby; Red Lion, Sibbertoft.
Park: Recreation Ground on the Haselbech road in Naseby
Difficulty: 1

A Woodland Walk in Charnwood Forest

A Leicestershire country park preserves many fascinating pockets of a vanishing landscape

WALK 123

Distance: 5 miles (8km)
Total ascent: 655ft (200m)
Paths: firm paths on Beacon Hill but can be muddy around Broombriggs
Terrain: woodland, heathland, fields and farmland
Gradients: gradual
Refreshments: a variety of pubs and restaurants at Woodhouse Eaves
Park: Broombriggs car park on B591 Beacon Road above Woodhouse Eaves
Difficulty: 1

6 The farm trail turns left, away from Woodhouse Eaves, passing through a couple of fields. Take the path on the right, rising towards Windmill Hill. When a path junction is reached at the top of the field, turn left. This will lead you down through fields to return to the car park.

1 From the car park, cross Beacon Road, walk uphill a few paces and turn right into Beacon Hill Country Park. A woodland path climbs up to join a broad, clear path. Turn left on this path, passing tall oak, beech and birch trees. Open heath is reached, which is being cleared of bracken and scrub.

2 Keep straight on, climbing gradually, while off to the left is a car park with toilets. To the right is the bare summit of Beacon Hill. Climb over grass and rocks to reach a trig point and an old AA toposcope.

3 Continue along the path, curving right as it descends. Banks of bilberry precede denser woods. When a gateway and car park are reached at the bottom, detour left to look at the Native Tree Collection, returning to the car park later. To continue the walk, exit from the car park near the toilets and follow a path uphill signposted for Broombriggs. Cross the road to return to the Broombriggs car park.

4 Broombriggs Farm Trail is marked with yellow rectangles, with separate paths for walkers and horseriders. Cross a stile and walk up through fields, parallel to Beacon Road, to enter Bluebell Wood. When the farm access road is reached, turn left, then turn right to pick up the next section of the trail. A broad, grassy strip has been fenced off and this climbs above the Hall Field to reach the Trust Field. This is the highest part of the farm and there are good views westwards.

5 Follow field boundaries, passing through gates and crossing several stiles. As the trail descends it turns left and runs to the right of Long Stye Wood. Notice boards along the way explain about farming at Broombriggs, with further reference to the surrounding countryside. There is an option to turn right at the bottom of the wood and detour into Woodhouse Eaves, if desired.

Map labels: SHEPSHED, Beacon Hill, Beacon Hill, toposcope, 245, Beacon Hill Country Park, Native Tree Trail, Out Woods, Ye Olde Bulls Head, golf course, Beaumanor Park, Beaumanor Hall Conference Centre, WOODHOUSE, Beacon Plantation, B591, Broombriggs Hill, Bluebell Wood, Broombriggs Farm, old windmill, Ye Olde Bulls Head PH, Quorndon, Long Stye Wood, WOODHOUSE EAVES, Pear Tree PH, Broombriggs Farm Trail, Curzon Arms PH, on Beacon Hill, Green Hill, MOUNTSORREL, Benscliffe Wood, B5330, stile in Charnwood Forest

WALK

124

ABOUT • CHESTER

The 20th legion of the Roman army was garrisoned in Chester onwards from ad 88 and a large civilian town grew up next to the fort. Apart from the Roman-Medieval walls, the city has a number of interesting Roman remains including an ampitheatre.

Central England

DISTANCE • 4 miles (6.4km)	**REFRESHMENTS** • many cafés and pubs in Chester
TOTAL ASCENT • 25ft (8m)	**PARK** • Little Roodee car park off Grosvenor Road; numerous other car parks; park-and-ride drops off in the city centre
PATHS • pavements	
TERRAIN • city streets	
GRADIENTS • one climb to the city walls	**DIFFICULTY** • 1

Roman Drama in the Heart of Chester

❶ Begin at The Cross in the city centre and walk west for 328yds (300m) along Watergate Street until you reach the junction with City Walls Road. Go right slightly to gain access to the red sandstone city walls and turn left to walk in an anti-clockwise direction along the walls, soon passing the Roodee Racecourse on your right.

❷ Cross over the A483 Wrexham road and follow the walls around for 437yds (400m), passing the early Norman Chester Castle, rebuilt from its ruinous state in the 19th century, on the left and following the course of the River Dee on the right. In 109yds (100m) cross Bridgegate. In 164yds (150m) the walls turn north, away from the river; the Roman Gardens are below on the right.

❸ Come down from the walls at New Gate and turn right into the Roman Gardens. After exploring the gardens, leave where you came in, turn right to see the Roman Amphitheatre in 55yds (50m), and the Chester Visitor Centre, which offers an excellent introduction to the city, further along on the far side of the road.

❹ Return to New Gate and continue the circuit of the walls. After 328yds (300m) swing west to cross Northgate and then St Martins Gate, then turn south to reach Watergate where you first ascended the walls.

❺ Descend the walls and turn left along Watergate Street, back to The Cross. Turn right down Bridge Street, with access to the Roman bath and hypocaust through the

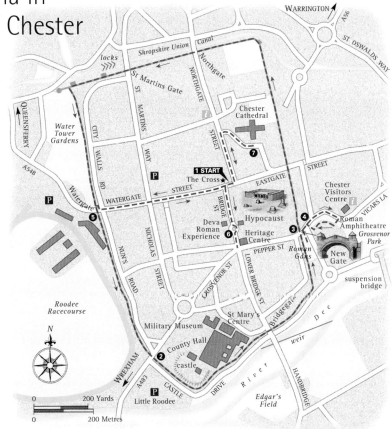

Spud-U-Like shop. (Not signed, but go in and down the stairs to the left of the counter.)

❻ Further down Bridge Street is the Chester Heritage Centre, well worth visiting before returning to The Cross. Here you turn right and immediately left up Northgate Street, until you reach Chester Cathedral which is set back slightly on your right.

❼ Spend some time exploring this fine 14th-century red sandstone cathedral with its fine Norman stonework and rich carvings. Once a Benedictine monastery until its dissolution in the 1540, unlike many Chester survived to become the cathedral for the Diocese of Chester just one year later. After visiting the cathedral, retrace your steps to The Cross to finish the walk.

DON'T MISS

Chester Zoo, to the north of the city, is one of the finest zoological parks in Europe, a pioneer in showing animals in their natural surroundings. At 110 acres (44ha), it is the second-largest in Britain after London Zoo.

WALK
125

ABOUT • MOW COP

Starting near the summit, you descend through woodland to the Ackers Wood railway, crossing the plain below, and following the Macclesfield Canal before climbing up to Mow Cop, where Hugh Bourne launched the Primitive Methodist movement.

Central England

DISTANCE • 5½ miles (8.8km)

TOTAL ASCENT • 600ft (183m)

PATHS • field and woodland paths, lanes and canal towpaths

TERRAIN • paths, especially descending to the canal, can be boggy

GRADIENTS • a gradual descent, level

towpath and then a steepish ascent to Mow Cop

REFRESHMENTS • The Rising Sun, Kent Green, near Scholar Green

PARK • National Trust car park at Mow Cop

DIFFICULTY • 2

One Man Went to Mow

❶ From the car park, head north, following the Gritstone Way and Mow Cop Trail signs, bearing left after 22yds (20m) on the broad track towards residential Wood Street. Turn right after crossing the road and then immediately left, signed Old Man of Mow.

❷ Take this track, passing the strange pinnacle of the Old Man of Mow on the right. Just before a prominent radio mast, follow a yellow waymark downhill to the left for 656yds (600m), across muddy fields (keep to the left-hand wall), and then steeply down through Roe Park Wood.

❸ Emerge from the woodland at a stile, follow the track through the field past a farm and through a gate to join a wide lane. In 109yds (100m) bear right around Wood Farm to eventually reach a metalled lane, which leads left to the Ackers railway crossing.

❹ Take care crossing the high speed line and enter Yew Tree Lane, turning right in 219yds (200m) at the junction into New Road to reach the canal bridge. Descend to the towpath on the far side of the bridge (No 85) via the steps on the right-hand side, hard against the bridge.

❺ Turn left and follow the canal towpath south for about 1½ miles (2.4km), with the tower of Mow Cop to the left and passing the fine, red-brick Georgian façade of Ramsdell Hall on the other bank.

❻ Just past the Heritage Narrow Boats marina at Kent Green, take the stile on the right before bridge No 87 and turn left on the road.

❼ Continue under the railway line and up the hill towards the village of Mount Pleasant.

❽ In 875yds (800m), at the top of the hill, Mount Pleasant Road turns sharp right. After 100yds (91m) take the track on the left (The Brake), signed Brake village.

❾ This soon becomes a footpath which goes straight and steeply up the hill on an embankment for 547yds (500m), towards Mow Cop village. Emerge on to a rough track and turn left. In 164yds (150m) go right up steps pass the Primitive Methodist Memorial Chapel.

❿ Cross Woodcock Lane, pass the village Post Office and Stores on the left. Turn left into the High Street and return to the car park at Mow Cop in 400yds (366m).

DIFFICULTY ✷✷

N

CONGLETON
A34
Moreton Hall
moat
Little Moreton Hall
Macclesfield Canal
The Rising Sun PH
SCHOLAR GREEN
A34
NEWCASTLE-UNDER-LYME
Ackers Crossing
Roe Park Wood
Wood Farm
farm
❺ ❹
❸
Ramsdell Hall
Heritage Narrow Boats Marina
❻
❼
❽ ❾
The Brake
MOUNT PLEASANT
radio mast
Old Man of Mow
1 START
❷
folly
post office
chapel
❿
MOW COP

0   ½ Mile
0   500 Metres

• DON'T MISS •

The Macclesfield Canal, part of the famous Cheshire Ring of canals, was begun in 1826, and took only five years to complete. The 28-mile (45km)-long waterway linked the Peak Forest Canal in Marple to the Trent and Mersey Canal at the Hardings Wood Junction.

The Goyt Valley

A circuit in one of the Peak District's most famously conserved valleys

WALK

126

1 Follow the nature trail signs leading up into the forest. Soon after entering the trees join a broad path and turn right, following and eventually crossing a stream. At a sharp bend and path junction, turn right to arrive at the partly reconstructed ruins of Errwood Hall.

2 Left of the Hall ruins, up way-marked steps, continue on the woodland walk as it leads off into the trees, past some gateposts and the remains of estate workers' cottages on the edge of open country

3 Turn right by the cottages, down to some steps which lead to a footbridge and a crossroads of paths, where you turn left, going up through the sparse trees to contour below wooded Foxlow Edge. Beyond the trees a short detour takes you to a circular shrine, erected in 1889 by the Grimshawes in memory of their childrens' governess.

4 Climb up the steps from the shrine, back on the main path which leads up to the road ahead, which is known as The Street. This was a packhorse route from Buxton to the west. Turn uphill on the road to its summit, known as Pym's Chair, after John Pym, the 17th-century Puritan leader.

6 From the summit, which is reached by crossing a ladder stile, drop down to a stile from which a broad green track heads left above Shooter's Clough (to the left), contouring gently down. Follow a well-marked path, reaching another path. Cross this through gateposts and continue down to the Errwood car park.

5 Cross the stile on the left of the road at Pym's Chair and walk along the 2 miles (3.2km) of partly restored path, alongside a wall to the south, to Shining Tor. At 1,834ft (559m), this is the highest point on the walk.

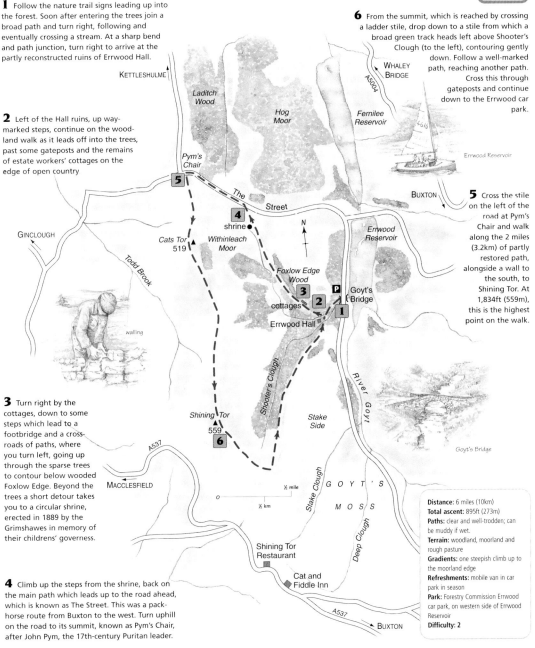

KETTLESHULME

Laditch Wood

Hog Moor

WHALEY BRIDGE

A5004

Fernilee Reservoir

Errwood Reservoir

Pym's Chair

5

GINCLOUGH

Cats Tor 519

Todd Brook

The Street

4 shrine

Withinleach Moor

N

BUXTON

Errwood Reservoir

Foxlow Edge Wood

3

cottages

P Goyt's Bridge

2

1

walling

Errwood Hall

Shooter's Clough

A537

Shining Tor 559

6

MACCLESFIELD

Stake Side

River Goyt

Goyt's Bridge

½ mile

0

½ km

G O Y T ' S

M O S S

Stake Clough

Deep Clough

Shining Tor Restaurant

Cat and Fiddle Inn

A537

BUXTON

Distance: 6 miles (10km)
Total ascent: 895ft (273m)
Paths: clear and well-trodden; can be muddy if wet.
Terrain: woodland, moorland and rough pasture
Gradients: one steepish climb up to the moorland edge
Refreshments: mobile van in car park in season
Park: Forestry Commission Errwood car park, on western side of Errwood Reservoir
Difficulty: 2

Lud's Church and the Green Knight

Legends haunt the strange rock shapes and hollows along and beyond The Roaches

WALK

127

1 From the bus stop below The Roaches, follow the broad track up towards the gap between The Roaches and Hen Cloud. Tucked away under rocks to the left is Rock Hall, now the Don Whillans Memorial Hut.

2 Turn left just before the col and follow a wall on the right, then bear right ascending on one of several paths that climb through the woodland and later aim for a gap in the ridge to gain the top. Turn left along the partly paved ridge path for 1½ miles (2.4km). Near the highest point, pass the hollow enclosing Doxey Pool.

3 Continue on the clear, boggy path to the highest point, marked by a trig point at 1,657ft (505m) and with fine views across the Staffordshire Plain and Shutlingsloe.

4 Drop down on the path, which is later paved, through wind-eroded tors to the road at Roach End. Cross the road through a gap in the wall and immediately turn right over a stile which leads right down through heather and birch scrub to Forest Wood.

5 Enter the forest and after 200yds (182m) bear left, taking the lower path, signposted Gradbach, (ignoring the upper path sign-posted Lud's Church) through the woodland, with Black Brook below you to the right. Contour along the side of the valley and later descend, following way-markers, to a guide post. Bear right (signed Danebridge) to a footbridge where the Black Brook joins the River Dane.

6 Don't cross the bridge but turn left and ascend, passing a large tree, and at the second waymarker turn right, gradually ascending to Castle Cliff Rocks. This is a good place for a refreshment stop.

7 Turn sharply left here, signposted Lud's Church, to take the upper path which leads, after 200yds (182m), to the con-cealed entrance to Lud's Church on your right. Take time, and care, to descend into the usually boggy depths of the chasm and emerge at the steep steps at the far end.

8 A sandy path leads left through birch scrub and moorland. Reaching a clearing after 300yds (273m), a sign points right to the ridge which leads back towards Roach End. The path leads to the top of the moor, where you turn left on a clear path and then follow a wall for ½ mile (800m) to return to Roach End.

9 Turn right and follow the minor road, forking left for Upper Hulme after ½ mile (800m), with the outcrops of Five Clouds to the left. Return to the bus stop beneath the Roaches, and the start.

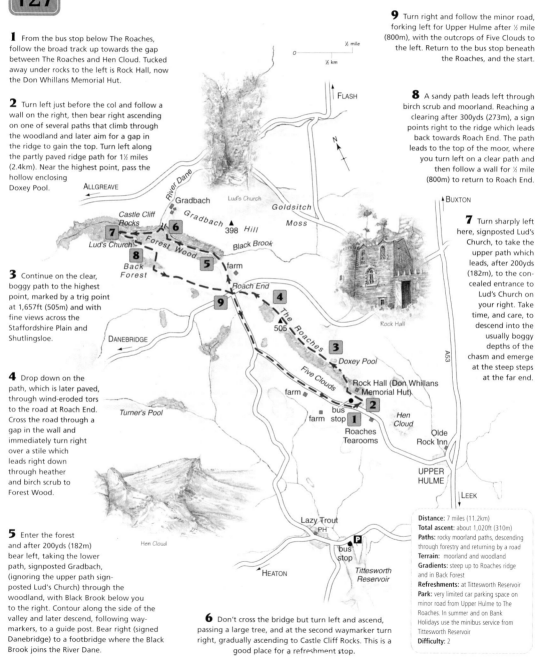

½ mile
0
½ km

FLASH

N

River Dane

ALLGREAVE

Gradbach   Lud's Church
Goldsitch
Castle Cliff   Gradbach   Moss
Rocks   398 Hill
7 **6**   Black Brook
Lud's Church Forest Wood
8   **5** farm
Back   Roach End
Forest   **9**   **4**
505   The Roaches
DANEBRIDGE   Five Clouds
Doxey Pool
farm   **3**
Turner's Pool   Rock Hall
farm   Rock Hall (Don Whillans
bus   **2**   Memorial Hut)
farm stop **1**   Hen
Roaches   Cloud
Tearooms   Olde
Rock Inn

BUXTON

A53

UPPER
HULME

LEEK

Lazy Trout
PH
P
bus
stop
HEATON   Tittesworth
Reservoir

Hen Cloud

Distance: 7 miles (11.2km)
Total ascent: about 1,020ft (310m)
Paths: rocky moorland paths, descending through forestry and returning by a road
Terrain: moorland and woodland
Gradients: steep up to Roaches ridge and in Back Forest
Refreshments: at Tittesworth Reservoir
Park: very limited car parking space on minor road from Upper Hulme to The Roaches. In summer and on Bank Holidays use the minibus service from Tittesworth Reservoir
Difficulty: 2

The Mass Trespass on Kinder Scout in 1932 led to prison sentences for five of the ramblers. However their brave action, combined with many years of peaceful campaigning, eventually led to the opening of the first National Park in the Peak District in 1951.

DISTANCE • 6 miles (9.6km)	**GRADIENTS •** stiff climb to the Kinder plateau, followed by a steep, boggy descent
TOTAL ASCENT • 1,475ft (450m)	
PATHS • lanes, moorland paths and tracks	**REFRESHMENTS •** Royal Hotel, Twenty Trees café in Hayfield
TERRAIN • high moorland, requiring boots, waterproofs, map and compass. **This route is for experienced hillwalkers only. It should not be attempted in poor weather conditions**	**PARK •** Bowden Bridge National Park car park (fee), Hayfield; or in the village
	DIFFICULTY • 3

The First National Park

❶ Start from the National Park car park at Bowden Bridge, turn left and follow the minor road beside the River Kinder. Branch right after ½ mile (800m) by a footpath sign near the waterworks gates. Cross the river, turn almost immediately left, through a gate on to a broad path by the side of the river. Eventually cross the river by a footbridge below the grassy dam of the Kinder Reservoir.

❷ Go through a gate on the right, signed White Brow, and follow the paved path which climbs, with a wall to your right, up the slopes of White Brow.

❸ The path levels and degenerates to a rocky and sometimes boggy footpath. Follow this through a gate and then around Nab Brow, with fine views across the Kinder Reservoir to your right towards the distant cleft of Kinder Downfall – the highest waterfall in the Peak.

❹ The path eventually descends into William Clough by a cascade. Turn left before a footbridge to follow the signed Snake Path up beside the clough (steep valley) into its narrowing confines.

❺ The rough, rocky path rises steeply, frequently crossing the stream or winding high on its banks, passing the point where the trespass took place. Eventually, after climbing a rocky reconstructed staircase of stones, it emerges beneath Ashop Head.

❻ About 20yds (18m) from the top of the stone staircase, a flagged path leads off to the right towards the prominent headland of Ashop Head. Climb the steep, award-winning reconstructed stairway, now on the Pennine Way

(south), which leads to the top of Ashop Head.

❼ Turn right at the top near a large cairn and go over a stile, marked by a sign stating that you are entering an Environmentally Sensitive Area. Follow the edge path up and below Mill Hill Rocks towards the next prominent headland of Sandy Heys, about ½ mile (800m) of rough walking ahead. This is where the victory meeting was held in 1932.

❽ When you reach the prominent rocks of Sandy Heys, which form the southwestern buttress of Kinder Scout, take the path leading off right (southwest) steeply down the crest of the ridge. Cross rocky

steps and boggy ground, then cross a stream in a dip, and head down towards the foot of William Clough.

❾ On reaching William Clough, cross the footbridge passed on your outward journey and retrace your steps around Nab Brow and White Brow above the reservoir, and down the Kinder Road back to the Bowden Bridge car park and the start of the walk.

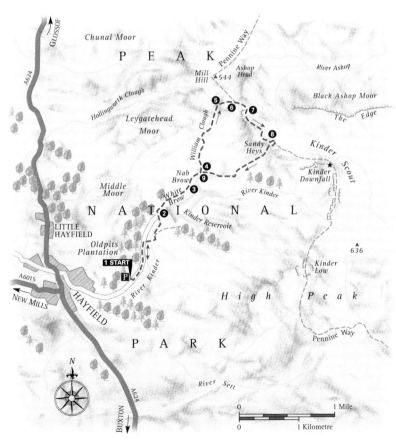

A Walk in the Dark Peak

Up to the bleak Kinder Plateau, where the Pennine hills first assert their mountain credentials

WALK
129

Distance: 6½ miles (10.5km)
Total ascent: 1,100 feet (335m)
Paths: mainly unsurfaced, some very rough; some short road sections
Terrain: fields, peat moorlands
Gradients: very steep in parts (do the walk in reverse for a more gradual ascent)
Refreshments: Ramblers Inn, Old Nag's Head, Edale
Park: Edale car park, signed off A625
Difficulty: 2

1 From Edale car park, go down the steps by the toilets and turn right. Walk past the railway centre and visitor centre.

2 Just before the Old Nag's Head, turn left to follow the Upper Booth and Pennine Way sign (through the Walkers Only gate). Follow the Public Footpath direction straight ahead, ignoring the Pennine Way markers going left. Cross the steep field to the gate at the top right corner.

3 Climb the stile and keep to the track. Climb on, continuing between the cairns. The upper reaches here are very steep and rocky, and should be climbed only if you have some experience and have sturdy footwear.

4 Keep to the narrow right-hand track skirting the knoll and continue to the head of the gorge. Cross the streams with extreme care. Turn right and head south, following the path alongside the stream you have just crossed, back along the other side of the gorge.

5 Take the track through the peat, past Upper Tor and Nether Tor. The path now begins its descent, and Edale appears in the valley below. After crossing Golden Clough, take the path right and keep right on a well-defined path.

6 Follow the path as it swings to the left, away from the village, then switches to the right again, down the slope of The Nab. Climb the narrow stile and follow the track alongside the Oller Brook.

7 At Ollerbrook Farm go through the narrow stile and continue along the path ahead. Cross the railway bridge and at the road turn right to return to the car park.

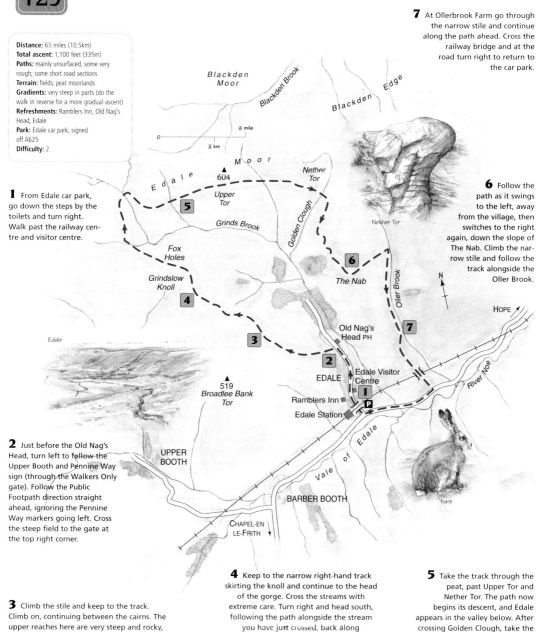

Blackden
Moor

Blackden Brook

Blackden Edge

Edale Moor

604

Upper Tor

Grinds Brook

Golden Clough

Nether Tor

Nether Tor

Fox Holes

Grindslow Knoll

The Nab

Oller Brook

HOPE

Edale

Old Nag's Head PH

EDALE

Edale Visitor Centre

River Noe

Ramblers Inn

Edale Station

519
Broadlee Bank Tor

UPPER BOOTH

Vale of Edale

BARBER BOOTH

hare

CHAPEL-EN LE-FRITH

½ mile
0
½ km

WALK
130

The Wonders of the Peak at Castleton

Early tourists were filled with awe at the sights around this Derbyshire village

Distance: 5 miles (8km)
Total ascent: 1,035ft (315m)
Paths: can be muddy if wet; ridge mostly paved
Terrain: rocky start then easy going on ridge and through fields
Gradients: one steep, 1,000ft (305m) ascent to the Mam Tor ridge
Refreshments: restaurants, pubs and cafes in Castleton, picnic tables at Mam Nick
Park: main car park, Castleton
Difficulty: 2

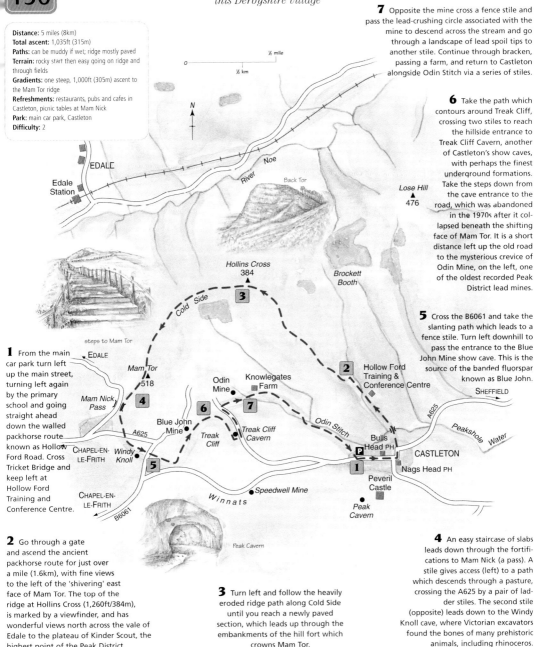

7 Opposite the mine cross a fence stile and pass the lead-crushing circle associated with the mine to descend across the stream and go through a landscape of lead spoil tips to another stile. Continue through bracken, passing a farm, and return to Castleton alongside Odin Stitch via a series of stiles.

6 Take the path which contours around Treak Cliff, crossing two stiles to reach the hillside entrance to Treak Cliff Cavern, another of Castleton's show caves, with perhaps the finest underground formations. Take the steps down from the cave entrance to the road, which was abandoned in the 1970s after it collapsed beneath the shifting face of Mam Tor. It is a short distance left up the old road to the mysterious crevice of Odin Mine, on the left, one of the oldest recorded Peak District lead mines.

5 Cross the B6061 and take the slanting path which leads to a fence stile. Turn left downhill to pass the entrance to the Blue John Mine show cave. This is the source of the banded fluorspar known as Blue John.

1 From the main car park turn left up the main street, turning left again by the primary school and going straight ahead down the walled packhorse route known as Hollow Ford Road. Cross Tricket Bridge and keep left at Hollow Ford Training and Conference Centre.

2 Go through a gate and ascend the ancient packhorse route for just over a mile (1.6km), with fine views to the left of the 'shivering' east face of Mam Tor. The top of the ridge at Hollins Cross (1,260ft/384m), is marked by a viewfinder, and has wonderful views north across the vale of Edale to the plateau of Kinder Scout, the highest point of the Peak District.

3 Turn left and follow the heavily eroded ridge path along Cold Side until you reach a newly paved section, which leads up through the embankments of the hill fort which crowns Mam Tor.

4 An easy staircase of slabs leads down through the fortifications to Mam Nick (a pass). A stile gives access (left) to a path which descends through a pasture, crossing the A625 by a pair of ladder stiles. The second stile (opposite) leads down to the Windy Knoll cave, where Victorian excavators found the bones of many prehistoric animals, including rhinoceros.

ABOUT • DERWENT DAM

Derwent Dam will forever be linked with 617 Squadron or 'the Dambusters'. In 1943, the squadron used this area as a practice ground prior to their successful air assault on dams in Germany, which fed vital Nazi armament factories.

C e n t r a l   E n g l a n d

DISTANCE • 6 miles (9.6km)

TOTAL ASCENT • 564ft (172m)

PATHS • lanes and moorland paths

TERRAIN • rough moorland paths, requiring boots and waterproofs

GRADIENTS • a gradual climb to Pike Low and steep descent down Abbey Bank

REFRESHMENTS • refreshment kiosk at Fairholmes

PARK • Fairholmes Visitor Centre, Upper Derwent Valley

DIFFICULTY • 3

The Dambusters' of Derbyshire

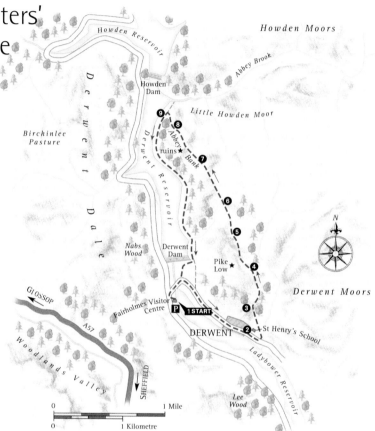

❶ From the Fairholmes Visitor Centre, take the signed path to the road which passes under Derwent Dam. Follow the road to the right, passing through Derwent hamlet.

❷ After about a mile (1.6km) St Henry's schoolhouse can be seen on the left-hand side. Three hundred yards (274m) further on there is a track off to the left with a gate and stile set slightly back off the road. Cross the stile and follow the path as it passes a ruined barn, left, and a private National Trust barn, right.

❸ Continue along the path to the left of the barn, cross the stile and ascend the steep tree-lined hollow way crossing several more stiles before reaching a farmhouse on the left. Here the path divides; follow the left-hand course as it ascends in zigzag fashion out on to Briery Side. Keep to the marked footpath to reach a wall and stile marking 'Open Country'. Here look back and admire the view down across Ladybower reservoir towards Bamford in the distance.

❹ Follow the path as it bears left for 200yds (183m) before turning right on to a broad track with a ruined wall on the right. Follow this for about ½ mile (800m) climbing past Pike Low, a Bronze Age burial mound (no access) at 1329ft (405m) on the left. This is the highest point of the walk.

❺ Continue on this track with the wall on the right. As the route nears a linear group of trees on the right the path bears left and crosses a ruined wall. Follow the path across the open moorland for about 250yds (229m) to another

ruined wall. Follow route signed Abbey and Howden Dam.

❻ With the ruined wall on the left, walk up the gradual slope and at a gate cross a stile. Here the path gradually descends. Continue to another signpost.

❼ Continue on the path that bears slightly left and downhill with the ruins of Bamford House Farm on

the left. Follow this path (ruined wall on left) down Abbey Bank; Howden Dam comes into view. The path bears left and descends steeply for about 50yds (46m) to a sign marking the way to the now submerged Abbey Grange. Follow this path as it drops steeply towards the reservoir.

❽ Go through the gap in the wall, leaving Abbey Bank behind, and

follow the path through the trees down to the reservoir service road.

❾ Turn left and follow the road for 2 miles (3.2km) along the eastern shore of the reservoir. At the dam turn right over a stile and follow the hedge-lined path down to steps which drop to the foot of the dam wall. At the bottom cut left across the grassed area to the road back to Fairholmes Visitor Centre.

Eyam – Village of the Damned

A fascinating walk around the village which sacrificed itself to save its neighbours from the plague

WALK
132

Distance: 5½ miles (9km)
Total ascent: 632 feet (193m)
Paths: mostly good; some parts narrow, rocky
Terrain: village roads, fields, woods, unsurfaced tracks
Gradients: very steep in parts
Refreshments: tea rooms and pubs in Eyam
Park: car park opposite Eyam Museum, Hawkshill Road, Eyam (west of Chesterfield, off A623)
Difficulty: 2

7 At the edge of the wood, follow the footpath along the wall to a gate. Go through the gate and take the steep path down through the wood to the road. Turn right through the gate and follow the road down to the museum and car park.

6 Retrace your steps to the signpost. Turn right, following the direction to Bretton, Hucklow and Abney. Continue along the road for some distance. At the public footpath sign, go left through the gate and cross the field towards the wood.

1 From the car park, turn left, then left again through the village, past Eyam Hall, the Plague Cottage and Eyam Church. At the square turn right up Lydgate and climb out of the village past the Lydgate Graves, then take the signed footpath to Stoney Middleton.

5 At the square, turn right, up Water Lane, and climb out of the village. At the top, follow the public footpath sign to the left. After a short distance, bear right onto a steep path up the field, and turn right through the gate at the top. Continue up the road and, at the signpost, head straight on towards Grindleford. Carry on a little further until you reach Mompesson's Well.

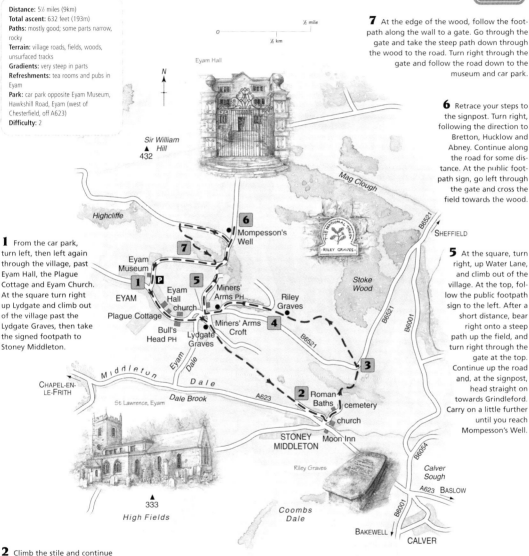

2 Climb the stile and continue along a single track road into Stoney Middleton, bearing left as you join the next road. Just before the stream, turn left towards the church. Follow the road past the Roman Baths and continue up the steep track that climbs out of the village past the cemetery.

3 At the top of the track, turn left, cross the road and pass through the narrow entrance by a gate. Follow the track alongside the stone wall. At the top corner of the field, by a trough, go through the gate ahead and continue climbing around to the right. At the top of a steep climb, turn left onto a farm track.

4 Beyond Riley Graves, continue ahead as you join the single track road that leads downhill through the trees. At the bottom, continue ahead into Eyam.

Packhorse Trails across the Peak

In the footsteps of the Jaggers, whose packhorses carried
goods over the moors before the industrial revolution

Distance: 5 miles (8km)
Total ascent: 206ft (63m)
Paths: generally good but sometimes indistinct
Terrain: moorland and woodland
Gradients: one slight climb to White Edge Moor
Refreshments: Longshaw Lodge cafe (seasonal), Fox House Inn or Grouse Inn
Park: Longshaw Estate National Trust car park off A625 Sheffield to Hathersage road, near Fox House Inn
Difficulty: 1

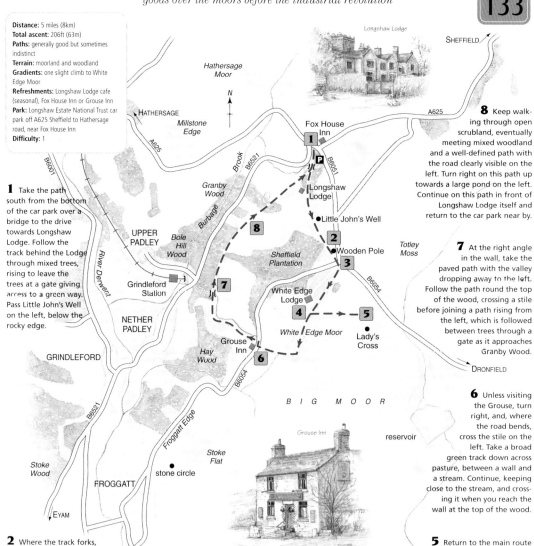

1 Take the path south from the bottom of the car park over a bridge to the drive towards Longshaw Lodge. Follow the track behind the Lodge through mixed trees, rising to leave the trees at a gate giving access to a green way. Pass Little John's Well on the left, below the rocky edge.

8 Keep walking through open scrubland, eventually meeting mixed woodland and a well-defined path with the road clearly visible on the left. Turn right on this path up towards a large pond on the left. Continue on this path in front of Longshaw Lodge itself and return to the car park near by.

7 At the right angle in the wall, take the paved path with the valley dropping away to the left. Follow the path round the top of the wood, crossing a stile before joining a path rising from the left, which is followed between trees through a gate as it approaches Granby Wood.

6 Unless visiting the Grouse, turn right, and, where the road bends, cross the stile on the left. Take a broad green track down across pasture, between a wall and a stream. Continue, keeping close to the stream, and crossing it when you reach the wall at the top of the wood.

5 Return to the main route and continue left (south) along the edge of White Edge Moor, ignoring gate in barbed wire fence on right, until you reach a gate in a wall. Don't go through gateway but take the path sharp right dropping down through the heather to a bridleway, which you join and follow to reach the B6054 near the Grouse Inn.

2 Where the track forks, bear left to reach a gate onto the B6055 Owler Bar road at the Wooden Pole waymark. This is a fine viewpoint.

3 Cross the road and at an Open Country access sign, cross the stile and follow the fence towards the brow of White Edge Moor. Do not follow track on the right to White Edge Lodge. Pass above two small, windswept plantations, with White Edge Lodge beneath you to the right. The way rises to the highest point of the walk, at 1,273ft (388m).

4 To visit Lady's Cross follow the footpath which leads off through the heather to the left. Lady's Cross is soon seen 50yds (46m) to the right of the path. First mentioned in a document dated 1263, it was a guide cross on the Hope–Chesterfield and Sheffield–Tideswell routes.

WALK
134

ABOUT • HARDWICK HALL

Discover one of the most fascinating women in British history in this walk around Hardwick Hall. Born in 1527, Bess wed four wealthy men, outlived them all and inherited their estates to become one of the richest women in England, only outdone by Elizabeth I.

Central England

DISTANCE • 6 miles (9.6km)	**GRADIENT •** gradual and comfortable
TOTAL ASCENT • 584ft (178m)	**REFRESHMENTS •** Hardwick Inn, café in the Old Hall
PATHS • mostly wooded, or surfaced; open fields can be muddy in wet weather	
	PARK • Hardwick Information Centre (signed)
TERRAIN • dense woodland opening out on to agricultural pastures. **Note: keep dogs on the lead whilst in the park**	**DIFFICULTY •** 2

Bess of Hardwick

❶ In the car park at the Tourist Information Centre, face the lake and take the wooded track to the left alongside Miller's Pond. Cross the bridge and at the end of the pond, bear left after passing through a kissing gate. Follow the grassy track to another kissing gate, and continue to Blingsby Gate on the left.

❷ Turn left, passing through Blingsby Gate and follow the firm gravel road. Pass a farm on the right and a blue sentry box on the left. Very soon pass through blue gates (entrance to Hardwick Park) to meet the road. Turn left, on the right is Stainsby Mill.

❸ Retrace your route back through Blingsby Gate, continue on the road and pass through the next gate. Immediately turn left and climb up over the meadow following the wire fence on the left which leads to another blue gate.

❹ Pass through the blue gate and take the right fork which leads to the village of Ault Hucknall. Emerge from the track immediately opposite the Church of St John the Baptist. Turn right along the road until a bend reveals a bridlepath, signed Rowthorne Trail, on your right. Cross cultivated fields to a stile and a road.

❺ Turn right, then right again to the entrance gates of Hardwick Park. Walk towards Hardwick Hall. At the main entrance to the house, and just before the Old Hall, turn right down a wide grass track. Pass through the kissing gate and immediately turn right, hugging the fence downhill.

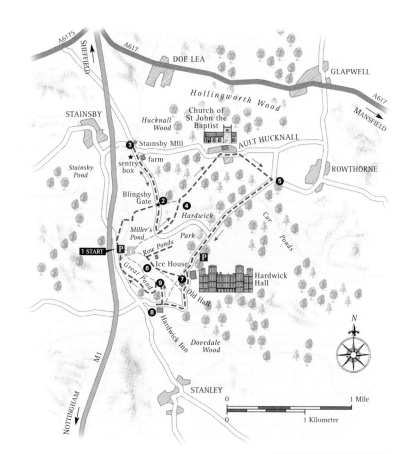

❻ Pass through another gate to the five historic Row Ponds. The Ice House can be seen between the third and fourth pond. Retrace your steps back to the Old Hall.

❼ Return to the road in front of Hardwick Hall, turn right and follow the road down through trees to another gate. This is another entrance/exit to the Park. On the left is Hardwick Inn.

❽ At the Park gate bear sharp left and walk across the field, hugging the fence as it circles round woodland. Eventually pass through a gate in the fence.

❾ Follow the path through the woodland, leading to the Great Pond on your right. Continue to the road and turn right to return to the car park and the start of the walk.

• DON'T MISS •

The church of St John the Baptist at Ault Hucknall holds the tomb of Thomas Hobbes (1588–1679), political philosopher and tutor to the 2nd and 3rd Earls of Devonshire. On its pews you will find rows of beautifully embroidered kneelers, each one crafted by one of the locals.

DH Lawrence's Nottinghamshire

*Tracing the characters and places of Lawrence's
once controversial writing in Eastwood and its
surrounding countryside*

WALK

135

1 From Durban House turn left up Mansfield Road, then left into Princes Street. Take the first right along Victoria Street.

2 Turn left onto Nottingham Road. Opposite the war memorial turn left up Walker Street and follow it round. Take the third right onto Lynncroft. At the end turn left onto Dovecote Road and continue into Moorgreen.

3 At the Horse & Groom pub turn right, then first left up New Road.

4 Follow New Road (tarmacked) for about 1¼ miles (2km) before turning left at the public footpath sign to Hucknall, Annesley and Underwood. The track swings left, running parallel with the M1, passing a sign for the footbridge over the motorway. Eventually it leads you into the woods. At the next junction turn right to continue alongside the motorway.

8 At the exit, turn left (Engine Lane); this long road eventually becomes Greenhills Road and leads back to Durban House.

7 Turn left towards Moorgreen (B600). Turn right at the entrance to Collier's Wood and take the left-hand path back into Eastwood.

6 Cross the stream by the little concrete bridge and enter the woods on the right. Take the track which runs parallel with the stream, leading eventually to a wider track (with a wooden fence). Moorgreen Reservoir will come into view on the right. Eventually this track leads onto a tarmac road, emerging at Beauvale Lodge.

5 At the next junction, follow the Public Footpath sign ahead to the edge of the wood, then turn left. After descending the hill, at the surfaced track, turn left to the site of Felley Mill Farm.

near Eastwood

SHEFFIELD

FRIEZELAND

UNDERWOOD

HOBSICK

Willey Spring
Felley Mill Farm

6

5

Morning Springs

Moorgreen Reservoir
High Park Wood

4

Watnall Copice

Beauvale Lodge

7

DH Lawrence Museum

Collier's Wood

8

Horse & Groom PH

3

Durban House

D H Lawrence Birthplace Museum

EASTWOOD

A608

1

2

war memorial

MOORGREEN

GREASLEY

Ram Inn
Pear Tree Farm

N

GILTBROOK

NEW EASTWOOD

A610

KIMBERLEY

Nottinghamshire landscape

HUCKNALL

NOTTINGHAM

½ mile

½ km

0

NOTTINGHAM

Distance: 8¼ miles (13km)
Total ascent: 230ft (70m)
Paths: mostly good. Some shallow steps; one stile; some tracks narrow and unsurfaced, and can be muddy, especially in woods
Terrain: urban, woodland, fields
Gradients: gradual
Refreshments: Restaurant in Durban House; cafés in Eastwood; Horse & Groom pub in Moorgreen
Park: at Durban House, Mansfield Road, Eastwood
Difficulty: 2

Land of Legend, Lair of Outlaws

*Robin Hood is believed to have roamed this lasting part
of the great Sherwood Forest*

WALK

136

1 From the visitor centre cafe, follow the waymarked path to Major Oak (not the path which goes through the complex and out the other side).

2 Go around the oak, following the path signed 'Visitor Centre 20 minutes', but turn almost immediately left onto the minor track.

3 After about 1 mile (1.6km), at a barrier and crossroads, turn left (before the Public Bridleway signs) on to a wide, straight route of red shingle. The path reaches the A6075 and swings right. Keep on the red path alongside the main road until it emerges on to it and you can cross safely. Take the tarmac path through the woods on the opposite side.

4 Beyond Archway House, cross the River Maun. Go under the railway bridge and turn right before the second bridge. Pass under another railway bridge (with signalbox) and follow this path to the end for a view of King John's Palace.

5 Retrace your steps to the river. Just beyond the bridge, turn right onto the waymarked track on the riverbank.

6 Continue to the Edwinstowe playing fields. Take the lower track (signed Public Bridleway) along the edge of the fields into the village.

7 Walk through the housing estate and along Sixth Avenue. Follow the road round to the left and turn right into Fourth Avenue. At the end, turn left and continue to the traffic lights; cross to St Mary's Church.

8 Leave the church by the Church Street gate (with steps, right). Continue up Church Street, out of the village. A footpath leads back to the visitor centre from the Sherwood Forest Country Park sign on the left.

Holborn Hill Plantation

WORKSOP BUDBY

A616

Budby South Forest

Hanger Hill

Robin Hood & Little John

BIRKLANDS

Robin Hood's Larder

Centre Tree

3

Major Oak

2

Major Oak

B6034

BILHAUGH

Sherwood Forest Country Park Visitor Centre

P

1

OLLERTON

A616

St Mary's Church

8

A6075

Royal Oak PH

EDWINSTOWE

A6075

7

playing fields

6

MANSFIELD

Archway House

River Maun

4 **5**

OLD CLIPSTONE

Eastfield Farm

Robin Hood PH

B6030

B6034

Dog & Duck PH

Remains of King John's Palace

B6030

Culloden Plantation

Archway House

CLIPSTONE

½ mile

0

½ km

N

Distance: 5½ miles (8.8km)
Total ascent: negligible
Paths: good; may be muddy
Terrain: woodlands and fields
Gradients: none
Refreshments: various in Edwinstowe; The Forest Table at visitor centre
Park: Sherwood Forest Country Park visitor centre, on B6034, north of Edwinstowe
Difficulty: 1

WALK 137

Laxton, a tiny village east of Ollerton, is a survival of the open-field system of agriculture, common during the Middle Ages. All the village farmers can use the land and the system is still administered by the Court Leet, which meets annually at the Dovecote Inn.

Central England

DISTANCE • 2½ miles (4km)

TOTAL ASCENT • 33ft (10m)

PATHS • field paths and lanes

TERRAIN • the deep hollow ways can be very wet and muddy after rain

GRADIENTS • none of any note

REFRESHMENTS • the Dovecote Inn, Laxton

PARK • Laxton village car park, next to the Dovecote Inn and Laxton Visitor Centre

DIFFICULTY • 1

A Little Bit of Old England

❶ From the village car park walk past the Dovecote Inn and turn left on the road, passing the site of the pinfold (for stray animals) down the Kneesall road for about ½ mile (800m), bearing right at the junction with the Moorhouse road.

❷ After about 200yds (183m), turn right by the second wooden footpath sign on to the broad, muddy trackway of the Langsyke. This leads up through a gate and an avenue of young beeches into a hollow way and out on to Mill Field, the largest of the three great open fields of Laxton. In summer, if the field is in arable use, you will be able to see different crops growing in the strips.

❸ Ascend the broad green headland for about 500yds (457m), turning sharp right at a prominent interpretative sign on to a metalled farm track which leads out to the Ollerton road. After crossing the road, follow a grassy, often wet hollow way, turning right at the junction with another towards the end of the main street of the village, with the church tower ahead.

❹ Just before reaching the street, turn left on to a farm track. After about 150yds (137m), leave the track, turning right over a stile by a notice board which is partly hidden by the hedge.

❺ Cross another stile which leads across the West Field via Hall, or Back, Lane, a muddy, deeply-hedged green track. Follow the lane for about 500yds (457m), where a gate and sign on your left leads across a field towards the motte and bailey castle, following

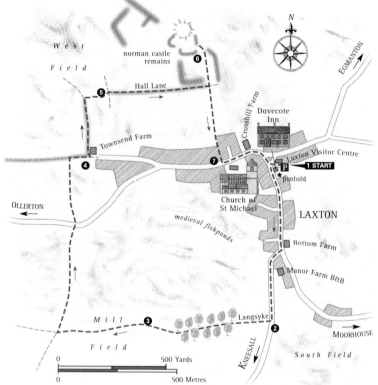

the green arrows of the former MAFF (Ministry of Agriculture, Fisheries, and Food) conservation walk.

❻ Retrace your steps back to the lane, where you go straight ahead arriving back in the village almost opposite the church.

❼ Turn left to walk down the main street and back to the car park.

• DON'T MISS •

It is worth stopping at the visitor centre in Laxton, which offers lots of information on the open-field system of farming. And don't miss the beautiful, mainly 13th-century, decorated parish Church of St Michael, the Archangel. The church had fallen into disuse and 'impious neglect' until it was remodelled by Earl Manvers, the lord of the manor, in 1854. He dismantled and rebuilt the tower, and shortened the nave by one bay. You'll also find the well-preserved mound of a motte-and-bailey castle in the village.

Huge Skyscapes above the Wash

The wind and tide add drama to an otherwise empty landscape

WALK

138

1 From parking space follow path signed Freiston Shore Marsh, passing through metal gate and crossing up and over inner sea bank. Follow path to left (Prison road signed right), then curve right almost immediately to go straight on towards outer sea bank. About ½ mile (800m) further on, just before pumping station, go right through 2 metal gates and onto outer sea bank. Follow bank to left.

7 Follow bank for 1 mile (1.6km) before route turns sharp left, then straight ahead to emerge onto another minor road. Turn right and walk towards distant houses. At T-junction turn left back towards parking area.

2 After 2 miles (3.2km) turn right by another pumping station, leaving outer sea wall, to follow path alongside drainage ditch for ¼ mile (400m) to inner sea bank. Ignore private farm road parallel to bank and climb stile onto inner sea bank, following it right for 1½ miles (2.4km), passing several pill boxes and crossing 3 stiles.

6 Bank emerges onto minor road opposite white house called Chimnies. Path continues to right of house, then into open ground with farmland below bank right and left. Inner bank clearly visible to left. In distance, right, the Stump of Boston's St Botolph's Church can be seen on a clear day.

3 At another brick pumping station and red stone tablet in middle of bank, turn left down track leading away from pumping station, with wide drainage ditch on right.

5 Stick to overgrown path as it passes buildings for short distance to road by pond on right. Turn right onto road, then almost immediately left as bank continues. Walk on road, with crest of bank to right. When road swings right, bisecting bank, clamber through woodland to left. Avenue of trees along top of bank persists, with arrows carved in some trees at intervals. After ¾ mile (1.2km), path takes sharp left turn and heads almost directly back towards second pumping station. However, after 120yds (109m) turn sharply right to continue in former direction for another ¾ mile (1.2km).

Distance: 8 miles (12.9km)
Total ascent: negligible
Paths: generally clear; some may be overgrown and muddy
Terrain: sea banks overlooking sea marshes and farmland
Gradients: some short steps up banks
Refreshments: none
Park: by the telephone kiosk in Freiston Shore
Difficulty: 2

4 In ½ mile (800m) continue down track 150yds (136m) beyond farm buildings on left to third, much older sea bank. As track cuts through bank, climb stile to left onto bank and go along crest. Natural avenue of trees marks route, crossing tracks as they cut through it. Eventually, after ¾ mile (1.2km), route springs out from trees into open land. Follow bank to farm visible in Benington Sea End, about ½ mile (800m) ahead.

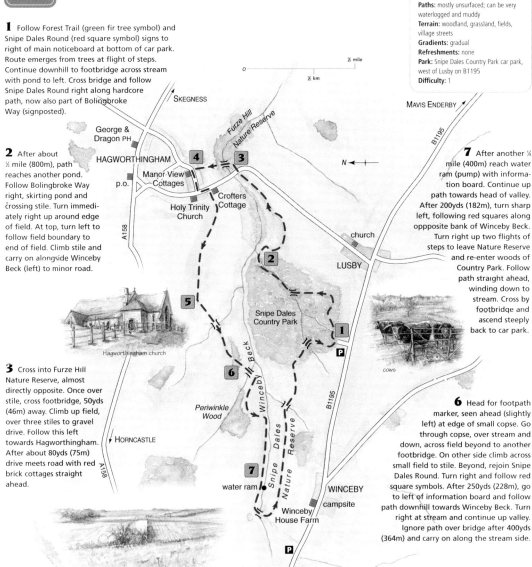

WALK 139

The Edge of the Wolds

*Rising from the flatlands, the Lincolnshire Wolds at
Snipe Dales conceal a rich variety of wildlife*

Distance: 5 miles (8km)
Total Ascent: 170 feet (51m)
Paths: mostly unsurfaced; can be very
waterlogged and muddy
Terrain: woodland, grassland, fields,
village streets
Gradients: gradual
Refreshments: none
Park: Snipe Dales Country Park car park,
west of Lusby on B1195
Difficulty: 1

1 Follow Forest Trail (green fir tree symbol) and
Snipe Dales Round (red square symbol) signs to
right of main noticeboard at bottom of car park.
Route emerges from trees at flight of steps.
Continue downhill to footbridge across stream
with pond to left. Cross bridge and follow
Snipe Dales Round right along hardcore
path, now also part of Bolingbroke
Way (signposted).

2 After about
½ mile (800m), path
reaches another pond.
Follow Bolingbroke Way
right, skirting pond and
crossing stile. Turn immediately right up around edge
of field. At top, turn left to
follow field boundary to
end of field. Climb stile and
carry on alongside Winceby
Beck (left) to minor road.

3 Cross into Furze Hill
Nature Reserve, almost
directly opposite. Once over
stile, cross footbridge, 50yds
(46m) away. Climb up field,
over three stiles to gravel
drive. Follow this left
towards Hagworthingham.
After about 80yds (75m)
drive meets road with red
brick cottages straight
ahead.

7 After another ¼
mile (400m) reach water
ram (pump) with informa-
tion board. Continue up
path towards head of valley.
After 200yds (182m), turn sharp
left, following red squares along
oppposite bank of Winceby Beck.
Turn right up two flights of
steps to leave Nature Reserve
and re-enter woods of
Country Park. Follow
path straight ahead,
winding down to
stream. Cross by
footbridge and
ascend steeply
back to car park.

6 Head for footpath
marker, seen ahead (slightly
left) at edge of small copse. Go
through copse, over stream and
down, across field beyond to another
footbridge. On other side climb across
small field to stile. Beyond, rejoin Snipe
Dales Round. Turn right and follow red
square symbols. After 250yds (228m), go
to left of information board and follow
path downhill towards Winceby Beck. Turn
right at stream and continue up valley.
Ignore path over bridge after 400yds
(364m) and carry on along the stream side.

4 Turn left and follow road through edge of village to road
back to Lusby. Turn left and head out of village for 100yds
(91m), where stile leads to footpath to right of Crofters
Cottage. Follow narrow, green belt between two houses to
another stile, then go straight ahead across several fields.

5 Path heads down after third field turning, first sharply
right, then left, before entering an open field. Cross footbridge at far edge of field and continue straight ahead to
stile. Cross this and another stile, heading straight ahead
then bearing left to top of rise in field.

WALK

140

Follow in the footsteps of the poet Alfred Lord Tennyson (1809–92). The walk begins at The White Hart Inn, frequented by Tennyson who is reputed to have enjoyed a drink by the fire, and takes you to his birthplace, a rambling, yew-fronted rectory.

Central England

DISTANCE • 5 miles (8km)	**REFRESHMENTS** • White Hart Inn and Cross Keys
TOTAL ASCENT • 65ft (20m)	
PATHS • good	**PARK** • White Hart Inn (ask permission beforehand)
TERRAIN • surface roads, grassy fields, cultivated fields	**DIFFICULTY** • 2
GRADIENTS • slight	

Tennyson's Home in Somersby

1 Turn left out of The White Hart Inn and follow the road round to the left through the village. Continue until you reach a fork in the road, take the right fork past the attractive stableyard on the right.

2 At the next junction, with Wood Farm on the right, turn left and continue past the old school building on the right.

3 Follow the road as it bends left past the new doctor's surgery and continue to the junction overlooked by a war memorial. Turn right at the memorial and continue towards the Cross Keys pub. Turn left on to the public bridleway just before the pub.

4 Stroll along this pretty, grassy track through the corridors of brambles before entering more open countryside. When the bridleway meets a public footpath ensure that you follow the bridleway, keeping the open fields to your left and the hedge and earth bank to your right. When the path meets a minor road, turn left and walk along the road alongside

a shallow wood.

5 As you walk along this road note the small carved face in the rocky outcrop set back to the left-hand side of the road. Pass the junction signed Ashby Puerorum and Horncastle and carry on into Somersby village. Look for Grange Cottage on the right with its white fence, and then next door, the

birthplace of Tennyson. Opposite is the church where Tennyson's father was rector.

6 Walk through the churchyard and around to a gate diagonally opposite the entrance. Turn left along the road until you come to Somersby House Farm. Turn right up the birdleway opposite the farm. Continue to Warden Hill Cottage. Turn left through the outbuildings, following the footpath signposts.

7 At the edge of Warden Woods turn left down a limestone path

with the wood on your right. As the path rises again at the end of the wood, turn right and follow the path along the bottom edge of the wood. At the T-junction turn left and follow the bridleway up and over the hill.

8 As you go down the hill note the no right of way over the stile. Follow the track down to the road, turn left then right on to a footpath over a footbridge. Trek across a lovely chain of fields to St Mary's Church in Tetford. Pass through the graveyard to the road, turn left and return to the White Hart Inn.

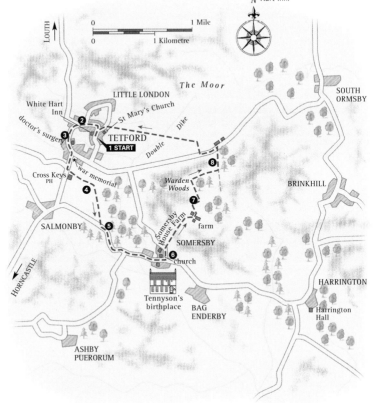

Northern England

Bounded east and west by the North Sea and the Irish Sea respectively, and along its northern frontier by the Anglo-Scottish border, the north of England possesses landscapes that are breathtakingly beautiful, exciting, wild and desolate. Here there are rugged heights, delectable dales, invigorating coastal margins, windswept moorlands, rivers, lakes, forests, towns, villages, folklore, wildlife, history, intrigue and mystery in great abundance.

Down the centre of the region, the Pennines form the geological 'backbone of England'. The Dales, of course, are renowned for their outstanding natural beauty and dramatic scenery, as at Malham Cove, a favourite with walkers, rock climbers and botanists alike. Above lies a spread of limestone pavement, one of Britain's rarest habitats. Apart from the fascinating shapes of the rock formations, the special interest of limestone pavement lies in its plant life, which includes 18 rare or scarce species, and in its record of glacial and post-glacial history.

Rare and beautiful too, are the landscapes of Cumbria and the North York Moors, the coast and the quiet folds of Northumberland and Durham.

That this landscape is an important part of our national heritage is demonstrated by the designation in this region of four national parks, six Areas of Outstanding Natural Beauty, 41 national nature reserves, and innumerable Sites of Special Scientific Interest.

At the northern edge stands Hadrian's Wall, the greatest extant example of Roman determination in Britain. Everywhere is at peace now but, long after the Romans had gone, the lands of the north were a violent and troubled place, where rustlers, outlaws and gangsters from both sides terrorised the Anglo-Scottish border, and spawned the building of fortified castles and strongholds.

Elsewhere, mystery surrounds the tales of witchcraft and stone circles, while the joys of wilderness walking lead you into the rolling fells of the Forest of Bowland. Literary associations are woven through the fabric of the north, with the Lake Poets, Lewis Carroll, and the Brontë sisters featuring here.

Best of the Rest

Wharfedale Most visited of the Yorkshire Dales, Wharfedale never fails to captivate with its rich and varied scenery. Away from the honeypots of Bolton Abbey and Grassington there is a wide choice of excellent footpaths across liberating open moorlands. On the moors between Grassington and nearby Hebden, extensive remains of lead-mining remind you that life was once much harder for Dales folk.

North York Moors The Cleveland Way follows the escarpment of the Hambleton and Cleveland Hills before turning south again to follow the coastline to Scarborough. The best parts of the inland, moorland section can be found above Osmotherley, with enormous views across the Vale of York and north towards County Durham the reward for comparatively little effort.

Cheviots In the last hills in England, deep valleys incise the huge rounded grasslands, making for excellent, remote, but quite straightforward walking. Around Ingram particularly, permissive paths have been linked up to make a series of walks which epitomise the Cheviot landscape of mountain sheepwalks and ancient settlement remains.

Howgills Like the Cheviots, the Howgills are rounded grassy mountains, cut by deep valleys leading to their remote heart. However, they cover a much smaller area, in the 'no-man's land' between the Yorkshire Dales and the Lake District, and all their exhilarating high ridges can be traversed in a few days of good walking. A favourite is the ascent of the Calf via Winder from Sedbergh, returning by Cautley Spout.

Duddon Bridge This is one of the quietest corners of the Lake District. Tourists are rarely noticed and local folk have a high regard for its hidden delights. The lovely Swinside Stone Circle sits in a quiet hollow in the hills high above the estuary of the River Duddon. It is a late neolithic or early Bronze Age structure, with its stones closely packed together, and it appears to be aligned on the Midwinter Solstice.

Garrigill The valley of the River South Tyne hides away in the North Pennines Area of Outstanding Natural Beauty. Amidst the high moorlands and below the shadow of Cross Fell, miners and farmers eked out a living from this hostile environment. Their legacy is a fine network of footpaths and bridleways across delightful meadows and high pasture, connecting hamlets and villages like Garrigill with the upland mining areas.

ABOUT • LIVERPOOL

Liverpool is the celebrated home town of the Beatles. This walk through the city takes you to all the famous Beatle landmarks from the Cavern Club on Mathew Street to the Empire Theatre, where the band made its last live appearance in 1965.

Northern England

DISTANCE • 5 miles (8km)

TOTAL ASCENT • 110ft (33m)

PATHS • footpaths

TERRAIN • city streets

GRADIENTS • very gentle

REFRESHMENTS • Tate Gallery Café at Albert Dock; the Philharmonic Pub

PARK • Plenty of free parking at Albert Dock

DIFFICULTY • 1

Liverpool: City of the 'Fab Four'

❶ Visit the Beatles Experience on Albert Dock. On leaving, turn right to the waterfront and right again for 700yds (640m) to the Mersey Ferry Terminal. Turn right into Water Street on the near side of the Royal Liver Building – with the unmistakable Liver Birds on top.

❷ Pass the Town Hall on your left, turn right into North John Street, continue for 200yds (183m) and turn left into Mathew Street and the Cavern Quarter. On the right is the reconstructed Cavern Club, next to the Cavern Walks shopping development.

❸ In 30yds (27m), on the left, is The Grapes pub, popular with the Beatles; the Beatles Shop is further along. At the end of Mathew Street turn left into Stanley Street to see the Eleanor Rigby statue in 20yds (18m) on the right.

❹ Walk back down Stanley Street, passing the site of Hessy's music shop on the right (currently unoccupied, next to Wade Smith). At the end, look to your right along Whitechapel, where the Ann Summers shop now occupies the NEMS shop, once owned by Brian Epstein's family.

❺ Turn left along Whitechapel, past the bus station, for 500yds (457m), and turn right along St John's Lane, passing St George's

• DON'T MISS •

*The **Maritime Museum** at Albert Dock is Liverpool's finest museum. It gives a vivid picture of life in the docks during the 18th century, and the Slavery Gallery does not flinch from showing that part of the city's seafaring history.*

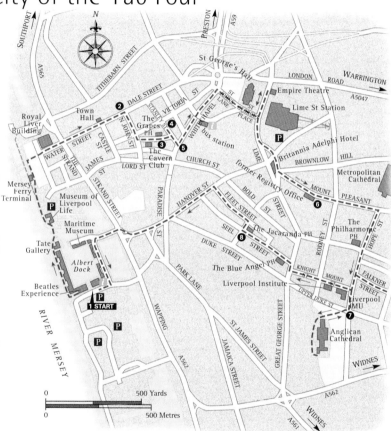

Hall, left. Cross to Lime Street Station and turn left to the Empire Theatre. Retrace your steps past the station and continue for 200yds (183m) past the Britannia Adelphi Hotel. Turn left, up the hill, on to Mount Pleasant. Note the former Registry Office on the right, now a cancer resource centre.

❻ Continue and turn right into Hope Street, opposite the Roman

Catholic Metropolitan Cathedral, down to the Philharmonic pub. Continue for 100yds (91m) and turn left into Falkner Street to No 36, John and Cynthia's first home together. Return to Hope Street and turn left. At the end, visit the Anglican Cathedral, which has several Beatles connections.

❼ Turn back along Hope Street and left into Mount Street just past

Liverpool John Moores University Hope Street Campus. Continue down the hill for 300yds (274m), turn right into Berry Street and left into Seel Street. The Blue Angel is on the left at No 108.

❽ Turn right into Slater Street, the Jacaranda is on the right at No 23. Left into Fleet Street for 500yds (457m) then left into Hanover Street to return to Albert Dock.

The Road to Wigan Pier (1936) by George Orwell is a moving testament to the poverty-stricken lives of those living in northern parts of Britain during the 1930s depression. Our walk begins at Wigan Pier which is, ironically, now a centre of enterprise.

DISTANCE • 9 miles (14.5km)

TOTAL ASCENT • 390ft (119m)

PATHS • mainly towpaths and surfaced pathways

TERRAIN • canalside pastures and country park woodland

GRADIENTS • gentle

REFRESHMENTS • Wigan Pier; the canalside Commercial Inn and the Kirkless Hall pub; Stables Café, Haigh Hall

PARK • car park at Trencherfield Mill, near the Mill at the Pier

DIFFICULTY • 2

George Orwell on the Road to Wigan

❶ From the car park near the Mill at the Pier, go past the barge *Roland* and through the Pier Gardens to reach the towpath of the Leeds and Liverpool Canal. Turn left and follow the towpath to Top Lock, the last in a long series of locks. On the way cross three busy roads, by pedestrian crossings.

❷ Beyond Top Lock the canal changes direction. Continue on the towpath to reach Bridge 60. Leave the canal and turn right over the bridge. Follow a surfaced driveway to eventually reach Haigh Hall.

❸ Pass to the right of Haigh Hall, and continue ahead until, directly opposite Haigh Golf and Visitor Centre, you turn left into a car park. Walk across the car park to the far right-hand corner, and turn left along a lane. Soon take the first turning on the left, a rough track descending to the Leeds and Liverpool Canal. Cross a bridge and go down to walk along the towpath.

❹ When you reach Bridge 60 again (this time from the opposite direction), climb steps to the right of the bridge, to regain the estate driveway. Turn right, ignore an early turning right, and continue descending gently through mixed woodland until, just as the

driveway makes a wide sweep to the right, you branch left on to a rough track alongside a stream.

❺ The track continues to the edge of a built-up area. Go forward to a road junction near the Parish Church of St Stephen. Turn left

and walk to the main road a short distance away. Cross the road with care, moving left to a nearby path signed the Leeds and Liverpool Canal. The path initially descends wooden steps, which can be slippery when wet, and joins the trackbed of a disused railway.

❻ Turn right along the trackbed and, always continuing to keep ahead, follow the on-going path to reach the towpath of the canal once more. Here, turn right and retrace your outward route to Wigan Pier and the car park near the Mill, at the Pier.

HAIGH

PRESTON

A49

A5106

BOAR'S HEAD

B5239

Haigh Hall Country Park

Stables Café & Visitors Centre

Haigh Hall ❸

ASPULL

B5238

golf course

Bridge 60 ❹

MARYLEBONE

B5376

NEW SPRINGS

TOP LOCK

Kirkless Hall PH ❷
Commercial Inn

Parish Church of St Stephen

❺

B5375

❻

B5238

WIGAN

Leeds & Liverpool Canal

SCHOLES

A49

N

Wigan Pier

Pier Café

A577

NEWTOWN

Pier Gardens

Mill at the Pier

1 START

A577

A571

JUNCTION 25 M6

B5238

INCE-IN-MAKERFIELD

A573

MANCHESTER

A577

0 ——— 1 Mile

0 ——— 1 Kilometre

High Pennine Byways over Blackstone Edge

A beautifully preserved section of ancient road leads over the moors between Yorkshire and Lancashire

WALK

143

1 From station take underpass beneath railway. Walk left, along tow-path, crossing canal at first set of locks, to follow path that emerges onto Ealees Road. Continue straight ahead on metalled track, passing a mill and Old Mill Cottage. As track curves right, take steps on your left and follow path uphill. Bear left, immediately before farm at top, to walk up a wooded valley. Cross footbridge; when path levels out, you see a canal drain. Don't cross it, but follow it to the left, to Owlet Hall.

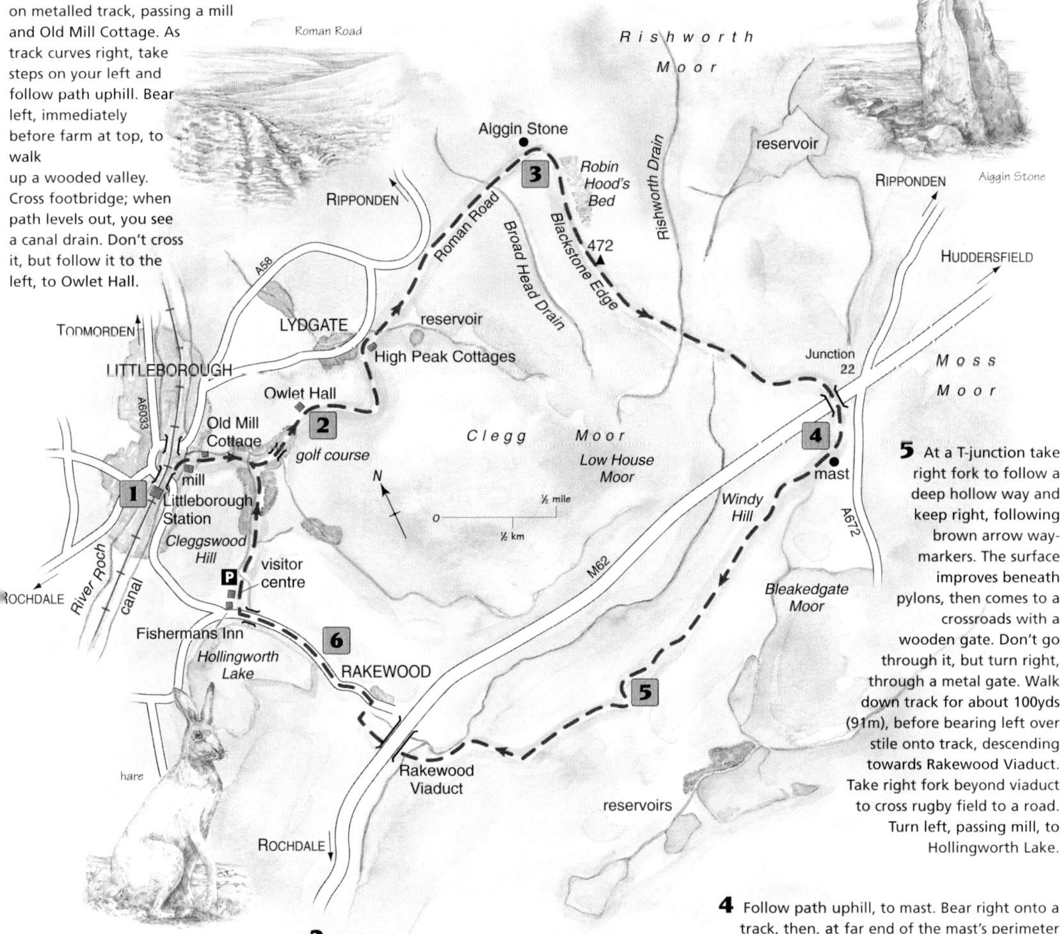

6 Keep to lakeside road before going right, past visitor centre. At far end of car park join metalled path. Cross footbridge and follow stream to bigger track. Go left here and retrace your earlier steps, keeping straight ahead on path to canal, and back along towpath into Littleborough.

2 Go through wooden gates and around front of house to join a field path, and follow a wall on your left with a golf course right. Go left along a stony track, keeping left past a farm, then turning left on bridleway to Blackstone Edge Road by High Peak Cottages. Turn right on path directly in front of cottages, continuing on a field path with a wall on right. At farm track go right for a few paces, then head left, up the hill on obvious path. Soon you are on the famous 'Roman Road' to the Aiggin Stone, a medieval waymarker.

3 Go right from the stone, through a gate, to join the Pennine Way. Small cairns mark the path along Blackstone Edge. Past a trig point (the highest point of the walk), follow a sandy track (aim for mast in the middle distance), bearing left to cross the M62 on a footbridge.

4 Follow path uphill, to mast. Bear right onto a track, then, at far end of the mast's perimeter fence, bear half-left on rutted track, downhill. Go through a wall-gap, then by a wall over Windy Hill. Eventually it becomes a walled track or hollow way.

5 At a T-junction take right fork to follow a deep hollow way and keep right, following brown arrow way-markers. The surface improves beneath pylons, then comes to a crossroads with a wooden gate. Don't go through it, but turn right, through a metal gate. Walk down track for about 100yds (91m), before bearing left over stile onto track, descending towards Rakewood Viaduct. Take right fork beyond viaduct to cross rugby field to a road. Turn left, passing mill, to Hollingworth Lake.

Distance: 9 miles (14.5km)
Total ascent: 1,148ft (350m)
Paths: mostly well-defined; may be boggy after rain
Terrain: mostly open moorland; best not attempted in bad weather or poor visibility
Gradients: mostly gradual
Refreshments: Littleborough
Park: Littleborough railway station
Difficulty: 3

Map labels: Roman Road · Rishworth Moor · Aiggin Stone · Robin Hood's Bed · reservoir · RIPPONDEN · Aiggin Stone · RIPPONDEN · Roman Road · Broad Head Drain · Rishworth Drain · Blackstone Edge · 472 · HUDDERSFIELD · A58 · TODMORDEN · LYDGATE · reservoir · High Peak Cottages · Junction 22 · Moss Moor · LITTLEBOROUGH · Owlet Hall · Old Mill Cottage · golf course · Clegg Moor · Low House Moor · mast · Windy Hill · A672 · Bleakedge Moor · mill · Littleborough Station · Cleggswood Hill · visitor centre · Fishermans Inn · Hollingworth Lake · RAKEWOOD · ROCHDALE · River Roch · canal · hare · Rakewood Viaduct · reservoirs · ROCHDALE · Clegg Moor · M62 · ½ mile · ½ km · N

ABOUT • MARSDEN

The rise of the textile industry brought great prosperity to a number of towns during the 19th century, including Marsden. The effect this had on the landscape is evident as you walk from the town and view its rows of terraced houses and mills.

Northern England

DISTANCE • 6 miles (9.6km)

TOTAL ASCENT • 920ft (280m)

PATHS • tracks, moorland paths and country lanes

TERRAIN • rough moorland, pastures and farmland

GRADIENTS • variable, steep in places

REFRESHMENTS • pubs and cafés in Marsden

PARK • parking places in Argyle Street, also plenty of roadside parking

DIFFICULTY • 2

The Wool Mills of Marsden

❶ From Argyle Street turn into Station Road. Climb to the station, turn right into Reddisher Road, and left into Spring Head Lane, a steep track rising to Inglenook. Turn right along a vehicle track to a radio mast. Turn left up a narrow, enclosed path, climbing steeply to a horizontal track at a top gate.

❷ Turn left and follow the track behind a farmhouse. A short way on, when the track forks, go left, descending. The track shortly turns right. Keep following the main track, which later becomes surfaced for a while, descending steeply. When the track next forks, just past Hey Cottage, bear right.

The route is obvious, enclosed by fences or walls. Go past farm buildings on the left and keep on the track until the next junction (waymarked). Turn right, soon leaving the lane for a walled path that breaks out on to the hillside.

❸ Keep forward on an obvious grassy path to a gate, beyond which it continues as a waymarked route across rough pasture, passing a derelict farmhouse to descend into a stream gully. Cross the stream, turn left, and climb beside a wall, go through a gate on to a

narrow lane. Turn left, continue to a bridge opposite the entrance to Hey Green Hotel. Cross the bridge and take a rising lane to the A62.

❹ Cross the A-road to a step stile, beyond which a rough path rises, right, on to Marsden Moor Estate. At an estate signpost, bear left, climbing across the hillside, below rock outcrops and through low, hummocky terrain.

❺ The route continues, always parallel with overhead power lines, and on to the Pule Hill part of Marsden Moor. Aim for the lower of two prominent ventilation shafts, beyond which an improving path strikes across the moor, finally, as it approaches the Carriage House pub, moving away from the power lines.

❻ When the path reaches a moorland road, turn left until, 80yds (73m) before a cattle grid, where you turn left into Old Mount Road. Almost immediately branch left on to an access track signed Hades Farm.

❼ Follow the farm track for 547yds (500m), past two paths to the right and branch right on to a grassy track beside the wall. Descend to a gate, beyond which the track, overgrown with rushes, continues between dilapidated walls. The distinct track continues towards a farm. Just before the farm, bear left, descending steeply beside a wall to a step stile below.

❽ Cross the stile and bear left across a hill slope, soon walking beside a wall until you meet a step-stile in a corner of a wall. Cross the stile, turn right and descend to meet the A62 again. Turn right and, near the church, turn left into Towngate. Take the first turning on the right, cross a bridge and turn left into Argyle Street to return to the start point of the walk.

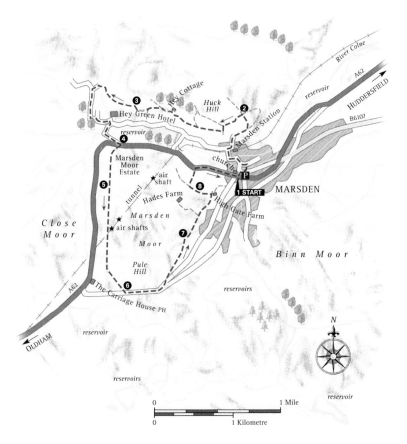

0 — 1 Mile

0 — 1 Kilometre

Cloth and Canal Folk in Calderdale

Explore Calderdale's charming tangle of lanes and bridleways between working villages

WALK

145

1 From the crossroads in the centre of Hebden Bridge go down Holme Street to the Rochdale Canal and walk right, along the towpath. After about 1 mile (1.6km) you come to a broadening of the canal, next to a mill and lock; immediately before the next bridge over the canal, go right to meet the A646.

2 Cross the road and walk right for 110yds (100m) to take a track left (signed Pennine Way), through a tunnel beneath the railway. Go steeply uphill on an unevenly paved, walled path, past old houses. At a high retaining wall and small graveyard turn sharp right, through a gate (signed as Pennine Way: official route).

3 Follow a grassy track then take stone steps past a waterfall issuing from a small stone building. Go left at the houses, on a more substantial track. Keep left at a house called Long Hey Top, then go immediately right along a waymarked field path, which leads to a road.

4 Cross the road and continue on the field path, then between walls, to meet an unmade track. (The New Delight Inn is left along this track.)

5 Walk steeply down to the beck – Colden Water – and cross it on a stone clapper-bridge. Climb steeply up the other side, to join a paved causeway at the top of the woodland. Follow the causeway over a stile to the left and over a field; at the second wall-stile bear slightly left to keep following the causeway, with a wall initially to your right and then your left. With Heptonstall church tower coming into view, turn right along a gravel path by a farm outbuilding. Keep left of a house, soon to go over a stile and onto a paved path.

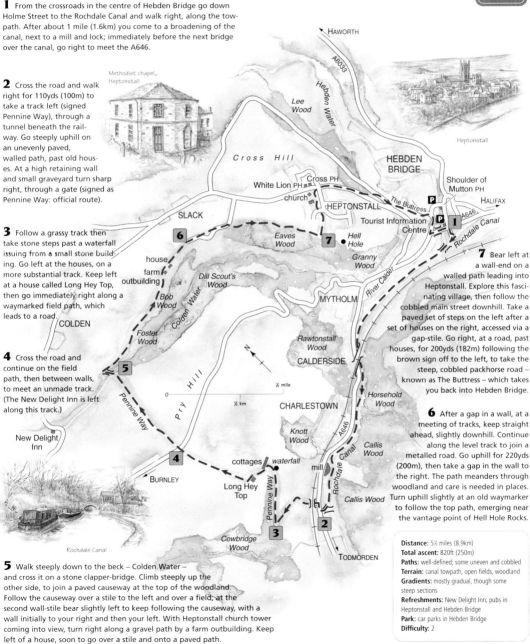

7 Bear left at a wall-end on a walled path leading into Heptonstall. Explore this fascinating village, then follow the cobbled main street downhill. Take a paved set of steps on the left after a set of houses on the right, accessed via a gap-stile. Go right, at a road, past houses, for 200yds (182m) following the brown sign off to the left, to take the steep, cobbled packhorse road – known as The Buttress – which takes you back into Hebden Bridge.

6 After a gap in a wall, at a meeting of tracks, keep straight ahead, slightly downhill. Continue along the level track to join a metalled road. Go uphill for 220yds (200m), then take a gap in the wall to the right. The path meanders through woodland and care is needed in places. Turn uphill slightly at an old waymarker to follow the top path, emerging near the vantage point of Hell Hole Rocks.

Distance: 5½ miles (8.9km)
Total ascent: 820ft (250m)
Paths: well-defined; some uneven and cobbled
Terrain: canal towpath, open fields, woodland
Gradients: mostly gradual, though some steep sections
Refreshments: New Delight Inn; pubs in Heptonstall and Hebden Bridge
Park: car parks in Hebden Bridge
Difficulty: 2

Slaidburn and the Forest of Bowland

Exploring the great tract of moorland which opens out between the Yorkshire Dales and the Lancashire Plain

WALK

146

Distance: 11 miles (17.7km)
Total ascent: 985ft (300m)
Paths: meadow paths, moorland roads and tracks.
Terrain: wild, open moors and hillsides, with steep stream valleys
Gradients: several longish gradual climbs, and one or two short sharp ones
Refreshments: Hark to Bounty Inn, Slaidburn; village shop, Dunsop Bridge
Park: public car park on edge of Slaidburn, 9 miles (15km) north of Clitheroe on the B6478
Note: not recommended in poor visibility
Difficulty: 3

1 Walk into the village to the Hark to Bounty Inn. From the inn turn right. Past the health centre, turn right ('Wood House' sign) on a path by Croasdale Brook, then through meadows. At a T-junction, go right down the grassy path to Myttons Farm.

8 Follow the farm track to the road, where you turn right for 600yds (548m), to reach the Hark to Bounty Inn at Slaidburn.

7 Go straight across a field, crossing first a wall stile, then a fence stile, then another wall stile. Aim diagonally right here across a field, bearing away from a fence. Keep left of a farm on your right, heading northeast until a gate and stile in a wall. Cross stile and follow the track to Pain Hill Farm. Go through farmyard, past buildings and out through a gate onto a track with several cattle grids.

2 Turn left to the road, then right for 1½ miles (2.4km) to go through a gate marked 'No vehicle access'. Turn immediately left up a bridleway, where a wall on the left soon swings away; follow the track uphill for 1 mile (1.6km) to a gate.

3 From this gate at the top of Dunsop Fell, bear diagonally right on a path, following yellow-topped marker posts for 1¼ miles (2km) down into Whitendale. Turn left on the road here beside the River Dunsop, for 3½ miles (5.6km), to Dunsop Bridge.

4 Turn left to cross the bridge then immediately left again up a marked bridleway. At Holme Head Cottages go through a gate (blue and yellow arrows) .In 20yds (18m), turn right to climb steps up a steep bank. Cross a wall stile and follow telegraph poles to Beatrix.

5 At Beatrix turn left along the road. Pass houses, and take the track to Back of Hill Barn. Follow arrow waymarks down to the valley bottom, cross the stream and climb the track to Rough Syke Barn.

6 Continue uphill, keeping on the right-hand track, eastward, to go through a gate. In 150yds (137m), turn left into a walled lane, for 600yds (548m) to a road. Turn right here, and in 250 yds (229m) go left over a stile with a footpath sign.

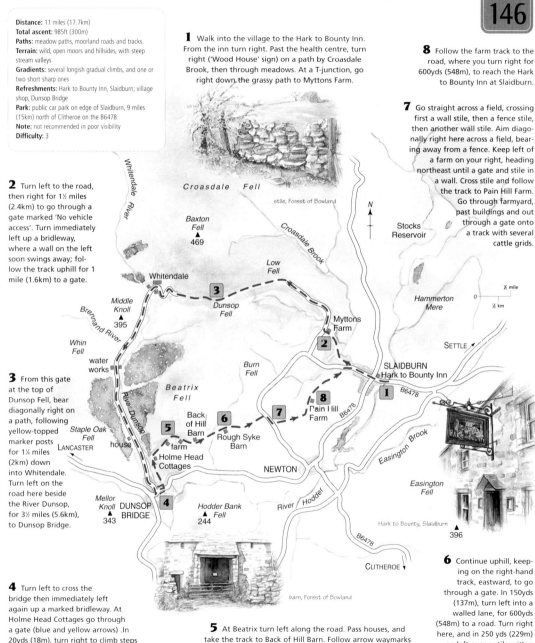

stile, Forest of Bowland

barn, Forest of Bowland

Hark to Bounty, Slaidburn

The Witches of Pendle Hill

*A walk up this prominent Lancashire hill reveals a
landscape where witches were once thought a problem*

WALK

147

Distance: 5½ miles (9km)
Total ascent: 1,310 feet (400m)
Paths: clear, but not obvious in poor
visibility; muddy in places
Terrain: mountain and upland pasture
Gradients: one steep ascent and a
lesser climb through a plantation
Refreshments: pubs, restaurant and
refreshments in Barley
Park: car park in Barley, north of
Burnley, off A6068
Difficulty: 2

1 From the car park, take the
path towards the village. Walk
past the Barley Mow restaurant,
and at Meadow Bank Farm turn
left beside a stream. At a footbridge, turn left onto a lane
and, just before Mirewater
Fishery, go through a kissing
gate on the right onto a footpath that leads to Brown House
Farm. Continue up a grassy bank
opposite the farm, to a stile.

2 Over the stile, cross a gully
and bear right in the next pasture, below power lines, to
another kissing gate. Ascend
the right-hand edge of the next
field. At the top, go through a
gate and across a sloping field
to more gates, where the steep
path onto Pendle Hill begins.
At the top, turn left beside a
wall, ignoring a ladder stile,
and following path towards
the summit trig point.

3 Cross the summit,
and descend to the
second of two large
cairns. Bear half-right,
following the path
across moorland. Near
a small cairn, branch
right to a waymarker
pole, continuing into
Boar Clough.

6 Climb out of the Newchurch-in-Pendle
and, at a road bend, turn right onto a
broad track. Follow this to a farm. Go past
the first house, and, just before you reach
the second, turn left to a gate giving onto
a field edge path going down to a walled
track. Turn left and go down this to meet
the road on the edge of Barley.

5 On leaving the plantation,
turn right, beside a wall. At the
top of the plantation, turn left
beside a fence. When a wall
appears, continue in the same direction. Follow the wall to the next waymark, then bear half-right across
rough pasture towards Newchurch-in-
Pendle, initially out
of sight. Aim to the
left of the church, to
locate a field corner
at the rear of houses.
Cross a stream and
stiles, before descending
steps to the road. Turn
left for Barley.

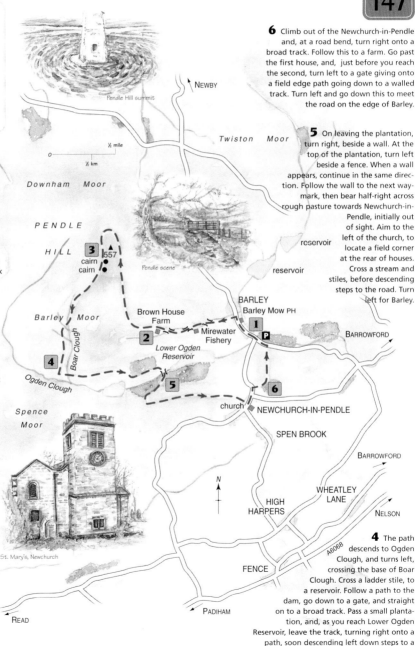

Pendle Hill summit

Pendle scene

St. Mary's, Newchurch

4 The path
descends to Ogden
Clough, and turns left,
crossing the base of Boar
Clough. Cross a ladder stile, to
a reservoir. Follow a path to the
dam, go down to a gate, and straight
on to a broad track. Pass a small plantation, and, as you reach Lower Ogden
Reservoir, leave the track, turning right onto a
path, soon descending left down steps to a
footbridge. Beyond, you climb into a plantation.

Haworth and the Brontë Moors

*The moors above the Brontë's West Yorkshire home were
a source of both inspiration and solace in their briefly
flourishing lives*

WALK

148

1 From the car park, go through gate posts opposite the museum and turn right. The lane soon becomes a paved field path that leads to the Haworth-Stanbury road. Walk left along the road and, after about 80yds (75m), take a left fork, signed to Peniston Hill. Continue along this quiet road to a T-junction.

2 Take the track straight ahead, soon signed Brontë Way and Top Withins, gradually descending to South Dean Beck where, within a few paces of the stone bridge, you'll find the Brontë Waterfall and Brontë Seat (a stone that resembles a chair). Cross the bridge and climb steeply uphill to a 3-way sign.

3 Keep left, uphill, on a paved path signed to Top Withins. The path soon levels out to accompany a dry-stone wall. Cross a stile and then keep left. Cross a tiny beck on stepping stones; a steep uphill climb brings you to a way-marker by a ruined building. A short detour of 200yds (182m), left, uphill, is needed if you want to investigate the lonely ruins of Top Withins.

7 From here you retrace your outward route: walk left along the road, soon taking a stile on the right, to follow the paved field path back into Haworth.

6 Bear right along the road through Stanbury, then take the first road on the right, signed to Oxenhope, and cross the dam of Lower Laithe Reservoir. Immediately beyond the dam, bear left on a road that soon reduces to a track, uphill, to meet a road by Haworth Cemetery.

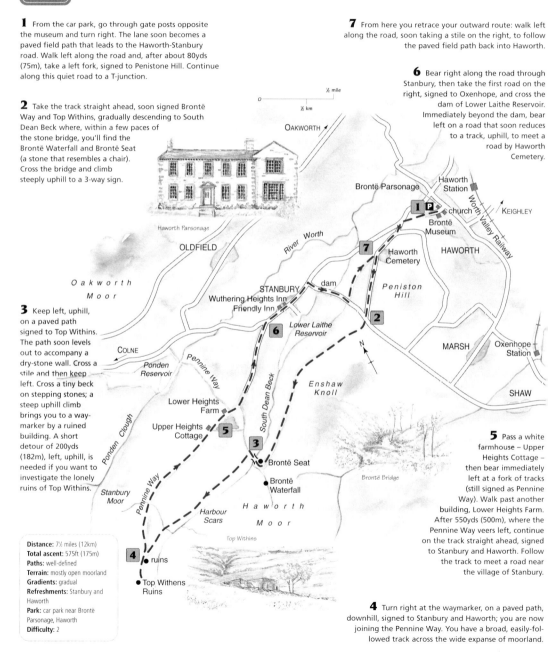

5 Pass a white farmhouse – Upper Heights Cottage – then bear immediately left at a fork of tracks (still signed as Pennine Way). Walk past another building, Lower Heights Farm. After 550yds (500m), where the Pennine Way veers left, continue on the track straight ahead, signed to Stanbury and Haworth. Follow the track to meet a road near the village of Stanbury.

4 Turn right at the waymarker, on a paved path, downhill, signed to Stanbury and Haworth; you are now joining the Pennine Way. You have a broad, easily-followed track across the wide expanse of moorland.

Distance: 7½ miles (12km)
Total ascent: 575ft (175m)
Paths: well-defined
Terrain: mostly open moorland
Gradients: gradual
Refreshments: Stanbury and Haworth
Park: car park near Brontë Parsonage, Haworth
Difficulty: 2

Saltaire's Model Streets and the Five Rise

Titus Salt built his vision of an industrial village beside the engineering triumph of the Leeds-Liverpool Canal

Distance: 8½ miles (13.7km)
Total ascent: 430ft (131m)
Paths: generally clear and well-signed; boggy in places
Terrain: canal bank, woodland and open moorland
Gradients: some steep sections
Refreshments: Saltaire, Bingley, Shipley Glen
Park: at Hirst Wood, 1 mile (1.6km) along Hirst Lane from A650 Saltaire roundabout
Difficulty: 2

1 Cross the canal by the swing bridge, turn left onto the canal towpath and follow the canal for 2 miles (3.2km) to Five Rise Locks.

2 At the locks' summit turn right over the metal bridge and walk up the road, bending right alongside the stone wall. Just before a road joins from the right, turn left up a narrow metalled lane between two walls.

3 Follow this path, with a stream on your right, uphill, crossing two roads and passing through a small housing estate, to reach the hilltop on Lady Lane, where you turn right.

9 Cross the river by a footbridge, then go straight on to the canal towpath, turning right to reach Hirst Wood after 1 mile (1.6km).

4 Turn left down College Road and walk towards the stone houses, with Lady Park Nursing Home to your right. The route bends left through a small estate called Nicholson Close to a signed footpath.

5 Go over a stile, turn right and follow the waymarkers through two fields to a stone stile. Cross and go left, passing farm buildings to reach a road. Turn left and then first right down a track.

6 After a right-angled bend beyond the cottages turn left, downhill on the packhorse track between walls. Pass the reservoir to reach a road, then turn right to reach Eldwick Hall on your right.

7 Turn left opposite the hall and follow the path through fields to reach a signpost. Turn right, along the Dales Way Link. On reaching a farm, go left over a stile and follow the farm drive to the road.

8 Cross the road to a farm and follow a path next to a beck until you reach a road, which you follow to the Glen Tramway entrance. Take the tramway down the hill, or the path beside it. At the foot of the hill go straight ahead through Roberts Park.

Bingley Moor

½ mile
0
½ km

EAST MORETON

MICKLETHWAITE

Lower Heights Farm

6 Eldwick cottages

Eldwick Hall

7

N

B6265

A650

KEIGHLEY

Five Rise Locks

5

Lady Park **4** Nursing Home

Golcar Farm

8

Glovershaw Farm

CROSS FLATS

ELDWICK

Baildon Moor

Salt's Mill

2

5 Rise Locks

3

Baildon Hill 283m

3 Rise Locks

BINGLEY

Leeds & Liverpool Canal

Bingley Station

Bracken Hall Countryside Centre

Old Glen PH

Glen Tramway

GUISELEY

CULLINGWORTH

B6429

grammar school

Roberts Park

9

A6038

Fishermans PH lock

aqueduct

Hirst Wood

church

Salt's Mill and Gallery

A657

Cottingley Park

A650

River Aire

Nab Wood

P

1

SALTAIRE Saltaire Station

LEEDS

Shipley Station

COTTINGLEY

MOORHEAD

SHIPLEY

B6269

BRADFORD

BRADFORD

Wartime Remains on Spurn Point

Exploring the wartime remains on this remote, curling finger of land in the Mouth of the Humber

1 Walk to the far end of the car park and follow the Spurn Footpath sign, ascending the bank and turning right. Cross a bridge and stile and turn left then right, to follow waymarkers along the edge of the cliff. After passing two bird hides, follow the path right to descend beside bungalows towards the road.

2 Follow the yellow waymarkers to the left of the road, through the dunes and past the 'No Through Road' sign. The path will eventually join the road; continue along it until it veers right, when the signed footpath again goes to the left.

3 The path rejoins the road briefly, then turns off to the right, following the telegraph poles. Go over a ladder stile and towards the Heligoland Bird Trap. Go over another ladder stile to reach a signpost.

4 Follow the Seaside Path sign, crossing the road and ascending the dunes. The waymarked path follows the coastline and passes the lighthouse, eventually descending via a boardwalk to Spurn Point Car Park.

Distance: 8½ miles (13.5km)
Total ascent: negligible
Paths: well-signed and mostly good;muddy in places; some road walking. Obey any diversions resulting from storm damage
Terrain: sand-dunes and grassland
Gradients: none
Refreshments: seasonal at Spurn Point
Park: car park, Kilnsea (east of the village, just beyond the crossroads)
Difficulty: 1

6 Go to the left of the information board at the north end of the car park, following the Riverside Path signs, past the former Low Light. The path joins the road briefly, but then goes left again, back to the Heligoland Trap. Go over the ladder stile and follow the outward route back to the car park.

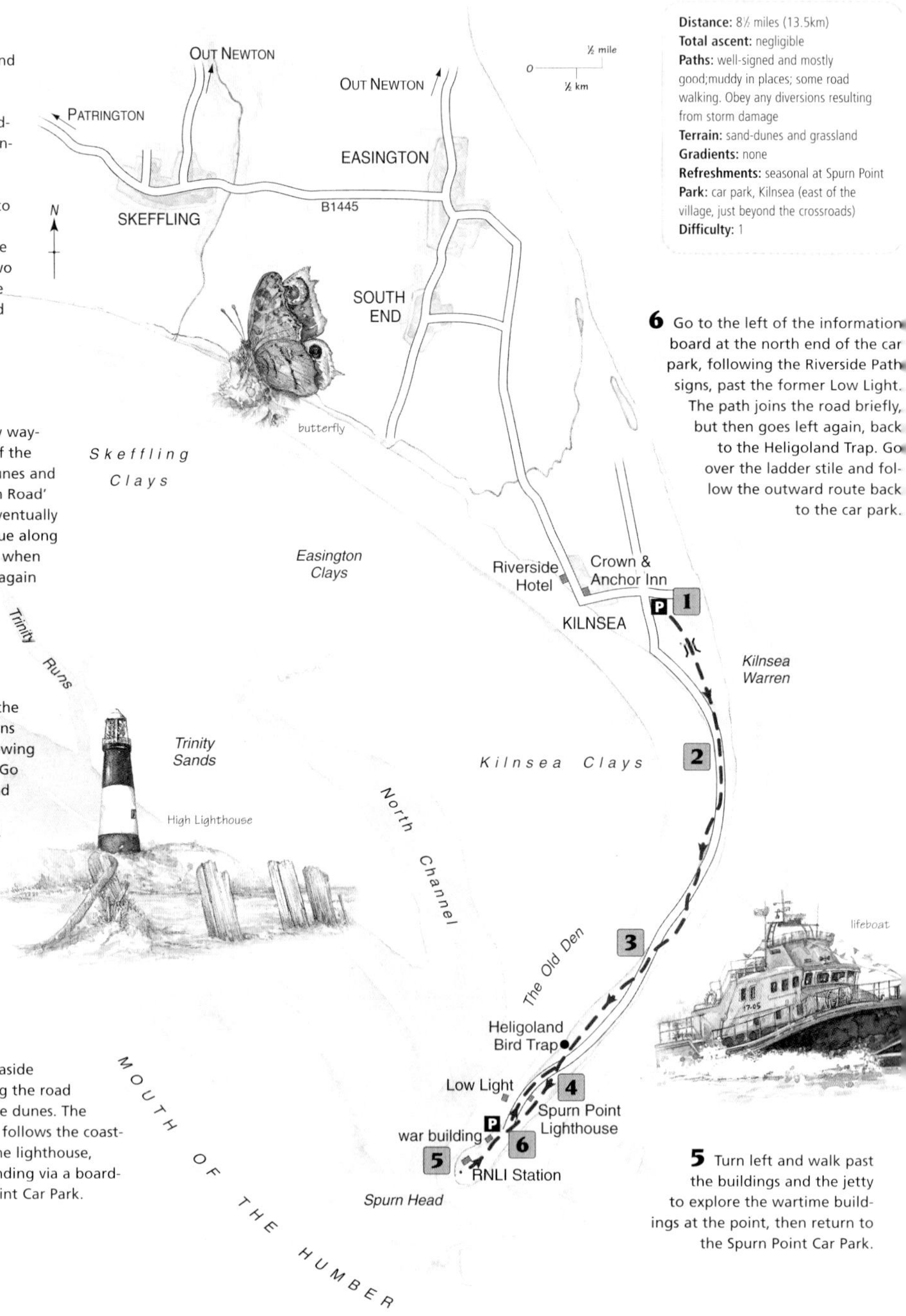

5 Turn left and walk past the buildings and the jetty to explore the wartime buildings at the point, then return to the Spurn Point Car Park.

OUT NEWTON

OUT NEWTON

PATRINGTON

EASINGTON

B1445

SKEFFLING

SOUTH END

butterfly

Skeffling Clays

Easington Clays

Riverside Hotel

Crown & Anchor Inn

KILNSEA

Kilnsea Warren

Trinity Runs

Trinity Sands

Kilnsea Clays

High Lighthouse

North Channel

The Old Den

lifeboat

Heligoland Bird Trap

Low Light

Spurn Point Lighthouse

war building

RNLI Station

Spurn Head

MOUTH OF THE HUMBER

WALK 151

ABOUT • WHARRAM PERCY

The discovery of Wharram Percy in 1948 led to extensive excavations revealing a 5000-year-old community. The village was deserted during the 15th century due to the Black Death which ravaged many settlements in England between 1338–79

DISTANCE • 8 miles (13km)

TOTAL ASCENT • 1,640ft (500m)

PATHS • field paths and track, some roads

TERRAIN • undulating chalk landscape

GRADIENTS • one steep climb through fields, one on road

Northern England

REFRESHMENTS • Middleton Arms, North Grimston

PARK • roadside parking in North Grimston, near the church, or in the Wharram Percy car park near Bella Farm

DIFFICULTY • 2

Plague and Pestilence in the Yorkshire Wolds

❶ Follow the main road south, past the Middleton Arms pub. Just beyond the speed derestriction sign take a track left over a cattle grid, towards Wood House Farm. Cross two more cattle grids. On the rise beyond, turn right at the Wolds Way sign.

❷ Go downhill and cross a bridge between two stiles. Bear slightly left and ascend the valley to a signpost. Turn left, going over a stile at another signpost. Then continue along the side of the field. At the next signpost go right, then go through the hedge on to a track.

• DON'T MISS •

In Wharram Percy's church there are a number of slabs that once covered the graves of important villagers. Some of them are decorated with crosses and other symbols. Excavations have revealed more than 1000 skeletons – almost half of them children.

❸ Follow the track across a road and downhill. At the next road turn left and walk uphill through Wharram le Street. At the crossroads turn right, towards Birdsall. Just beyond the houses on your left, go over a stile, signed Wolds Way.

❹ Follow the field edge to a road, then go straight ahead, passing Bella Farm. Beyond the farm, follow the sign for Medieval Deserted Village. Go through the car park and down the track. After the second kissing gate veer right to another gate.

❺ Go through the gate and down the steps on to the former railway line. To visit Wharram Percy, cross and follow the lane opposite. Return to the same point and turn left (not under the bridge). Follow the disused line to a road.

❻ Go straight ahead, and follow the road to a crossroads. Turn right, signed North Grimston. Follow the road, turning left at a T-junction by the entrance to Wharram Grange Farm. Go over a cattle grid, and right at a T-junction near Luddith Farm.

❼ After the next cattle grid turn right, signed CW. Follow the field edge then go through a gate and ahead, left of the stream. After another gate, pass under the railway bridge. Follow the path on to the road. Turn left to return to the start point.

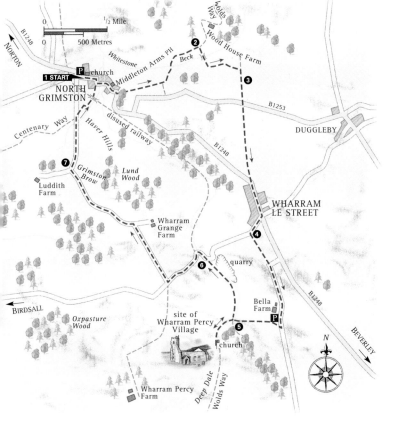

ABOUT • SCARBOROUGH

By the end of the 18th century Scarborough was a magnet for people of good fashion – ever since Elizabeth Farrer discovered medicinal waters springing beside the beach. The waters, no longer thought fit to drink, still flow from a niche near the spa.

Northern England

DISTANCE • 6¾ miles (10.8km)

TOTAL ASCENT • 590ft (180m)

PATHS • town pavements and beach, tides permitting

TERRAIN • two wide bays set either side of headland

GRADIENTS • one gradual climb form North Bay; ascent to castle entrance quite steep

REFRESHMENTS • plenty of hotels, pubs, restaurants, cafés and tea rooms throughout Scarborough

PARK • Albion Road car park on the South Cliff, off A165 Bridlington road

DIFFICULTY • 2

Scarborough, Queen of Watering Places

❶ From the car park, follow Albion Road towards the sea. Turn right and by Esplanade Gardens take the cliff lift (tramway) down, or the winding path beside it, to the spa buildings. At the seashore, turn left, along the beach or the road.

❷ Walk towards the harbour. Pass the lifeboat station and follow the road past the harbour, bending left through an archway on to Marine Drive (closed in bad weather). Follow Marine Drive for 1½ miles (2.4km) to a roundabout.

❸ Turn left, and left again at the next roundabout, then take the next left. Turn left again, along Queen's Parade. Follow the road along the cliff top. Go left of the Boston and Norbreck hotels, to descend along Mulgrave Place to a crossroads.

❹ Turn left to visit the castle. Return from the castle to the crossroads, and turn left. Anne Brontë's grave is behind the wall to your left. Follow the lane downhill, going left along Paradise, then bending right. Take the second turning right, Longwestgate.

❺ Go left down St Mary's Street. Continue downhill by the Leeds Hotel, bending right down a cobbled path for 22yds (20m) to join a main road. Turn right, uphill. At the traffic lights turn left along St Nicholas Street, bending right by the Royal Hotel. The Grand Hotel is to your left.

❻ Continue along Falconers Road. At the roundabout, take the second exit (the Crescent Hotel is now on your right) and walk round

the Crescent. Turn left by the Chessington Hotel, cross the next road and go straight on. At the top, turn left and then left again at the traffic-lights.

❼ At the next traffic-lights go right towards Tesco. Follow the road as far as Falsgrave signal box and turn left. At the bottom turn left, then left again after 33yds (30m) down Valley Road. Cross at the roundabout beyond Valley Bridge, then bear left to pass the Rotunda Museum.

❽ Continue up the slope and steps and over Cliff Bridge. At the end bear right up steps beside the Spa Chalet. Follow the road past the Crown Hotel, and go right at the Villa Esplanade along Albion Road to the car park.

• DON'T MISS •

*Scarborough's **Rotunda Museum** is a fascinating collection of local treasures, housed in a domed building. A spiral staircase rises to the main room, with paintings of Yorkshire geology above the 19th-century display cases. The museum was inspired by William Smith (1769–1839) who is known as the father of English geology.*

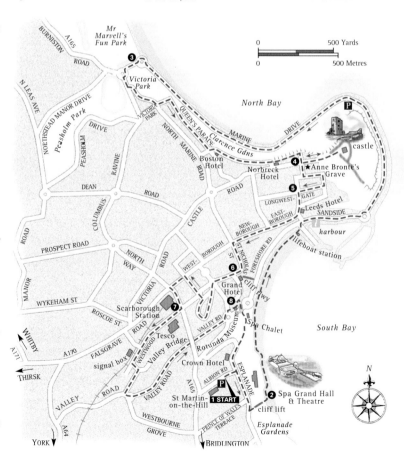

In the Hole of Horcum

*Exploring this spectacular dip in the moorland plateau
of the North York Moors*

WALK

153

Distance: 8½ miles (13.7km)
Paths: tracks and woodland paths; often muddy
Total ascent: 1,015ft (309m)
Terrain: moorland ridges and wooded valleys
Gradients: moderate; some steep sections
Refreshments: Levisham, or caravan in car park
Park: car park on the A169, 12 miles (19.2km)
north of Pickering and 3 miles (4.8km) north of
Lockton
Difficulty: 2

7 At a signpost for Saltergate turn left,
go over two footbridges and turn left
at the waymark beyond it. The path
follows the valley into the Hole of
Horcum, passing a former farmhouse, then ascends to a ladder
stile beside the A169. Turn right
to reach the car park.

6 At the top of the
green take the lane to
the right of the
Horseshoe Inn. At a stile
beside a gate across
the lane, go right and
descend to follow a
path along the nar-
rowing valley,
beside the stream.

1 From the car park cross
the road and walk north,
following the road's sharp
left bend and then going
ahead over a stile onto
an uphill track as the
road hairpins right.
Follow this track for
2½ miles (4km), pass-
ing left of a pond,
to reach signpost
by a second pond.

5 After 500yds
(457m), turn right
along a bridleway,
going downhill and
left at a crossing track.
The path winds
through woodland
and eventually
reaches a road,
where you turn
left up into
Levisham village.

4 At the second
gateway take the
track uphill,
through a gate into
woodland.
Continue uphill
where a track joins
from the right,
turning left at a
crossing track,
which eventually
becomes metalled.

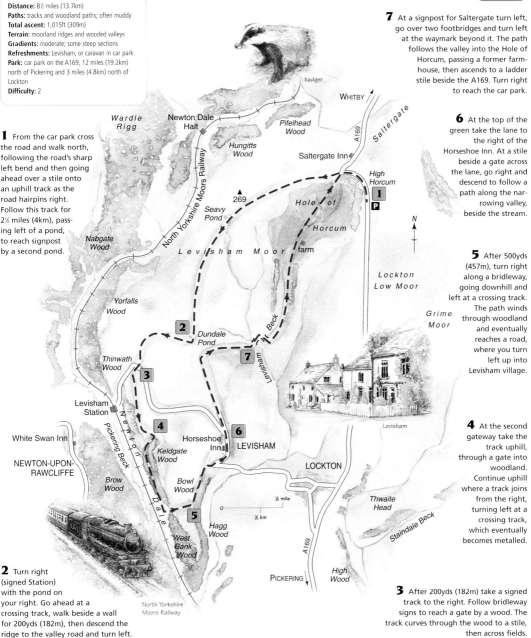

2 Turn right
(signed Station)
with the pond on
your right. Go ahead at a
crossing track, walk beside a wall
for 200yds (182m), then descend the
ridge to the valley road and turn left.

3 After 200yds (182m) take a signed
track to the right. Follow bridleway
signs to reach a gate by a wood. The
track curves through the wood to a stile,
then across fields.

High and Deep on Yorkshire's Coast

From the soaring cliffs above pretty Staithes to the hidden depths of Boulby Mine, this walk shows the contrasts of the North Yorkshire coast

WALK

154

1 From the top of the car park walk left, past garages, along a path by allotments. Turn right up the valley and follow the footpath signs through the houses to eventually meet the main road. Cross, go over a stile, through the field and cross a track by two more stiles.

8 At a crossing track (the Cleveland Way), turn right and follow it to Staithes, following signs to Cowbar. Descend to the harbour, cross the footbridge and turn right at the main village street up to the car park.

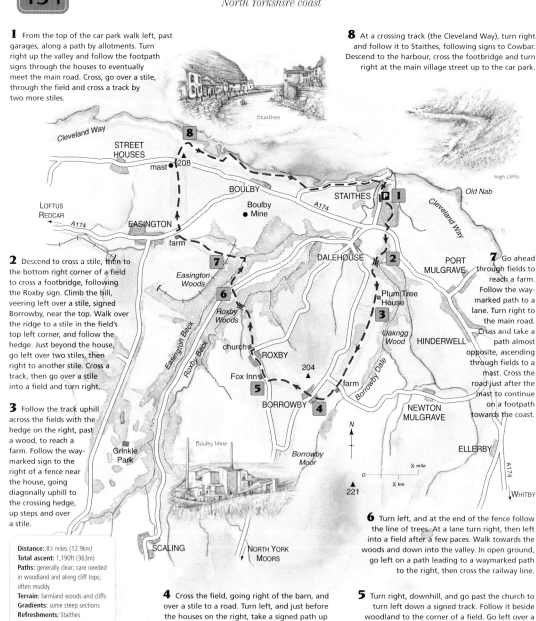

2 Descend to cross a stile, then to the bottom right corner of a field to cross a footbridge, following the Roxby sign. Climb the hill, veering left over a stile, signed Borrowby, near the top. Walk over the ridge to a stile in the field's top left corner, and follow the hedge. Just beyond the house, go left over two stiles, then right to another stile. Cross a track, then go over a stile into a field and turn right.

7 Go ahead through fields to reach a farm. Follow the way-marked path to a lane. Turn right to the main road. Cross and take a path almost opposite, ascending through fields to a mast. Cross the road just after the mast to continue on a footpath towards the coast.

3 Follow the track uphill across the fields with the hedge on the right, past a wood, to reach a farm. Follow the way-marked sign to the right of a fence near the house, going diagonally uphill to the crossing hedge, up steps and over a stile.

Distance: 8½ miles (12.9km)
Total ascent: 1,190ft (363m)
Paths: generally clear; care needed in woodland and along cliff tops; often muddy
Terrain: farmland woods and cliffs
Gradients: some steep sections
Refreshments: Staithes
Park: Staithes car park, off A174
Difficulty: 2

6 Turn left, and at the end of the fence follow the line of trees. At a lane turn right, then left into a field after a few paces. Walk towards the woods and down into the valley. In open ground, go left on a path leading to a waymarked path to the right, then cross the railway line.

4 Cross the field, going right of the barn, and over a stile to a road. Turn left, and just before the houses on the right, take a signed path up steps and over a stile. Cross three stiles, and as the hedge bends left, go diagonally across the fields to meet a lane.

5 Turn right, downhill, and go past the church to turn left down a signed track. Follow it beside woodland to the corner of a field. Go left over a stile into woodland. Follow waymarkers to cross a footbridge. Turn left, uphill, and left again where paths fork, ascending to a stile.

WALK

155

Like so many other monasteries in England, Furness was a victim of Henry VIII's split with the Catholic Church. Abbot Roger Pele and his monks rose up against the king but were quickly forced into submission and the abbey looted and destroyed.

DISTANCE • 6 miles (9.6km)	
TOTAL ASCENT • 260ft (79m)	
PATHS • field paths, lanes and tracks	
TERRAIN • rolling farmland, can be muddy in winter	
GRADIENTS • easy	

Northern England

REFRESHMENTS • cafés and inns at Dalton and the Farmers Arms at Newton

PARK • Goose Green car park at the bottom of Church Street opposite Furness Park Garage

DIFFICULTY • 2

The Abbot of Furness

❶ Turn left out of the car park, signed Public Footpath, Mill Wood, and pass through a gate at the end of the lane, signed Public Footpath to Broughton Road. Take the raised path beyond, following a beck and passing under a railway bridge before continuing through three tall gates into another field. At the far side, turn left across a footbridge, go under another railway bridge, and follow an enclosed path to the road.

❷ Cross the road before turning right along a field-edge path through the Vale of Nightshade. Pass under another railway bridge and left along the road to abbey.

❸ Swing left at the junction beyond the abbey. Pass the car park and just beyond a left-hand bend, follow a clear but unsigned path on the right. Cross the railway with care and turn right by the cottage to follow a Mill Beck. Cross the beck on a slab bridge, before recrossing it at Bow Bridge.

❹ Turn left along the lane. After 300yds (274m) a footpath sign points the way uphill over two fields to Newton. Turn half-right past The Village Inn, then left, passing the Farmers Arms and out of the village.

❺ Go left at the T-junction. After 200yds (183m) take the path on the right, which cuts diagonally northeast across fields, crossing primitive stiles before coming out on to another lane. Continue along an enclosed muddy track, which is staggered slightly right across the road, to pass Malkin Hall. Turn right along the next lane for 50yds (46m), then left up a gravel track.

❻ Beyond some outbuildings, climb a raised bank on the left of the track and head north on an old mine railway trackbed. Continue through a bush-lined cutting past a water-filled mining hollow, then descend beside a hedge towards Standing Tarn.

❼ Turn left though a squeeze stile above the tarn and head diagonally away from the tarn at the top right-hand corner of a large field. Staggered to the right, across a rough farm track, the next path begins at a squeeze stile and continues by a field edge. Turn left beyond the next stile and descend on a winding lane past some cottages, then pass beneath the railway to reach the main street in Dalton.

❽ Turn left up the main street, past the shops and the castle. Turn left along Church Street, descending past the Brown Cow Inn back to the car park.

MAP

N
A595
A595
A590
BARROW
Mill Wood
DALTON-IN-FURNESS
iron mines (disused) ★
Dalton Castle ⑧
Brown Cow Inn P
1 START
station
iron mines (disused) ★
ULVERSTON
A590
★iron mines (disused)
Standing Tarn
⑦
⑥
❷
Abbot's Wood
Vale of Nightshade
The Village Inn
Farmers Arms PH
Furness Abbey
❸ P
❹
Bow Bridge
NEWTON
❺
Malkin Hall
iron mines (disused) ★
STAINTON WITH ADGARLEY
BARROW-IN-FURNESS
DENDRON
0   1 Mile
0   1 Kilometre

• DON'T MISS •

Dalton Castle where you can view a display of restored armour from the Civil War. Built by the monks of Furness Abbey, following 14th-century raids on their territories by the Scots (including one by Robert the Bruce), the castle has been both a courthouse and a prison. Today, it is in the care of the National Trust.

WALK
156

ABOUT • KENDAL CASTLE

Climbing Castle Hill leads to Kendal Castle, home of the ruling barons of Kendal from the 13th century. The Parr family lived here and their long and intriguing history only became known when Catherine Parr became the only wife to outlive HenryVIII.

Northern England

DISTANCE • 7½ miles (12km)

TOTAL ASCENT • 650ft (198m)

PATHS • well-defined, firm paths

TERRAIN • limestone hills and town streets

GRADIENTS • steady climb from the town back to Kendal Scar

REFRESHMENTS • Castle Inn, Castle Street; the 1657 Chocolate Shop, off Finkle Street

PARK • Scout Scar car park, Underbarrow Road

DIFFICULTY • 2

Kendal Castle

❶ Go through the kissing gate across the road from the signed car park and climb through scrub hawthorns towards Scout Scar. Follow the edge path south.

❷ Turn left at a large cairn and follow the limestone path across the plateau. Beyond the second access (a kissing gate) through crosswalls, the path traverses a field to reach a country lane.

❸ Turn left along the lane over the by-pass down towards Kendal. Take the right fork on the edge of town, then turn right down Gillinggate. Go straight across the main road at the bottom, into Dowker's Lane, and through the arched stone gate into the recreation ground. Take the left-hand path through the recreation ground and cross the footbridge spanning the River Kent.

❹ Cross the road, turn right then go left up Parr Street (which becomes Sunnyside) before climbing the path to the castle.

❺ Head north along the grassy ridge back into Kendal. Turn left along Castle Road, then left again along the A684. Where this bends right go straight ahead to cross the river at Stramongate Bridge.

❻ Continue along Stramongate and Finkle Street, then turn left along Stricklandgate. Turn right by the Tourist Information Centre to climb up Allhallows Lane and Beast Banks. Turn right by the triangular green in to Mount Pleasant (leading to Serpentine Road). At the main road turn right, then take the left fork into Queens Road.

❼ Go left up a narrow tarmac lane, signed footpath to Helsfell

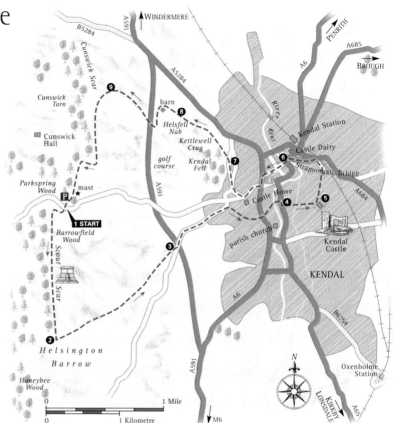

Nab. Half-way up the hillside this becomes a gritty track heading northwest on the slopes of Kendal Fell.

❽ Beneath Kettlewell Crag the path turns right over a stile (look for a small yellow arrow) and follows the right-hand field edge beneath Helsfell Nab. Beyond an old barn swing left on a path parallel to the by-pass. Cross two ladder stiles before reaching a third to cross the footbridge over

the by-pass. Cross another ladder stile to leave the footbridge and then cross one more over the wall to the right. Continue on the faint footpath across the field, aiming for the grassy hilltop ahead.

❾ Beyond the stile in the left corner of the field, swing half left to the edge of Cunswick Scar. Head south along it, crossing a stile, then turn right, following the permissive route signed to Scout Scar. Go over the stile into the

woods and take the right fork back to the car park.

• DON'T MISS •

The 14th-century Castle Dairy on Wildman Street is Kendal's oldest building. It was probably part of a dowry given by Sir Thomas Parr to his daughter Agnes on her wedding to Sir Thomas Strickland in 1455.

WALK 157

This walk follows in the footsteps of Beatrix Potter. It passes Far Sawrey and climbs the rolling hills to Moss Eccles Tarn. Passing through the forests of Claife Heights, you will catch glimpses of Bowness and Windermere through the tree boughs.

Northern England

DISTANCE • 6 miles (9.6km)

TOTAL ASCENT • 850ft (259m)

PATHS • field paths can be muddy in winter

TERRAIN • rolling hills and woodland

GRADIENTS • Steady but gentle climbs. The descent back to the car park can be slippery after rain

REFRESHMENTS • Tower Bank Arms in Near Sawrey

PARK • National Trust car park above Windermere Ferry landing stage

DIFFICULTY • 2

The World of Beatrix Potter

❶ From the south of the car park follow the footpath signed to Far Sawrey, Near Sawrey and Hill Top. After a short way it crosses the road, eventually to emerge on the High Cunsey Lane (not named), close to its junction with the B-road.

❷ Turn right, then left, up the B-road. At a sharp left-hand corner turn right, along a track marked to Far Sawrey, Near Sawrey and Hill Top. Follow it northwest through woodland and past a few cottages.

❸ Rejoin the B-road, turn right, then first left, descending along the lane towards St Peter's Church. Go right through a kissing gate by a whitewashed cottage, then follow the clear cross-field path towards Near Sawrey. The path returns to the road just short of Hill Top Farm.

❹ Through the village turn right along the lane opposite a post-box. This becomes a stony track that climbs past Moss Eccles and Wise Een tarns before entering the Claife Heights conifer plantations.

❺ Ignore the footpath on the left, and instead stay with the forestry road. Turn right along a path signed to the ferry and Far Sawrey. White waymark posts (look out for these as path may be unclear after major tree felling) highlight the route from here back to the car park. The winding path climbs to the Claife Heights viewpoint, where you can look down the length of Windermere.

❻ The continuing path crosses a wide forestry track. Turn right to reach High Blind How (the viewpoint is off the path). Just south of the viewpoint the path rounds some huge rocky outcrops. Beyond the outcrops follow the path to the left back into thick woodland.

❼ Turn right at a junction of paths and head south, signed Far Sawrey. The path becomes a wide track on entering an open area of pasture and crag with a wall on the left. Turn left at the T-junction of tracks, following the signed route to Windermere ferry and the lakeshore. At the next signpost turn right through a kissing gate, signed to ferry.

❽ After traversing high fields with a view to Bowness the path re-enters the woods and zigzags down steep slopes to the ruins of the old viewing station. Beyond these, descend the stepped path back to the car park.

• DON'T MISS •

Explore the places in Windermere that were home to Beatrix Potter – where Peter Rabbit, Tom Kitten and others came to life on the pages of her books.

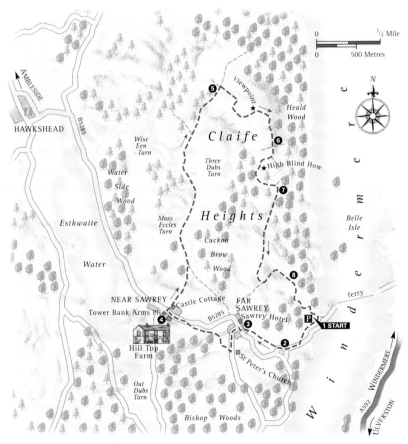

ABOUT • HARDKNOTT FORT

From the Duddon Valley you see the fort as the high point of your journey. After rounding the craggy Harter Fell, you climb, in the invaders' footsteps, to reach the outer walls of the fort – against a backdrop of the mighty Cumbrian mountains.

Northern England

DISTANCE • 6 miles (10km)

TOTAL ASCENT • 1,509ft (460m)

PATHS • mountain paths, can be muddy and indistinct in places. Compass advised

TERRAIN • forest and rugged fellside

GRADIENTS • two steady climbs

REFRESHMENTS • none on the route. Newfield Arms, Seathwaite; Bower House Hotel, near Eskdale Green

PARK • Birks Bridge car park, near Birks

OS MAP • 3

The Roman Fort at Hardknott

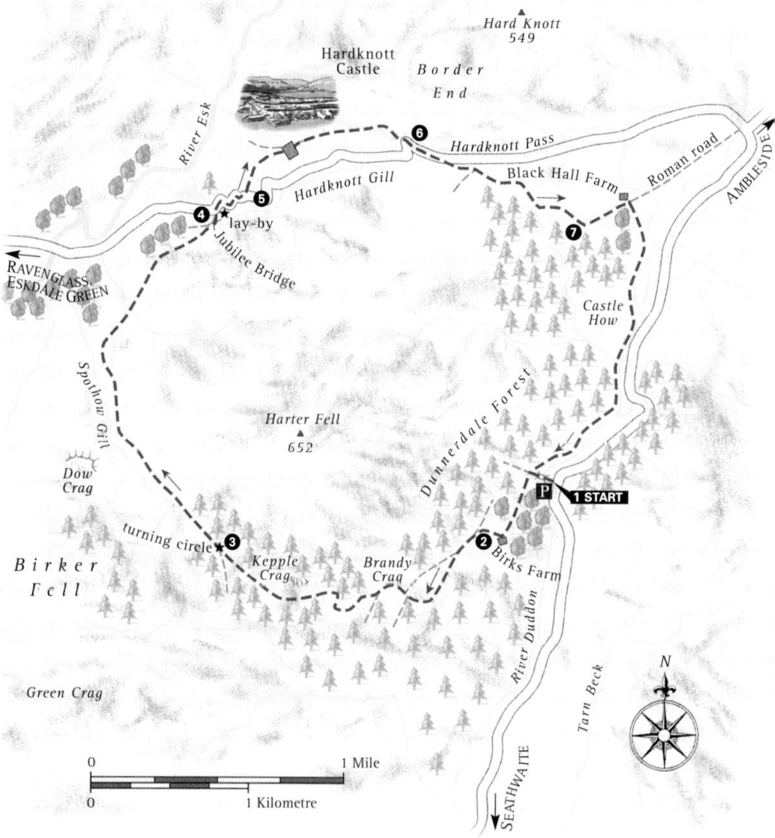

❶ Cross the bridge over the River Duddon and immediately turn left along the waymarked bridleway which heads south before climbing through oak woods to Birks Farm. Once through the gate into the yard (caution – farm dogs), veer right on to a forestry road.

❷ Turn left at a T-junction of forestry roads, ignoring the bridleway signed to Harter Fell, the waymarked footpath to the right, and the two left forks. The track climbs steadily through the trees and rounds the southern flanks of Harter Fell before ending at a vehicle turning circle.

❸ Continue on a rocky bridleway traversing the west side of the fell for 500yds (457m) before leaving the forest through a gate. Stay close to Spothow Gill for ½ mile (800m) then swing right, cross a small gill and go through a gate to descend the bracken-clad slopes beneath Birker Fell's crags. Pass through another gate and cross Dodknott Gill to reach Jubilee Bridge, which spans Hardknott Gill.

❹ Climb out past a small car park to the Hardknott Pass road. Turn right here to climb paths that take short cuts between bends in the road. If you prefer, you can continue along the road but it can be very busy in summer.

❺ A footpath signpost (32in/81cm high) points the way left up the fellside to the fort at Hardknott. Continue on the faint path from the back of the fort towards the crags of Border End. Swing right short of the crags to emerge on the roadside just before the summit of Hardknott Pass.

❻ Climb the short stretch of road before turning right on the bridleway, signed to Birks. At the highest point, the summit of Hardknott Pass, ignore the right turn, and descend south-eastwards down peaty slopes, keeping the spruce trees of Dunnerdale Forest on your right.

❼ At the foot of the slope go through a gate into a small enclosure, turn left over a step stile in the wall and through another gate, then continue on a grassy track towards Black Hall Farm. On reaching the farm, go over a stile, then turn right on a track heading towards the River Duddon. The well-defined track traverses rough pasture between the river bank and the forest to reach the bridge at the back of the car park.

Map labels: Hard Knott 549; Hardknott Castle; Border End; River Esk; Hardknott Pass; Black Hall Farm; Roman road; AMBLESIDE; Hardknott Gill; lay-by; Jubilee Bridge; RAVENGLASS, ESKDALE GREEN; Spothow Gill; Harter Fell 652; Dunnerdale Forest; Castle How; Dow Crag; turning circle; Birker Fell; Kepple Crag; Brandy Craa; Birks Farm; 1 START; P; Green Crag; River Duddon; Tarn Beck; SEATHWAITE; N; 0   1 Mile; 0   1 Kilometre

• DON'T MISS •

The Ravenglass and Eskdale steam-driven narrow-gauge railway, which runs from Ravenglass to Dalegarth, near Boot. Built as a 3ft (1m)-gauge line in 1875 to carry iron-ore, it was converted to the present 15in (38cm)-gauge in 1915, when the mine closed.

The Contrasts of Upper Eskdale

*From a lowland vale to England's highest mountains,
following the River Esk into the remote heart of
Lakeland*

WALK

159

1 Begin from a roadside parking area at the foot of Hardknott Pass, and descend to follow the access to Brotherilkeld Farm (right, by the telephone box). As you near the farm, branch left on a path parallel with the River Esk. Ignore a footbridge and continue up-river.

2 Beyond a gate follow a broad track crossing rough pasture. This leads past a series of delightful waterfalls, and ultimately arrives at Lingcove Bridge, directly below the crags of Throstle Garth.

3 Cross the bridge and climb left, still alongside, but well above, the river. Two pronounced rises follow before the path reaches Scar Lathing, where the river makes a distinct bend westwards. Cross an inflowing stream, and bear left to pass beneath Scar Lathing, beyond which lies the bleak arena of Great Moss, spread below the soaring heights of Sca Fell and the lower cliffs of Cam Spout Crag.

4 The moss is invariably waterlogged and paths sketchy, but the objective is now to cross the river. This is usually best accomplished at or just above the confluence with How Beck, and is rarely completed dryshod. Once across, head towards the base of the waterfall from How Beck, then turn left and contour along the base of a rocky slope to reach a small knoll with massive boulders, known as Sampson's Stones.

5 A short way further on a sheepfold is reached. From it a clear path begins a gentle climb away from the river into a little-known landscape of knolls, streams, low crags and bogland.

7 A short way beyond the bridge, take the lower of two ladder stiles, and follow an improving track to Taw House Farm. Immediately turn left over a ladder stile and go down an enclosed path to the footbridge across the Esk encountered at the start of the walk, and from there retrace your steps to the valley road.

6 The path, passing below Silverybield Crag, Round Scar and Rowantree Crags, is clear throughout, but occasionally resorts to evasion tactics before breaking free of the rocks on reaching Scale Gill. Now a clear green path zigzags down through bracken, turns right at the bottom and crosses Scale Bridge, where the gill puts on an impressive show of force.

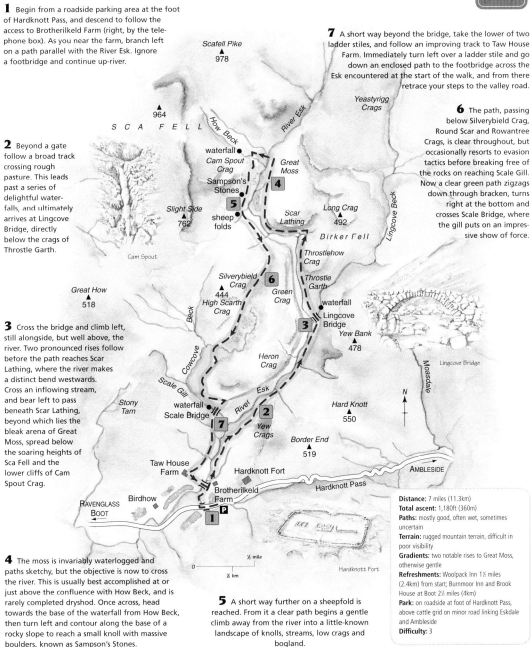

Distance: 7 miles (11.3km)
Total ascent: 1,180ft (360m)
Paths: mostly good, often wet, sometimes uncertain
Terrain: rugged mountain terrain, difficult in poor visibility
Gradients: two notable rises to Great Moss, otherwise gentle
Refreshments: Woolpack Inn 1½ miles (2.4km) from start; Burnmoor Inn and Brook House at Boot 2½ miles (4km)
Park: on roadside at foot of Hardknott Pass, above cattle grid on minor road linking Eskdale and Ambleside
Difficulty: 3

A Poet's View of the Buttermere Valley

The poet Coleridge stepped this way across a tranquil Lakeland scene

1 From the Bridge Hotel walk down to the left of the Fish Hotel, then through a gate, signposted to Scale Force and Scale Bridge. Go over a bridge, through a gate and turn right.

2 In ¼ mile (400m), after crossing a stream via a footbridge, take the path to the left which runs along the base of a rocky slope with occasional cairns. Eventually reach a gap in a wall. Descend to cross a footbridge. Scale Force waterfall is on your left.

3 Ascend for a few paces, then turn right, downhill, on a bank with a stream on your right. At the confluence with another stream, cross a footbridge then turn right. Later the path veers away from the stream towards the shore, then left alongside the lake.

4 Towards the end of the lake the track divides. Take the right-hand path through the gate and follow the water's edge. Go ahead at next gate and, just past a broken-down wall, turn left to pass a ruin, then aim for a group of pine trees by the shore. Pass through a kissing gate and then along a wall to a pumping station. Continue along the shore to cross a foot-bridge over a river. Later turn right over two bridges. Continue on shore path through Lanthwaite Woods and later past a boat house, then along by the lake. The path leads over several stiles and small bridges until it bears left at a wall.

5 Go through the gate and turn right onto the road to a parking area. Branch left across the hillside and soon cross the river and follow the bridleway. Go through a gate, to a footbridge. Cross over, then turn right to double-back and go down hill.

6 At the road walk left for a few paces then back up the bridle-way leading uphill and over a shoulder. Follow the path, keeping the lake on your right. When it comes back to the road, continue to a group of pine trees.

7 Pass through a kissing gate and follow the shore, then take a gravel path through woods. At the far end cross a footbridge, then go through a kissing gate. Turn left up field to another kissing gate, then immediately turn right around foot of crag. On reaching a foot-bridge, cross it and turn left, signed Buttermere village, and follow riverside path back to car park.

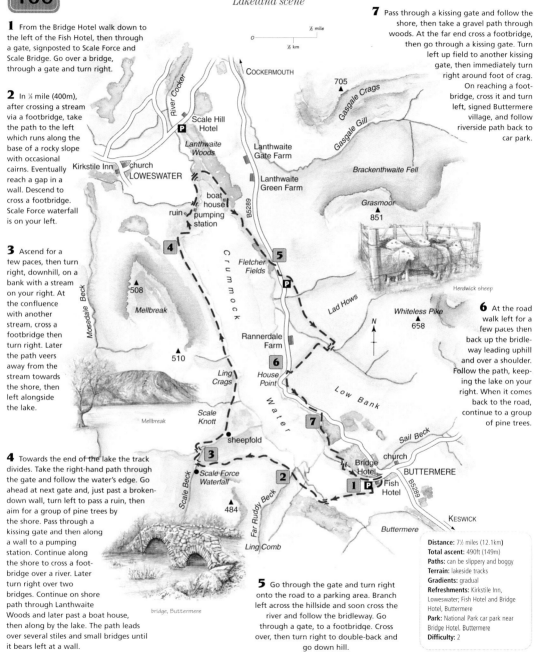

½ mile

0

½ km

COCKERMOUTH

River Cocker

705 ▲

Gasgale Crags

Gasgale Gill

Scale Hill Hotel

P

Lanthwaite Woods

Lanthwaite Gate Farm

Kirkstile Inn church

LOWESWATER

Lanthwaite Green Farm

Brackenthwaite Fell

boat house

ruin pumping station

B5289

Grasmoor
▲
851

4

C
r
u
m
m
o
c
k

Fletcher Fields

5

P

▲ 508

Mosedale Beck

Mellbreak

Lad Hows

Whiteless Pike
▲
658

N

6 At the road...

Rannerdale Farm

▲ 510

Ling Crags

House Point

6

W
a
t
e
r

Low Bank

Herdwick sheep

Mellbreak

Scale Knott

sheepfold

3

Scale Force Waterfall

Scale Beck

7

Sail Beck

church

Bridge Hotel

BUTTERMERE

B5289

2

1 P Fish Hotel

Far Ruddy Beck

▲ 484

Ling Comb

Buttermere

KESWICK

bridge, Buttermere

Distance: 7½ miles (12.1km)
Total ascent: 490ft (149m)
Paths: can be slippery and boggy
Terrain: lakeside tracks
Gradients: gradual
Refreshments: Kirkstile Inn, Loweswater; Fish Hotel and Bridge Hotel, Buttermere
Park: National Park car park near Bridge Hotel, Buttermere
Difficulty: 2

High Pike – the Last Lakeland Hill

*The Cumbrian Mountains end at a lonely viewpoint
high above the Solway Plain*

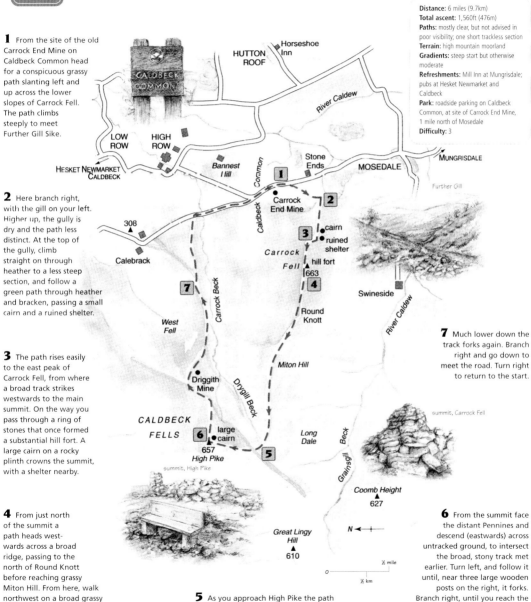

WALK
161

Distance: 6 miles (9.7km)
Total ascent: 1,560ft (476m)
Paths: mostly clear, but not advised in poor visibility; one short trackless section
Terrain: high mountain moorland
Gradients: steep start but otherwise moderate
Refreshments: Mill Inn at Mungrisdale; pubs at Hesket Newmarket and Caldbeck
Park: roadside parking on Caldbeck Common, at site of Carrock End Mine, 1 mile north of Mosedale
Difficulty: 3

1 From the site of the old Carrock End Mine on Caldbeck Common head for a conspicuous grassy path slanting left and up across the lower slopes of Carrock Fell. The path climbs steeply to meet Further Gill Sike.

2 Here branch right, with the gill on your left. Higher up, the gully is dry and the path less distinct. At the top of the gully, climb straight on through heather to a less steep section, and follow a green path through heather and bracken, passing a small cairn and a ruined shelter.

3 The path rises easily to the east peak of Carrock Fell, from where a broad track strikes westwards to the main summit. On the way you pass through a ring of stones that once formed a substantial hill fort. A large cairn on a rocky plinth crowns the summit, with a shelter nearby.

4 From just north of the summit a path heads westwards across a broad ridge, passing to the north of Round Knott before reaching grassy Miton Hill. From here, walk northwest on a broad grassy track, passing Red Gate, an obvious cross-track, which offers a quick escape route northwards if necessary.

5 As you approach High Pike the path curves northwards to pass the top of Drygill Beck, a steep-sided ravine, beyond which it ascends easy grassy slopes to the summit, on the way crossing a broad stony track.

6 From the summit face the distant Pennines and descend (eastwards) across untracked ground, to intersect the broad, stony track met earlier. Turn left, and follow it until, near three large wooden posts on the right, it forks. Branch right, until you reach the top of a narrow gully. Bear right again, alongside the gully and soon cross it to pursue an old mining track above Carrock Beck.

7 Much lower down the track forks again. Branch right and go down to meet the road. Turn right to return to the start.

HUTTON ROOF
Horseshoe Inn
CALDBECK COMMON
River Caldew
LOW ROW
HIGH ROW
HESKET NEWMARKET
CALDBECK
Bannest Hill
Stone Ends
MOSEDALE
MUNGRISDALE
Further Gill
Common
Caldbeck
1
Carrock End Mine
2
cairn
3 ruined shelter
308
Carrock Fell hill fort 663
Calebrack
4
Swineside
West Fell
Carrock Beck
7
Round Knott
Miton Hill
River Caldew
summit, Carrock Fell
Driggith Mine
Drygill Beck
CALDBECK FELLS
6 large cairn
657
High Pike
summit, High Pike
5
Long Dale
Grainsgill Beck
Coomb Height 627
Great Lingy Hill 610
N
0 ½ mile
½ km

ABOUT • CASTLERIGG STONE CIRCLE

Castlerigg is one of Britain's earliest stone circles and is made up of 48 stones. Called the Druid's Circle, it was probably used as a type of ancient planting calendar. This is a challenging walk but the views on show have inspired poets and painters.

Northern England

DISTANCE • 5½ miles (8.8km)

TOTAL ASCENT • 590ft (180m)

PATHS • some of the field paths to the circle can be muddy in winter

TERRAIN • woodland and pasture

GRADIENTS • short, steep climb from the car park, then easy gradients

REFRESHMENTS • none on the route. Many inns and cafés in nearby Keswick

PARK • Great Wood car park (NT), Borrowdale Road, by Derwent Water

DIFFICULTY • 3

Castlerigg's Ancient Stone Circle

❶ From the back of the car park, go through a gate by a ticket machine and climb along the woodland path. Ignore the first left turn; at the next major junction of paths turn left to climb, steeply at first, beneath Walla Crag. Take the waymarked right fork, signed to the forest's edge, before following an enclosed path across fields.

❷ Turn right on meeting a path by a stream. Cross the footbridge over the stream and climb to the lane north of Rakefoot Farm. Go left for a few paces, then right on a sunken path signed Castlerigg Stone Circle. Follow a wall on the left, across fields, before it swings left beyond a ladder stile.

❸ Turn right along the A591 (ignore sign for Castlerigg Stone Circle). After 200yds (183m) turn left down the drive of The High Nest. A well-defined field path continues north across several fields.

❹ Turn left on meeting a lane, then left again through the next gate to reach the stone circle. Beyond the stile at the top right-hand corner of the field, follow Castle Lane back to the A591 and Point ❸ of the walk. Retrace the outward route to Point ❷. Now stay with the riverside path, bearing left at the junction of two paths, before descending further past Springs Farm.

❺ Follow the road beyond the farm and turn left along the enclosed path to Castlehead Wood, signed Castlehead and Lake Road. Take the widest path ahead, then the second right fork by the field

boundary, to emerge on the Borrowdale Road. Turn left along the path across the road, then go right towards Cockshot Wood.

❻ Once in the wood, turn left. Beyond a gate at the southern edge, the path cuts across a field

to Strandshag Bay, on the shore of Derwent Water.

❼ Turn left along the path into the woods, then right along a stony lane passing Stable Hills (NT), back to the lake shore.

❽ After following the shore past Broomhill Point to Calfclose Bay the path goes inland through the wood. Pass an NT collection box to reach Borrowdale Road opposite the pedestrian access to the Great Wood car park.

• DON'T MISS •

Near Broomhill Point you'll pass close to the Centenary Sculpture. Known as the Hundred Year Stone, it was sculpted by Peter Randall Page from a split glacial Borrowdale boulder. The sculpture is dedicated to the first 100 years of the National Trust, from the early pioneers like Canon Hardwicke Rawnsley to the 20th-century trust members.

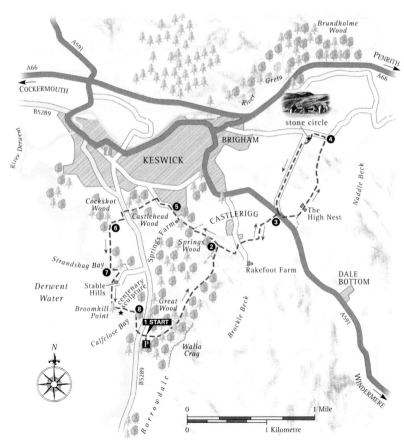

Swindale and the Eastern Fells

*Exploring forgotten valleys on the Lake District's
eastern fringe*

WALK

163

1 Leave Keld on a moorland road to Tailbert Farm. At Tailbert, abandon the road for a track across the hillside, later descending through bracken and gorse into Swindale. Cross a ford or a nearby bridge. Turn left, follow the minor road to Swindale Head Farm and go through gates onto a bridleway signed Mosedale.

2 After a final building on the left, branch left through glacial moraine, and climb through the rocky outcrops of Selside Pike. Cross open moorland to a fence at Swine Gill. Go through a gate and continue to a dilapidated building and a collapsed wall nearby.

6 When the river makes a pronounced bend to the right, move away from it to a wall. Go past Steps Hall, following a rough track towards Thornship Farm. Opposite the farm continue alongside the river to reach Keld once more.

5 Follow the road to a cattle grid. Here leave the road, turning left alongside the River Lowther. Cross a road and continue beside the river.

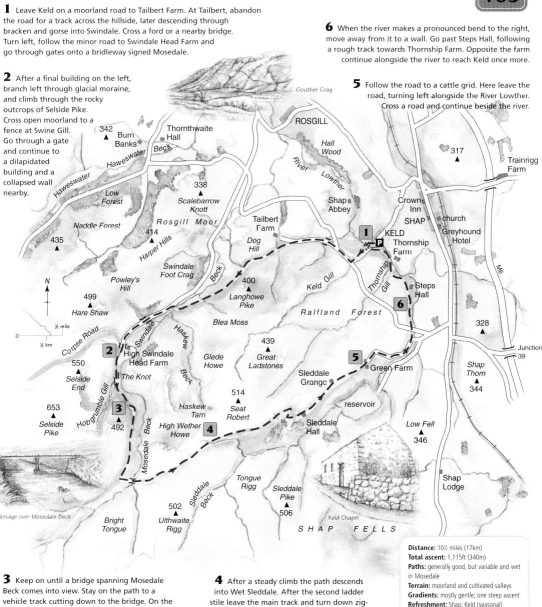

3 Keep on until a bridge spanning Mosedale Beck comes into view. Stay on the path to a vehicle track cutting down to the bridge. On the other side ascend one of the tracks which climb onto a broad grassy ridge, rising to a fence and gate. Beyond, a grassy track climbs further. When this forks, branch right.

4 After a steady climb the path descends into Wet Sleddale. After the second ladder stile leave the main track and turn down zig-zags to Sleddale Hall. Here go down to a lower track, through a gate beside a barn and forward to Sleddale Grange. Beyond this follow a rough-surfaced road to Green Farm.

Distance: 10½ miles (17km)
Total ascent: 1,115ft (340m)
Paths: generally good, but variable and wet in Mosedale
Terrain: moorland and cultivated valleys
Gradients: mostly gentle; one steep ascent
Refreshment: Shap; Keld (seasonal)
Park: Keld, on minor road west of A6 at Shap
Difficulty: 3

Long Meg and Lacy's Caves

A spectacular stone circle and intriguing Gothic caverns are linked by a walk in the verdant Eden Valley

Distance: 6 miles (9.7km)
Total ascent: 230ft (70m)
Paths: mainly good, but some muddy sections
Terrain: fields, woodland and riverside
Gradients: slight; one short steep section
Refreshments: The Watermill, Little Salkeld
Park: beside small village green in Little Salkeld, 1½ miles (2.4km) north of Langwathby and the A686 Penrith-Alston road. Turn left off road to Glassonby at sharp right bend
Difficulty: 1

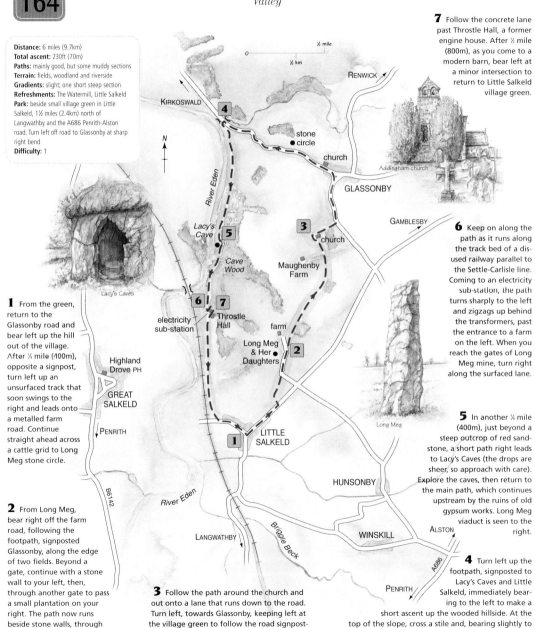

Addingham church

Lacy's Caves

Long Meg

7 Follow the concrete lane past Throstle Hall, a former engine house. After ½ mile (800m), as you come to a modern barn, bear left at a minor intersection to return to Little Salkeld village green.

6 Keep on along the path as it runs along the track bed of a disused railway parallel to the Settle-Carlisle line. Coming to an electricity sub-station, the path turns sharply to the left and zigzags up behind the transformers, past the entrance to a farm on the left. When you reach the gates of Long Meg mine, turn right along the surfaced lane.

5 In another ¼ mile (400m), just beyond a steep outcrop of red sandstone, a short path right leads to Lacy's Caves (the drops are sheer, so approach with care). Explore the caves, then return to the main path, which continues upstream by the ruins of old gypsum works. Long Meg viaduct is seen to the right.

4 Turn left up the footpath, signposted to Lacy's Caves and Little Salkeld, immediately bearing to the left to make a short ascent up the wooded hillside. At the top of the slope, cross a stile and, bearing slightly to the right, follow the field edge above the river. Keep along the path as it descends gently to the riverbank and runs upstream, later through woodland.

1 From the green, return to the Glassonby road and bear left up the hill out of the village. After ¼ mile (400m), opposite a signpost, turn left up an unsurfaced track that soon swings to the right and leads onto a metalled farm road. Continue straight ahead across a cattle grid to Long Meg stone circle.

2 From Long Meg, bear right off the farm road, following the footpath, signposted Glassonby, along the edge of two fields. Beyond a gate, continue with a stone wall to your left, then, through another gate to pass a small plantation on your right. The path now runs beside stone walls, through fields that can be very muddy, and crosses a farm lane to reach Addingham church.

3 Follow the path around the church and out onto a lane that runs down to the road. Turn left, towards Glassonby, keeping left at the village green to follow the road signposted to Kirkoswald. The road winds downhill for 1 mile (1.6km) to a bridge across a stream, with a lay-by to the left.

Map labels:
RENWICK
KIRKOSWALD
stone circle
church
GLASSONBY
Lacy's Cave
Cave Wood
Maughenby Farm
GAMBLESBY
church
electricity sub-station
Throstle Hall
farm
Long Meg & Her Daughters
Highland Drove PH
GREAT SALKELD
PENRITH
LITTLE SALKELD
HUNSONBY
WINSKILL
ALSTON
LANGWATHBY
PENRITH
River Eden
Briggle Beck
B6142
N
½ mile
½ km

The Edge of an Empire on Hadrian's Wall

*Walking on the wall which, for a while,
marked the northern limits of the Roman Empire*

WALK

165

Distance: 6 miles (9.6 km)
Total ascent: 560ft (171m)
Paths: mostly good but can get boggy
Terrain: fields, open country
Gradients: gradual
Refreshments: Haltwhistle town centre
Park: by Haltwhistle Railway Station
Difficulty: 2

1 From the station, walk straight ahead to the main street, then right along Westgate. Follow the main road through the town, then turn left up a flight of steps, immediately before the Grey Bull Hotel. Cross the next road, to join a private road to a kissing gate and path down to Haltwhistle Burn.

2 Almost at the burn, bear left alongside a playing field to join a lane. Shortly, turn right beyond some old works, over the bridge and left through a gate. After 200yds (182m), bear left, recross the burn and turn right on a lane to Lees Hall Farm.

3 Keep to the right of the farm to a gate on the far side. Follow the track to the next gate then cross the main road, turning right, then left by a house. Keep on the tarmac road, through a gate, across the burn, then later over a cattle grid until you reach a farm – the site of Aesica, Great Chesters Fort.

4 Within the fort, turn left towards a round fenced area. Go through the gap in the wall and follow the Pennine Way markers, over ladder stiles and past Cockmount Hill Farm, keeping along the wall.

5 Turn left off the Pennine Way after a ladder stile beyond Turret 44B. Turn left again at a muddy lane, crossing a cattle grid, then after 200yds (182m), turn right on a path signed Fell End. Go through a gate to the left of a building then follow the wall around to the left. Just beyond a waymarker, go down the course of an old wall and straight on where it ends to the far side of the field. Pass through a gate then bear left to ascend to the lowest gap in the ridge ahead. Near the top, pass through a gate and cross the next field to a stile at the main road.

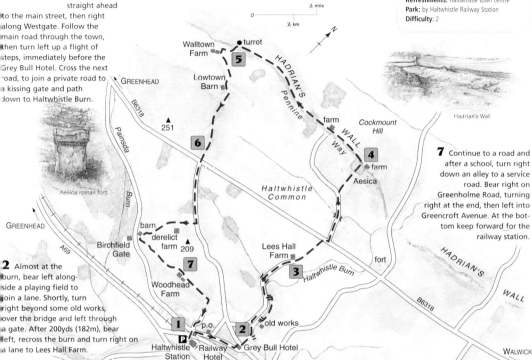

7 Continue to a road and after a school, turn right down an alley to a service road. Bear right on Greenholme Road, turning right at the end, then left into Greencroft Avenue. At the bottom keep forward for the railway station.

6 Cross the road signposted Haltwhistle and after 400yds (366m), where the road bends left, turn right on a path signposted Birchfield Gate. Head across the field to a ladder stile. Go down the centre of the next field towards a house. At the next gate, bear right, cross a burn and head for the left corner of a barn. Turn left here, recrossing the burn and ascending to the right hand corner of the field. Cross four stiles to a field on the left. Continue, to the left of Woodhead Farm, through two more gates and keep ahead, crossing a stile in the right hand corner of the field.

Cross Fell – the Pennine Giant

Rising up above the Vale of Eden, the Pennines' highest hill is a wild and spectacular vantage point

1 In Kirkland head up the road alongside Kirkland Beck. Beyond the last buildings a walled track heads out onto rough upland pastures, eventually looping north to skirt High Cap above Ardale Beck.

2 The gradient, nowhere unduly steep, is eased by a few bends. Within sight of the summit plateau, and not far from a bothy, the ascending track bears sharply left. Here leave it to strike eastwards on a cairned and grassy path, crossing the watershed and passing around the northern scree slopes of Cross Fell to locate the Pennine Way.

7 Onwards a broad green path descends easily through bracken to a sheepfold and across a tract of rough ground to Wythwaite Farm. At the farm turn right through gates, and follow a broad track back to Kirkland.

½ mile

0

½ km

Cross Fell

Green Fell
▲ 740

Brown Hill
▲ 666

Skirwith Fell
▲ 786

Fallow Hill
▲ 787

Rake End
▲ 696

▲ 535

Thack Moor

The Screes

Greg's Hut **3**

Ardale Beck

2

bothy

Kirk Dale

Pennine

Cross Fell
▲ 893

Kirkland

High Cap
▲ 546

Kirkland Beck

4 Way

Tees Head

River Tees

Cock Lock Scar

Grey Scar

5

Swath Beck

Kirkland Fell

Little Dun Fell
▲ 842

church

SKIRWITH

KIRKLAND
P

Wildboar Scar

6

Middle Tongue

Great Dun Fell
▲ 847 • masts

Skirwith Beck

1

Ranbeck Farm

MILBURN

FOREST

Hanging Walls of Mark Anthony

Wythwaite

ford

7 412

Grumply Hill

Crowdundle Beck

Iron Howe
▲ 613

6 Wildboar Scar is simply an abrupt escarpment of boulders and grass, and has a much clearer path. Ahead lies the dome of Grumply Hill, with the path keeping north of it to join a tributary of Crowdundle Beck.

Blencarn Beck

BLENCARN

CULGAITH

High Slack
▲ 269

Ellen Gill

MILBURN

3 A waymarker indicates the line of the Pennine Way, initially wet underfoot and clear enough to follow. It soon dries out, and a few large cairns guide you to the summit shelter-cairn and trig pillar.

4 In poor visibility the surest way down is to retreat. Otherwise, press on across the summit plateau, aiming for the distant summit of Great Dun Fell and its conspicuous masts and radar station. Near the edge of the Cross Fell plateau large cairns mark the way down to Tees Head.

5 From Tees Head a cairned path, not obvious, and narrow in places, leaves the Pennine Way and heads southwest across bouldery terrain to a cairn on the edge of Wildboar Scar. If you can't locate the line of cairns leaving Tees Head, drop beneath the downfall of scree and boulders and skirt along its lower edge until cairns appear in the far distance, and head for them.

Distance: 9 miles (14.5km)
Total ascent: 2,265ft (690m)
Paths: good on ascent, thereafter sketchy
Terrain: high mountain plateau
Gradients: moderate
Refreshment: none nearby
Park: alongside river, opposite church in Kirkland, 5 miles (8km) east of A686 in Langwathby
Note: this route requires good navigational skills and should not be attempted in poor visibility
Difficulty: 3

WALK
167

This walk visits Appleby Castle, restored in 1651 by the extraordinary Lady Anne Clifford. She won fame as a great adversary of Cromwell and for her prolific building and restoration work, including St Anne's Hospital and St Michael's in Bongate.

Northern England

DISTANCE • 6½ miles (10.4km)

TOTAL ASCENT • 375ft (114m)

PATHS • field tracks and farm lanes

TERRAIN • pastureland and town

GRADIENTS • no steep ascents

REFRESHMENTS • several pubs and tea shops in Appleby. The Royal Oak on Bongate is next to the start of the walk

PARK • roadside parking by the war memorial and St Michael's Church at the top of Mill Hill on Bongate

DIFFICULTY • 2

The Indomitable Spirit of Lady Anne Clifford

❶ Walk down Mill Hill to cross Jubilee Bridge over the River Eden by Bongate Mill. Walk up the hill and turn right at the top for 200yds (183m). Cross the road to the shop opposite, go along Colby Lane for 15yds (14m) to a footpath on the left signed Bandley Bridge.

❷ Cross the stile and go along the left-hand edge of the field to another stile. Turn right down a green lane for 10yds (9m) and turn left at a metal stile. Go over the rise in the field, cross the stile and turn right on to a green lane. As the track turns right, turn left over

a stile along the edge of a field. Soon turn right over next stile.

❸ Continue through the middle of the next field, aiming for a gate just below the horizon. Cross the stile by the gate and continue through the middle of the field. Over the brow of the hill, descend to the right-hand corner to cross a beck at the bottom. Turn right through a gate in a wall then left to cross Bandley Bridge. Cross a stile by a gate, turn right through a grassy field and a gate. After a

ruined wall, bear left up the bank towards a marker pole. At the top, bear left through a gate, then right on to a track to Nether Hoff.

❹ Go through the farmyard, then along the lane over a bridge and past some modern houses. At the junction with a road, cross to a footpath through a garden diagonally opposite, signed Village Green and Colby Hall. Go through a gate and across a field to a footbridge then, bearing right, cross over two stiles. Bear left, round the base of the bank on your left and at the end of the field go through a gate on to an access road. In 30yds (27m) turn right over a bridge to follow a concrete track over the hill. As Colby Laithes comes into view turn right up a footpath signed Appleby.

❺ Follow this track as it turns sharp right, then left, and becomes indistinct. Go through several fields and join a track coming in from the left. As the track bends right through a gate, cross a stile and turn left. By bungalows at the field corner join a path behind gardens. Pass a playground and turn left on a snicket (alley) into Appleby. Turn left on Holme Street, pass the fire station and cross Holme Bridge. Turn right through a metal gate signed Sands. Another gate leads to a woodland path, which eventually drops down to join a metalled road. Continue to the Sands (the road by the river) and turn right over the Eden.

❻ Walk along Bridge Street into Boroughgate, turn right through the Cloisters to St Lawrence's Church. After visiting the church return to walk up the left-hand side of Boroughgate. Pass the Hospital of St Anne, left, to the castle gates then follow Shaws Wiend, descending to Scattergate. Pass the rear entrance to the castle, retrace your steps down to Jubilee Bridge and Mill Hill.

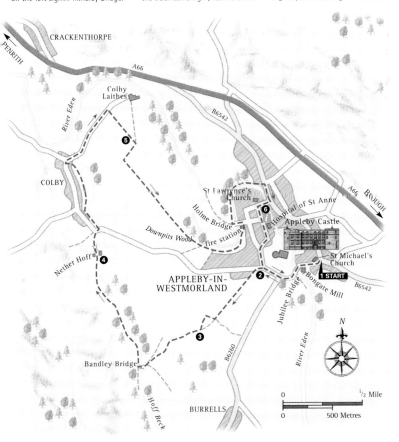

ABOUT • LYVENNET VALLEY

This walk visits a series of sites including Ewe Close and Ewe Locks, part of the ancient kingdom of Urien, warrior king of Rheged. The Rheged Visitor Centre, on the edge of Penrith, celebrates the time of this old British kingdom and is well worth a visit.

Northern England

DISTANCE • 6½ miles (10.4km)

TOTAL ASCENT • 720ft (219m)

PATHS • some unclear. Can be extremely muddy

TERRAIN • pastureland and open fell

GRADIENTS • some steep grassy slopes

REFRESHMENTS • The Butchers' Arms, Crosby Ravensworth

PARK • by the village hall in Crosby Ravensworth

DIFFICULTY • 3

Valley of the Kings

❶ Cross the bridge opposite village hall, turn right down left bank of beck. Turn left, signed Wickerslack, bear left between sheds, join track zigzagging up field beyond. At the top go ahead through a gate, cross field between telegraph poles. Over crown of the hill, aim for field corner nearest buildings. Cross stile and immediately another, walk diagonally across to a stile behind Crake Trees farm.

❷ Behind farm, turn left to a gate and a zigzag track up a field. The path is indistinct by remains of a stone enclosure. Follow its left-hand edge to a post and a thorn bush to your left. Cross ditch by the thorn and follow it to a wall. Turn right, wall on left, through two gates to a junction of tracks.

❸ Left through gate then right up road. In 100yds (91m) go left, pass a farm and down a lane, signed Haber. At the end, go through gate, bear right to a track. At the end, go through a gate into a field. Go half-left to bottom left-hand corner. Take right-hand gate, continue down the field; cut the corner at the bottom to go right, through gate. Bear left to Haber farm and go left of buildings. Turn left below cow sheds, go right through a gap in field boundary. Cross field and through a gap in wall. Turn left on to a muddy track, continue to the bottom.

❹ Turn right. Pass High Dalebanks. On grassy track follow signs to Oddendale (wall left). When track is enclosed by boulders, turn left to a bridge. Cross bridge and a stile, climb bank, bear right, between two humps. Walk to Slacks ruin. In farmyard bear right, through gate. Turn left to Lane Head. At top of farmyard (ruin) go through gate to open fell. Turn left, follow grassy

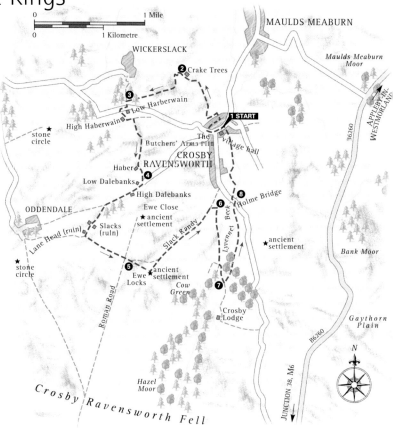

MAULDS MEABURN

Maulds Meaburn Moor

WICKERSLACK

❷ Crake Trees

❸

Low Harberwain

High Haberwain

1 START

stone circle

The Butchers' Arms

CROSBY RAVENSWORTH

Haber

❹

Low Dalebanks

High Dalebanks

ODDENDALE

Ewe Close

★ ancient settlement

❻

Holme Bridge

❽

Slacks (ruin)

Lane Head (ruin)

Slack Randy

stone circle

❺

Ewe Locks

★ ancient settlement

Cow Green

❼

★ ancient settlement

Bank Moor

Crosby Lodge

Gaythorn Plain

Roman Road

N

Hazel Moor

Crosby Ravensworth Fell

JUNCTION 38, M6

B6260

track. In 100yds (91m) go right, to corner of wall on left. In 30yds (27m) beyond fence in field on left, the Roman road crosses your track. Beyond is Ewe Close.

❺ As track descends, carry on across fell (no footpath) for 200yds (183m) to Ewe Locks. Turn left downhill for ¾ mile (1.2km) on to track, Slack Randy. Turn right, by a boulder to a good track.

❻ Right again through metal gate; double back across fellside. Follow path down to gate in left corner of field. Fence on right, pass through another gate. At crossroads of paths go left, to Lyvennet Beck.

❼ Ford beck (footbridge 200yds/ 183m upstream). Go through gate, turn left over a bridge to another gate. Ascend track to a gate. Turn left across field to a stile next to a

gate, continue through three fields to Holme Bridge.

❽ Left over bridge then right over a footbridge into a field. At the far side, cross a stile and continue with beck on your right. Follow the path along the bottom of a steep bank, cross a stile and turn right over a ladder stile by a bridge. Turn left through a gate on to a lane, at the end turn left to village hall.

Up Gunnerside Gill with Swaledale Miners

*A fine ramble up through classic Dales scenery reveals
a landscape shaped by the search for lead*

1 From the bridge in the centre of Gunnerside take the track on the eastern side up the beck, beginning opposite the Kings Head. After 100yds (91m), at a white gate, take stone steps to the right, then a walled path, emerging into open fields. The path descends to the beck as the valley broadens out. Cross a side beck on a tiny bridge, take two gap-stiles, close together, and follow a wall. Beyond two little gates you reach the beck again, and the first evidence of lead ore processing.

2 Pass two ore-dressing floors, one each side of the beck, and the entrance to a mining tunnel, known as a 'level'. Continue on the riverside path, following the yellow arrows, then go uphill, away from the beck. Cross a stile in the fence before going through a gap-stile in a wall. The path climbs gradually, as the valley becomes steeper-sided. Keep a wall to your left as the path levels out into the principal mining area.

3 Soon the Bunton mining complex comes into view. Pass through it and leave on a stony path uphill, with huge hushes on all sides. After 100yds (91m) uphill, fork left, downhill.

7 Keep left (the track soon becomes more distinct), heading for the roofs of Gunnerside that soon appear. The path gradually becomes clearer and leads you downhill. Go through a little wooden gate and back into the village.

6 Follow this track to the left, through a gate and past a little waterfall in Botcher Gill, before making a gentle descent. Across the valley the landscape changes back to a more familiar one of farms, walls and barns. When the track makes a long right turn, go left on a grassy path, by a small cairn.

ore wagon

Blakethwaite

Gunnerside Moor

Friarfold Moor
▲
589

Blind Beck

4 limekiln
Blakethwaite Smelting Mill

N

Gunnerside Gill

5

Bunton mining
complex

3

MELBECKS

Botcher Gill

6

Silver Hill

MOOR

Winterings Edge

▲
566

Jingle Pot
Edge

mine buildings

2

Gunnerside
Pasture

Birkbeck
Wood

Gunnerside

Elias's Stot
Wood

cairn ●

7

1

GUNNERSIDE

½ mile

0

½ km

IVELET

DALE

Kings
Head PH

REETH

B6270

SWALE

River Swale

SATRON

B6270

B6270

THWAITE

CRACKPOT

Distance: 6 miles (10km)
Total ascent: 660ft (201m)
Paths: good
Terrain: steep-sided Pennine valley
Gradients: gradual
Refreshments: Kings Head, Gunnerside
Park: opposite Kings Head, Gunnerside, on B6270 between Reeth and Kirkby Stephen
Difficulty: 2

4 Approach Blakethwaite Smelting Mill, on a cramped site where Gunnerside Beck meets Blind Beck. Take a small bridge made from a slab of stone. Behind the mill the flue (mostly collapsed) rises steeply uphill. From the mill, the return path is clear, following a well-defined path gradually climbing up the west flank of Gunnerside Gill.

5 Cross another hush on a stone parapet; soon the southern end of Gunnerside Gill comes into view. Follow the track as it becomes stonier, makes a hairpin turn to cross Botcher Gill and joins a more substantial track.

Limestone Landscapes around Malham

Above the spectacular face of Malham Cove lies a less-visited world of classic limestone scenery

Distance: 5 miles (8km)
Total ascent: 985ft (300m)
Paths: good; some steep, stepped sections
Terrain: limestone landscape and upland pasture
Gradients: mostly easy, apart from steps by cove
Refreshments: pubs and cafés, Malham
Park: car park by visitor centre, Malham
Difficulty: 2

1 From the car park walk into the village. Where the road forks at the little bridge over Malham Beck, keep left, signed to Settle. About 200yds (182m) past the last building, go through a pair of gates on the right, to follow the well-trodden path towards Malham Cove. Descend to accompany Malham Beck, passing a little clapper-bridge on the way.

2 Just 300yds (274m) from the base of the cliff, take steps on the left climbing steeply to the extensive limestone pavement on top of the cove. Cross the pavement (with care) to a wall, and follow it to the left, along the dry valley of Watlowes. Beyond a wall-stile the valley narrows into a rocky gorge, that you leave by steps at the far end.

3 Take a step-stile at the top. Ignore a track to the right (signed Malham Tarn) to continue straight ahead alongside the wall. After just 30yds (27m), take a ladder stile on the left, over the wall. Follow the wall on your right; a finger post indicates Langscar Gate. Walk up to a road, cross it, and continue in the same direction, now on a rutted track. Follow the track uphill to a meeting of walls.

4 Take the gap in the walls and bear half-left to join a grassy track, uphill, to a gate in a wall. Continue in the same direction, through two more gates, after which you bear half-left towards Nappa Cross, a stone pillar on top of a wall (a medieval guide-stone). Follow the wall uphill to a gate and a three-way fingerpost. This, at 1,640ft (500m), is the highest point of the walk

5 Go through the gate (signed to Cove Road), and follow a path downhill. Pass a way-marker sign (Malham 2 miles) and head towards Malham Cove in the distance. Descend gradually, going through a gate near where dry-stone walls meet and continuing down the broad track to a minor road. Walk right, down the road, for 200yds (182m), to a sharp hairpin bend to the left.

6 At this corner, take a gate on the right onto a field track (signed Malham 1 mile), soon enclosed between limestone walls. Follow this green lane past the water treatment works to join another, stonier track to a T-junction of tracks. Go right to return to Malham car park.

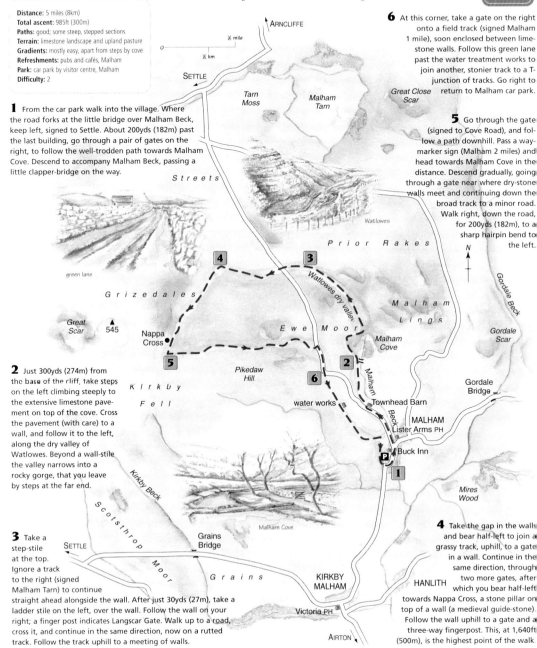

ABOUT • ARKENGARTHDALE

Lead has been mined here for thousands of years but it wasn't until the 17th century that intensive mining began and small 'frontier' towns began springing up. This walk has plenty of history to offer as it wends its way through the Yorkshire Dales.

Northern England

DISTANCE • 8 miles (13km)

TOTAL ASCENT • 1,213ft (370m)

PATHS • mostly clear tracks; a little walking on heather moor

TERRAIN • steep, mined valleys and moorland

GRADIENTS • two stiff climbs, but generally gradual slopes

REFRESHMENTS • Red Lion in Langthwaite and the CB Inn in Arkengarthdale

PARK • car park at southern end of Langthwaite village

DIFFICULTY • 3

Arkengarthdale's Mining Legacy

❶ From the car park, turn right, then right again. Cross the bridge, continue ahead between cottages and climb the hill. Follow the lane to the hamlet of Booze (note that hamlets in Arkengarthdale are early Norse settlements). Pass the farmhouse and a stone barn and follow the track to a gate.

❷ Beyond the gate, where the track bends left, go ahead, beside a tumbled wall. Bear right to pass a ruined cottage and follow the path to the stream. Walk upstream, pass through a gate, and cross the stream on stepping stones.

❸ Follow the course of the steam through moorland to a wooden hut. Turn left along the track beyond. Go straight ahead at a crossing, then turn left at a T-junction. Where the wall on your right ends, take the path, right, down to a gate.

❹ Follow the gill downhill to go through another gate. Turn right along the track beyond it. Continue through a gateway and on to another track by a barn. Follow the track, which bends left by a stone wall and passes farm buildings, through two gates to a white gate.

❺ Go through the gate into Scar House grounds. Bear right down the drive, over a bridge and cattle grid and turn right on to a track. Continue to a road. Turn left, then right at a T-junction. After a cattle grid, turn left on a signed track.

❻ Bear right at a gravelled area and continue uphill on the track. Where it divides, go left beside slag heaps and pass the junction of two flues. The track bends right then left, uphill, to a T-junction. Turn left here. Follow the track downhill to a road.

❼ Turn left. Beyond the farmhouse turn right at a bridleway sign towards the house, and turn left before reaching it. Follow the signed track though a gate. Continue downhill and turn left before a small barn. Go over four stiles to the road. Turn left back to the car park.

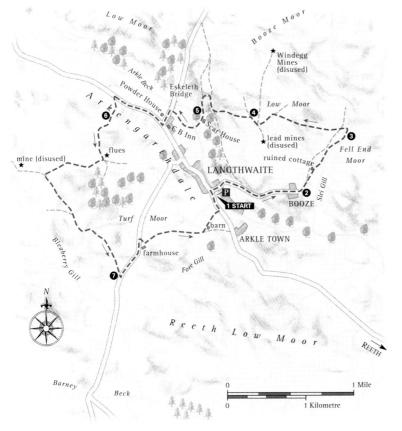

• DON'T MISS •

*The attractive village of **Reeth**, set around a wide, sloping green, has been a market town since 1695 and still holds sheep sales. It formerly had an important knitting industry.*

WALK
172

ABOUT • DURHAM

Above the River Wear sits Durham's imposing cathedral and castle – once the centre of power of the prince-bishops.In the 11th century William I conferred wide-ranging powers on the bishopric – effectively making them kings of the north.

Northern England

DISTANCE • 1½ miles (2.4km)

TOTAL ASCENT • 300ft (91m)

PATHS • city pavements and riverside paths

TERRAIN • fortress rock with castle and cathedral, and ravine of the River Wear

GRADIENTS • moderate climbs from Market Place to Palace Green and from river bank to St Oswald's Church; otherwise easy

REFRESHMENTS • available throughout the centre of Durham, including on Palace Green and in the cathedral

PARK • city centre car parks in Durham, the Prince Bishop car park is the most convenient

DIFFICULTY • 1

The Prince-Bishops of Durham

• DON'T MISS •

*In the cathedral treasury is the 13th-century **Conyers Falchion**, a fearsome knife, that represents the defence of the bishopric. It is still presented, as for centuries past, to each new Bishop of Durham at the bridge over the River Tees at Croft, as he first enters the Palatinate officially.*

❶ From the statue of Lord Londonderry in the Market Place, follow his horse's nose to pass the Nationwide building society and go up Saddler Street. Ascend the hill for 164yds (150m) and turn right up Owengate, signed

Cathedral and Castle, and on to Palace Green.

❷ At the top of the hill, turn right, to follow the wall for 55yds (50m) to the entrance of the castle. After visiting the castle return to the

entrance and keep ahead to enter the cathedral by the north door.

❸ After your visit, leave by the door opposite the one you entered by. Walk ahead down the cloisters. The treasury is to the right at the

end. After visiting, continue around the cloisters and go right, signed Norman Undercroft Exhibition, into an irregular square, The College.

❹ Follow the wall on your left until you reach the arch. Go through the arch and turn right on to South Bailey. Descend slightly for 273yds (250m) to Prebends Bridge. Do not cross, but turn right along the lower riverside path.

❺ Follow the path for 328yds (300m) passing the Old Fulling Mill Museum of Archaeology. Continue ahead for another 328yds (300m) and ascend a slope then steps up on to Silver Street. Turn left and cross Framwellgate Bridge. Over the bridge, turn left down steps by the Coach and Eight pub to the banks of the River Wear.

❻ Go straight ahead, passing behind the riverside buildings to reach the end of Prebends Bridge. Do not cross, but continue beside the river for 600yds (656m) until the path ascends into St Oswald's churchyard. Go through the churchyard on to Church Street and turn left.

❼ At the traffic lights continue on the main road – New Elvet. At the next crossroads turn left over Elvet Bridge and ascend the slope at the end. Turn right, back to the Market Place.

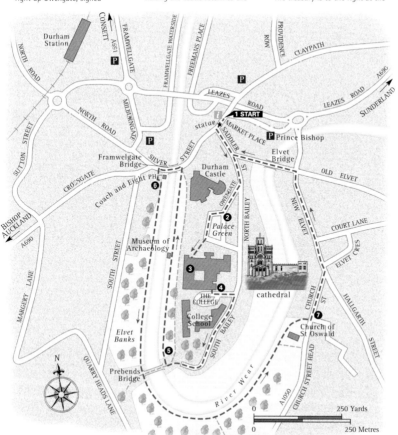

Northern England

DISTANCE • 5 ¼ miles (8.4km)

TOTAL ASCENT • 460ft (140m)

PATHS • field paths, roads and farm tracks

TERRAIN • undulating farmland and fine coastland with grassy dunes

GRADIENTS • moderate

REFRESHMENTS • Bark Potts café and Robson's fish restaurant, Craster; Cottage Inn, Dunstan

PARK • signed car park at entrance to Craster

DIFFICULTY • 2

Dunstanburgh – Castle of Legends

❶ From the car park, take the path behind the tourist information centre signed Craster South Farm. Fork left near a bench and at a kissing gate bear half-right across the field and uphill. Go through another gate on to a lane.

❷ Turn right, then right again at a crossroads. Go through the archway across the road then turn left through a gate, signed to Dunstan (the nearby Dunstan Hall is believed to have been the birth place of Duns Scotus, a famous 13th-century philosopher). At the next gate go half-left, through another gate and past the row of houses to the road.

❸ Turn right and follow the road as it bends left. Go straight on at the next junction, towards Embleton. Take the next lane right, signed Dunstan Square. Pass the houses then bend left though the farmyard. Go straight on through a gate, signed Dunstan Steads.

❹ Follow the farm road for a mile (1.6km). As you approach the hamlet of Dunstan Steads, go

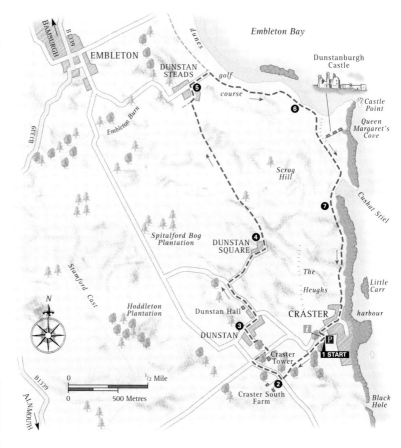

through a gateway and wind between farm buildings to a road. Turn right, and follow the road as it bends left to reach a lane.

❺ Turn right, following a sign to Dunstanburgh Castle. At the bottom of the lane, go through a gate and turn right beside the golf

course. The path goes alongside a green to a kissing gate by a National Trust sign.

❻ Go through the gate and follow the path inland round the castle rock, to arrive at the gatehouse entrance. After visiting the castle, leave the gateway and continue

straight ahead along the ridge to reach a kissing gate.

❼ Continue ahead along the coast, through another kissing gate to enter Craster village by a gate on to a lane. Pass the houses to reach a T-junction above the harbour, and turn right, to the car park.

Flodden's Bloody Field

Scotland invaded England for the 'auld alliance' and the flower of its nobility was slaughtered in this Cheviot pastureland

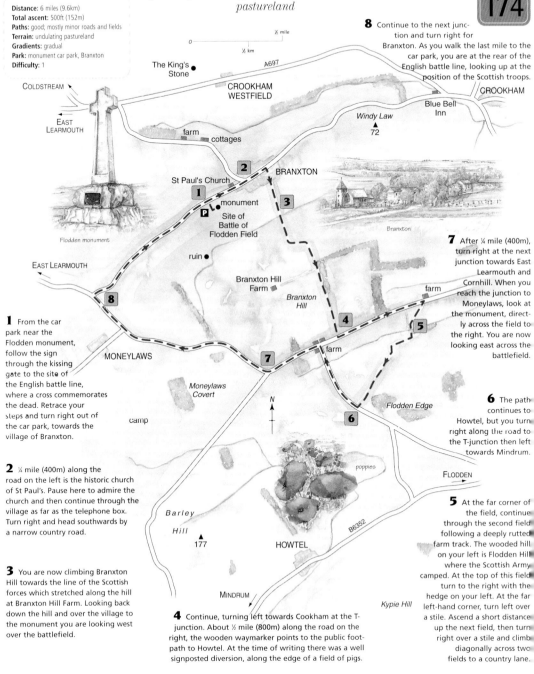

WALK

174

Distance: 6 miles (9.6km)
Total ascent: 500ft (152m)
Paths: good; mostly minor roads and fields
Terrain: undulating pastureland
Gradients: gradual
Park: monument car park, Branxton
Difficulty: 1

0   ½ mile
    ½ km

8 Continue to the next junction and turn right for Branxton. As you walk the last mile to the car park, you are at the rear of the English battle line, looking up at the position of the Scottish troops.

1 From the car park near the Flodden monument, follow the sign through the kissing gate to the site of the English battle line, where a cross commemorates the dead. Retrace your steps and turn right out of the car park, towards the village of Branxton.

2 ¼ mile (400m) along the road on the left is the historic church of St Paul's. Pause here to admire the church and then continue through the village as far as the telephone box. Turn right and head southwards by a narrow country road.

3 You are now climbing Branxton Hill towards the line of the Scottish forces which stretched along the hill at Branxton Hill Farm. Looking back down the hill and over the village to the monument you are looking west over the battlefield.

4 Continue, turning left towards Cookham at the T-junction. About ½ mile (800m) along the road on the right, the wooden waymarker points to the public footpath to Howtel. At the time of writing there was a well signposted diversion, along the edge of a field of pigs.

5 At the far corner of the field, continue through the second field following a deeply rutted farm track. The wooded hill on your left is Flodden Hill where the Scottish Army camped. At the top of this field turn to the right with the hedge on your left. At the far left-hand corner, turn left over a stile. Ascend a short distance up the next field, then turn right over a stile and climb diagonally across two fields to a country lane.

6 The path continues to Howtel, but you turn right along the road to the T-junction then left towards Mindrum.

7 After ¼ mile (400m), turn right at the next junction towards East Learmouth and Cornhill. When you reach the junction to Moneylaws, look at the monument, directly across the field to the right. You are now looking east across the battlefield.

Berwick's Bulwark against the Scots

The streets, ramparts and surrounding countryside of this historic border town make for a splendid circular walk

WALK 175

1 From the Maltings car park go left, down the hill. At the bottom, cross the road, then keep ahead over Berwick Old Bridge. Once over, turn right. At corner of Blakewell Road take path to the right, beside the river.

2 Keep following this route by the river, taking care as it can be extremely muddy and wet and subject to high tides. Later go through a gate and follow the path, keeping to the line of the fence and up to the sewage works.

3 Go over the stile and follow the path, then go through the gate and turn left. At the next gate turn right onto the road. Go to the corner of the field and take the path along its right-hand edge, above the little hut.

4 Continue into the next field. At the end take the right-hand path and descend past a ruined hut and over a little bridge. Ascend and go over the stile to the picnic area with toilets.

5 Go over the next stile, by the main road, then turn right over the bridge. Take the footpath to the right, down the steps. Go over the stile and back along the river, keeping to the line of the hedge. After ½ mile (800m), veer right to follow a series of waymarks. At the end cross the wooden bridge then a ladder stile and ascend through woodland. At the top of the wood turn right along a woodland path. (If the tide is in, stay with the hedge on your left to cross the stone bridge and turn right into the woodland.)

Distance: 5 miles (8km)
Total ascent: 100ft (30m)
Paths: undefined in places; can be muddy
Terrain: fields, town
Gradients: some steps
Refreshments: plenty in town
Park: the Maltings car park, Berwick upon Tweed
Difficulty: 1

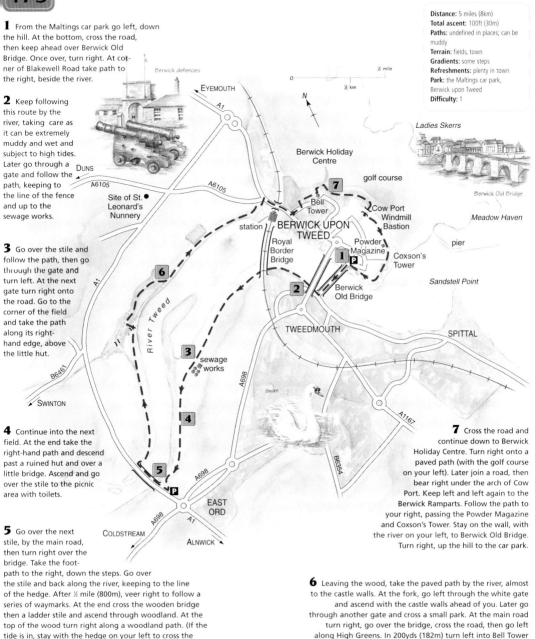

Berwick defences

Ladies Skerrs

Berwick Old Bridge

Meadow Haven

6 Leaving the wood, take the paved path by the river, almost to the castle walls. At the fork, go left through the white gate and ascend with the castle walls ahead of you. Later go through another gate and cross a small park. At the main road turn right, go over the bridge, cross the road, then go left along High Greens. In 200yds (182m) turn left into Bell Tower Place then, at a school, keep right to the Bell Tower.

7 Cross the road and continue down to Berwick Holiday Centre. Turn right onto a paved path (with the golf course on your left). Later join a road, then bear right under the arch of Cow Port. Keep left and left again to the Berwick Ramparts. Follow the path to your right, passing the Powder Magazine and Coxson's Tower. Stay on the wall, with the river on your left, to Berwick Old Bridge. Turn right, up the hill to the car park.

Scotland

Scotland displays many faces, even on first acquaintance: the rolling hills of the Southern Uplands, the industrial urban belt between the Clyde and the Forth, then the Highlands in all their splendour, breaking up west and north into a succession of headlands and sea lochs, islands and stacks. A tour of Scotland offers the chance to see Britain's landscape on a grand scale – all the island's highest mountains lie north of the border, along with an incredibly rugged coastline and vast tracts of wilderness. There is also a greater degree of freedom to roam than elsewhere, and a distinct culture and tradition evident wherever you travel.

The weather can be extreme on the high ground, so approach with due caution. You can approach the Cuillins from Sligachan on Skye without too much difficulty, but to grapple with the high ridges requires rock-climbing skills. You can wander in the wilds of the Flow Country, but you need to know when it's time to turn back. If the really high mountains look daunting, there are plenty of smaller hills you can climb.

The ancient Caledonian pine forest at Rothlemurchus is a mere remnant of a much more widespread wildwood. Even in the apparent wilds of Scotland most of the landscape is man-managed. The first rough highways through the glens and high passes were trodden by drovers, and the first attempt to establish a real road network came under the auspices of General Wade after the 1745 Jacobite Rebellion.

Wherever you look, you can find evidence of strife: Largs, Bannockburn, Stirling and Culloden all saw great and decisive battles. Then there are shameful episodes painfully seared into the folk memory: the Massacre of Glen Coe, and the brutal Clearances of the 19th century, in which thousands were evicted from the land.

Scotland is a land of conflicts and contrasts, of lovely scenery and loveless battlefields. Romantic-looking castles sit uneasily with their history of appalling bloodshed. Craggy peaks can look welcoming one moment, then threatening the next, as the weather clouds over. This endless variation is an essential part of Scotland's fascination.

Best of the Rest

Trotternish There is something surreal about the pillars and spikes of Quiraing, the intriguing end to the Trotternish uplands of northern Skye. Walkers who approach from the road crossing the centre of the island are rewarded by an unfolding view of towers and pinnacles. Although the pillars present problems to even the most experienced scrambler, there are good paths around the strange arenas created by this unique rock formation, making them accessible to most fit walkers.

Trossachs The Victorians were first drawn by the scenic splendours of the Trossachs, another point of entry from the lowland world to the upland wilds of the Highlands, and the area became a fashionable stopping place for tourists. As the road from Callander winds its way through forests and past lakes, the placenames turn from Anglicised lowland Scots to bewildering Highland Gaelic. The difference should not be lost on walkers who will find much to delight and challenge them here.

Glen Clova Glen Clova strikes out into the rising eastern Highlands, offering many Lowlanders the first glimpses of the great mountain ranges beyond the Highland line. Jock's Road is an ancient highway linking Kirriemuir with the splendour of Royal Deeside and can be used to access the Caenlochan National Nature Reserve.

Sandwood Bay Few places epitomise the essence of remote northwest Scotland than this spectacular sweep of sand on Sutherland's wild Atlantic coast. Accessible only on foot from a road end three miles (4.8km) away, walkers who make it this far (the drive out to the roadend is as challenging as the walking) are rewarded by solitude and a perfect beach.

Merrick The feral goats which loiter on the wild hillsides of the Southern Uplands are often the only company walkers have as they make their way up southern Scotland's highest peak, the Merrick. From the campsites and facilities in Glen Trool there is a good track, though very steep in places, to the upper parts of this lonely mountain, and the views in clear weather are unsurpassed.

Arran Often fêted as Scotland in miniature, there is a wealth of good walking at all levels on this Clyde island. For an introduction to Scottish mountain walking, the ascent of Goat Fell, the island's highest peak, from Brodick Castle by Glen Rosa and the Saddle, is hard to beat.

Scotland

Following St Ninian on the Isle of Whithorn

A coastal walk where St Ninian's early church thrived

1 At the harbour, beyond The Steampacket Inn, follow the signpost for St Ninian's Chapel. Follow the track through the children's play area and head for a cairn marking the end of the Pilgrims Way. Look for the chapel to your left.

2 Follow the path to a large, square, white tower which looks across the Solway to Cumbria. Then enter the chapel grounds via a kissing gate beside a cairn, raised in 1997 to celebrate the foundation of Ninian's church 1600 years earlier.

3 Retrace your steps, walking round the harbour past the tumbledown red village store, the parish church and the post office. At the Queen's Arms Hotel, turn left into Tonderghie Row, following the sign for Burrow Head Holiday Park past Cutcloy Farm.

8 Follow the road past Orfasey Cottage and on until it terminates at a T-junction beside an old barn. Turn right and, at the next junction, turn right again, following the road back round the harbour to your starting point.

7 Nearing a farm, where the path has fallen away, cross the fence into a field. Follow the track in the field through a gate between two dry-stone walls. Follow the right-hand wall along to another gate then turn left alongside the far wall and over a gate onto the farm road at Morrach and turn right onto a track.

6 The path is easy to follow along the coast, although it may be overgrown at points. Keep close to the barbed-wire fence or cross it temporarily until the obstruction is passed.

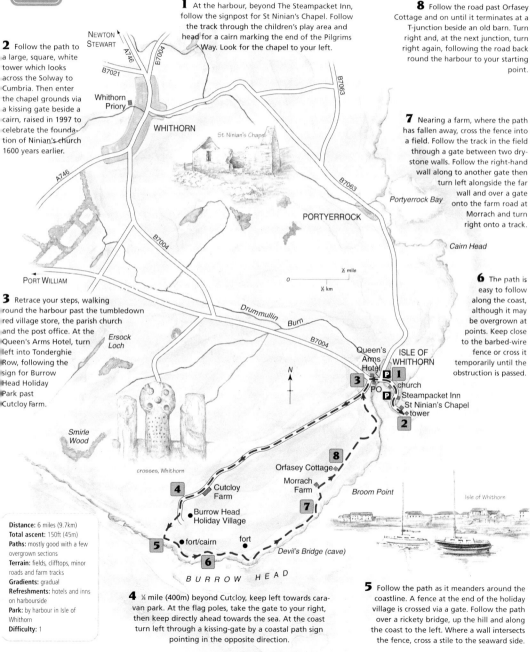

Distance: 6 miles (9.7km)
Total ascent: 150ft (45m)
Paths: mostly good with a few overgrown sections
Terrain: fields, clifftops, minor roads and farm tracks
Gradients: gradual
Refreshments: hotels and inns on harbourside
Park: by harbour in Isle of Whithorn
Difficulty: 1

4 ¼ mile (400m) beyond Cutcloy, keep left towards caravan park. At the flag poles, take the gate to your right, then keep directly ahead towards the sea. At the coast turn left through a kissing-gate by a coastal path sign pointing in the opposite direction.

5 Follow the path as it meanders around the coastline. A fence at the end of the holiday village is crossed via a gate. Follow the path over a rickety bridge, up the hill and along the coast to the left. Where a wall intersects the fence, cross a stile to the seaward side.

WALK 177

ABOUT DUNDRENNAN ABBEY

Mary, Queen of Scots, spent her last night in Scotland in this abbey, founded in 1142 by a Cistercian order of monks from Rievaulx in North Yorkshire. No early written records of the abbey have survived but the remains suggest a wealthy past.

Scotland

DISTANCE • 6 miles (9.6km)

TOTAL ASCENT • 98ft (30m)

PATHS • good, but can be very muddy in wet weather

TERRAIN • country lanes, farm tracks, fields and a section of A-road

GRADIENTS • gentle

REFRESHMENTS • none on route. The Selkirk Arms, Kirkcudbright

PARK • car park, Dundrennan Abbey

DIFFICULTY • 2

A Simple Life at Dundrennan Abbey

• DON'T MISS •

Kirkcudbright is one of the most colourful towns in Scotland, with streets of brightly painted Georgian houses. The town has a rich history which dates back to the 13th century when the fortress of Castlemains came into the possession of John Balliol, the Lord of Galloway, and Edward I is believed to have stayed here during this time. In the late 19th and 20th centuries, Kirkudbright prospered under a new trade – brought by the artists of the day – and quickly gained a reputation as an artists' haven for the quality of its light. A number of famous artists were attracted to the town, including EA Hornel, who donated his home at Broughton House to the town – the house is now a museum.

❶ From the car park in Dundrennan village return to the A711 and turn left. Take the first turning on the left, signed Port Mary, and continue along this road. At the next junction go left again avoiding the military road.

❷ Follow this road as it winds round the farm steading and past the entrance of Port Mary House. Stop for a moment and consider the fate of Mary Queen of Scots. She fled here after her disastrous defeat at Langside in 1568 and

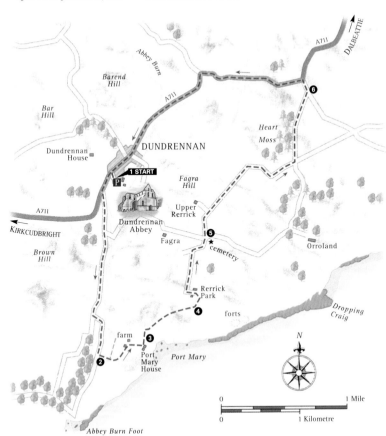

set sail from here for England, hoping to receive the protection of Elizabeth I, but she was never to return. Go through the gate at the end of the road, along a farm track and through a second gate.

❸ Walk ahead for approximately 100yds (91m), then turn right and cross a small burn. Head across the field parallel to the telegraph poles and look for the gate in the far side. Go through it.

❹ Turn left and follow the line of the burn then turn left again, cross the burn and enter the steading at Rerrick Park farm. Turn left on to the road, which runs up the side of the farm house and then turns sharp right.

❺ At the crossroads, beside a cemetery, go forward on the middle road. Pass the entrance to Upper Rerrick on the left and follow the road as it turns first right and then left to end at a T-junction.

❻ Turn left and at the junction with the A711 turn left again. Continue along this quiet road for about 2 miles (3.2km) to reach the village of Dundrennan (note that the stone from the ruined abbey was used in the construction of the village) and return to the abbey car park.

Scotland

Four Kingdoms from Criffel

England, Ireland, Scotland and the Isle of Man are all visible from this looming moorland eminence above the Solway Firth

Distance: 9 miles (14.5km)
Total ascent: 1,867ft (569m)
Paths: mostly good; very boggy in winter and in wet weather
Terrain: road, fields, woodland, heather moorland and farm tracks
Gradients: very steep up Criffel
Refreshments: Abbey Tea Room at car park.
Park: Sweetheart Abbey car park
Difficulty: 2

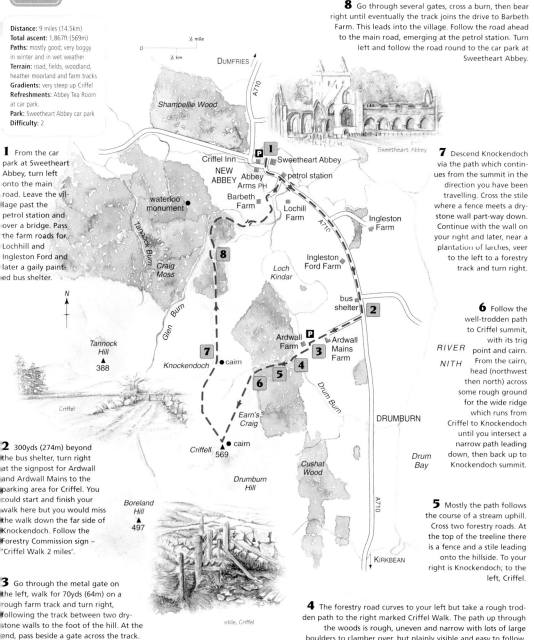

½ mile

0   ½ km

8 Go through several gates, cross a burn, then bear right until eventually the track joins the drive to Barbeth Farm. This leads into the village. Follow the road ahead to the main road, emerging at the petrol station. Turn left and follow the road round to the car park at Sweetheart Abbey.

1 From the car park at Sweetheart Abbey, turn left onto the main road. Leave the village past the petrol station and over a bridge. Pass the farm roads for Lochhill and Ingleston Ford and later a gaily painted bus shelter.

7 Descend Knockendoch via the path which continues from the summit in the direction you have been travelling. Cross the stile where a fence meets a dry-stone wall part-way down. Continue with the wall on your right and later, near a plantation of larches, veer to the left to a forestry track and turn right.

6 Follow the well-trodden path to Criffel summit, with its trig point and cairn. From the cairn, head (northwest then north) across some rough ground for the wide ridge which runs from Criffel to Knockendoch until you intersect a narrow path leading down, then back up to Knockendoch summit.

2 300yds (274m) beyond the bus shelter, turn right at the signpost for Ardwall and Ardwall Mains to the parking area for Criffel. You could start and finish your walk here but you would miss the walk down the far side of Knockendoch. Follow the Forestry Commission sign – 'Criffel Walk 2 miles'.

3 Go through the metal gate on the left, walk for 70yds (64m) on a rough farm track and turn right, following the track between two dry-stone walls to the foot of the hill. At the end, pass beside a gate across the track.

5 Mostly the path follows the course of a stream uphill. Cross two forestry roads. At the top of the treeline there is a fence and a stile leading onto the hillside. To your right is Knockendoch; to the left, Criffel.

4 The forestry road curves to your left but take a rough trodden path to the right marked Criffel Walk. The path up through the woods is rough, uneven and narrow with lots of large boulders to clamber over, but plainly visible and easy to follow.

stile, Criffel

Caerlaverock and the Rich Solway Marshes

In the shadow of this unusual castle a nature reserve protects a rich marshland habitat

1 From the car park, turn back along the approach road for ½ mile (800m) then turn left, passing Scottish National Heritage's information point on your left.

2 In 300yds (275m), bear left by a house, along a hedged track to the edge of the Merse (saltmarsh). Turn right before the next fence and keep left for 150yds (136m) then turn right along a low bank for 1 mile (1.6km). Near the end, veer left to cross two wooden bridges and then a stile.

Distance: 6 miles (9.5km)
Total ascent: 310ft (95m)
Path: country roads, lanes and foreshore tracks; very muddy after rain
Terrain: flat estuary foreshore, saltmarsh, grassland
Gradients: one fairly gentle hill
Refreshments: tearoom at Caerlaverock Castle
Park: car park at the Wildfowl and Wetlands Trust's East Park Centre at Caerlaverock, signposted off the B725 nine miles (14.5km) south of Dumfries.
Note: entrance fees are charged for entry to the Wildfowl and Wetland Trust facilities and Caerlaverock Castle
Difficulty: 1

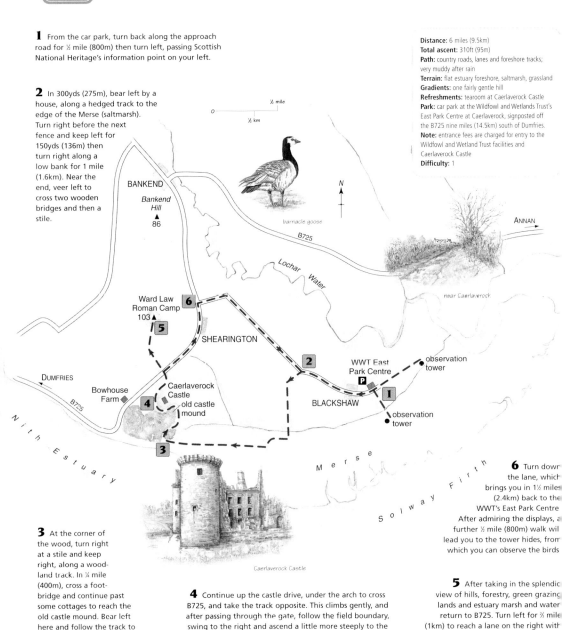

Caerlaverock Castle

3 At the corner of the wood, turn right at a stile and keep right, along a woodland track. In ¼ mile (400m), cross a footbridge and continue past some cottages to reach the old castle mound. Bear left here and follow the track to pass Caerlaverock Castle.

4 Continue up the castle drive, under the arch to cross B725, and take the track opposite. This climbs gently, and after passing through the gate, follow the field boundary, swing to the right and ascend a little more steeply to the ramparts of the roman camp on Ward Law Hill.

5 After taking in the splendid view of hills, forestry, green grazing lands and estuary marsh and water return to B725. Turn left for ⅔ mile (1km) to reach a lane on the right with a Wildfowl and Wetlands Trust sign

6 Turn down the lane, which brings you in 1½ miles (2.4km) back to the WWT's East Park Centre. After admiring the displays, a further ½ mile (800m) walk will lead you to the tower hides, from which you can observe the birds

WALK 180

ABOUT • GLEN TROOL

This walk takes you to southern shores of Loch Trool where Robert the Bruce and his 300 men routed the superior force of the English troops. Their victory marked the turning point in Scotland's fight for independence and their ultimate goal, the Crown.

Scotland

DISTANCE • 5 miles (8km)

TOTAL ASCENT • 150ft (46m)

PATHS • good; firm footing even in wet weather

TERRAIN • forest paths, gravel paths and single-track roads

GRADIENTS • moderate

REFRESHMENTS • House of Hill, Bargrennan, 4 miles (6km) southwest off the A714

PARK • car park at entrance to Caldons Campsiteweather

DIFFICULTY • 2

Robert the Bruce, Ambitious Patriot

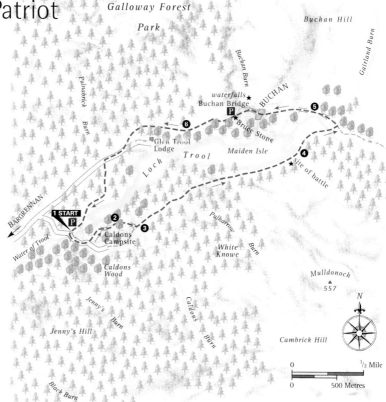

① From the car park at the entrance to the campsite, turn left following the waymarks for the Loch Trool Trail. Go over a bridge, enter Caldons Campsite and turn left on to the path which follows the river. Cross another bridge and pass between two toilet blocks.

② Continue following the waymarks as the trail winds round a picnic area and crosses a green metal bridge. Continue on the path then veer right across the grass to join a trail which heads uphill into the forest.

③ Keep on this path as it goes uphill and crosses a bracken covered clearing. Go through a kissing gate, continue through the clearing, re-enter the wood and keep walking to the interpretation board marking the site of the battle. It is at this point you can imagine Robert the Bruce's men lying in wait to ambush the 1,500-strong English force. When the English were lured to the southern shores of Loch Trool, and unable to form a tight battalion, then Bruce's soldiers attacked, blocking their escape route and hurling boulders from the slopes above.

④ Continue on the path from the interpretation board as it emerges from the woods and go downhill towards the end of Loch Trool. Turn left, cross a stile and a footbridge on to the Southern Upland Way and turn left.

⑤ Go through two gates and cross a wooden bridge. Soon after the stone Buchan Bridge, look out for a track branching to the left and go uphill toward the Bruce Stone and one of the best views of the loch.

⑥ Continue on the track past the Bruce Stone – laid in memorial for one of Scotland's greatest warriors – and turn left on to the road through the car park. Keep going until you see a waymark on the left then turn left on to a forest trail to eventually return to the start of the walk and your car.

• DON'T MISS •

*St Ninian founded the first Christian church in Scotland in the 5th century at nearby **Whithorn**, which thus became known as the Cradle of Scottish Christianity. Archaeologists have recently uncovered his church and can be visited at the dig. There are also the remains of a 12th-century priory. The archaeological visitor centre offers guided tours and exhibitions, and the museum contains the 5th-century Latinus Stone, Scotland's oldest Christian artefact and memorial. St Ninian's cave lies to the south, with 8th-century carvings, once used as his retreat.*

WALK

181

ABOUT • CULZEAN CASTLE

General Eisenhower was presented with the gift of an apartment in Culzean Castle in recognition for his contribution during World War II. An exhibition at Culzean tells about his role as Supreme Commander of the Allied Expeditionary Force.

Scotland

DISTANCE • 5½ miles (8.8km)

TOTAL ASCENT • 150ft (46m)

PATHS • very good, although some stretches can be boggy in wet weather

TERRAIN • estate roads, farm tracks, forest paths, beach, old railway line and roads

GRADIENTS • moderate

REFRESHMENTS • restaurant at visitor centre

PARK • visitor centre car park

DIFFICULTY • 2

Culzean Country Park

❶ Go diagonally through the visitor centre courtyard and turn left on to a path. Turn right at the junction, then second left, through an arch and into the castle forecourt. Keep left, go through a gate and at the next gate turn left.

❷ Go down some steps, about turn and follow the path to the sign for the Battery, Cliff Walk and Swan Pond. Turn right, go through the trees, through a gate, across a grassed area and down some steps into the Battery.

❸ Turn left, exit at the other end and turn right on to a forest path. Follow this until you reach a path signed Cliff Walk and turn right. Go right at the T-junction by the Swan Pond.

❹ Turn right again at the sign for Barwhin Hill and Port Carrick. In 200yds (183m) turn right and go down some steep steps to Port Carrick beach. Turn left and head back uphill by the next steps. Turn right.

❺ Follow the cliff path until it descends by some wooden steps to Maidenhead Bay. Turn left and walk along the beach until the pavement beside it turns left.

• DON'T MISS •

The Robert Burns National Park in Alloway, which has a superb audio-visual version of his poem Tam O' Shanter. Follow the trail of the hapless Tam as he was pursued by witches from the auld haunted kirk to the Brig O' Doon.

as it turns into a farm road and then turn left at a derelict World War II building and head for Shanter Farm. Turn left and enter the farm steading.

❼ Cross the farm yard diagonally and exit at the other side. Then continue to follow the farm road round the side of a cottage then turn left, go through a gate and follow the line of the fence until you can cross it and continue along the old railway.

Cross the grassed area diagonally towards a white cottage with a red roof.

❻ Turn left into Kirkoswald Road and then first right into Shanter Road. Continue to follow the road

❽ Continue through a caravan park, fork left, turn right on to the A719 and follow it for just over a mile (1.6km) to pass Morriston Farm. Just past the sign for Souter Johnnie's Cottage is a farm track.

❾ Turn left along here, right and down some steps at a railway bridge and follow the line of the old railway to the next bridge. Exit right, via the steps, turn right, then left on to the estate road and follow it to the car park.

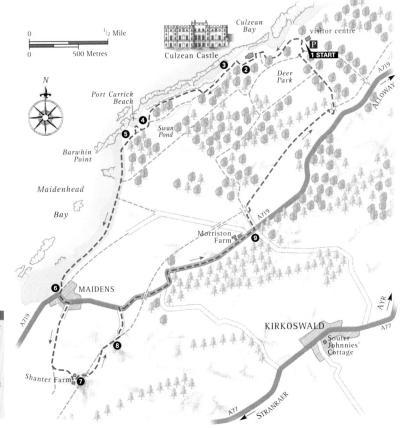

Burns' Alloway and the Brig o' Doon

A landscape much changed, yet still recognisable as the one-time home of Scotland's national poet

Distance: 7 miles (11.3km)
Total ascent: negligible
Paths: good; can be muddy
Terrain: old railway, fields, beach, golf course and woodland
Gradients: some steps
Refreshments: visitor centre at car park
Park: Tam O'Shanter Experience car park, Alloway, near Ayr
Difficulty: 1

1 From Tam O'Shanter Experience, walk to end of car park, furthest from entry road. Go right down path into Burns Monument Gardens. Follow path anti-clockwise around monument then towards Auld Brig (Brig o'Doon) ahead. Visit Statues House, then continue to top of steps down to right. Descend to road, turn right and cross over. Just short of large white hotel, go down steps on left into Riverside Gardens.

2 Walk around gardens by river towards Auld Brig. Leave by steps back up to road, turn right and cross Auld Brig. Continue up path, under old railway bridge to top, swinging right on to main road.

3 Turn right and follow main road back over river. Just over newer bridge, cross over and turn left, up steps, into Auld Alloway Kirkyard (opposite parish church) to Burns' parents' graves.

4 Leaving kirkyard by steps, turn left and go along the road until level with Tam O'Shanter Experience. Cross right into Murdoch's Lone and go left immediately beyond a low white pumping station, steeply down to old railway line. Turn left through two tunnels and beyond.

5 Eventually, emerge on main road at Burton Farm road end. Turn right and follow road over old railway, then turn left on other side into lane, turning back on itself before swinging right towards sea. Continue past estate house on left to cottages at end of track.

6 Go between cottages and leave lane as it swings right, going through gate and down field, through gate to beach. Turn right along beach past Greenan Castle and car park to river mouth.

7 Turn right up road with river to left, to T-junction, opposite garden centre. Turn left over river bridge and cross road, turning right into Greenfield Avenue.

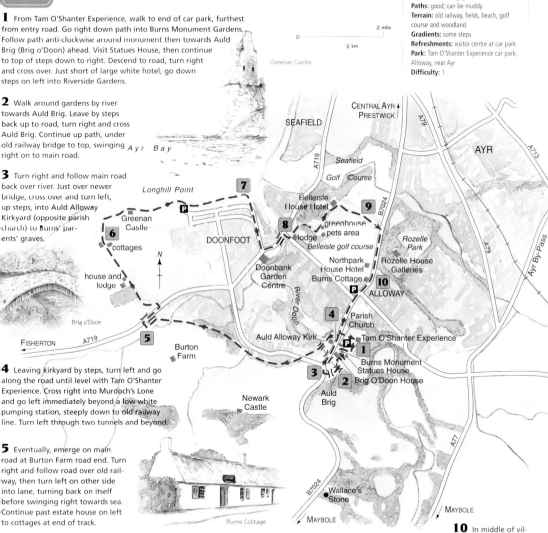

8 As Greenfield Avenue curves, go left through gates by lodge into Belleisle Park. Continue with golf course on right, through trees and then curve off right to pets area. Just before this, turn left into walled garden and carry on into second garden with large greenhouse. Leave by path from far left corner, up to rear of Belleisle House Hotel. Pass in front of golf shop and in 150yds (136m) turn right across golf course, following signs to Practice Area.

9 At path's end, go through green gates to main road and turn right. Follow past Rozelle Park on left and Northpark House Hotel on right, until road curves right into Alloway.

10 In middle of village, pass Burns Cottage on right and continue on main road (B7024) past cricket ground to return to Tam O'Shanter Experience on left.

Magic Waters from Hart Fell

*In the Southern Uplands with the magic of Merlin and
the healing waters of the Hartfell Spa*

WALK

183

1 From Annan Water Hall, follow the signpost to Hartfell Spa. Follow the path along the Auchencat Burn, then through a gate in a dry stone wall. The track heads up away from the burn. Beyond the next wall, the first waymarker can be seen.

2 The path continues along the edge of the hill. Go through the gate in the wall and keep the fence on your right. Cross the stile at the next waymarker.

3 Descend to the burn and cross two bridges made from telegraph poles. Ignore the third bridge. A small sign points the way to the spa. The glen starts to widen at the next waymarker.

4 Head towards the narrow ravine for ½ mile (800m), past some sheep pens on the right and across another path. As you ascend, the ravine narrows just before a rocky outcrop on the left. The spa is on the right. Retrace your steps to the sheep pens.

5 Turn left up the main valley to a wire fence after ½ mile (800m). Head left along it and ascend to an opening. Turn right then ascend northeastwards across featureless terrain for ¾ mile (1.2km) to a small cairn on Arthur's Seat. Beyond it, continue north-easterly to pick up a track to Hart Fell summit.

Distance: 7 miles (11.2km)
Total ascent: 2,400ft (732m)
Paths: generally good but indistinct in places
Terrain: fields, riverbank and grassy mountain
Gradients: slight to moderate; one very steep section
Refreshments: Star Hotel, Moffat
Park: Annan Water Hall, near head of minor road north of A701 in Moffat
Difficulty: 3

9 Keep ahead, passing farm sheds on your left. Cross two cattle grids to reach the lane. Turn left along the lane to return to Annan Water Hall.

8 Bear right on a track for 100yds (91m), then bear left to a gate. Beyond, cross a plank bridge and continue across a field to the left hand corner of a wooded ravine. Keep ahead, with the wood on your right to reach a gate to the right of a grey-roofed shed. Continue down the track to the next gate by a bridge.

7 Towards the end of the ridge, bear right to a sheep pen then descend on a faint track ahead, in the direction of Annan Water Hall, to a gate.

6 Return by way of Arthur's Seat to the gap in the wire fence. Take the path directly ahead and in 100yds (91m), take the right fork.

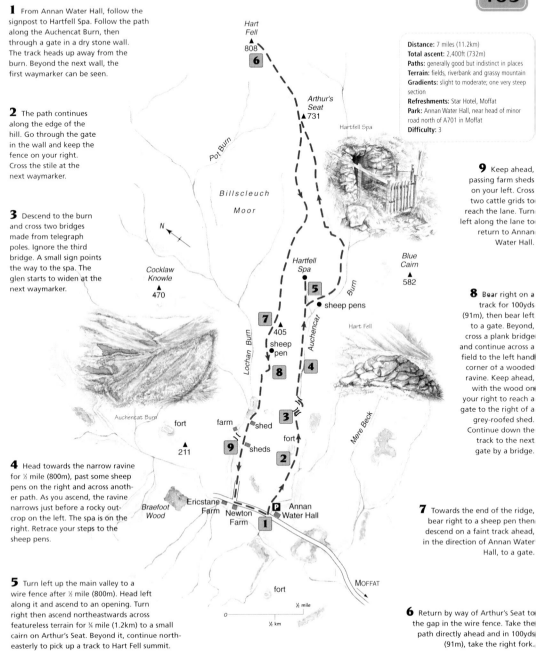

WALK 184

ABOUT • NEW LANARK

David Dale, a Glaswegian banker and industrialist, was the visionary behind New Lanark's town planning. In an age where the chasm between the rich and poor was largely ignored, he provided social housing and 'cradle to the grave' care of its townsfolk.

Scotland

DISTANCE • 8 miles (13km)

TOTAL ASCENT • 200ft (61m)

PATHS • mostly firm but some muddy stretches

TERRAIN • woodland and riverside gorges

GRADIENTS • steep in some sections, but with steps to ease ascents

REFRESHMENTS • Mill Hotel in New Lanark

PARK • car park above New Lanark

DIFFICULTY • 2

Around New Lanark

• DON'T MISS •

Near by you'll find the Falls of Clyde, part of a Scottish Wildlife Trust reserve, which offers a full ranger service including badger watching and bat walks (between May–September). Plus, an open hide, manned 24 hours a day, offering unrivalled views of breeding peregrine falcons (telephone 01555 665262).

❶ From the car park take the path down to New Lanark, where there are a number of buildings open to the public and exhibitions of the community's history.

❷ Beside Robert Owen's School, bear left off the road along a path that continues through a gate into Scottish Wildlife Trust's nature reserve. Follow the path up steps and along the river, past the thundering Dundaff Linn and weirs that once powered the cotton mills.

❸ Turn right at the approach drive to Bonnington Power Station, which in 1927 was Britain's first hydro-electric scheme. At the power station, fork right off the drive to follow a footpath signed to Falls of Clyde. The waterfalls, Corra Linn and Bonnington Linn, are most dramatic after prolonged heavy rain, when there is more water than the power station needs, and the excess flows freely through the gorge.

❹ Keeping to the path, cross the river over Bonnington Weir, then turn right down a woodland track into the Corehouse Estate. After 200yds (183m), turn right on to a footpath down towards the river. From here there are spectacular views of the falls.

❺ Keep to the riverside path, ignoring other paths up to the left. Beyond the ruins of Corra Castle, there are views of New Lanark on the opposite bank. At a junction with a track, turn right and continue until you reach some houses on your left. Just beyond their gardens, climb the bank to your left and follow a faint path through the trees to a gap in the wall along Kirkfield Road. Turn right and then right again at the

bottom of the hill into St Patrick's Lane and follow signs for Clyde Walkway.

❻ Cross the river on Clydesholm Bridge, then turn right through the gate of Old Brigend (private property). Follow the Clyde Walkway up to the treatment

works, then climb steeply, with several steps, and bear right to follow a lane to Castlebank Park. Just beyond a sign to Jookers' Johnnie, turn right down the drive to Castlebank House. Follow the path signed Clyde Walkway down from Castlebank Park to river level and on to New Lanark and your car.

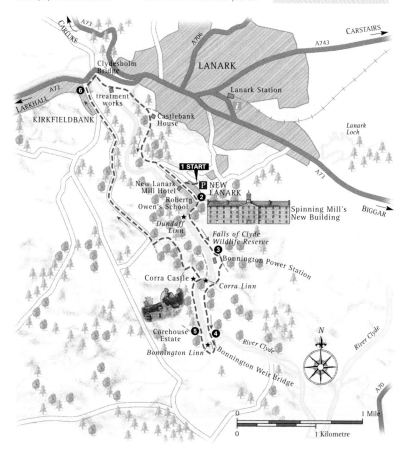

WALK 185

ABOUT • RULLION GREEN

The Covenanters, having refused to accept the authority of bishops or kings over church matters, were pursued here and routed by Scottish troops. The Battle at Rullion Green was part of a 30-year-long dispute, which caused the death of 18,000 men.

Scotland

DISTANCE • 5 miles (8km)

TOTAL ASCENT • 1,300ft (396m)

PATHS • mostly well-maintained and dry, but rough descent from Turnhouse Hill

TERRAIN • mostly mountain moorland and wooded waterside. Dogs must be kept on leads. The Pentland Hills Regional Park is

grazed by sheep and a habitat for ground nesting-birds

GRADIENTS • steep on Turnhouse Hill

REFRESHMENTS • Flotterstone Inn

PARK • car park at Flotterstone Information Centre

DIFFICULTY • 3

Bloodshed in the Pentland Hills

❶ From the car park, follow the footpath up the glen beside the metalled drive. Glencorse Burn, which has now been tamed by dams and reservoirs further up the valley, would have been a broad, ferocious torrent at the time of the battle.

❷ At the end of the footpath cross the road and bear left through a gate on to a track signed Glencorse. At the end of the stone wall on your left, turn left and follow the path across a footbridge. This is probably the point where Dalyell crossed the burn, when he brought his army through the hills on the north side of the valley.

❸ Following the burn upstream, the path fords a shallow rivulet and then climbs to the top of the ridge. Only at this point would Dalyell's army have been spotted by the Covenanters, camped half a mile (800m) away beneath the southern slope of Turnhouse Hill. The path continues down into the valley beside a ruined drystone wall before starting on the long ascent of Turnhouse Hill.

❹ From the summit, you will have a grandstand view of the battlefield below. The Covenanters occupied the higher ground, ranged along a spur, now crowned with trees over to the right. Dalyell was attacking from the left and failed to outflank his enemy owing to the steepness of the hill. When he lost every skirmish, he quickly abandoned subtle tactics and used his great superiority in numbers to launch a sustained frontal assault across open ground.

❺ Continue along the path, to the bottom of a deep cleft in the hills. Cross a stile and turn immediately right to follow a faint path downhill beside a drystone wall. Crossing a small stream, the path drops down into the valley, where there is a footbridge, which crosses Logan Burn.

❻ Once over the bridge, turn right along the metalled drive, which runs along the shore of Glencorse Reservoir. This did not exist at the time of the battle and on his march to Rullion Green Dalyell would have passed the ruins of St Catherine's Chapel, which now lie beneath the water.

❼ Just beyond Glen Cottage, at the end of the reservoir, turn right through a gate to follow a path through pine woods and past the 19th-century filter beds. The path continues beside Glencorse Burn

• DON'T MISS •

The 19th-century filter beds used to clean the reservoir's water can now be seen as works of art, with their strange iron ventilation shafts thrusting from the roots of trees. The beds themselves have been transformed into attractive water-gardens and tree-nurseries.

to rejoin the metalled drive back to the car park.

The Mysteries of Rosslyn

*On the trail of the Holy Grail in a wooded glen near
Edinburgh's suburbs*

WALK
186

1 From the car park, take the path leading towards the river and cross the metal foot-bridge. Follow the path uphill and pass under the arch of the castle bridge. At the T-junction, turn left along Gardener's Brae.

5 From the cairn, continue along the road into Roslin itself. At the end of the road, follow the signs to the left, to Rosslyn Chapel. From the chapel, retrace your steps, then turn left towards the cemeteries and left again between the cemeteries, towards the castle. Return from the castle to the steps on the left, which will return you to the car park.

2 Follow the path along the side of the river. This will take you uphill to a wall on the left. Keep the wall on your left as you follow the path back down towards the river, then continue over three stiles

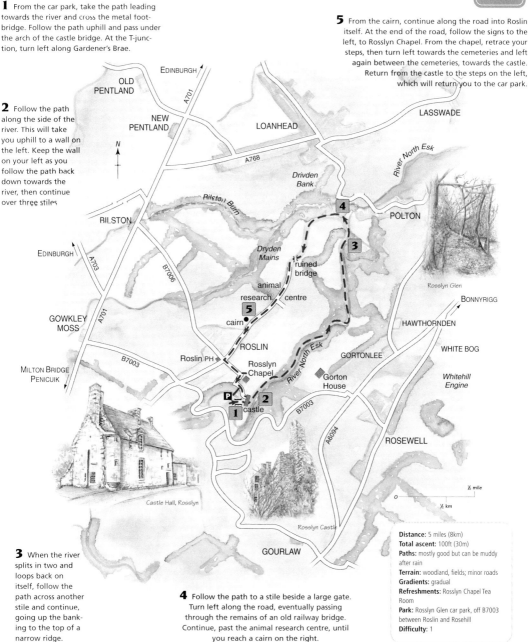

Rosslyn Glen

Castle Hall, Rosslyn

Rosslyn Castle

3 When the river splits in two and loops back on itself, follow the path across another stile and continue, going up the banking to the top of a narrow ridge.

4 Follow the path to a stile beside a large gate. Turn left along the road, eventually passing through the remains of an old railway bridge. Continue, past the animal research centre, until you reach a cairn on the right.

Distance: 5 miles (8km)
Total ascent: 100ft (30m)
Paths: mostly good but can be muddy after rain
Terrain: woodland, fields; minor roads
Gradients: gradual
Refreshments: Rosslyn Chapel Tea Room
Park: Rosslyn Glen car park, off B7003 between Roslin and Rosehill
Difficulty: 1

Edinburgh's Literary Past

*A walk around the elegant streets of the Scottish capital,
with a proud tradition of literature*

Start: Edinburgh Waverley railway station
Distance: 5 miles (8km)
Paths: pavements throughout
Terrain: city streets
Gradients: a few short, steep sections
Refreshments: plenty in city centre
Park: Waverley Station
Difficulty: 1

1 From Waverley Station, turn right, then left into Princes Street. Walk down to the Scott Monument, cross over, continue down Princes Street, then right into Frederick Street. Take the second turning on your left, George Street, then next left into Castle Street.

2 Walk down and cross, turning right into Rose Street. Continue along Rose Street to the end. At this junction, turn right and right again, into George Street. Cross over and turn left down North Castle Street until you reach Queen Street. Cross over, turn left, then right down Wemyss Place and right into Heriot Row.

3 Walk down Heriot Row to Dundas Street, turn left, cross over, then right into Great King Street. Cross at the end, then turn sharp right into Nelson Street, then left into Drummond Place. Follow Drummond Place into London Street, then turn right, up Broughton Street. Keep going to the main road junction at the top of the hill, then turn left into Picardy Place.

4 Cross the road opposite the Playhouse, turn left, then right at the roundabout with the clock and immediately right up Blenheim Place. Take the path on the right by Greenside Church, climbing up to Calton Hill. Taking the the left hand path, walk across towards the Edinburgh Experience and descend by the path leading to Waterloo Place.

5 Turn right, cross over then turn left at the Balmoral Hotel and up North Bridge. Turn left down the High Street (Royal Mile) and walk down to Holyrood Palace. Walk back up the other side of the road.

6 Turn left along Melbourne Place (George IV Bridge). Cross over and walk down to the statue of Greyfriars Bobby on the corner. Go sharp right down Candlemaker Row, then left into the Grassmarket.

7 Go right up West Bow into Victoria Street. Opposite Byzantium Market, go up the steps leading to Castlehill and the Castle. Walk up to the Castle Esplanade to enjoy the views, then return down the hill of Lawnmarket until you reach Bank Street on the left.

8 Turn left along Bank Street, following the road down and keeping walking down the hill until you reach Princes Street. Turn right and walk back to Waverley Station.

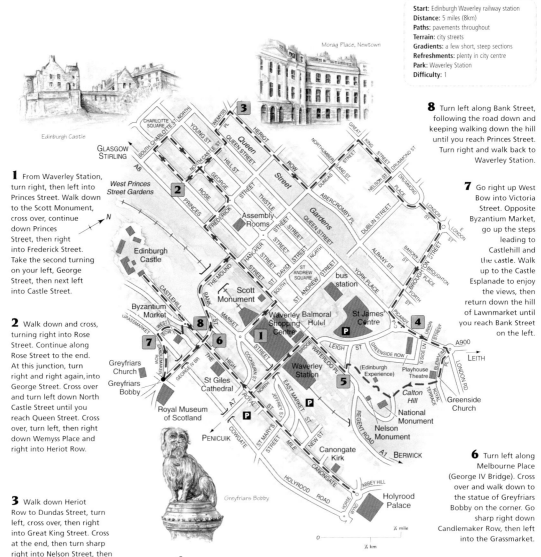

Morag Place, Newtown

Edinburgh Castle

Greyfriars Bobby

The Antonine Wall

*The boundary that once marked the Roman Empire's northern
limit, between the Forth and the Clyde in Scotland*

A Frontier for Brittania

Once the Romans had abandoned their ambition to include the
whole of Britain in the empire, they had to decide on a northern
frontier. In terms of controlling local tribes and protecting the rich
province from invasion, they could rely on strategically positioned
forts and military roads, but in times of peace a more formal
frontier was required. There were taxes to be levied on imports;
there were criminals and other undesirables whose movements
needed to be checked. Most importantly, travellers should be
suitably impressed when entering the greatest empire in the world.

The most substantial and long-lasting of these frontiers was the
wall constructed on the orders of the Emperor Hadrian following
his visit to Britain in AD 122. But within 15 years of completion a
new emperor, Antoninus Pius, decided on a frontier 100 miles
(160km) to the north, retaking lands in southern Scotland that the
Romans had abandoned some 60 years before.

A Wall of Turf

The Antonine Wall spans Britain's narrowest land-crossing, running
40 miles (64km) from the Firth of Forth to the Clyde. Unlike its
predecessor, it was built of turf, but was nonetheless substantial,
and 16 forts were built at regular intervals along its length. There
were also signal stations, a military road and complex secondary
defences to deter attack by cavalry or chariots. Trees now cover
some of the site but the turf ramparts over the stone foundations of
the Roman fort are still clearly visible.

Manned, according to inscriptions, by auxiliaries from distant
corners of the empire, the frontier served its purpose for some 20
years until about AD 158, when a further change in policy led to a
withdrawal back south and the re-commissioning of Hadrian's Wall.
One of the best-preserved sections of wall is at Rough Castle, near
Bonnybridge, where its course may be followed to both west and
east of the public car park.

A PATROL ALONG THE FRONTIER AT ROUGH CASTLE

Scotland

❶ Having parked, return down
the lane for about 300yds
(274m) and turn right through a
gate into a park-like field of
trees and open grassland. The
Roman frontier is still
unmistakable: a deep, wide ditch,
or vallum, overlooked by a
substantial bank – all that
remains of the turf wall.

❷ As you follow its course back
to the car park and beyond,
picture it when newly built. Set
on stone foundations, it was a
massive 15ft (4.5m) in width and
stood at least 10ft (3m) high,
with a timber palisade along the
parapet. You may notice stones
from the foundations half-buried
in the turf, but your mind must

recreate the watch-towers and
beacon-platforms.

❸ Beyond a burn tumbling
through a sheltered glen is
Rough Castle fort: a four-square
compound protected by
ramparts. This was the base for a
small garrison, together with
administrative clerks and an
officer elite. Enter through the
west gate and imagine the
barrack blocks and granaries on
your route to the principia, or
headquarters building.

❹ Turning left, exit through the
north gate. Ahead of you is a
serried grid of pits; each one
contained a bunch of sharpened
stakes, known as lilia, or lilies,

that could prove most effective
in deterring an assault. Turning
to the right and recrossing the
frontier, you can explore the
fort's 'annexe'. This contained the
bath-house, potteries,
blacksmiths and other
workshops.

❺ Beyond the annexe, a stile
leads on to a woodland path that
follows the frontier for a further
mile (1.6km) and, although the
earthworks are overgrown, it is
here that one can best imagine
the landscape of 2,000 years
ago. To the south lay an empire
that stretched to Africa and Asia;
to the north lay mountains and
impenetrable forests haunted by
barbarians. The wall was a

boundary between two opposing
worlds.

Distance: 2½ miles (4km)

Total ascent: 50ft (80m)

Paths: firm grass to west of
Rough Castle; muddy stretches
through woods to east of fort

Terrain: open grassland and
woods

Gradients: easy

Refreshments: pubs and cafés in
Bonnybridge and Falkirk

Park: car park at Rough Castle

OS Map: Explorer 349 Falkirk,
Cumbernauld & Livingston

Difficulty: 2

Scotland

Glasgow's Not-so-mean Streets

*Architectural wealth softens the edges of
Scotland's biggest city*

8 Turn right, then left into Sauchiehall Street. Turn right along Hope Street, then left along St Vincent Street and back into George Square.

7 Turn left and keep walking round to the three towers of Trinity College. Go left into Lynedoch Street and right at the end into Woodlands Road. At traffic lights turn right and walk over the footbridge. Walk along Renfrew Street past the School of Art and dental hospital to Dalhousie Street.

6 Go over the bridge, turning right at the roundabout into Gibson Street. Follow this road then, at a mini-roundabout, turn right, uphill, into Park Avenue, just by Glasgow Caledonian University buildings. Turn left at the top into Park Drive, then right up Cliff Road.

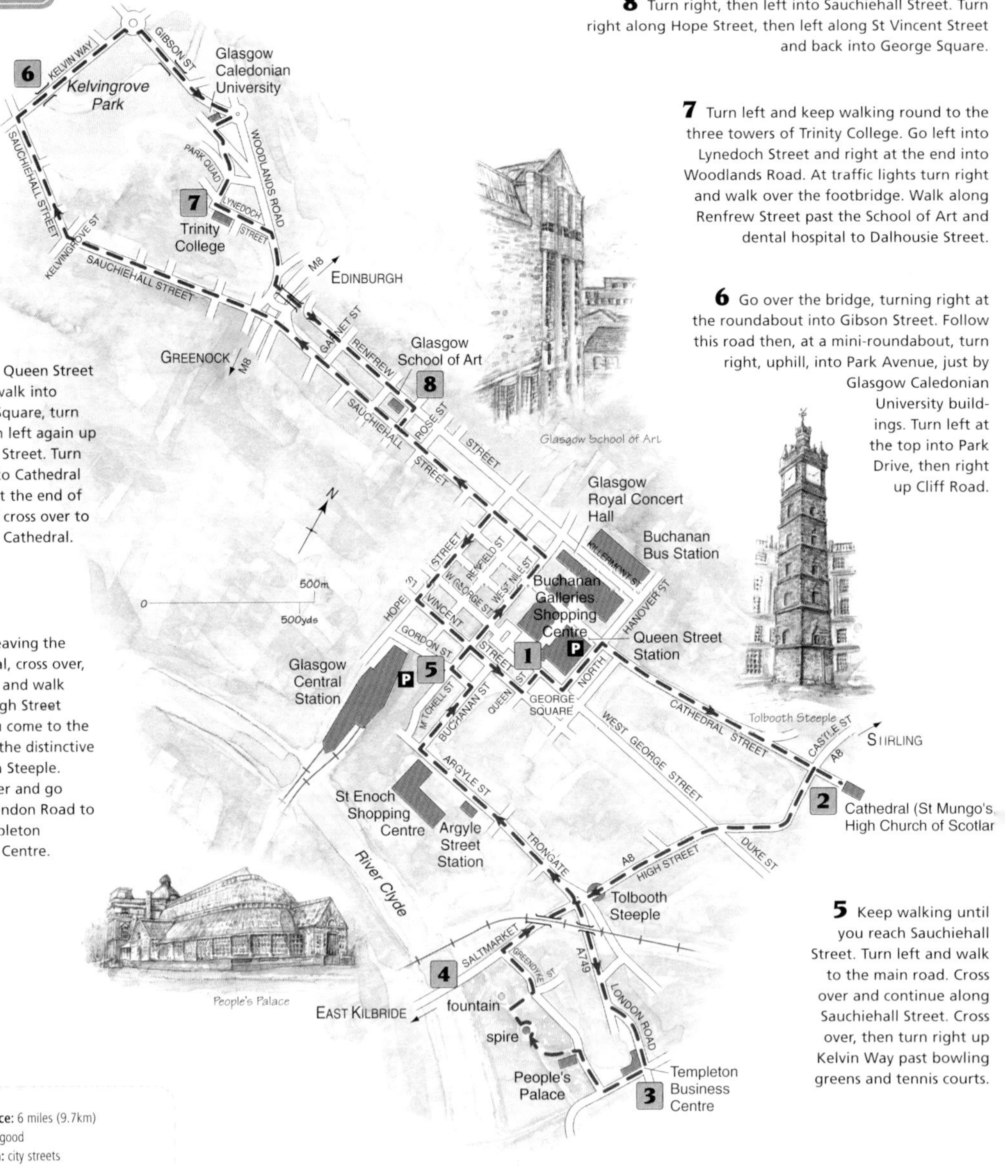

1 From Queen Street Station walk into George Square, turn left, then left again up Hanover Street. Turn right onto Cathedral Street. At the end of the road cross over to Glasgow Cathedral.

2 On leaving the Cathedral, cross over, turn left and walk down High Street until you come to the clock of the distinctive Tolbooth Steeple. Cross over and go along London Road to the Templeton Business Centre.

5 Keep walking until you reach Sauchiehall Street. Turn left and walk to the main road. Cross over and continue along Sauchiehall Street. Cross over, then turn right up Kelvin Way past bowling greens and tennis courts.

Distance: 6 miles (9.7km)
Paths: good
Terrain: city streets
Gradients: some short steep sections
Refreshments: plenty in city centre
Park: Buchanan Galleries multi-storey, Cathedral Street
Difficulty: 1

3 Walk right round the building, turning right and up the path on the other side. Just past the People's Palace, take the track on the left across Glasgow Green. Pass the spire, go right onto Greendyke Street then left to Saltmarket.

4 Turn right, then go left at the Tolbooth Steeple to walk along Trongate, into Argyle Street, then go right into Buchanan Street. Walk up until you reach Gordon Street. A short way along turn right into West Nile Street.

WALK

190

Stirling, Cockpit of Scottish History

The history of Scotland has been played out on the streets of this strategic burgh

Distance: 5 miles (8km)
Total ascent: 100ft (30m)
Paths: good; mostly paved but some dirt tracks
Terrain: town trail and riverside
Gradients: gentle, one short steep section
Refreshments: Castle Tea Room
Park: car park, Castle Esplanade, Stirling
Difficulty: 1

Robert the Bruce

Cambuskenneth Abbey

CAMBUSKENNETH

bowling club

farm

RIVERSIDE DRIVE

QUEENSHAUGH DRIVE

River Forth

ABBEY MILL

ABBEY ROAD

River Forth

ABBEY

rowing club

MILLAR PLACE

N

Old Stirling Bridge

Forth

DEAN CRESCENT

SHORE ROAD

SEAFORTH PL

Stirling Station

A9

LOVERS WK

FORTH STREET

6

7

BURGHMUIR ROAD

GOOSECROFT RD

MURRAY PL

FRIARS ST

KING ST

hospital

UNION STREET

COWANE STREET

BARNTON STREET

BAKER STREET

8

COW LN

CORN EX RD

DUMBARTON ROAD

A84

LOWER BRIDGE ST

5

UPPER BRIDGE ST

ST MARY'S WYND

BARN RD

SPITTAL ST

ST JOHN ST

BROAD ST

Municipal Building

ALBERT PLACE

Gowan Hill

Portcullis Hotel
CASTLE WYND

OLD TOWN

Upper Back Walk

Stirling Castle

Beheading Stone and Cannon Pair

UPPER CASTLE HILL

4

1

P

2

cem

Valley Cem.

Mar's Wark

Pyramid

Church of the Holy Rood

3

Stirling Castle

1 From the castle car park, head downhill, passing the visitor centre on your left. Follow the sign to the right for the Back Walk, passing the old Grammar School, now a hotel called the Portcullis. On the Back Walk, the cemetery is to the left and the Pyramid to the right.

2 Turn into the cemetery by the iron gates opposite the Pyramid. Climb the Ladies' Rock for a view over the historic sites of Stirling and the Forth Valley and exit by the back gate. Turn right and continue until you see a fork to the left.

3 Ignore the steps to the left and take the path alongside as far as a narrow tarmac road. Cross the road via two kissing gates and continue on the path, ignoring two forks to the left and passing Gowan Hill with a pair of cannons on top.

4 Continue on the path, ignoring a right uphill fork. At the houses turn left down a lane with the Wallace Monument ahead in the distance. At the T-junction bear left on a lane, then take the narrow, grassy track on your left up to Gowan Hill.

5 Return to the lane and continue to the main road. Cross and turn left, heading through the pedestrian underpass. Old Stirling Bridge is to your left and accessible through the hospital grounds. Retrace your steps from the bridge and turn left into an underpass to the centre of the roundabout. Turn left again through another underpass which exits beyond the road bridge.

6 Follow the riverside path under the railway bridge and continue until the river begins to bend left. Take the path on the right behind the bowling club and follow the riverside path again to the footbridge to Cambuskenneth. Cross the bridge, head up the street and turn right at the T-junction to reach Cambuskenneth Abbey. Retrace your steps back over the bridge and turn left, then right to continue along Abbey Road towards the town.

7 At the station, cross the railway bridge and take the underpass to Maxwell Place. Follow the curve of the street to the left to the post office. Cross into Friars Street. At the end turn left and follow the road up and around to the right, to Corn Exchange Road on the left.

8 On Corn Exchange Road, beyond the Municipal Building and opposite the library, take the cobbled lane to the right signposted Upper Back Walk. Head uphill, with the old town walls on your right. You can investigate the Old Town as you ascend, finally arriving back at the castle car park.

½ mile

¼ km

WALK 191

A steep, demanding climb is rewarded with panoramic views over Fife, with the Highland mountains on the far horizon. The moor is a wild place and not so very different from when Mary, Queen of Scots, rode the hillside with a falcon on her wrist.

DISTANCE • 5 miles (8km)

TOTAL ASCENT • 1,148ft (350m)

PATHS • mostly good, but some stretches muddy in wet weather

TERRAIN • woods and open moorland

GRADIENTS • steep on East Lomond Hill

REFRESHMENTS • tea rooms, restaurants and pubs in Falkland

PARK • near the town hall

DIFFICULTY • 2

The Royal Palace of Falkland

❶ Follow the lane out of the car park and turn left up Back Wynd. Bear right at the factory entrance gates, then turn left at the crossroads into East Loan. Continue uphill where the road turns into a track with the factory entrance on the left.

❷ After 60yds (55m) fork right on to the signed track. Soon take the signed footpath left to climb a long flight of steps, with a handrail, cut into the hillside through trees.

❸ Continue up the steps to an attractive area of beech wood. The route, now a path, levels off slightly. As you gain height the path becomes steeper entering coniferous pines. The woodland clears to reveal an expanse of moorland and heather. The path is well-defined until near the summit where it becomes steep and demanding. Look back for views of Falkland and its palace almost directly below.

❹ The only evidence of the Pictish hill fort is the ramparts which encircle the site. Ben Lomond can be seen to the west, the Grampian Highlands to the north, the North Sea and the East Neuk of Fife to the east and the Firth of Forth and Edinburgh to the south. From the far side of the summit follow a faint path downhill to the left to join the straight clear track that can be seen further down the slope, cutting across the moorland.

❺ Pass through a kissing gate, bear right along the clear track, an old limestone-burners' road enclosed by drystone dykes. In August and September the heather moorland is a purple blaze of colour. The track (take care in wet conditions as the track can be muddy and boggy) leads down to a minor road.

❻ At the junction with the road turn right. Here there are toilets, a picnic area and car park. Continue on the road downhill,

with woodland on your left, for 2 miles (3km) into Falkland. Enter the town and pass a number of well-restored cottages dating back to the 17th and 18th centuries. One, the Old Room, opposite Mill Wynd, is now a cunningly disguised electricity sub-station. Many cottages have 'marriage lintels', engraved with initials, hearts and dates above their doors.

❼ Having visited the palace, then turn right into Beck Wynd to return to the car park.

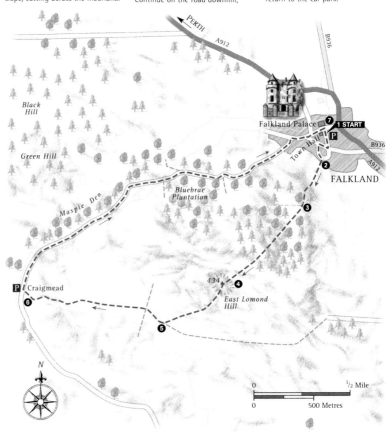

ABOUT • ARDOCH ROMAN FORT

Unlike its more southerly neighbours, the hostile Scottish tribes proved no easy conquest for the Roman troops. Remains of the marching camps, forts and garrisons all point to Rome's might, 2000 years ago, and the strength of resistance they encountered.

Scotland

DISTANCE • 4 miles (6km)	**GRADIENTS** • minimal
TOTAL ASCENT • minimal	**REFRESHMENTS** • Braco Hotel
PATHS • firm, but there can be puddles after rain	**PARK** • on roadside in high street of Braco village
TERRAIN • woodland and fields	**DIFFICULTY** • 2

The Roman Campaign Headquarters at Ardoch

• DON'T MISS •

Ardoch Old Bridge, just upstream from the present crossing, was built in the early 18th century to carry a military road from Stirling up into the Highlands. It formed part of a system involving roads and garrisons, intended to suppress the northern clans whose distant ancestors may have possibly battled with Agricola in Roman times

❶ Park in the high street and walk through the village on the A822 Crieff road. Cross a bridge over the River Knaik, a stream which, under various names, flows from the foothills of the Highlands to the Allan Water and the Firth of Forth.

❷ Immediately beyond the bridge, turn right and enter Ardoch Fort through a small wooden gate. Following the forts' massive inner rampart, you can appreciate the complexity and strength of its defences. Walk in an anti-clockwise direction around the perimeter fence. (The land on the other side of the fence belongs to the Ardoch Estate.) Within the fence are a large number of impressive angular ditches built as a series of defence mechanisms. The great marching camps extend for more than ½ mile (800m) to the north, but are best seen from beside the road to Comrie. Once you have explored the site, return to the entrance and go back across the bridge.

❸ On the village side of the bridge, turn right through the stone-piered entrance of a private road. Follow the track through attractive woodland above the river's waterfalls and rapids, before veering to the left to reach a crossroads.

❹ Turn left, continuing on the track between two duck ponds. The hills on the south-east horizon are the Ochil Hills, which include the summit of Ben Cleuch at 721m. Behind you, to the north, you can glimpse the bracken-covered foothills of the Highlands. The Romans realised that if they were to conquer Scotland, they first had

to control this broad and fertile valley through the hills now known as Strathallan.

❺ Turn left at a T-junction. Looking back across the fields from this point there is a good view of Braco Castle, an imposing mansion with medieval origins that, just like

a Roman villa would be, is the focus of a large, well-run estate. The track skirts cultivated fields, grazing lands and managed woodland. Turn left at the juction with the B8033, opposite the remains of the tower of Braco Free Church (1845), and return to Braco high street and your car.

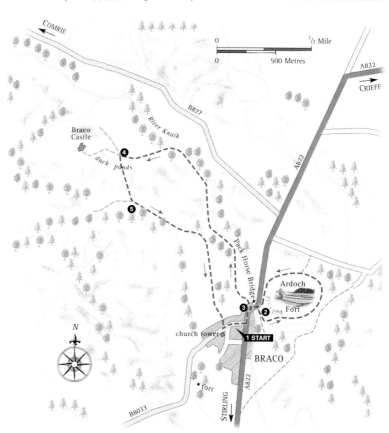

Rob Roy and Balquhidder

Legend and reality merge in the tales of a Highland hero on the braes of these lovely mountains

WALK
193

Distance: 7 miles (11km)
Total ascent: 1,750ft (533m)
Paths: good but boggy on hillside
Terrain: mostly forestry roads; some hillside
Gradients: moderate to steep
Refreshments: Kingshouse Hotel
Park: Balquhidder church, Balquhidder, off A84 between Callander and Lochearnhead
Difficulty: 3

8 Eventually this road turns back on itself and goes downhill to join the road beside the burn. Turn left, continuing past the bridge on your right and the water works back to Balquhidder church and the car park.

7 This road is at a higher altitude and will let you see all of the glen before you. After about 1 mile (1.6km) or so look for the magnificent view to your right over Loch Voil and the Braes of Balquhidder.

1 From the church at Balquhidder take the track that goes around to the right, signposted to waterfall. At the back wall of the church there is a stile over a fence and a Forest Enterprise sign for Kirkton Glen.

2 Follow the path uphill, through the woods and past the water works, keeping the burn on your left. A newly made logging road crosses the burn from the left. Continue uphill with burn on the left. There has been a lot of felling work here and it is now possible to see the shape of the Glen.

3 The road follows the line of the burn. It forks after 1½ miles (2.4km) and to your right there is a sign for Glen Dochart Pass. Follow a narrow but well-trodden path going uphill to the left of the sign.

4 Follow the path, crossing the burn at a fence then over the fence at a stile further up, and head for a range of crags as the path becomes indistinct. Follow it as it turns right then curve up to the left through the crags to the Lochan an Eireannaich.

6 Retrace your steps down the hill to rejoin the forestry road. Here you have the choice of three directions. Take the turning to the left and head off down the glen.

5 From here cut across the shoulder of Meall an Fhiodhain, the hill on your right, keeping to the high ground and going through a ruined fence. Your reward is the spectacular view along the course of the Ledcharrie Burn to Glen Dochart.

WALK

194

ABOUT • PASS OF BRANDER

Enjoy fine views over the Pass of Brander, as you follow the route taken by Robert the Bruce in 1308 into the territory of the Macdougall clan to settle a blood-feud. The successful ambush demonstrated Bruce's skills as a guerrilla fighter and as a tactician.

Scotland

DISTANCE • 11 miles (17.7km)	**REFRESHMENTS** • Kilchrenan Inn (erratic winter opening)
TOTAL ASCENT • 320ft (98m)	**PARK** • pull-in on roadside below Kilchrenan church
PATHS • mainly firm, but some very muddy sections around Tervine	**DIFFICULTY** • 3
TERRAIN • woods and mountain moorland	
GRADIENTS • gentle	

Guerrilla Warfare in the Scottish Hills

1 From Kilchrenan church, follow the road down to Kilchrenan Inn and turn left up the lane to Ardanaisaig. After passing modern forestry plantations, the road enters a wood (about 3 miles/ 4.8km from the start) where huge oaks tower above a lower canopy of hazel, silver birch and alder. Such forests covered almost all the Highlands at the time of Bruce.

2 At the end of the public road, turn left in front of the gatehouse of Ardanaisaig Hotel to take the private road towards Tervine. Soon, you will see the Pass of Brander up ahead, with the steep, scree-covered slopes of Ben Cruachan plunging down into the loch.

3 Just beyond the second white cottage on your left, turn left through a gate (faint marker for Fank's Cottage) over rough ground. Turn left through a gate towards a sheepfold, then immediately right through another gate on to a muddy track beside a drystone wall. At the end of the wall the track swings downhill to the right and fords a shallow burn.

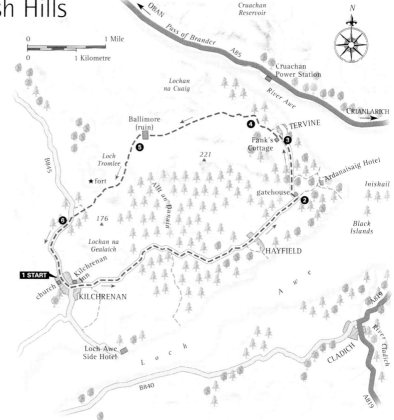

• DON'T MISS •

Kilchrenan Church, an attractive building dating from the early 18th century, contains the grave-stone of Sir Colin Campbell, who was killed in a skirmish with the clan of the Macdougalls in 1294. His descendants were given vast tracts of their territory by Bruce and the Campbells eventually became the most powerful clan in Scotland.

4 Passing a small clump of fir trees, the track swings to the left. There are stepping stones across a burn, which the track then follows upstream. The path is very faint across the grassy hillside, but is marked by a slight embankment. Stay close to the burn. Beyond a gated fence the path rises to the watershed with dramatic views

towards the west, then swings round to the right below a craggy hill. Beyond another gate, it drops down to a ruined farmhouse.

5 From the shell of Ballimore there is a firm, clear track to Loch Tromlee. On an island in the loch are the remains of a small medieval fortress, stronghold of the

MacCorquodales of Phantilands, sacked by the Macdonalds in 1646. The track continues through a forestry plantation before reaching the Kilchrenan road.

6 Turn left down the road, which was once an important route to a ferry on Loch Awe, to return to the village of Kilchrenan.

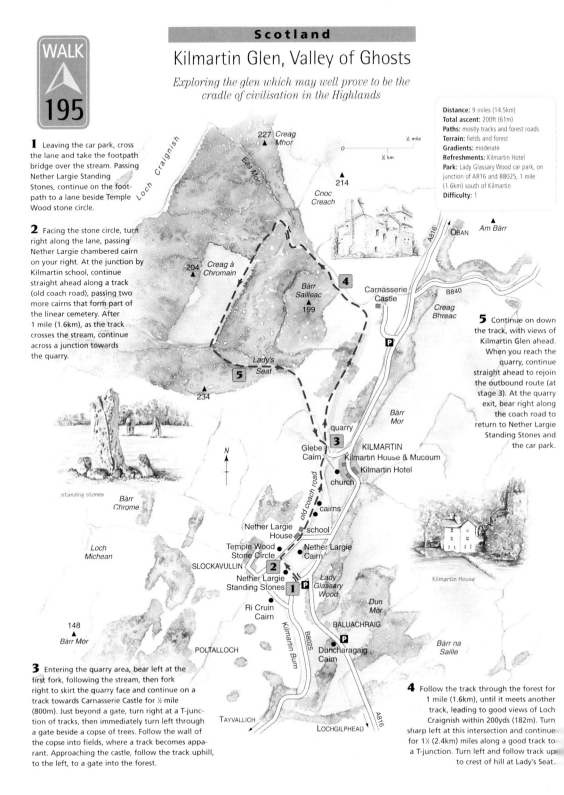

Kilmartin Glen, Valley of Ghosts

Exploring the glen which may well prove to be the cradle of civilisation in the Highlands

WALK
195

Distance: 9 miles (14.5km)
Total ascent: 200ft (61m)
Paths: mostly tracks and forest roads
Terrain: fields and forest
Gradients: moderate
Refreshments: Kilmartin Hotel
Park: Lady Glassary Wood car park, on junction of A816 and B8025, 1 mile (1.6km) south of Kilmartin
Difficulty: 1

1 Leaving the car park, cross the lane and take the footpath bridge over the stream. Passing Nether Largie Standing Stones, continue on the footpath to a lane beside Temple Wood stone circle.

2 Facing the stone circle, turn right along the lane, passing Nether Largie chambered cairn on your right. At the junction by Kilmartin school, continue straight ahead along a track (old coach road), passing two more cairns that form part of the linear cemetery. After 1 mile (1.6km), as the track crosses the stream, continue across a junction towards the quarry.

3 Entering the quarry area, bear left at the first fork, following the stream, then fork right to skirt the quarry face and continue on a track towards Carnasserie Castle for ½ mile (800m). Just beyond a gate, turn right at a T-junction of tracks, then immediately turn left through a gate beside a copse of trees. Follow the wall of the copse into fields, where a track becomes apparent. Approaching the castle, follow the track uphill, to the left, to a gate into the forest.

4 Follow the track through the forest for 1 mile (1.6km), until it meets another track, leading to good views of Loch Craignish within 200yds (182m). Turn sharp left at this intersection and continue for 1½ (2.4km) miles along a good track to a T-junction. Turn left and follow track up to crest of hill at Lady's Seat.

5 Continue on down the track, with views of Kilmartin Glen ahead. When you reach the quarry, continue straight ahead to rejoin the outbound route (at stage 3). At the quarry exit, bear right along the coach road to return to Nether Largie Standing Stones and the car park.

WALK
196

ABOUT • IONA

Iona is still considered a sacred island and has long been associated with the spread of Christianity in Britain. In 563 St Columba landed on the island and founded a monastery. The monks deserted in 825 when the monastery suffered a series of savage Norse raids.

Scotland

DISTANCE • 6 miles (9.6km)	**REFRESHMENTS** • in summer, restaurant and tea rooms in village
TOTAL ASCENT • 140ft (43m)	
PATHS • mostly good, even in bad weather	**PARK** • car park at the jetty on Fionnphort; ferry to Iona
TERRAIN • made-up roads, farm tracks, hill paths, grass and beach	**DIFFICULTY** • 2
GRADIENTS • flat to moderate	

The Missionaries and Myths of Iona

❶ After leaving the ferry, walk straight ahead, passing the Spar shop and the entrance to the nunnery. At the end of the road turn left, go through a gate and continue along a rough road until it reaches a collection of farm buildings.

❷ Turn left and follow a straight road until you reach a crossroads. Turn right and head west, along another straight road, towards the coast. Go through a metal gate, fork left and cross the machair (low lying land formed from sand and shell fragments) to the beach.

❸ Turn left and walk along the beach of a double bay then turn left and head across the machair until you reach a stony path. Turn right on to this and continue up hill until you reach a lochan.

❹ Take the left-hand path round the lochan. Follow it across a heather moor, past a series of mounds and downhill to the beach at St Columba's Bay, where Columba first landed in AD 563.

❺ Return by the same route but at the end of the stony path keep

• DON'T MISS •

*The neighbouring island of **Staffa** can be reached on a boat trip from Iona. From the landing spot you can walk along the top of the natural hexagonal basalt columns and enter Fingal's Cave, where the sound of the sea in the cave inspired Felix Mendelssohn to write Hebrides Overture.*

straight along the line of a fence and when it ends follow the faint track and a series of stone markers back to the road and the gate.

❻ Turn right through the gate and head east along the road. At the coast follow the road left to the village. Turn left at the jetty and right into the nunnery, exit by the far gate and follow the road to the

abbey. The abbey and nunnery, founded in 1203 by monks of the Benedictine order were only restored in the early twentieth century and the cell where St Columba slept excavated.

❼ Turn right through the gate into the graveyard. Note that only three of the tall crosses built here remain: the 9th-century St John's

Cross, 10th-century St Martin's Cross and 15th-century Maclean's Cross mark the remains of the eight Norwegian and many Scottish kings that were buried here. Follow the path anti-clockwise and exit by the far gate. Turn right into the abbey grounds. From here return to the road, turn left and follow it back to the village.

Remote Moidart's Citadel

By the peaceful lochside at Castle Tioram, once home to a Clan Ranald chieftain

1 Turn right out of the car park, passing through a gate to follow the shoreline path.

5 Cross a field at the bottom of the valley, go over a stile and turn right along the road to return to the car park.

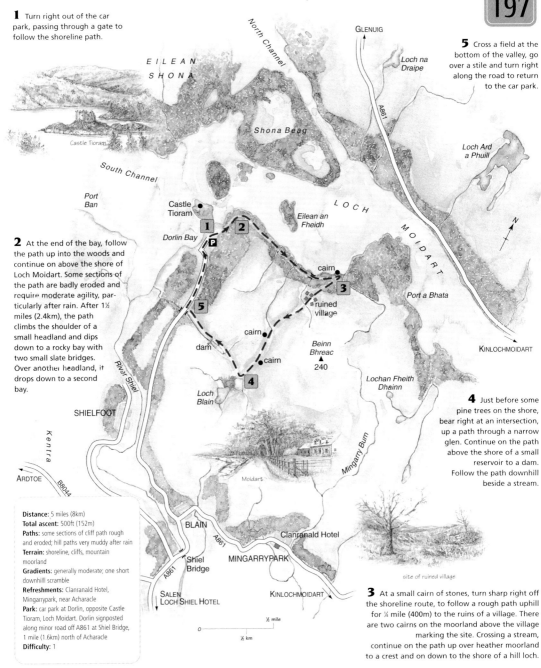

2 At the end of the bay, follow the path up into the woods and continue on above the shore of Loch Moidart. Some sections of the path are badly eroded and require moderate agility, particularly after rain. After 1½ miles (2.4km), the path climbs the shoulder of a small headland and dips down to a rocky bay with two small slate bridges. Over another headland, it drops down to a second bay.

4 Just before some pine trees on the shore, bear right at an intersection, up a path through a narrow glen. Continue on the path above the shore of a small reservoir to a dam. Follow the path downhill beside a stream.

Distance: 5 miles (8km)
Total ascent: 500ft (152m)
Paths: some sections of cliff path rough and eroded; hill paths very muddy after rain
Terrain: shoreline, cliffs, mountain moorland
Gradients: generally moderate; one short downhill scramble
Refreshments: Clanranald Hotel, Mingarrypark, near Acharacle
Park: car park at Dorlin, opposite Castle Tioram, Loch Moidart. Dorlin signposted along minor road off A861 at Shiel Bridge, 1 mile (1.6km) north of Acharacle
Difficulty: 1

3 At a small cairn of stones, turn sharp right off the shoreline route, to follow a rough path uphill for ¼ mile (400m) to the ruins of a village. There are two cairns on the moorland above the village marking the site. Crossing a stream, continue on the path up over heather moorland to a crest and on down to the shore of a hill loch.

ABOUT • CALEDONIAN CANAL

Of all the canals built during this era the Caledonian Canal, designed by Thomas Telford and completed in 1847, is undoubtedly the most impressive. Its 60 miles (97km) length includes an impressive flight of eight locks known as Neptune's Staircase.

Scotland

DISTANCE • 5 miles (8km)

TOTAL ASCENT • 64ft (19m)

PATHS • firm, dry path

TERRAIN • waterside and woodland

GRADIENTS • level, apart from one short descent

REFRESHMENTS • hotels in Banavie, Corpach and Fort William

PARK • Banavie Station or at Neptune's Staircase and cross canal by lock gate

DIFFICULTY • 1

Telford's Caledonian Canal

❶ From the car park at Banavie Station, cross the main road (A830) and go through a metal gate on to the canal towpath. On your left is Neptune's Staircase, a flight of eight locks that raises the canal 64ft (19m) in height. Above the locks, yachts lie moored in a sheltered pool.

❷ Follow the towpath, with the canal on your left, for approximately 2½ miles (4km). The ground drops steeply to the right and through gaps in the woodland there are fine views of the Ben Nevis range and of Inverlochy Castle Hotel, a Gothic mansion that is now one of Scotland's most exclusive hotels.

❸ The canal and towpath bridge a stream, with some houses visible below. Continue for 20yds (18m), then turn right down a path between the trees. Beyond the gate at the bottom, turn sharp right to follow the stream through the tunnel under the canal and past a weir. Reaching an

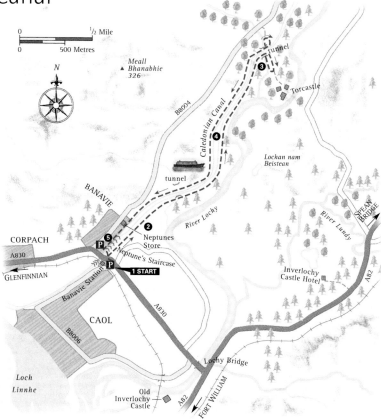

intersection, turn sharp right to return to the canal and right again along the towpath.

❹ On the return walk there are fine views along Loch Linnhe to the Corran Narrows and of the 4,406ft (1,343m) summit of Ben

Nevis, Britain's highest mountain. The town of Fort William, on the east shore of the loch, was still a military garrison at the time of the canal's construction.

❺ Pass Neptune's Store, a small post office and shop, offering

tourist information, toilets and facilities for yachtsmen (limited winter opening). The bow-windowed cottages overlooking Neptune's Staircase date from the early 1800s. Cross the canal by the lock gates to return to the car park.

Scotland
The Lost Valley of Glen Coe

*Hidden in the mountainous walls of this famous
Highland glen, a hanging valley once sheltered the
Macdonald's cattle from raiders*

1 Start on the path leading down from the car park, to join the main path through the Pass of Glencoe. Walk down east, then turn south to cross the footbridge over the River Coe, located just downstream of the Meeting of Three Waters. Climb the opposite bank, go through the birch scrub and up over a ladder stile at fencing.

2 After a further 100yds (91m) or so, leave the main path and climb a zigzagging path rising steeply off to the right. This leads up to the higher path, the one above the tree-fringed gorge of the Allt Coire Gabhail. Having enjoyed a gentle stroll for a while, and just before a large boulder, descend through the trees to make the crossing of the river. Take care traversing a few awkward rocks and roots on the way down.

3 Stepping stones make the river crossing easy. Continue the climb up along the left bank, clambering over an outcrop of rocks before reaching the point overlooking the distinctively flat, alluvial plain of the Coire Gabhail (Lost Valley).

Distance: 3½ miles (5.2km)
Total ascent: 855ft (261m)
Paths: rough but clearly defined on ascent; less obvious on the short circuit around the Lost Valley
Terrain: confined, steep-sided gorge through woodland giving way to more open mountainous aspect at the top
Gradients: short but steep over rocks
Refreshments: Clachaig Inn, 3 miles (4.8km) west of car park
Park: westernmost car park in the Pass of Glencoe on A82 between Tyndrum and Ballachulish
Difficulty: 2

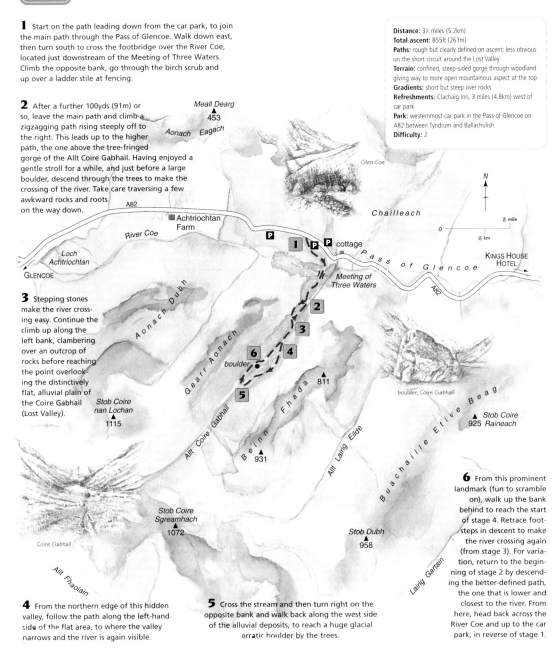

4 From the northern edge of this hidden valley, follow the path along the left-hand side of the flat area, to where the valley narrows and the river is again visible.

5 Cross the stream and then turn right on the opposite bank and walk back along the west side of the alluvial deposits, to reach a huge glacial erratic boulder by the trees.

6 From this prominent landmark (fun to scramble on), walk up the bank behind to reach the start of stage 4. Retrace footsteps in descent to make the river crossing again (from stage 3). For variation, return to the beginning of stage 2 by descending the better-defined path, the one that is lower and closest to the river. From here, head back across the River Coe and up to the car park, in reverse of stage 1.

WALK 200

ABOUT • KILLIECRANKIE

The first victory of the Jacobite Rebellion by followers of James VII took place in 1689 in Killiecrankie. The terrifying Highland Charge overwhelmed the government troops and their leader, General Hugh MacKay, in just ten minutes.

Scotland

DISTANCE • 6½ miles (10.4km)	**REFRESHMENTS** • Killiecrankie Centre and Boating Station
TOTAL ASCENT • 500ft (152m)	
PATHS • good trails, metalled roads	**PARK** • forest car park at Faskally Boating Station
TERRAIN • forest trails and country roads	
GRADIENTS • moderate	**DIFFICULTY** • 2

The Battle at Killiecrankie

❶ From the car park walk past the boating station and continue uphill following the lochside path for Killiecrankie which leads underneath both the A9 flyover and Clunie footbridge.

❷ Follow the loch, past the viewing point where the Old Bridge of Clunie stood before it was demolished for the hydro-electric scheme in 1950. Loch Faskally is a man-made feature following the deep, natural river valley.

❸ Keep left on the single-track metalled road towards Killiecrankie. Just before the entrance to Faskally House, turn left on to the signed footpath following the lochside. Pass the point where the rivers Tummel and Garry meet.

❹ Pass under the Garry Bridge and a short distance further on turn left and cross the river on a metal footbridge.Turn left up the steep slope to Garry Bridge car park. Immediately after the car park, turn right on to an unclassified metalled single-track road that climbs up past Tenandry Parish Kirk. Soon after there are views of the valley and east towards the mountains.

❺ After 1½ miles (2.4km), turn sharp right and then bear right and cross the River Garry on a stone bridge. Cross the rail bridge and turn right on to the B8079 and follow the footpath past the primary school. The path peters out and after a very short distance bear right on to a track leading downhill following the riverside, but still to the east of the railway.

❻ Continue to the Killiecrankie visitor centre (where you will find refreshments and toilets). From here continue on the path downhill, passing Soldier's Leap and the railway viaduct. You are now on the east bank of the River Garry. Continue southwards, passing Balfour's Stone, to the metal footbridge.

❼ Take the path on the left here, uphill and over the railway bridge to exit on to the B8079. Turn right and follow the B-road, continuing straight ahead as it becomes the B8019 at Garry Bridge, eventually returning to the car park.

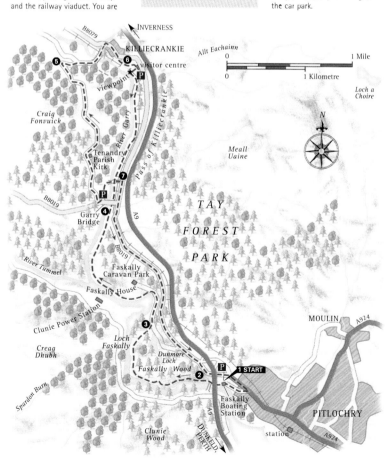

Scotland

On General Wade's Road

Discovering a section of the great military occupation road near Newtonmore

8 Continue on this road towards the A9. Cross the A9 and turn right, then take the first left onto a minor road, signposted from the A9 'Farm Access 200yds'. Continue down this road, past the lane to Nuide Farm, until you return to the car park at Ralia.

1 From the visitor centre car park at Ralia turn right and walk 330yds (300m) to the road that runs parallel to the A9. When the A9 exit for Newtonmore joins this road, cross over and take the minor road (signposted to Ralia and Nuide) to the right.

2 A short distance along here on the right, at the gap in the trees, climb a gate and follow the track uphill. Cross another gate and turn left onto the A9. About 350yds (320m) further along you reach Ralia Kennels (unmistakable but unsigned).

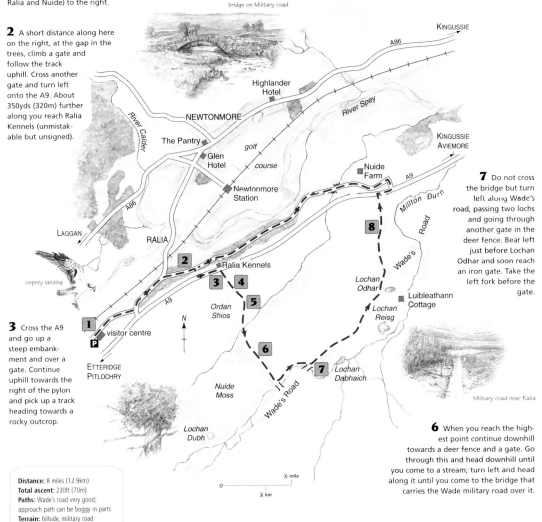

bridge on Military road

KINGUSSIE

A86

Highlander Hotel

River Spey

NEWTONMORE

River Calder

The Pantry

golf

Glen Hotel

course

KINGUSSIE AVIEMORE

Nuide Farm

A9

Newtonmore Station

Millton Burn

Road

A86

LAGGAN

RALIA

Ralia Kennels

Wade's

Lochan Odhar

Luibleathann Cottage

osprey landing

Ordan Shios

Lochan Reisg

Military road near Ralia

visitor centre

ETTERIDGE PITLOCHRY

Nuide Moss

Wade's Road

Lochan Dabhaich

Lochan Dubh

½ mile

0

½ km

3 Cross the A9 and go up a steep embankment and over a gate. Continue uphill towards the right of the pylon and pick up a track heading towards a rocky outcrop.

7 Do not cross the bridge but turn left along Wade's road, passing two lochs and going through another gate in the deer fence. Bear left just before Lochan Odhar and soon reach an iron gate. Take the left fork before the gate.

6 When you reach the highest point continue downhill towards a deer fence and a gate. Go through this and head downhill until you come to a stream; turn left and head along it until you come to the bridge that carries the Wade military road over it.

Distance: 8 miles (12.9km)
Total ascent: 230ft (70m)
Paths: Wade's road very good; approach path can be boggy in parts
Terrain: hillside, military road
Gradients: moderate
Refreshments: visitor centre
Park: Ralia visitor centre, off A9 near Newtonmore
Difficulty: 2

4 Cross a stile at the fence and continue on the track towards the left-hand side of the hill. On a good day it is worth detouring up to the summit to enjoy the panoramic views of the surrounding area.

5 Follow the path round the back of the hill and then turn left. Go downhill and across some boggy ground before rising again to meet a farm track passing in front of you. Cross this and continue on a line uphill.

Rothiemurchus – Heart of the Caledonian Pine Forest

A memorable ramble through ancient woodland

WALK 202

1 Start on the footpath immediately to the right of the Rothiemurchus Camp and Caravan Park entrance, signposted Public Path to Braemar by the Lairig Ghru. Walk south along the track into the forest, then on through a gate by Lairig Ghru Cottage.

2 Where the track divides take the right fork, signposted for Gleann Einich, passing a large cairn on the left. Soon after, go over a stile at the cattle grid. The track then rises to more open country.

3 Having gained about the highest point along the track, turn sharp right for another track leading up over the heather. Reach a tarmac lane by a cattle grid, turn left and continue to where the lane terminates at Whitewell Croft. From there, bear left down a path for Rothiemurchus footpath. A short deviation leads first to a large memorial cairn on the left.

4 Walk down from the cairn and, on regaining the track for Gleann Einich, turn right for 700 yds (637m) to arrive at a major crossroads of estate tracks. There are fire beaters and signposts here. Follow the Lairig Ghru track to the left, passing pine-fringed Lochan Deo and walking beyond where the other path from Coylumbridge joins from the left. Soon after, reach the Cairngorm Club footbridge over the Allt na Bheinn Mhor.

5 Go over the bridge and turn right on a rough track heading upstream of the river. From where the waters of the Am Beanaidh and the Allt Druidh join forces, veer southeast, passing close to a ruined house on the left before rising gently up to Piccadilly.

6 Piccadilly is the Rothiemurchus Estate name for this other major junction of tracks, a focal point marked by a large cairn. Walk northeast from here, following the Loch Morlich track. Shortly after passing through a stile at Tilhill, turn left joining the track from Rothiemurchus Lodge to Loch Morlich and continue through a further 2 miles (3.2km) of pine forest.

7 Join the road to Glen More and the ski centre by the western shore of Loch Morlich. At certain times of the year the road is served by buses connecting with Aviemore (check with local tourist information), which offers a convenient return; alternatively it is a further 1 hour of walking by the roadside to return to Coylumbridge.

Cairngorm Club footbridge

Distance: 5 ½ miles (8.9km) or 8 miles (12.9km) if walking back from Loch Morlich
Total ascent: 510ft (155m)
Paths: mostly good, level tracks; wet in places after rain
Terrain: pine forest, heather moorland
Gradients: gradual
Refreshments: Coylumbridge Hotel and in Aviemore
Park: by roadside, just west of entrance to Rothiemurchus Camp and Caravan Park, near Coylumbridge, 2 miles (3.2km) southeast of Aviemore
Difficulty: 2

AVIEMORE
INVERDRUIE
Coylumbridge Hotel
River Druie
NETHY BRIDGE
B970
COYLUMBRIDGE
Lairig Ghru
Rothiemurchus Camp and Caravan Park
cairn
Loch an Eilein
Whitewell Croft
cairn
Scots pine
GLEN
MORE
River Luineag
Allt na Bheinn Mhor
Lochan Deo
Cairngorm Club Footbridge
Am Beanaidh
Allt na Doire
FOREST
PARK
ROTHIEMURCHUS
ruin
cairn
Piccadilly
Allt Druidh
Lochan nan Geadas
Loch Morlich
GLENMORE LODGE
cairn
Rothiemurchus Lodge

½ mile
0
½ km

N

WALK
203

ABOUT • ABERDEEN

Oil caused havoc in the 1970s as rising prices led to government cuts and threats of petrol rationing but in 1975 oil was stuck in the North Sea. This walk around the old fishing port celebrates the prosperity and tragedy that oil has brought to Aberdeen.

Scotland

DISTANCE • 6 miles (9.6km)
TOTAL ASCENT • negligible
PATHS • excellent in all weather
TERRAIN • mainly roads and pavements with a short section of beach (underwater at high tide)
GRADIENTS • fairly level throughout

REFRESHMENTS • Aberdeen Maritime Museum or Harry Ramsden's
PARK • outside Harry Ramsden's on the Esplanade or Queen's Link Leisure Park
DIFFICULTY • 2

Around Aberdeen

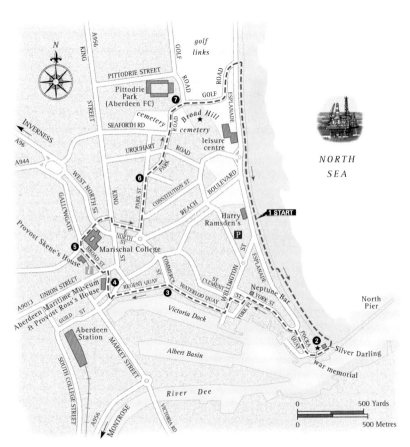

and John Ross's House, Provost of Aberdeen between 1710–1711.

❹ From here head along Exchequer Row, turn left into Union Street, continue and turn right into Broad Street, where you will find Provost Skene's House and the Tourist Information Office on the left, behind the offices.

❺ Continue past Marischal College (which houses the Marischal Museum), turn right into Littlejohn Street, cross North Street. At the end of Meal Market Street turn right into King Street and then left into Frederick Street. At the junction with Park Street turn left and keep walking until the road crosses the railway.

❻ Shortly after this is a roundabout. Head along Park Road, almost straight ahead. Follow it through the cemetery and towards Pittodrie Park, home of Aberdeen Football Club, and its junction with Golf Road.

❼ Turn right into Golf Road and walk through the golf links. Detour to the top of Broad Hill, the mound behind the cemetery, for magnificent views to the north and out to sea. The road turns sharply left towards its junction with the Esplanade. Cross the Esplanade and turn right on to the promenade which you can follow back to the start of the walk.

❶ Head southwards on the promenade beside the shore with the sea on your right. Go down the slipway on to the beach and continue for a short distance. Step over the rocks to reach the wooden steps on the right and leave the beach into a children's play area.

❷ Walk past the Silver Darling restaurant and into the harbour area. Continue past the war memorial, keeping the blue storage tanks on your left, and along Pocra Quay. Turn left into York Street and at the Neptune bar, turn left into York Place. Then, take the first right, the first left

and first right again to emerge on Waterloo Quay.

❸ Where Waterloo Quay becomes Commerce Street, turn left into Regent Quay and at the T-junction cross the road at the pedestrian lights. Turn left, then first right to reach Aberdeen Maritime Museum

In the Executioner's Shadow, Deep in the Cuillins

*Am Bàsteir means 'the Executioner' in Gaelic, but this is
a relatively gentle walk beneath its awesome profile*

WALK

204

1 From the Sligachan Hotel, walk along the A863 for about 200yds (182m). Take one of the paths on the left, opposite the top of a slip road to the hotel. Most lead across boggy ground to cross the Allt Dearg Mor at the footbridge. Walk south on the gently rising footpath towards Sgurr nan Gillean, the easternmost peak of the mountains seen clearly on the skyline ahead.

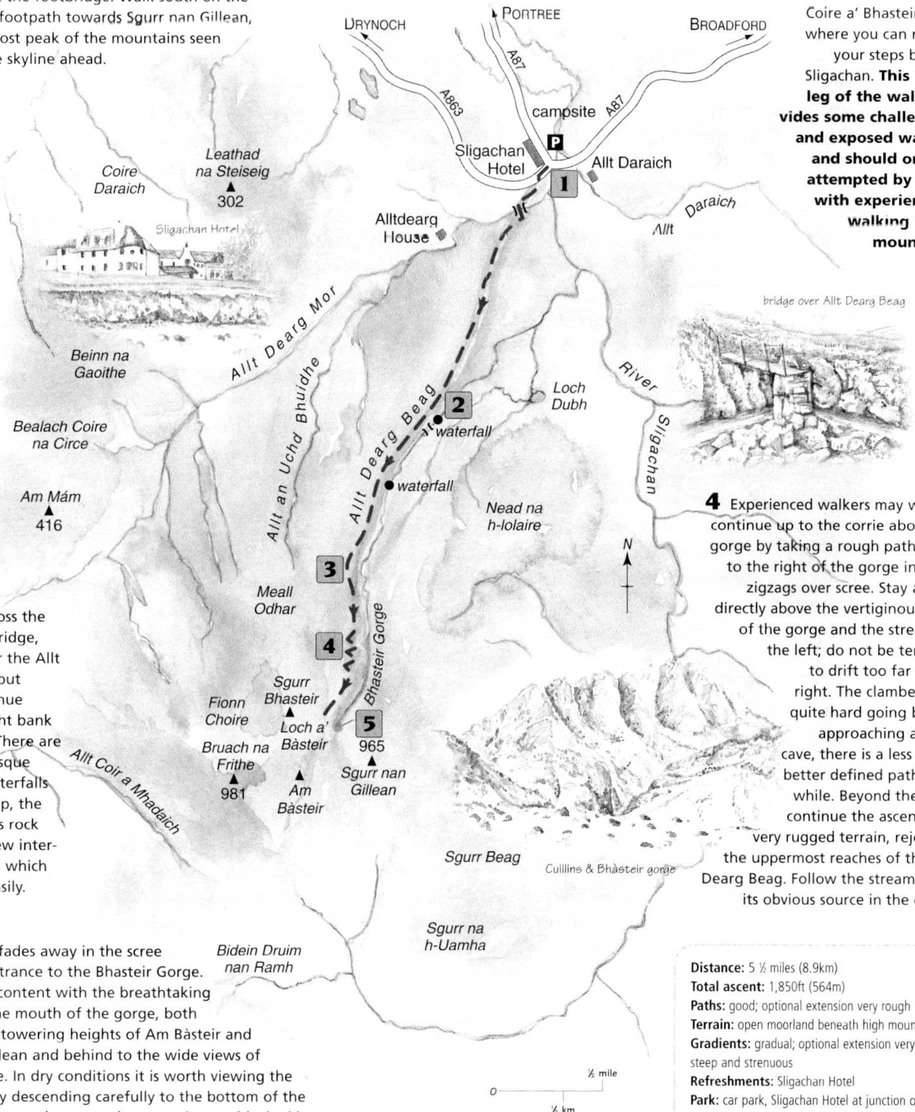

5 The path ends at Loch a' Bhasteir, the tiny body of water held in the secluded recesses of Coire a' Bhasteir, from where you can retrace your steps back to Sligachan. **This upper leg of the walk provides some challenging and exposed walking and should only be attempted by those with experience of walking in the mountains.**

bridge over Allt Dearg Beag

4 Experienced walkers may wish to continue up to the corrie above the gorge by taking a rough path rising to the right of the gorge in steep zigzags over scree. Stay almost directly above the vertiginous sides of the gorge and the stream on the left; do not be tempted to drift too far to the right. The clambering is quite hard going but on approaching a small cave, there is a less steep, better defined path for a while. Beyond the cave, continue the ascent over very rugged terrain, rejoining the uppermost reaches of the Allt Dearg Beag. Follow the stream up to its obvious source in the corrie.

2 Do not cross the second footbridge, this time over the Allt Dearg Beag, but instead continue along the right bank of this river. There are many picturesque pools and waterfalls and, higher up, the path traverses rock slabs and a few intervening burns, which are forded easily.

3 The path fades away in the scree below the entrance to the Bhasteir Gorge. Most will be content with the breathtaking views from the mouth of the gorge, both ahead to the towering heights of Am Bàsteir and Sgurr nan Gillean and behind to the wide views of northern Skye. In dry conditions it is worth viewing the gorge itself by descending carefully to the bottom of the ravine. Passage up the gorge, however, is soon blocked by deep pools and precipitous waterfalls. Return to Sligachan by retracing footsteps back down the upward path.

Map labels: PORTREE, DRYNOCH, BROADFORD, A87, A863, campsite, Sligachan Hotel, Allt Daraich, Allt Daraich, Coire Daraich, Leathad na Steiseig ▲ 302, Alltdearg House, Sligachan Hotel, Beinn na Gaoithe, Allt Dearg Mor, Allt an Uchd Bhuidhe, Allt Dearg Beag, Loch Dubh, River Sligachan, Bealach Coire na Circe, Am Mám ▲ 416, waterfall, waterfall, Nead na h-Iolaire, N, Meall Odhar, Bhasteir Gorge, Fionn Choire, Sgurr Bhasteir, Loch a' Bhàsteir ▲ 965, Bruach na Frithe ▲ 981, Am Bàsteir, Sgurr nan Gillean, Allt Coir a Mhadaich, Sgurr Beag, Cuillins & Bhàsteir gorge, Sgurr na h-Uamha, Bidein Druim nan Ramh, ½ mile, 0, ½ km

Distance: 5 ½ miles (8.9km)
Total ascent: 1,850ft (564m)
Paths: good; optional extension very rough
Terrain: open moorland beneath high mountains
Gradients: gradual; optional extension very steep and strenuous
Refreshments: Sligachan Hotel
Park: car park, Sligachan Hotel at junction of A87 and A863, Isle of Skye
Difficulty: 2

WALK
205

ABOUT • RAASAY

The defeat of the Jacobites at Culloden in 1746 ended all hopes to return a Stuart to the throne and led to a relentless manhunt for Bonnie Prince Charlie. This walk takes you to Raasay, one of his final hiding places in Scotland, before he fled into exile.

Scotland

DISTANCE • 6 miles (9.6km)

TOTAL ASCENT • 540ft (165m)

PATHS • mostly good but can be muddy after heavy rain

TERRAIN • green lanes, moorland, hillside and tarmac road

GRADIENTS • mostly gentle

REFRESHMENTS • Raasay Hotel

PARK • parking area before the last house on the road to North Fearns

DIFFICULTY • 2

Escape to Raasay

❶ From the car park at the end of the road continue along the green lane. The sea is on your right and you will have a superb view across to the islands of Scalpay, Longay and Pabay.

❷ After a mile (1.6km) look up to the left as you pass the impressive cliffs of Beinn na' Leac. Continue on past the headland of Rudha na' Leac, beyond which you will see a memorial cairn on the path.

❸ Stop at the cairn to read the inscription to the gaelic poet Sorley McLean, who was from Raasay, and also to those who were cleared from the land to make way for sheep. McLean's poem Hallaig is reproduced here. From here the path narrows, entering woodland and passing a ruined building. Follow the path out of the wood and where it forks, keep left. Re-enter woodland, go downhill and cross the Hallaig Burn where it meets the path.

❹ Climb uphill from the burn and veer right towards the top corner of a drystone wall. At the corner

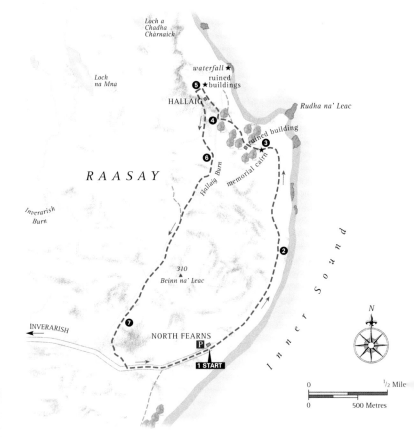

you can see the best preserved of the houses of Hallaig township which was cleared of people in the 18th and 19th centuries to make way for sheep.

❺ Continue by following the track round the rest of the ruins, heading towards a rocky crag in the north, then turn left and head

uphill. Turn left again and with the crag behind you head south towards another crag on the distant hills.

❻ When you intersect the Hallaig Burn, turn right and follow its course uphill until it disappears. Then pick up the rough track, heading round the back of Beann

na' Leac. Eventually the track will disappear but by then you will see the road below.

❼ Descend the hill heading towards the road. When you reach the burn turn left and walk along it until it flows under the road. Turn left and return to your car.

WALK

206

Brochs, built from 100 bc, are found only in Scotland. On this scenic and remote walk you'll see two, Dun Telve and Dun Troddan. Their builders and purpose are a mystery, but these bell-shaped, dry-stone towers remain as a testimony to the skills of the engineers.

Scotland

DISTANCE • 8 miles (13km)	**REFRESHMENTS** • none on route. Five Sisters Restaurant, Sheil Bridge, 9 miles (14.5km) from Glenelg
TOTAL ASCENT • 148ft (45m)	
PATHS • mostly good, but can be muddy after heavy rain	
TERRAIN • metalled and forest roads; beach	**PARK** • at the war memorial near the end of Glenelg village
GRADIENTS • mainly flat, one section with a gentle gradient	**DIFFICULTY** • 3

The Iron Age Brochs of Glenelg

❶ From the war memorial head south, following the signs for Glenelg Brochs. About a mile (1.6km) past the turning to Sandaig, the remains of a hill fort can be reached via a faint track leading up towards some rocky crags on the left.

❷ From the fort continue on the faint track to return to the road. Turn left and continue to the Dun Telve Broch on your right. Dun Troddan Broch is just a little further, on the left, a short distance up the hillside. Notice the proximity to good agricultural land which was essential to the Iron Age inhabitants and a notable feature of the location of many of the brochs in this part of Scotland.

Access is via the kissing gate and a path.

❸ Visible from Dun Troddan is a wooden house with a turf roof. Just beyond it, and before some caravans, is a turning on the right

leading to a bridge over the river. Cross here and turn left on to a forest road.

❹ The road climbs gently from here, then forks. Go left, through a gate, then downhill towards a bridge over the river. Cross it, but take great care as it is in poor repair, then climb a gate on to a dirt track.

❺ Follow the track left, bear left where it joins the farm road and

continue past Balvraid farm. About 200yds (183m) past the farm look out for the chambered cairn on the right –a mound of stones covered in grass.

❻ From here continue on the road, cross a bridge by a modern bungalow and go left following this road for just over a mile (1.6km) back past the brochs to the outskirts of Glenelg. Leave the road here and walk along the beach back to the war memorial.

GALLTAIR

SHIEL BRIDGE

Glenelg Bay

Glenmore River

war memorial **1 START**

GLENELG

Loch a' Mhuilinn

Meall a' Chaisteil

Allt na Seana Gheid

hill fort

Loch Beinn a' Chaoinich

❷

SANDAIG

❸ Dun Troddan Broch

Meall Breac

Dun Telve Broch

❹

bungalow

❻★chambered cairn

Balvraid

❺

N

Allt an Fharaig

Sròn an Fheadain

0   1 Mile

0   1 Kilometre

742
▲
Beinn a' Chapuill

A Scottish Millennium Forest

Renewal of the ancient Caledonian Forest

Scotland's Native Trees

Once the Scots pine was an object of worship and ancient druids lit bonfires of them at the winter solstice to encourage the return of the sun. Glades were hung with lights to represent the divine light of the stars, rituals that became, in time, the modern customs of decorating a Christmas tree or burning a yule log.

Once, most of Scotland, like England was covered in a dense forest. Huge, majestic pine trees, birch and rowans covered the land. The bears, wolves and wild boar that roamed free, using the forest as a source of food and shelter and feeding on a host of smaller creatures, were hunted in turn by the greatest predator of all, *Homo sapiens*.

As well as hunting, early humans gathered nuts, berries and roots, and in time they acquired the skills of husbandry, abandoning their nomadic lifestyle and becoming farmers. They cleared vast areas of the forest to provide land on which to grow crops, and harvested the timber to build their houses and barns, and stockades to contain their domesticated animals. As the pace of development increased, so too did the amount of timber required. Eventually, whole areas were cleared to the extent that today only one per cent of Scotland's original native woodland survives today.

Restoration of the Native Pine Forests

What remains of the native forests represents specimens that descended from the trees that grew here at the end of the last ice age – over eight thousand years ago. Scots pine is renowned for its long life and many of the specimens that grow around Loch Affric are extremely old and knotted. (It is worth noting that the same trees, which you see today, provided shelter for Bonnie Prince Charlie when he fled from Government forces after the Battle of Culloden in 1746.) It is quite possible that many of the trees were mere seedlings back when wolves, bears and lynx still lived here. However, as these natural predators became extinct the forest came under serious threat from increased numbers of red deer, browsing the forests for food.

By the end of World War II, most of the remaining trees were reaching the end of their lives. Continual grazing of deer and sheep meant that none of the young seedlings were surviving to replace them, and the forest faced extinction.

Fortunately, in 1951, the Forestry Commission acquired control of the woodland. In response to the failing forest, they erected fences and started controlling the numbers of deer within the enclosures. They also started a planting programme of young trees,

raised from seeds gathered in the Glen, in an attempt to kick-start the regeneration process of the forest. Eventually, as the numbers of deer reduced, so the seedlings began to survive and it was no longer necessary to continue planting.

On this walk, you will enter a new enclosure funded by the Millennium Forest for Scotland Project. This is part of a nationwide scheme to increase the area of native woodland that is being managed for conservation.

Scotland

AROUND LOCH AFFRIC THROUGH THE MILLENNIUM FOREST PROJECT

❶ From the car park, head back to the road and turn left. At the fork in the forestry road keep left, go over a bridge and then through a gate in the deer fence. Continue on the forest road. Pass a cottage on your right, cross another bridge; go uphill and across a cattle grid. The area on either side of the track is now part of the pinewood regeneration. Follow the road as it winds round the side of Loch Affric. After a couple of miles you will reach the houses at Athnamulloch. Cross the river by the bridge and follow the track uphill.

❷ This path leads to the youth hostel at Altbeith just over three miles away, but keep a sharp lookout for the narrower track that branches to the right in approximately quarter of a mile. Turn right and follow the track uphill. Although it can be muddy at times of high rainfall, the going is generally easy. Pass through another gate in the deer fence and

re-enter the regeneration area.

❸ Continue along the track and enjoy the grand view over Loch Affric – but be sure to apply a powerful insect repellent, particularly on this section, to ward off the horse-flies. Exit the regeneration area via another gate and continue on the path past Affric Lodge and back to the fork in the road, and from there return to the car park.

Distance: 8 miles (13km)

Total ascent: 320 feet (100m)

Paths: very good, except in wet weather when some stretches can become boggy

Terrain: forest roads, hill tracks and heather

Gradients: mainly gentle

Refreshments: none available

Park: car park at the end of the road at Loch Beinn a Mheadhoin.

Difficulty: 3

The Stuarts' Last Stand at Culloden

*Around the woods and moors of Culloden, where the
Stuart cause died in battle*

WALK

208

1 Turn right onto the B9006, then first left for Balloch, then right onto a forestry road. Turn right at a T-junction, left when you reach a bungalow and complete a circuit returning to the main road and turn left.

Distance: 6½ miles (10.5km)
Total ascent: negligible
Paths: mostly good but can be muddy after wet weather
Terrain: moorland, woodland, fields, forestry road and minor roads
Gradients: none
Refreshments: visitor centre
Park: Culloden battlefield visitor centre car park, off B9006 between Inverness and Croy
Note: the site is owned by the National Trust for Scotland and an entrance fee is payable
Difficulty: 1

2 Return to the visitor centre and enter battlefield site. Turn right at first junction, passing the yellow flag. Go straight on at the junction to a second yellow flag.

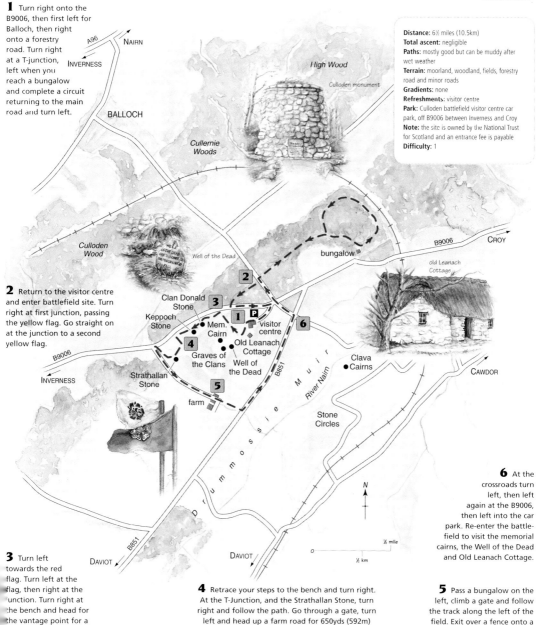

3 Turn left towards the red flag. Turn left at the flag, then right at the junction. Turn right at the bench and head for the vantage point for a view over the battlefield.

4 Retrace your steps to the bench and turn right. At the T-Junction, and the Strathallan Stone, turn right and follow the path. Go through a gate, turn left and head up a farm road for 650yds (592m) with the battlefield on your left.

5 Pass a bungalow on the left, climb a gate and follow the track along the left of the field. Exit over a fence onto a minor road and turn left.

6 At the crossroads turn left, then left again at the B9006, then left into the car park. Re-enter the battlefield to visit the memorial cairns, the Well of the Dead and Old Leanach Cottage.

Ullapool and the Drove Roads

Following the tracks of drovers bringing cattle across
from the isles

WALK

209

1 From the car park next to Safeway supermarket, exit to Latheron Lane and turn left into Quay Street. At the Riverside Hotel, where the road curves right, turn left into Castle Terrace. Go down the steps to the river on the right and cross a bridge.

2 At the far side, turn right and follow the path along the side of the river. Continue by the riverside to a wooden bridge and up some steps. Turn right at a cattle grid to the main road.

7 When the path forks, go left up the side of the hill. Eventually the track curves to the right. From here the view over Loch Broom, the Summer Isles and Ullapool is breathtaking. The path now winds down the side of the hill, through a kissing gate and out to the main road. Turn left and follow the main road, passing the Far Isles Bar and Restaurant on the right hand side, to the church. Here, turn right and follow the signs back to the car park.

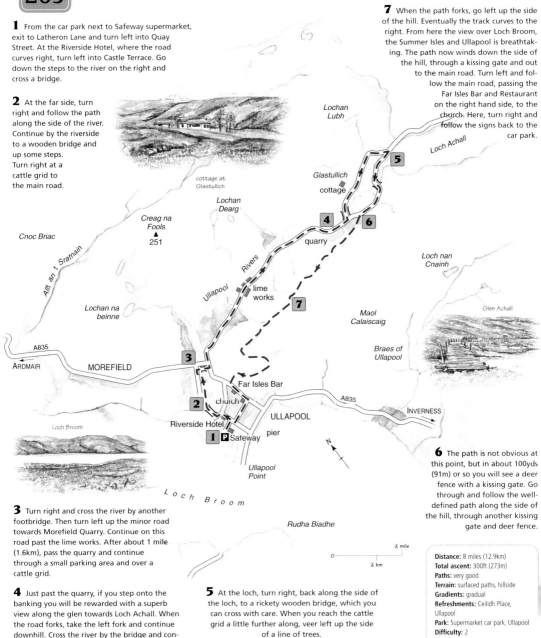

3 Turn right and cross the river by another footbridge. Then turn left up the minor road towards Morefield Quarry. Continue on this road past the lime works. After about 1 mile (1.6km), pass the quarry and continue through a small parking area and over a cattle grid.

4 Just past the quarry, if you step onto the banking you will be rewarded with a superb view along the glen towards Loch Achall. When the road forks, take the left fork and continue downhill. Cross the river by the bridge and continue past the cottage on your left.

5 At the loch, turn right, back along the side of the loch, to a rickety wooden bridge, which you can cross with care. When you reach the cattle grid a little further along, veer left up the side of a line of trees.

6 The path is not obvious at this point, but in about 100yds (91m) or so you will see a deer fence with a kissing gate. Go through and follow the well-defined path along the side of the hill, through another kissing gate and deer fence.

Distance: 8 miles (12.9km)
Total ascent: 300ft (273m)
Paths: very good
Terrain: surfaced paths, hillside
Gradients: gradual
Refreshments: Ceilidh Place, Ullapool
Park: Supermarket car park, Ullapool
Difficulty: 2

WALK 210

ABOUT • STRATHNAVER

This walk is a reminder of the brutal clearances of Strathnaver (1785–1850). Ten thousand tenants were evicted from Strathnaver by Elizabeth, Countess of Sutherland and her ruthless factor, Patrick Sellar, to make way for intensive sheep-farming.

Scotland

DISTANCE • 5 miles (8km)

TOTAL ASCENT • 50ft (15m)

PATHS • mostly good but can be a little muddy in wet weather

TERRAIN • metalled road, forest roads, moorland and forest trails

GRADIENTS • mainly flat with a few slight gradients

REFRESHMENTS • none on the route; seasonal coffee shop near the Strathnaver museum at Bettyhill

PARK • off the road at the corner of the junction of the B873 and the B871 at Syre

DIFFICULTY • 2

The Dispossessed of Strathnaver

1 From Syre church head south along the B873. Look out for the memorial to Donald MacLeod on the right-hand side of the road. Rosal village is across the river from here but hidden by the forest.

2 Continue along the road for a mile (1.6km), then cross the river via two anglers' bridges. Take great care when crossing, particularly in wet weather conditions. A forest road runs parallel to the River Naver but access is prevented by a deer fence.

3 Turn left and continue to follow the track beside the deer fence for about ¾ mile (1.2km) until you reach a stile. Cross the fence and walk up the fire break to reach the forest road.

4 Turn left on to the road and continue until a large, green waymarker indicates the entrance to Rosal village. Leave the road and turn right on a track through the trees leading to a gated enclosure. Through the gate is the

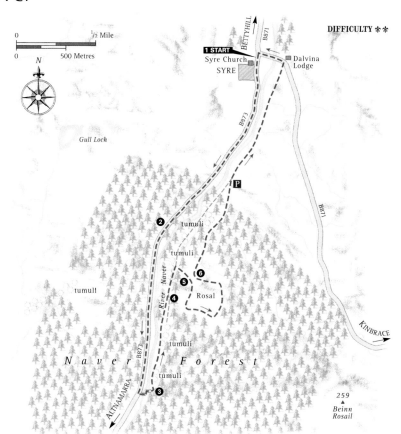

DIFFICULTY ✸✸

• DON'T MISS •

Strathnaver Museum in the former St Columba's Parish Church at Bettyhill, some 12 miles (19km) north of Syre, tells the story of the Sutherland clearances in graphic detail, featuring models and artefacts from the period. While you are at the museum look out for the intricately sculptured Pictish Cross, located in the church graveyard, which dates from about ad 800.

Rosal village.

5 Walk clockwise round the village following the numbered interpretation boards, which tell the story of the clearances. (At the top cairn turn around and shout in the direction of Beinn Rosail and listen to the echo.) Continue on the trail, then leave through the enclosure gate and retrace the path for 20 yds (18m) to the right.

6 Follow a very faint track uphill and into the forest, where it becomes a well waymarked trail. When it rejoins the forest road turn right and go through a gate. Continue to the junction with the B871, turn left and return to the start and your car.

The Flow Country

*A unique landscape of extensive peatlands is glimpsed
from its northern edge*

WALK
211

1 From the lay-by to the southeast of Melvich, cross the road and head up a farm track to the left of a small loch. The track goes through a gate and curves to the left behind a derelict cottage. You will encounter two gates across the track close together.

2 Midway between the two gates, take the rough peat-cutters track that goes uphill on your left. Continue to follow this track, keeping left when it forks, until it disappears. Then continue in this direction heading for the highest point, where you will see Loch Sgiathanach slightly to your left.

3 Head for the left-hand edge of the loch and follow the course of the Allt a Ghlasraich burn, which flows from here to Achridigill Loch.

4 Where the burn meets the loch, turn 90 degrees to the right. You should be heading to the mid-point between two small hills. Loch Baligill lies at the foot of the hills. Follow the shore-line along the right-hand side of the loch.

5 At the end of the loch, turn right and, keeping the hills on your left, head for the highest point in front of you. Climb a short, steep slope and from the top you should see the hill of Cnoc Eipteil ahead of you.

Distance: 8 miles (12.8km)
Total ascent: 500ft (152m)
Paths: some good others very boggy or indistinct
Terrain: extensive peatbog, hillside
Gradients: moderate to steep
Refreshments: Melvich Hotel
Park: lay-by on A836 southeast of Melvich
Note: this is remote and difficult terrain and the walk should not be attempted in wet weather or poor visibility
Difficulty: 3

8 If you don't spot it, walk in that direction and eventually you will cut across it. This track will take you back to the main road. Turn right and follow the road through the village and beyond, to where you started.

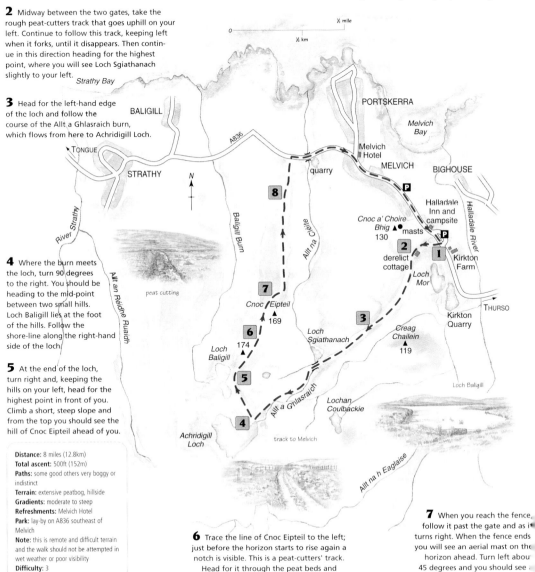

6 Trace the line of Cnoc Eipteil to the left; just before the horizon starts to rise again a notch is visible. This is a peat-cutters' track. Head for it through the peat beds and trenches and continue through it.

7 When you reach the fence, follow it past the gate and as it turns right. When the fence ends you will see an aerial mast on the horizon ahead. Turn left about 45 degrees and you should see a peat-cutters' track in the distance.